P9-DZY-181

Leonard Bernstein

Leonard Bernstein

A Life

Meryle Secrest

Alfred A. Knopf · New York · 1994

This Is a Borzoi Book
Published by Alfred A. Knopf, Inc.

Copyright © 1994 by Meryle Secrest Beveridge

Library of Congress
Cataloging-in-Publication Data
Secrest, Meryle.
Leonard Bernstein : a life / by Meryle Secrest. — 1st ed.
p.   cm.
Includes bibliographical references and index.
ISBN 0-679-40731-6
1. Bernstein, Leonard, 1918–1990.
2. Musicians—United States—Biography.   I. Title.
ML410.B566S43   1994
780'.92 — dc20
[B]   94-12664   CIP   MN

Manufactured in the United States of America

First Edition

In memory of
Lowell Pierson Beveridge,
1905–1991

By the . . . composers they love, ye shall know the texture of men's souls.

— JOHN GALSWORTHY

Contents

Acknowledgments   *xi*

The Tzaddikim   *3*

Rocking the Cradle   *38*

Wrong Note Rag   *57*

Tanglewood, 1940   *73*

Paid with Interest   *99*

All-American Boy   *121*

"Music I Heard with You"   *139*

The Elegant Construction   *162*

The White Suit   *181*

"Wow, I'm Famous!"   *199*

The Omnipotent One   *222*

Maestro   242

The Kissing Bandit   270

To Have Is to Be   293

The Right to Fail   310

Questions Without Answers   327

Haywire   347

Amberson   365

Tadzio   379

Tanglewood, 1990   398

Notes   417

Index   451

Acknowledgments

I met Leonard Bernstein in 1963 when I was sent to interview him by the Washington *Post*. Young as I was I realized at once that I was in the presence of an uncommon personality and fell an instant victim to his verve, his erudition, his seriousness of purpose and his unique charm of manner. I was eager to embark upon this study.

Shortly after starting work, however, I learned I would not be able to consult the vast Bernstein archives—which are said to fill a warehouse and contain everything from the suit he wore for his famous New York Philharmonic debut to his first European airline ticket, not to mention original scores and thousands of photographs—because the estate had commissioned an authorized biography and given exclusive access to another biographer. Similarly, I was told by one of Bernstein's three trustees that he could not talk to me because he was contractually bound not to do so. Various family members, close friends and colleagues, including Bernstein's brother, Burton; his three children; Lauren Bacall; Isaac Stern; Carlos Moseley; Jack Gottlieb; Harry Kraut; Michael Tilson Thomas; John Mauceri; and Rosamond Bernier declined for a variety of reasons. Some expressed their unwillingness to act in contradistinction to the family's wishes. I also encountered a surprising number of young musicians who guardedly explained that they would be placing their careers at risk by being interviewed. These, however, were in the minority, as the following list demonstrates. I am deeply indebted to all those who gave a great deal of help for this study, which, it should be noted, is not meant to assess Bernstein's position in the hierarchy of American composers but aspires to be a general biography as J. Christopher Herold defined it. An assessment of Bernstein as composer is much needed; others are more qualified to make that than I.

I am most of all indebted to Shirley Bernstein, Leonard Bernstein's sister, who generously gave me a great deal of time and help, answered my queries with refreshing candor, and helped clarify a number of issues that had been obscure to me. She has been an invaluable guide.

For those who also agreed to be interviewed, I extend my warmest thanks to Ellen Adler, Edward Alexander, Victor Alpert, Marin Alsop, Leonard Altman, Alison Ames, Amy Antonelli, Bettina Bachmann, Thomas G. Bagg, Julius Baker, William Ballard, Ann Barak, Stephanie Barber, Michael Barrett, Mrs. Alan Barth, Harry Beall, Evangeline Benedetti, Annette Elkanova Berger, Professor Walter Berns, the Honorable Livingston L. Biddle, Edward Birdwell, William Bolcom, R. Sumter Brawley, Byron E. Bray, Ruth Buffington, the late Leonard Burkat, Professor Stephen Burton, Maggie Carson, Mitchell Cooper, John Corigliano, Frank Corsaro, William G. Dakin, Jon Deak, Antonio de Almeida, Dr. Anna Lou DeHavenon, Mrs. Irene Diamond, Harry Ellis Dickson, Wayne Dirksen, Stanley Drucker, John Duffy, Richard Dyer, Roger Englander, Helen Epstein, Matthew Epstein, Alan S. Evans, Noel Farrand, Martin Feinstein, Verna Fine, Elizabeth ("Candy") Finkler, Barbara Firger, Leon Fleisher, Henry Fogel, Murray F. Foss, Jacqueline "Kiki" Speyer Fouré, Robert Freeman, Lloyd Garrison, Robert Gartside, Judy Gordon Gassner, Edwin Geller, Milton Goldin, Ralph Gomberg, Eric A. Gordon, James Gordon, Walter Gould, Naomi Graffman, John Gruen, Julia Gruen, Daniel R. Gustin, Jerry Hadley, Daron Hagen, Connie Hammond, Earl Hammond, Pat Handy, Mr. and Mrs. J. Patrick Hayes, the late Hans Heinsheimer, Eve Helman, Josephine Hemsing, Derek Hill, Raphael Hillyer, Joseph Horowitz, Richard Horowitz, Lois Howard, William Huckaby, Eugene Istomin, Gail Jacobs, Alexei Junghans, Rabbi Israel Kazis and Mrs. Kazis, Cal Stewart Kellogg, Leighton Kerner, Jack L. Kirkman, Susan Koscis, Yuri Krasnopolsky, Robert Kreis, Dana Kruger, Ken LaFave, Dorothy Lang, Arthur Laurents, the late Mrs. Fred Lazarus III, Marion Leach, Benjamin Lees, Bethel Leslie,

Professor Jonathan Levy, Barbara Lewis, Bobbie Lewis, Jean Battey Lewis, Laura Longley, Stefan Lorant, Robert and Elaine Newman Lubell, Joseph McLellan, John McLennan, Leonard Marcus, Mr. and Mrs. Jacques Margolies, Gustav Meier, Carol Tilson Miller, Ouida Mintz, Kenneth Mirkin, Jim Mosher, Tom Mullaney, Peter Munves, Thomas P. Muraco, Orin O'Brien, Susanne Oldham, Kurt Ollmann, the late Will Parker, Kenneth Pasmanick, Ellice F. S. Patnaik, Maurice Peress, Shirley Rhoads Perle, Thomas D. Perry, Jr., W. Stuart Pope, Hal Prince, Phillip Ramey, Frank Rizzo, John Rockwell, Mary Rodgers, Ann Ronell, Stephen S. Rosenfeld, Friede Roth, Julius Rudel, Evelyn Saile, Greg Sandow, Hanna Saxon, the late Peter Mark Schifter, Daniel Schorr, Mark Schubart, Thomas J. Schwab, Daniel B. Schwartz, Nancy Scimone, Norman Scribner, Corinne Semon, Philip Setzer, Cantor and Mrs. Gregor Shelkan, Bright Sheng, Ethan Silverman, Joseph Silverstein, Edward Skidmore, Dr. Bertram Slaff, Leonard Slatkin, Mary H. Smith, Maynard Solomon, Zachary Solov, Stephen Somary, Stephen Sondheim, Stephen Spender, Paul Sperry, André L. Speyer, Christian Steiner, Mark Stringer, Nathan Stutch, Rose Styron, Dr. Bluma Swerdloff, Addice Thomas, Vera Tilson, Joan Tower, the late Tatiana Troyanos, Jonathan Tunick, Noel Tyl, Joan Vanoni, Josh Waletzky, Nick Webster, Arnold Weinstein, Sally Weller, John Wells, Jane White, Richard O. White, Angus Whyte, Richard Wilbur, Harold W. Williams, Jane Wilson, Tom Wolfe, Dr. Russell Woollen, Rosemarie Tauris Zadikov and Bruno Zirato, Jr.

I wish to record my special thanks to Mildred Spiegel Zucker and her husband, Harry, who entertained me nobly at their home in White Plains, New York, showed me photographs and documents and a sixteen-page letter from Leonard Bernstein giving a remarkable insight into his relationship with his father. Mrs. Zucker also prepared summaries of her friendship with Bernstein and a detailed summary of her important collection of letters and postcards, most from the early years. I am also greatly indebted to the composer David Diamond, another lifelong friend, who spent a weekend talking to me about his friendship with Bernstein, generously lending me photocopies of letters and photographs from his extensive collection. His insights and tireless help are deeply appreciated. I am especially grateful for similarly extensive help from the composer Ned Rorem, who was never too busy to answer my queries and entertained me munificently when I visited his New York apartment. I also wish to record my thanks to Shirley Rhoads Perle, for lending copies of her letters, to Verna Fine for similar courtesies, and to Andrew Pincus, music critic of the Berkshire *Eagle,* who was particularly generous with time and help, allowing me to interview him shortly before facing a serious operation. He also provided me with a group of important interview notes gathered for a project of his own. I have been helped and guided by the wonderful and sage Richard Bales, composer and conductor, whose career at the National Gallery of Art is nationally known and who knew Bernstein from the days when both were students of Koussevitzky.

Many others provided courtesies large and small. Dean David Rubin of the Newhouse School of Public Communications at Syracuse University is one of the very few authorities who have actually studied music as a business. He and I spoke at length and he provided copies of his own valuable articles on this complex and intriguing subject. Then there was Mrs. Merle Orren, who found me on her doorstep in Newton, Massachusetts, one day and kindly allowed me to see the house in which Bernstein had lived and to point out the spot in the living room where his piano is said to have been. Tim Page, music critic of *Newsday,* was a major influence on this study, suggesting names and approaches, giving me the benefit of his extensive knowledge, searching his files, never too busy to talk and always sympathetic and encouraging—qualities not always to be found in professional critics. Then there was Johanna Fiedler, daughter of the famous Boston Symphony Orchestra conductor and a friend and colleague of long standing, who was never too busy to commiserate with me—she is engaged on a biography of her father—and suggest new approaches. Last but not least there were a number of close associates and friends of Bernstein's who felt, for various compelling reasons, that they should not be mentioned by name. I have respected their wishes; they know who they are, and to them go my heartfelt thanks.

Biographers are invariably kind to other biographers, but some, it seems to me, went above and beyond the call of duty in giving me help. Barbara Heyman, Samuel Barber's biographer, was kindness itself, as was Philip Hart, author of the major study *Orpheus in the New World* and the biographer of Fritz Reiner, who shed much light on many obscure corners of music history. I also wish to thank Don Ott, who is in charge of the Mitropoulos archive and was particularly helpful.

A number of institutions were consulted for this study, and valuable help and expertise was given. I particularly wish to thank Dr. James W. Pruett, chief of the Music Division at the Library of Congress, and members of his staff—including John Newsom, assistant chief; Elizabeth Auman, donor relations officer; Gillian Anderson; and Ray White—for their detailed and invaluable help in guiding me through the library's important collection of materials relating to Bernstein's career. I spent many months in their company. I am similarly indebted to Jeff Flannery, reference librarian at the Manuscript Division of the Library of Congress, who gave me important information. While at the Performing Arts Library at the Kennedy Center, Peter Fay, music specialist, was most helpful and knowledgeable.

The officers at Tanglewood, the summer home of the Boston Symphony Orchestra, went out of their way to be helpful when I went there to conduct interviews in the summer of 1991, a year after Bernstein's last performances there. I am particularly indebted to James E. Whitaker, chief coordinator, and Carol Woodworth for steering me in the right directions. Considerable help was also provided by the New York Philharmonic Orchestra and its former administrator, Frank Milburn, and Barbara Haws, archivist; my thanks go to them. Betsy Walker, librarian at the Curtis Institute of Music, went to great trouble to answer my queries when I went to study there, as did Bridget P. Carr of the Boston Symphony Orchestra Archives; I appreciate their help. I also wish to thank Elizabeth Schaaf, archivist at the Peabody Conservatory in Baltimore; Patricia O'Kelly, managing director of public relations for the National Symphony Orchestra; and the librarians at the Jewish Community Center of Greater Washington.

My further thanks are due to the following people who gave help, advice, information and their valuable time: the editor William Abrahams, Cleveland Amory, Gladys Bashkin, Joanne Belk, Marie Bernard, Albert J. Beveridge III, Naneen Boyce, John Malcolm Brinnin, Robert E. Browne, Robert Bunshaft, Lois Butka, Jacob Canter, Richard Carter, Stephen Cera, Lee Cheek, Noma Copley, Diana Stomzick Corto, David J. Rau, associate curator, Mark Coir, director of archives, and Roy Slade, president of the Cranbrook Academy of Art, Jeffrey Dane, Fredric Dannen, David Davis, Peter G. Davis, Gervase de Peyer, Gina di Medio, William Dunlap, Edith Eisenberg, Milton Esterow, Roberta Fels, Virginia Fitzgerald, Jane Fluegel, the late Andor Foldes, Lukas Foss, Lillian Frankel, Dr. Arnold Freedman, Florence Freund, Yvonne R. Freund, Sarah Garrison, Edward Geller, Thomas A. Goldman, Barbara Gordon, Ellsworth Grant, Regina Greenspun, Herbert Grossman, Julius Grossman, Ed and Evy Halpert, Barbara Barry Harnick, John R. Harpold, Rosalie Harris, Phoebe Hoban, Professor Richard B. Hovey, Professor A. Hurwitz, Penn Jillette, Denise Kahn, Martin Kasden, Austin H. Kiplinger, Clarice Kornette, Tom Godell of the Koussevitzky Recordings Society, Marcia Kraus, Dr. Bernard E. Kreger, Alan Kriegsman, Joseph Laitin, Maestro Joel and Dr. Susan Lazar, Dr. E. James Lieberman, Helen Lillie, Professor Ralph Locke, James Lovell, David Lowenherz, president of Lion Heart Autographs, Clay McDaniel, John Maxtone-Graham, Mrs. Loudon Mellen, Jeffrey Meyers, Elmer Michelson, Alan Miller, Hermine R. Mittelman, Professor Hugh S. Moorhead, Gerson Nordlinger, Jr., Jeanne Paul, Vivian Perlis, Joan Peyser, Andrew Porter, Father Cormac Rigby, Marcella Rittner, Jerome Robbins, Don Roberts, music librarian at Northwestern University at Evanston, Angela Robinson, Richard Rodzinski, Roz Rosenblatt, Jane Rosenbloom, Leo Rost, Norman Rosten, Etta Schiff, Michal Schmidt, Harold C. Schonberg, Marie Schwartz, Nell Davenport Schwartz, Nancy Jean Seigel, Professor Howard Shanet, Arthur Shimkin, Ethel Siegel, Marie Siegrist, Nancy Sies, George Silberman, Maggie Smith, Thomas W. Smith, William Jay Smith, Boris Sokoloff, Mary Gene Sondericker, department of Special Events at the Metropolitan Opera, Dorle Soria, Caroline Stoessinger, Brian Stuart, Mrs. Sydney Sugerman, Howard Taubman, Philip Taubman, Gloria Felix Thompson, Elle Tracy, Dr. Ferdinand Trauttmansdorff, cultural attaché at the Austrian embassy, Walter N. Trenerry, Cecilia A. Vogel, Vincent Wagner, Morris Wald, Marion L. Weil, Lea Weinberg, William A. Whitcraft, Jr., Ronald Wilford, Marie Winn, Curt Wittig, Professor Christoph Wolff, acting director of Harvard University Libraries, Bill Wright, Jack L. Yohay and Harriet Zinnes.

On my numerous trips to New York for interviews, Clara and Bevis Longstreth generously allowed me to make their spacious apartment my home away from home, often on very short notice. I cannot thank them enough for their repeated hospitality; I owe them more than I can say. Anne Biddle similarly welcomed me to her elegant house outside Philadelphia when I was studying at Curtis and entertained me generously and warmly. So did my great friends in London, Anne Ellis and Audrey Stevenson, whose hospitality is a reflection of their warmth of spirit; the same is true for Jean Pierre and Michèle Epron in Paris. My agent, Murray Pollinger, has followed the course of this study with his usual close, informed and eloquent interest. Victoria Wilson, my editor, has given me the benefit of her tactful and incisive advice and suggested many valuable additions. As always I wish to thank my husband, the composer and conductor Thomas Beveridge, who has advised, suggested and encouraged, and cast a professional eye over the results. I hasten to add that the remaining errors, if any, are mine. This book is dedicated to the memory of my father-in-law, the late Dr. Lowell P. Beveridge, a most "parfit, gentil knyght" and a musician of rare gifts.

Leonard Bernstein

The Tzaddikim

Faster, my Kronos, give your horses the whip . . .

— GOETHE, "AN SCHWAGER KRONOS" (TO THE POSTILION KRONOS); MUSIC BY FRANZ SCHUBERT, OP. 19, NO. 1

"In the beginning was the Note, and the Note was with God," Leonard Bernstein wrote. "Whosoever can reach for that Note, reach high, and bring it back to us on earth . . ."

Given the pinnacles Bernstein would eventually attain, the fact that he showed no interest in his chosen field until he was nine or ten is considered unusual for a musician, if not anomalous. The most popular version of the story is that he was ten before the idea of playing a piano occurred to him, and his interest was accidental, his aunt Clara's piano having been placed in the house for safekeeping. He struck a chord, it is said, and screamed for music lessons.

There is, however, respectable evidence that his prodigious talent showed itself in babyhood. According to this story his mother went to visit a neighbor, took him along and put him on the living room carpet.

He began a purposeful crawl, or totter, towards a piano in the next room. Hauling himself up by one of its legs, he planted a fist firmly on the keys. Another account has him taking music lessons at the age of nine, at the urging of a music teacher who lived across the street and used to see him drumming out melodies on the windowpane. Supposedly, he was practicing fingerings on the windowsill, which would argue for a well-established piano passion some time before the arrival of Aunt Clara's massive carved upright. The fallow period between the infant Lenny's marked interest and the arrival of the piano is usually explained by lack of parental interest. It is said that even if they had known their son was destined to be a musical prodigy, they would not have done anything about it.

To assume from that that the Bernstein family life was devoid of music would be erroneous. Samuel Bernstein, Leonard Bernstein's father, was descended from a long line of Hasidim, followers of Israel ben Eliezer (or the Baal Shem Tov), an eighteenth-century charismatic leader who would redefine traditional Jewish values. Instead of the rabbinical emphasis on formal learning, doom-ridden visions and the sophistry that passed for much Talmudic thought, Israel ben Eliezer's approach to his faith was direct and positive. One should take the time to praise the simple pleasures of life. Worship should be a joyful experience. Leo Rosten wrote, "God can be worshiped anywhere, said the *Baal Shem Tov*, directly and simply: God requires no synagogues, except 'in the heart.' Prayers should be spontaneous, personal, happy—not the formalized, automatic rote of the *shul*. . . . The Chasidim preferred gay songs to magisterial invocations. They danced and clapped hands while singing out the Lord's praises, and they invited group expressions of religious rapture. The Chasidic celebration of God offered poor Jews a new kind of communion—warm, intimate, personal . . ." Since coming to God with a full heart counted for more than purely intellectual understanding, the expression of faith through music became one of the central tenets of the Hasidic movement, and in the nineteenth century three-quarters of the Jewish population of Eastern Europe was Hasidic. Since God was present in all things—eating, drinking, praying, making love—he was present in music as well, and the more abandoned one's emotion as one sang, shouted, rocked and leapt into the air, the more one was worshipping God; the more one identified with God. "The founder of Hasidism taught that music heightened spiritual awareness and made it easier to appreciate the beauty of the world . . ."

Music as an acceptable outlet for feeling would be all the more important for a society in which so much emphasis was placed upon ritualistic behavior. As Irving Howe has pointed out, life in the European *shtetl* was highly formalized. "The 613 *mitzvot,* or commandments, that a pious Jew must obey, which dictate such things as the precise way in which a chicken is to be slaughtered; the singsong in which the Talmud is to be read; the kinds of food to serve during the Sabbath; the way in which shoes should be put on each morning . . . these were the outer signs of an inner discipline."

From childhood Bernstein was brought up listening to Hasidic melodies, those tunes perhaps borrowed from Arabic, Greek, Turkish or Spanish roots and collected by Najara in the sixteenth century, and watching the faithful singing, dancing, clapping and swaying. Once he could play the piano, he accompanied his father while he "sang and acted out the old story of a group of pilgrims visiting a rabbi on a holiday and being so moved by his ardent prayers that they offered to sacrifice themselves . . ." Sam Bernstein dancing and clapping—it is not the usual image presented of Bernstein's father, but it must have had an effect upon his impressionable son.

Since book learning was not expected of the Hasidim, they needed educated leaders, called *tzaddikim,* or righteous men. These men had "reached the ideal of communion in the highest degree and therefore appeared before God as 'one of his own.' " Each *tzaddik* or *rebbe*'s sole function was to mediate between God and his followers, to help them not only spiritually but in earthly affairs as well. Each had his own group of followers, some of whom believed that to imitate him in every word and gesture, even to the way he tied his shoes, would somehow bring about the necessary spiritual transformation. To that extent, his life and personality became an integral part of theirs. As the Hasidic movement spread, dynasties were established. Fathers passed to sons their power to mediate, as it were, in perpetuity.

Samuel Bernstein claimed to trace his own lineage back to the tribe of Benjamin—a fairly common Hasidic conceit. More recent ancestors were rabbis, that is to say, scholars, legal authorities and teachers as far back as sixteenth-century Prussia and Poland. Samuel was born on January 5, 1892, in a *shtetl* near the town of Berezdov (in Yiddish, Beresdiv) on a tributary of the Korchyk River midway between Kiev and Rovno in the Ukrainian area of the Pale of Settlement. He was named Yiroel Yosef ben Yehuda, but the name Yiroel disappeared before he was circumcised, and he was always known as Shmuel. His stories about the family usually contained frequent references to Bezalel Bernstein, Leonard's great-grandfather, a heroic blacksmith who died in his thirties while trying to rescue a tool chest from his burning blacksmith shop, and his own father, Rabbi Yehuda, or Yudel, ben Bezalel. Yudel, who was only twelve when his father died, "wrapped himself for protection in Hasidism, Talmud, and Torah, and grew up to become another scholar-rabbi—his slight, flaccid body hunched over his books, rocking more or less constantly to the rhythms of devout prayer," Burton Bernstein, Leonard's brother, wrote. "He cultivated a beard and long sidelocks. He wore a black caftan and a fur hat—the uniform of the ultra-Orthodox. He knew and cared little for the world beyond the walls of his room, the yeshiva, and the synagogue."

Yudel's wife, Dinah Malamud, Leonard's grandmother, from the nearby town of Korets, possessed the practical attributes her scholar-husband lacked. She established, or continued, a Bernstein family pattern of strong, capable women who sustain the exalted intellectual goals of their physically susceptible men. She was delicately fair-skinned, blue-eyed and blond, but her fragile appearance was belied by her physical stamina. She ran their farm with her capable hands, as big as a man's, plowed their fields and tended their animals, besides bearing and bringing up their children.

Yudel and Dinah would eventually emigrate to the United States and, since they never changed, Shmuel's three children would learn at first hand about their stiff-necked pieties, their insularity and the gulf that separated the American-born Bernsteins from these adherents of an ancient culture, as well as the enduring links. If Yudel was a God-fearing man, he was an unyielding one. "Judaism entered into every cranny of daily life: no question was too small to be answered by one religious dictum or another . . . no sin against God . . . too trifling to go unpunished." Once Shmuel's yarmulkah fell off during evening prayer and he was severely beaten. After she arrived in America, Dinah refused to enter a room unless a mezuzah was affixed to its doorpost. An Orthodox Jew, crossing such a threshold, touched his finger to the mezuzah and then to his lips whenever he entered or left. The mezuzah symbolized that the home was consecrated, that it was an altar to wisdom, or *chachmah,* that word which Samuel Bernstein loved so much.

The excessive regimentation of conduct within the *shtetl* and the barriers placed between it and the outside world is said to be a consequence of lives lived with the ever-present threat of hostility, sacrilege and brute force. Jews in tsarist Russia could legally live only in the Pale of Settlement, an area of about a million square miles stretching between the Baltic and the Black Sea. Beresdiv was in the historic province of Volhynia, which had contained Jewish settlements as far back as the twelfth century and which had become, by the sixteenth, a center of Jewish culture.

Jews in nineteenth-century Volhynia were at the mercy of whichever Russian tsar was in power. For a time, they enjoyed the modest liberal reforms of Alexander II, but when he was assassinated in 1881, to be followed by Alexander III, the old pattern of pogroms and intolerance was reinstated. Jews had been emigrating to the United States since Colonial times, but never with such desperation or in such numbers. Between the assassination of Alexander II and World War II, almost a third of Eastern European Jews crossed the borders of Germany and Austria-Hungary and made their way to freedom.

One of the ways of persecuting Jews in the early nineteenth century was compulsory military service for youths, the younger the better. During Nicholas I's thirty-year reign (1825–55) pathetic children were torn away from their families at the age of eight or nine, treated as adults and taken on forced marches. "Well, they cough and cough until they cough themselves into their graves," one onlooker said. A young conscript's period of service could be as long as twenty-five years, during which he would be under constant pressure to convert to Christianity. The outbreak of the Russo-Japanese War in 1904 revived some terrifying memories and put further pressure on Jews in the Pale of Settlement to flee before the draft took them. By chance, Shmuel Yosef knew an escape route. His uncle Herschel Malamud, his mother's younger brother, had left Korets in 1903 and managed to reach Hartford, Connecticut, where he took up a new life as Harry Levy and was training as a barber. Harry Levy's relatives in Korets knew the best way of smuggling oneself across the Prussian border. They had the address of the United Hebrew Charities in Danzig and advice about how to get passage to Liverpool and thence to America. In 1908, Harry Levy sent his nephew the money, and Shmuel, aged sixteen, packed up his clothes. Since he was the firstborn son, his parents had hoped he would continue the ancestral tradition and become a rabbi, or *rebbe,* as the Hasidim said. Shmuel had been educated at the local *heder,* or religious primary school, and went on to the yeshiva, or rabbinical college, to study and discuss the Torah and the Talmud and become a learned man like his father. To leave his native land for an uncertain future was tantamount to closing the door, not just on his family, but their hopes. Whether from guilt or prudence, he did not say goodbye to his parents but stole away.

After the frightful crossing in steerage that might have been predicted, Shmuel arrived at Ellis Island, where Uncle Harry was waiting to greet him and post the necessary twenty-five-dollar bond needed for his admittance. A clerk renamed him Samuel Joseph Bernstein, and Sam was ready for work—any work. Harry Levy could not yet afford to apprentice him as a barber, but he knew where a boy just off the boat, speaking no English, could earn enough money to survive: Manhattan's Fulton Fish Market along the South Street docks.

The terrible conditions there left a permanent scar on the memory of the young immigrant. He was used to heavy farm work, but even he was appalled at the numbers of fish he was required to clean every week. At first he trimmed and gutted for no wages. "Customers used to drop pennies in a tin box and Sam Bernstein . . . used to average $1.40 a week—for the labor of cleaning two tons of fish." In those days he lived on a piece of herring, which cost a penny, and a hunk of black bread, which cost two cents. Eventually he got steady work, a weekly wage of five dollars, and a work day of twelve hours, six days a week. It was a useful experience, his son Burton wrote, since it helped him acquire a rudimentary English. He discovered that he was no worse off than his co-workers and, "anything could happen in this America."

He lived in New York for four years, lodging first in a grimy East Side tenement, then in better quarters in Brooklyn. He took English classes at night and tried to pass Post Office examinations to become a postman. He said, "I wanted to wear the uniform of my country. So I studied and scrimped, and finally it came time to take the examination. And what happened? I failed—on spelling!" Then Uncle Harry offered him a job in his barbershop, so Sam moved to Hartford, where he swept floors and sterilized combs and scissors. Shortly after that he was hired as a stockboy by the firm of Frankel and Smith, wholesalers to barbers, and dealers in a line of wigs and switches woven from Oriental and European hair. Frankel and Smith were starting up a new branch in Boston, so Sam moved again. He had, purely by chance, discovered the field in which he would demonstrate a natural aptitude. He would eventually own the biggest beauty-supply company in New England.

Sam married Jennie Resnick in 1917. By then he was an assistant manager at Frankel and Smith, with a salary of fifteen dollars a week. Jennie, too, was an immigrant. Her family had come from a small village not far from Beresdiv and found work at wool factories in Lawrence, the manufacturing town just outside Boston. Pictures of Sam taken at the time of their marriage, wearing the respectable suit and stiff collar of his Sabbath best, along with owlish glasses, made him look like a bookkeeper. His ears stuck out, the way his son's would, a trait he shared with every member of the Malamuds, his mother's family; and he lacked stature. Jennie, who was enchantingly pretty, judged him to be barely acceptable. Their daughter, Shirley, said that her mother was not in love and neither was her father. "I found out my father had fallen in love with a Gentile he knew he couldn't marry and married my mother on the rebound." What Jennie liked about Sam was his sense of humor. "He always had a good story to tell," she told her son Burton. She was, by all accounts, fun-loving and intelligent but, because she had been obliged to go to work in the mill at age twelve, indifferently educated. "Orthodox Jews in those days disdained their women," Theodore White wrote. She detested her factory work, and marriage to Sam, a young man with a future, was her escape route.

Yet their differences were basic. For Sam, whose true world was the life of the mind, Talmudic study and how to prosper in business, Jennie was a hopeless lightweight; she liked dances, parties, gossip, movie magazines and cheap romantic novels. Once married, he attacked her for her "common" Resnick relatives and, Shirley Bernstein recalled, refused to have them in his house. She mocked his relentless ambition, his stringent economies and his obsession—in her eyes—with religion. The conflict was so immediate that Jennie left Sam and moved back with her parents after just a year of marriage, and did it again about two years later. However, the arrival of their firstborn, Leonard, on August 25, 1918, gave them a common purpose in life. (Leonard was named Louis, a name he never used and legally changed when he was sixteen.) Sam dreamed about educating Lenny, and his career was thriving. He became manager at Frankel and Smith, with another increase in wages, and resolved to have his own business. The marriage lurched along for the next few years. In the autumn of 1923, five years after Leonard's birth, Shirley Anne arrived, and Sam opened his own business, the Samuel Bernstein Hair Company. (Sam and Jennie then had their last child, Burton, born on January 31, 1932.) In his memoir, *Family Matters,* written while his mother was still alive, Burton Bernstein made no secret of his parents' troubled relationship and implied they would have divorced had such a course been open to them. Leonard Bernstein explored the theme of an unhappy marriage in two works thought to be at least partly autobiographical. Shirley Bernstein saw her father as

Sam and Jennie, a 1917 engagement picture

The young Leonard Bernstein, age four, with his
parents, Jennie and Sam Bernstein, circa 1922

unpredictable and her mother as a benumbed victim. "My father knew she didn't love him. When he felt she and we were turning against him he'd be very miserly. He'd make her beg for money. I remember one Tuesday morning when Burtie was an infant I asked my mother for a quarter for banking day at school. She was only wearing a housecoat, so she asked my father for the money, and he said, '*You* give it to her.' Things got ugly and he went to throw a bottle of milk and my mother fled to the baby's room. Lenny spread-eagled himself against the door and my father calmed down."

Once the family had settled into a comfortable house at 8 Pleasanton Street in Roxbury—at this stage they could afford a maid—Sam and Jennie joined the conservative congregation of Mishkan Tefila, a handsome neoclassical building of Indiana limestone that had been built facing Franklin Park on the corner of Seaver Street and Elm Hill Avenue a few blocks away. Mishkan Tefila is now in ruins, its beautiful walls defaced, its windows shattered, its roof gone and its noble facade obscured by trees that have grown right up to the steps. But when the Bernsteins were living in Roxbury it was the *stadt shul,* a great central synagogue attracting adherents from a wide area. The conservative movement, as Mishkan Tefila's famous rabbi, Herman H. Rubenovitz, wrote, sought to offer a middle path between the rigidities of the Orthodox *shuls* and the reform synagogues, so "reformed" that the Hebrew language had practically disappeared and the traditional Sabbath observance had given way to Sunday-morning services. Mishkan Tefila offered children a proper Hebrew training, and its congregation observed the Jewish calendar. However, in contrast to Orthodox *shuls,* men and women sat together, and there was a handsome organ played by its music director, Professor Solomon G. Braslavsky, and mixed choirs. Sam became an active member. Just after World War II he was vice-president of the temple and sat on the dais with its cantor, Gregor Shelkan.

That Sam should take his family to a conservative congregation when a Hasidic *shul* existed—Beth Pinchas, in the West End of Boston—had to do with the pressures of daily life in his adopted land. "In Boston, as in every American city, immigrants might continue to practice their religion as their fathers had, and the wives would try—at home—to preserve the old customs," Theodore White wrote. "But the men had to learn the ways of American small business to survive, the mothers had to feed their children into the suction of American schools.

So there perished first the old religious orthodoxy, then the old-country customs . . ." Burton Bernstein, who realized how torn his father felt, noted that while Jewish dietary laws were observed at home, outside the house the children could eat whatever they liked. One of the songs from Leonard Bernstein's *Candide,* a tango, notes ironically, "I am so easily assimilated . . ."

Sam made heroic efforts to adapt to his alien culture. Yet the one from which he had fled, which he called "a prison," engendered conflicts that were never resolved. His daughter said, "My father suffered from large swings of mood, and one never knew what to expect; he'd either be very up, dancing and singing, or very depressed. I do remember the emotion very strongly. We'd be playing and someone would say 'Daddy's home!' and I would stiffen. Sometimes there would be scenes at the dinner table and terrible silences and he'd say, 'Tell your mother to pass the salt,' and call her ugly names under his breath. That's why to this day I have a bad stomach."

When Sam was in a good mood, one could hardly stop him from talking, or rather, pontificating. Leonard said, "If you say to him 'pass the salt,' he's already teaching you something: 'You know, Moses said about salt . . .' " As Leonard wrote, his father was unable to spend any time with a customer without reaching for his Bible and beginning a rambling lesson on, for example, the Book of Judges, chapter 14. Sam might have abandoned all ambition to become a rabbi, but could not help believing, with his culture, that "a man's prestige, authority and position depended to a considerable extent on his learning." So from time to time he went to services at Beth Pinchas, where he was also a member, and "where the women sat upstairs, and the men, almost invisible in their prayer shawls, keened loudly, and not one syllable was cut from the lengthy liturgical services." There, a man's longing for God could be expressed unreservedly; indeed, to be overwhelmed with feeling was almost required.

"To the child, the father is God," Leonard Bernstein wrote. On learning that God had made Adam from dust, Lenny, aged four, decided on a practical experiment. He dumped some earth into a basin, turned on the tap and awaited the transformation. As for Sam, he would instruct, exhort, admonish and mold, with the goal of creating a *ruach Elohim,* godly spirit. Once the baby Leonard began to speak, he talked straightaway in grown-up sentences, "like a little old man," his mother said. Sam would say, "I live to give that boy the opportunity I didn't have." Both Sam and Jennie hovered over their son; but while Sam wres-

Lenny and Shirley with their parents in 1933

tled with his soul, Jennie fretted over his health. From childhood, Bernstein suffered from periodic attacks of asthma, a life-threatening disease which left him gasping and wheezing. The kind of running and jumping games most children can play were proscribed for him at first, because violent exertion exacerbates the symptoms, which can be triggered by anything from cat dander and dust mites to paint fumes and car exhaust. He was only aware of being skinny, scared and miserable.

Until he was thirteen Bernstein lived in Roxbury, then a Jewish suburb (it has now become black), within the boundaries of which he felt safe. However, to the west of Franklin Park, a dividing line, lay the homes of the "lace-curtain" Irish, parents of tough working-class youths who systematically attacked Jewish children. This happened to Bernstein more than once. Years later he said, "You know what I lack talent in? Boxing. I can't hit anybody. It's one of the real shames of my life. I remember being attacked by a bully when I was just a kid, maybe because I was Jewish. I couldn't fight back."

Bernstein attended William Lloyd Garrison School, and Sam took him to Mishkan Tefila. The first time he heard the choir, Bernstein found himself in tears. As for the organ, "It was the Mighty Wurlitzer itself to me"; before long he had persuaded Professor Braslavsky to give him organ lessons. Mitchell Cooper, who grew up across the road and also attended Mishkan Tefila, recalled that Bernstein had a very good voice as a boy and was cantor for the youth service. From the age of eight on, Bernstein was enrolled in the Hebrew school, a building that adjoined the temple on the Elm Hill side. He went there for two hours every day after school. His contemporary Theodore White, who studied at a similar Boston Hebrew school, Beth-El, recalled that his teachers were mostly European immigrants enrolled at Boston universities and earning their living teaching Hebrew. "They were rigorous in their teaching of the young and violent of temper when the tired children failed to respond." After some preliminary work translating from English, the Bible was taught in Hebrew; "it was explained to us in Hebrew, pounded into us in Hebrew, and we were forced to explain it to one another in Hebrew." White took courses in the Bible from Genesis through the Prophets and was expected to know everything from memory. "Memory was the foundation of learning . . . and the memory cut grooves on young minds that even decades cannot erase," he wrote. Bernstein's own memory for names, dates, languages, faces and whatever he had heard was generally agreed to be phenomenal, and must have owed something to that early training. Once, when Bernstein and Aaron Copland had gone for a walk and spent twenty minutes in an aimless conversation, Copland "was finally moved to wager that neither of them could remember a word of what they had been saying. Never a man to withdraw meekly from a dare, Bernstein promptly repeated the entire conversation, not only verbatim but backward."

As Bernstein grew older his ability to tolerate physical activity improved. To Cooper, he was a "thoroughgoing kid" who played on the street, a boy among boys, not effete, mannered or shy. "We both belonged to the same youth organization, and he once made me play hooky from school, which I always felt badly about." As for taking music lessons, Cooper said, "everyone did. I took piano lessons for two years before I changed to banjo, and so did my brothers. I think it would have been stranger if he *hadn't* taken piano lessons."

Bernstein's first piano teacher, when he was nine, was a lady in Dorchester named Frieda Karp, who charged a dollar a lesson. He made rapid progress and, a year later, opened her recital with Paderewski's Fantasy. It was clear he needed a piano of his own. "Well, I didn't want it much," Sam Bernstein said of Aunt Clara's piano. "It wasn't any beauty, and it cost five dollars to move, but finally I said I'd take it, and the minute Lenny sat down at that—ah, I tell you, I knew that boy wanted music and nothing else."

Bernstein recalled that the piano had to go in the hallway as there was nowhere else to put it. It had a middle pedal that could make it sound like a mandolin. "And I remember *touching* it . . . and that was it. That was my contract with life, with God. From then on . . . I had found my universe, my place where I felt safe. This thing suddenly made me feel supreme . . ."

Bernstein clung to the notion that Aunt Clara's piano was the talisman that changed his life. "One day I was a scrawny little thing that everybody could beat up, and the next time I looked around I was the biggest boy in the class. I could run faster, jump higher, dive better than almost anybody, and all the girls wanted to feel my muscles."

In 1929, when he was just eleven, Bernstein entered Boston Public Latin School. This illustrious institution, in which he would spend the next six years of his life, was founded in 1635 (a year before Harvard University) and, down through the centuries, retained its reputation for having trained some of the country's most famous men and women, from Benjamin Franklin, John Quincy Adams and John Hancock to Ralph Waldo Emerson and John Fitzgerald Kennedy. It was open to all—Irish, Jewish, Italian, Oriental—but its standards were exacting and only the best and brightest survived to graduate to the next step: Harvard University.

Bernstein said that he took the streetcar from Roxbury with a friend of his to present their report cards from Garrison School. They stood in a line and were accepted. Once they were back in the street they jumped up and down in excitement because both of them had such good grades that they had been excused from taking an entrance exam.

In retrospect Bernstein believed that his most valuable experience at Boston Latin was the training he received in synthesizing information. He termed it "interdisciplinary cognition—that is, learning to know something by its relation to something else." Learning to love learning was the goal. But according to Theodore White, who was there at the same time, little emphasis was placed on joy. What mattered was the ability to pass stiff monthly exams, usually based on previous College Board questions, and the passing grade was 50, rather than 60 as elsewhere: evidence of the superior standards to which the students were being held.

When Bernstein arrived a wing was being built onto the school, and so he took classes across the road in the High School of Commerce and, the following year, on Pinckney Street in Beacon Hill. "Since we were like orphans, being farmed out . . . it wasn't until the [third year] that I began to develop a very strong school spirit," Bernstein said later.

One of the teachers he remembered was Aaron Gordon, a "young, handsome, blond-haired kid" who taught him English, history and Latin. He also remembered Philip Marson, his first English master. "He made an incredible impression on me. He revealed the English language to me in some magical way and I fell in love with poetry that year, largely due to his influence." Some twenty-five of Bernstein's essays from Boston Latin, most of them written during his final year, have survived. (A fragment of one essay is a defense of a performance of Serge Koussevitzky's that had been criticized; how dare anyone attack the great man's interpretations of Beethoven, Tchaikovsky and César Franck?) Bernstein's penmanship was rhythmical and his capital letters executed with a flourish. His literary style, however, was stilted; his phrases sound quaintly archaic. His teacher repeatedly urged him to use simpler, more direct language. One of Bernstein's essays in particular was a masterpiece of equivocation. Discussing his future, he conceded that he wanted to be a musician but said that his father had other plans for him. It was true that a Harvard background could be quite useful for a businessman. As for their disagreement, his son would have to bide his time.

That guarded description alluded to a conflict that raged throughout his adolescence once it became clear that music was more than a passing interest. Sam wanted his firstborn to take over the thriving family business. Even if Leonard were to become a rabbi, that would be no disgrace. Although Sam quite liked the idea of Leonard having an avocation, something a cultured man of the world could take up on weekends for relaxation, the idea of music as a career was out of the question, or so he said then. Bernstein usually explained his father's opposition with the comment that, in the *shtetl,* a musician was simply one of a raffish band of traveling players who drifted from town to town, performing at country fairs and weddings. "As characters, the shabby klezmorim were familiar to all Ashkenazic Jews," Leo Rosten wrote; "they were regarded as drifters, odd types . . ."

Mitchell Cooper commented, "You have to place this disapproval in the context of a community of immigrants struggling to survive in a reasonably hostile environment, who had made it. It would have taken an amazing man *not* to have wanted his son either to become a professional or go into business. Here you have a father who is wondering what's going to happen to the business and how is it going to look with his contemporaries? They are going to say, 'Poor Sam, what a disappointment, and look at all the money he spent.'" Or, as Sam Bernstein quipped, "How did I know he was going to become Leonard Bernstein?" He also said, with some bitterness, "You know, every genius had a handicap. Beethoven was deaf. Chopin had tuberculosis. Well, someday I suppose the books will say, 'Lenny Bernstein had a father.'" Leonard Bernstein said, "We developed an enmity, a hatred over this subject . . ."

The first pieces Bernstein learned from Frieda Karp were a schottische called "The Mountain Belle" and a march, "On to Victory." He thought she was very pretty and was perfectly happy with her for the next two years, but then she married and moved to California. Bernstein trotted off to the New England Conservatory and was accepted. The fee was three dollars an hour. After a painful scene, Sam agreed to allow Lenny to go if he would forfeit all but twenty-five cents of his weekly allowance to pay for lessons. It was a marvelous opportunity, but the experience almost destroyed him as a pianist.

"Watching him play for the first time, the new teacher declared that he had 'no system.' 'You have humps,' she added, pointing to his hands. 'Only a camel has humps . . .' The lady, it appeared, sternly disapproved of the way most pianists, including the very best ones, arch their hands over the keyboard, and she had invented a system of playing in which the hands were held rigid, with the knuckles down and only the fingers moving." For two years Bernstein faithfully practiced this ruinous method. Father and son reached a temporary truce after Lenny gave a speech in Hebrew for his bar mitzvah that aroused universal admiration. His reward was a Chickering grand and a cruise down the Panama Canal.

Miss America receives a permanent wave, with the
newfangled permanent wave machine, in 1926.
Opposite: above, The Boston Latin School; *below,*
Burton Bernstein with the family dog and car

The family house in Newton, Massachusetts: a contemporary view

"The first night, after dinner," Sam related, "Lenny and I took a walk through the ship. He spotted a beautiful big piano. It was about seven-thirty. Most of the passengers were still at dinner. Lenny sat down at the piano. In about an hour, the whole salon was filled. At midnight he was still playing . . ."

As might be guessed from the lavish presents, Sam had become a man of property. At the time of the great stock market crash, when "millionaires were . . . selling apples in Times Square," as Bernstein put it, Sam had struck gold: he had managed to outbid the competition for the New England franchise of the new, improved Fredericks Permanent Wave machine. It was such a profitable coup that the Samuel Bernstein Hair Company expanded almost overnight from a small office to two floors, employing fifty people. That was in 1927. During the Depression years that followed, against all logic, the hairdressing business continued to expand. In 1932 Sam built a red-shingled summer cottage in Sharon, and in 1933, a winter home for the family in the middle-class suburb of Newton, Massachusetts.

The house in Sharon, a summer resort colony popular with Bostonians in the 1930s because it was on a railway line, is now painted dark green. It is substantial, with glassed-in porches and a pleasant garden, and situated on an unpretentious, winding street. Massapoag Lake, a short distance away, is bordered with sandy paths and trees bent out of shape by the almost constant wind, no doubt the reason why it was chosen as a refuge for Sam's oldest son, with his agonizing allergy to pollen. The Newton house is a square red-brick center-hall colonial with Georgian details, yellow trim and half-moon cutouts on the shutters. It stands on a narrow, deep lot and is somewhat closer to the street than its neighbors. In a picturesque area graced with handsome Tudors and elegant colonials well placed on manicured lots, the Bernstein home is a notable exception. Large, solid and prosaic, it faces the street with an uncompromising air, as if created by an armor-plated imagination.

The Newton house had a two-car garage, a great luxury. Bernstein's friend the late Leonard Burkat said, "Lenny used to talk about poverty and misery and wretchedness, but by the standards of his friends they were indescribably rich." Lenny would arrive at school in his mother's Plymouth convertible or perhaps another car the family had, a brown Dodge, and wearing a camel hair coat, and create a sensation. He was always well dressed, Burkat remembered, and had fancier bow ties than anyone else. Most of the boys of his generation had to work after school delivering groceries or doing other odd jobs, but not Lenny.

Years later Bernstein claimed there had been no music at all at Boston Latin School. However Burkat, a classmate, said that there were extracurricular music and art lessons. "We got instruments and rehearsal rooms, that was true; they were generously provided," he said. Sports played no great part in their lives. "We were infant intellectuals and artists."

In 1932 Bernstein, whose pianistic progress had been stunted by his teacher's theory, went in search of new inspiration. He had heard about Heinrich Gebhard, then the most influential teacher in Boston, who charged the immense sum of twenty-five dollars a lesson. Nancy Jean Seigel, granddaughter of Helen Hartness Flanders, who was one of Gebhard's pupils, remembered him as "a funny-looking man. Short and bald, with twinkly eyes. He had one tiny, malformed ear." He was born in Germany but had lived in the United States since the age of eight and studied piano with Clayton Johns, finishing his studies under Theodor Leschetizky and Richard Heuberger. He was known for his beauty of tone; his forte as a soloist was the French school, which he had begun to explore in 1903. Gebhard said, "We revelled in this new impressionistic idiom—the new harmonies, the new pianistic effects. What fun it was to experiment with the damper and soft pedal trying to recreate the . . . poetry of this exquisite music." Leonard Altman, who also studied with Gebhard, said, "He was one of the old Viennese-German school, clicking heels and kissing ladies' hands. I remember he did that once to an aunt of mine and she almost fainted. He was a man of great enthusiasms. Not great on technique. Musically he was much sounder. He left you alone. You left wanting to practice."

If Gebhard was the best, Bernstein wanted him. But Bernstein was rejected on the basis of inadequate technique and Gebhard's secret belief, a friend said, that the young man did not have a real gift. Gebhard suggested Bernstein study with his assistant, Helen Coates. Coates, red-haired, dimple-cheeked, was only twenty-one when she met the fourteen-year-old Bernstein. She had studied with Gebhard and might have had a performing career but was more interested in teaching. Bernstein's letter asking for his first lesson was written in the autumn of 1932. She penciled on it an appointment for Saturday at one p.m. a week later.

Much remedial training was needed to correct Bernstein's disastrous technique. Coates soon realized that exercises bored her gifted pupil (as Gebhard had suspected, he hated rote learning), but he could be drawn into it if the challenge was interesting enough, for instance, a Chopin étude. At home he went on playing and composing, with his mother as chief listener. As an evening wore on, Jennie Bernstein would threaten to go to bed, but Lenny could always keep her there a little longer by flattery: he wanted to know which particular ending of a new piece she liked best. She said, "Lenny *always* wanted an audience. And, in the beginning, I was his audience."

Bernstein was every teacher's ideal, the natural pupil. As with most teachers, Helen Coates succumbed to the human temptation to become part of his life. She was old enough to be a mentor, young enough to take part wholeheartedly in his private world of hopes, and hopes deferred. She knew soon enough that a career in music was a constant bone of contention between father and son. The problem seemed to be not that Sam was unalterably opposed but that he vacillated. Some time after he bought Lenny his Chickering grand, Sam was writing to Miss Coates to say that he had almost given up thoughts of his son becoming a businessman and now wanted Lenny to make a brilliant career in his chosen field. That was in the summer of 1933; a year later, Sam had retreated to his former position. He now hoped Lenny would not try to make a living as a musician. No doubt the father problem was the subject of extended conversations. Bernstein wrote Miss Coates a boastful letter about his grades when he graduated from Boston Latin in the

At age eleven

summer of 1935. His average was 82 and he was expecting to be accepted by Harvard. He sent her notes and picture postcards when he was on holiday. In Sharon one summer he wrote that he had bought himself a Smith American Piano Company upright and was teaching sister Shirley how to play the bass parts. Once he discovered opera, Lenny would rush over to his teacher's and spend his lesson singing and playing an act of an opera he had just discovered; his teacher said that "he could read, sing and memorize anything." One day he appeared with a mammoth piano concerto in the style of Tchaikovsky and Liszt that he had written. He was just fourteen.

When his son had become an overnight success, Sam Bernstein said:

That Lenny, what a boy! So emotional! So sensitive! Sometimes I'm ready to kill him. Like when I have a big day at the office, some important men coming, a big deal and what happens!

At 2 o'clock in the morning I wake up from a sound sleep. I hear something crashing downstairs. The piano! Chords are crashing, Lenny is playing like mad.

"Damn you, Lenny," I shout down the stairs. "You make so much noise and I got a big day at the office tomorrow."

And my boy, he replies, "But papa, I have to do this, it's in my head now and I got to put it down!"

The battles continued. Shirley Bernstein said that as a little girl, she never went to bed without hearing her brother playing the piano. If her parents wanted peace and quiet they left the house. Just the same, Sam and Jennie never gave Lenny a curfew hour, as any sensible parent would have done. Jennie appeared to take the indulgent view that Lenny could do whatever he liked. Sam, while protesting against his son's inconsiderate behavior, appeared to believe he was powerless to prevent it. Lenny could "get away with" being outrageous. Naturally enough, he looked for any kind of justification that would assuage his guilty conscience and pitied himself loudly on the rare occasions when he was brought up short. One of those took place during his freshman year at Harvard. He had brought a group home for the weekend, the kind of people whom Jennie would like—artists, musicians, and so on—and Sam would regard with suspicion. They appeared at about three in the morning, which upset Sam. The next night they went to a roadhouse and straggled back well after midnight. That did it. Sam insisted that everyone leave. After they had departed Lenny was loudly indignant. He immediately "came down with the 'flu." The doctor had called, the invalid was in bed taking pills and writing a long letter of self-justification to his friend Mildred. How could a father, who had everything to live for, destroy everyone's happiness? he asked her. The whole family was upset about it, or so he claimed.

No doubt Sam felt it his role, as a conscientious parent, to try to instill at least some of the 613 *mitzvot,* badgering his children with constant admonitions which they learned they could defy and even joke about. Shirley Bernstein said that when she was appearing in a play as an adolescent she drove to Cambridge for rehearsals every night even though she was too young to have a driver's license. She said, "I was very sassy about it. I would drive right up to the cops and get directions." Meantime her father did not prevent her from taking the family car but, instead, fulminated about it, saying, "I hope you get caught" and, "You won't get a license for years."

Shirley Bernstein recalled that she took piano lessons and enjoyed them, but her brother was so far ahead of her that she became discouraged. Nevertheless, she had learned how to read music, and her brother soon recruited her into playing four-hand arrangements of symphonies, including Beethoven's Sixth through Ninth. When she made a mistake, he hit her, probably an echo of the treatment he had received at Hebrew school. When she was barely nine or ten Shirley was enlisted to sing operatic roles. "He would take out operas from the public library and we'd learn them together," she said. She attributes her husky voice to the punishment her vocal cords received as she screamed out the leading roles in *La Bohème, Aïda* and *Madama Butterfly.* She played and sang, and when she could no longer sing soprano they turned to the music of Bessie Smith and Billie Holiday. He was her friend, her mentor, more of a parent than her own parents. At the same time she found herself unconsciously comparing other boys with her brother and finding them wanting: "If within, say, three days, I didn't have the emotional intimacy I had with Lenny, I'd reject the person." Shirley, a friend said, "absolutely positively idolized her brother, to a point where it may have affected her whole life. You could say she was in love with him, in the sense that she was totally absorbed by him."

Leonard Bernstein was ignorant about sex until the day his mother went to hospital to give birth to Burton, he later told his brother. The maid explained everything he wanted to know because Bernstein, then thirteen, was "crazed with curiosity." This gap in his education would have been typical of his generation, particularly for those with a Hasidic background. As with other conservative sects, among the Hasidim sex was not considered an expression of a close relationship, but an obligation. The Bible decreed that a man should be fruitful and multiply; therefore the function of marriage was procreation, but also a source of temptation. All pleasures of the flesh must be regarded as suspect, and care taken not to eat too much or even sleep too long; sex was simply another taboo. A boy must be on his guard against excitement and masturbation; similarly, a girl must be modestly dressed and "protect the palace of her body from the corruption of all other lustful passions."

As the son of a *rebbe,* Sam waged a constant war against impurity. He would periodically inspect his wife's perfectly clean kitchen for signs of sloppy housekeeping and carry the battle forward himself, shouting triumphantly if he managed to find any evidence. One had to be forever on one's guard against dirt, vermin and bugs. Sam's obsession seemed to stem from the belief that some food was *trayf.* The word originally meant an animal not slain according to the ritual laws, but to Sam it came to mean anything "impure." When his mother, Dinah, came to live with them during World War II, the whole house had to be inspected with a magnifying glass lest it contain a spare germ that would make it *trayf*. Shirley and her girlfriends were warned not to appear before their grandmother with bare arms and legs, because a display of female flesh was *trayf*. A proper example was set by Dinah not long after her arrival. She had gone to bed when it occurred to her that she had forgotten to kiss the mezuzah. On her way downstairs to remedy the oversight she fell and broke her arm. Such was her feeling of what was right that, when the doctor came to set the bone, she refused to roll up her sleeve.

Not surprisingly Sam, who spent his day in the company of women professionally occupied with paint, powder and similar frivolities—which they bought from him—was contemptuous of them in private. He liked to call them "a bunch of two-dollar whores." Shirley Bernstein said, "I showed up one day at his office with a group of girls and I was wearing lipstick. He looked at me as if I was a whore and took a handkerchief to wipe it off." He lost perhaps his most lucrative opportunity because of his preoccupation with *trayf*. He was offered the chance to make a modest investment in a New Jersey cosmetics company specializing in nail polish. It was being run by a young man named Charles Revson, whose Revlon company would become a phenomenal success. Sam took the offer as a personal affront. "You're making American women into whores!" he said. "You're painting their nails so they'll look like two-dollar whores! Get out of my office!" Like a proper Victorian, Sam seemed appalled at the very idea that sex, that sordid business, and a man's baser passions should have anything to do with nice women, one's sisters and wives. A poem Bernstein wrote reveals his early indoctrination into this point of view. At the age of eleven or twelve he was approached by some rough boys and accused of "laying" a girl who sat in front of him in class. Bernstein had to ask what that meant. He wrote:

> I didn't I didn't:
> I wouldn't have, either,
> Or thought of it, even.
> Much less do it.
> I did love Millie Long.
>
> . . . .
>
> But that night in my bed
> I knew very hard
> That I loved Millie Long
> No longer.

Ouida Mintz at Tanglewood with Bernstein at right,
Aaron Copland, far left, and David Glazer,
clarinetist, circa 1940

Temple Mishkan Tefila in its present ruined state

Bernstein described himself at that period as someone who, in early adolescence, headed straight for the piano as soon as he walked into a room and who "stayed there until they threw me out. It was as though I didn't exist without music." Friends invariably recall that their first sight of Bernstein was at the piano, usually wearing the coat he had forgotten to take off. He was performing on stage as well. His first professional appearance was at his temple, Mishkan Tefila, when he was thirteen; by the age of sixteen he was appearing with the Boston Public School Symphony Orchestra, made up of the best performers from local high schools. Victor Alpert, who was concertmaster at his own school, Roxbury Memorial High, and played in the Boston School Symphony, remembered the stir Bernstein caused when he performed the first movement of the Grieg Piano Concerto in the spring of 1934. Naturally Bernstein was the star turn at his teacher's recitals. In the summer of 1935 he played the first movement of Beethoven's *Waldstein* Sonata, Chopin's Nocturne in F-sharp Major, Liszt's Piano Concerto No. 2 (with his teacher at the second piano), and *Malagueña* by the Cuban composer Ernesto Lecuona. A friend, Ouida Mintz, who was a pupil of Gebhard's, said, of the *Malagueña,* "He loved it and used to fake the runs."

From the earliest days he tried his hand at contests, entering them with a casualness that was the despair of his friends. Ouida Mintz, who went on to become a fine pianist, recalled one contest held at the New England Conservatory for which the first prize was a Mason and Hammond grand piano. Bernstein played the *Malagueña,* and she tackled the Chopin Scherzo in B-flat Minor, which she claimed was much harder. He held her hand while they waited for the verdict; they both lost. They entered another contest, sponsored by a newspaper and Victor Records. "You had to recognize excerpts from Victor recordings after hearing a couple of measures," she said. "Lenny and I reached the semifinals. To cram for the finals I went to a Boston music store and listened to record albums for hours. Lenny couldn't be bothered. One day a group of us drove out to Revere Beach, Boston's answer to Coney Island. I sat on the beach and sang themes for him, including the slow movement of the Brahms Violin Concerto. This was one of the extracts played, and he was so thrilled when he got it right. He got second prize, which was a trip to Tanglewood, but since he was going there already they gave him some records."

Bernstein's offhand manner concealed the fact that he was shrewd, calculating and intensely singleminded, almost from the start. While a freshman at Harvard he was already looking for a famous and influen-

The family house in Sharon, a recent view

tial mentor and decided it was going to be José Iturbi, the Spanish pianist, then conductor of the Rochester Philharmonic Orchestra. He wrote excited letters to Helen Coates and his girlfriends saying he was almost certain he had an audition, but nothing came of it.

Those were the days when a crowd of boys and girls hung out together during their summers in Sharon. Jennie always held open house on Lake Avenue and there were constant parties. Jerome Lipson, for many years violist with the Boston Symphony Orchestra, said, "We would go to a house party on a Friday or Saturday night and it would always end up the same way. He'd be at the piano playing and talking, everybody listening to [Lenny] because he had so much to say." Bernstein was their leader and immensely good-natured about helping others. Dorothy Alpert, a violinist like her husband, Victor, recalled that Bernstein substituted for her pianist at short notice when she had to play an audition for the director of her conservatory. "He had never seen the Wieniawski D-Minor Concerto before, and it was incredible the way he sight-read it. I got a good mark." Dorothy Alpert was a member of the Madison Trio, along with cellist Sarah Kruskall and pianist Mildred Spiegel, who was studying with Gebhard and was also a friend of Bernstein's. One of Bernstein's first compositions was written for them. "It was a good piece," Dorothy Alpert recalled, "sort of light, easy, with

Helen Coates, 1966

some technically difficult passages but on the whole very playable."
Friends would usually return the favor when he needed help. Sam Bernstein's company briefly sponsored a Saturday-morning radio program,
"Avol Presents," named for his brand of beauty supplies. The day
Leonard appeared on his father's program, Robert Lubell turned the
pages for the old warhorse *Malagueña*. Leonard Burkat said, "The curious thing is we were a sizable gang of kids whose paths crossed and perhaps as many as ten of us took up music as a profession with a certain
amount of success. Everyone knew how much better Lenny was, but no
one was jealous. He was *ours*."

Bernstein took to performing in a small jazz group to help pay for
lessons. They appeared at weddings and bar mitzvahs just like klezmorim, Bernstein said, and at the end of a long evening he might go
home with two more dollars. After that he played jazz piano at a nightclub called the High Hat in Roxbury Crossing, where he picked up the
sideman's habit of banging the pedal in time to the music, to the con-
sternation of Miss Coates. Leonard Altman said the nightclub was "a
dreadful place, the Forty-second Street of his day. His allowance had
been cut off because his father realized he was serious about music."

Those who knew him attest to his buoyant temperament; he made everything seem like a game. Ouida Mintz said that Bernstein's favorite afternoon expedition was a drive to Revere Beach for hot dogs and a ride on the roller coaster, which she hated. "He had a passion for them and usually went down backwards." His was an antic, pratfall kind of humor, fueled by sheer high spirits. His favorite game in the city, for instance, was to place some object on a sidewalk, duck into the nearest doorway and watch the impromptu ballet as people tried to decide whether or not to pick it up.

Since there was an endless stream of his friends in and out of his house each summer, and having nothing better to do, Bernstein thought he might as well put on some shows. He would one day complain, "I'm always hearing about my 'facility' and my 'versatility.' What never gets mentioned is that I work hard." Work he did. He did the casting and rehearsing, hired the ballroom of a local hotel, hung the curtain, designed the posters, printed up the tickets, arranged for scenery and costumes, coached, played and acted as well. For several years in a row he gave productions of Gilbert and Sullivan. Shirley, aged eleven, sang Yum-Yum in *The Mikado,* and in *H.M.S. Pinafore* the family maid, Lilia Jiampietro,

Lenny, at left, and Sam, second from right, with unidentified friends at the beach, circa 1935

Beatrice Gordon and her dog, Teddy, in Sharon,
August 1935

Mildred Spiegel, left, and the other members of the
Madison Trio: cellist Sarah Kruskall, center, and
violinist Dorothy Rosenberg Alpert

revealed unsuspected talents singing the role of Josephine. Victor Alpert played Ralph Rackstraw, Shirley had one of the walk-on roles as an Egyptian dancer and Bernstein himself was Captain Corcoran. Bernstein said, "The house was always filled with dozens of young people screaming for hours. I don't know how [my mother] stood it."

The Gilbert and Sullivan ventures were an outgrowth of the success of his first production, in the summer of 1934, Bizet's *Carmen* in drag. Bernstein and a friend wrote a new libretto, full of puns, double entendres and topical jokes, and the Sharon audience loved it. Bernstein played the piano and sang the role of Carmen. Victor Alpert was Escamillo and Beatrice Gordon played Don José.

The composer David Diamond, who knew Bernstein for most of his life, claimed that Bernstein never showed any interest in girls, but this hardly seems to be the case. His first adolescent romance happened one summer in Sharon. Beatrice Gordon's aunt owned a cottage diagonally opposite the Bernstein home. Lenny and Beatrice met when they were both twelve. By the age of thirteen, Bernstein was playing her excerpts from *Tristan und Isolde* and calling her his "first love." Mildred Spiegel said, "I remember he invited her to an open-air performance of *Aïda* and sat with his arm around her." His poems, signed "Lamb's Ear" to Beatrice, his "Rosebeam" now sell for handsome sums.

Barbara Firger, Beatrice Gordon's niece, said that she "looked like a Russian princess, petite, with dark eyes and beautiful black hair." She was interested in literature, studied piano and wrote poetry of an otherworldly, ethereal sort. Bernstein would spend hours at her house and send her his writings. From the age of thirteen he seems to have been obsessed by the notion that he was going to be famous. They decided that Beatrice would write his biography, and he sent her all his Boston Latin School essays—along with little notes on what to include—and whatever poems he was writing. Most of them are fairly high-toned and moralistic. There is one, hardly more than a fragment, in which he shows a side of himself that was usually well hidden. He absolutely had to have people around him, he wrote, as a bulwark against some unbearable feelings of loneliness and severe inner doubts about his future.

Bernstein in love was ardent, eager, impulsive and fairly inconstant. "He was surrounded by girls," Mildred Spiegel said. "Any mother who met him and had a daughter would invite him home for dinner." There was Helen Bock and someone named Lill. There was Marcella Weiner, a girl who shared the same piano teacher for a while when Bernstein was at Boston Latin School. They went around in the same crowd, and although she insists there was nothing between them, her father discouraged him as a boyfriend because he was a piano player and would never amount to anything. There was also Ouida Mintz, who liked him and said he once kissed her. She added, "He was not too attractive to me. He had a bad case of acne that was disfiguring, and he had pockmarks all his life. Besides, I had to have someone who was mine alone. He would dance with anyone." Bernstein went on being friendly with many of his girls even when a gulf had separated them. He wrote letters to his Beatrice after he went to Harvard and she, being penniless, was working in a fish factory.

Mildred Spiegel, later Zucker, in particular was a lifelong friend. She found him playing the *Malagueña* one day in the empty auditorium of her school, Roxbury Memorial High, surrounded by an admiring audience. His playing was unpolished and undisciplined but full of drama, verve and a kind of naïve authority. She was sixteen and he was two years younger. She was so convinced of his gifts that she announced shortly after they had met that he was a genius and would one day be famous. He replied, "Do you really think so?"

"I was like a big sister, and the idea of marriage never entered our heads," she said. "The chemistry wasn't there." She was generous and, sensing his insecurity and the family opposition to a career in music, did her best to reassure him. They teamed up as entertainers and performed at parties, where she would sing arias like "Je veux vivre" and "Sempre libera" and he would accompany her. Or they might perform their favorite duet, *Rumbalero* by Morton Gould. He would often appear at her house without warning. "He would bounce up the stairs, run into the kitchen, give my mother a big bear hug and lift the pot covers to see what was cooking." Mildred, who was official pianist for the Boston School Symphony, was a much more accomplished pianist than Bernstein, something he was aware of. When she played the Beethoven Piano Concerto No. 1 with the symphony, he rehearsed with her, playing the orchestra part. Then he flatteringly asked to borrow her copy of the concerto and returned it in a ruined state. The same thing happened to her copy of *The Well-Tempered Clavier*, but she did not mind. Lenny was the kind of person who could be counted upon to do the unexpected. One time, coming home from a concert, they danced Chopin mazurkas all the way to the subway. She said, "I must say, nobody affected me like Lenny. He made a dent."

He wrote a piano piece for her twenty-first birthday and a second, Music for the Dance II, a year later. She also may have been the source of inspiration for the song cycle *I Hate Music*, because she used to say

Elaine Newman

Arthur Fiedler

that to make him laugh. He would drop notes in her mailbox decorated with bars from music they were working on. Once he left an empty cigarette box as a calling card. At the age of fourteen he began to smoke.

Then there was Elaine Newman. They met when she was a sophomore in private school and he was a senior at Boston Latin. Once they went to a formal party at which she wore a long white silk taffeta gown with a black top hat, cane and gloves stenciled on the skirt. Years later he wrote her a letter about her "top hat" dress, the smell of her perfume and the distinctive color of her notepaper, full of a 1930-ish nostalgia. She said, "He was more than just a date, but there was no real commitment." Then one summer he left for Sharon and asked his best friend at school, Robert Lubell, to "occupe-toi d'Amélie." From then on Robert was an integral part of the Elaine-Lenny scene: "I could be walking down the street with Lenny on one side and Bob on the other, each of them squeezing my hand." This may be why, at about that time, Bernstein wrote a spoof of a Cole Porter ballad and dedicated it to Elaine. The second verse went:

> You little trollop
> You need a wallop
> I think
> To sum it all up,
> You stink.

Although she eventually married Bob, she was always drawn to Lenny and his improvisational spirit. "I remember meeting him in Boston one time. I had just bought a suit, and he insisted on taking it out of the box and having me model it, right in the middle of Tremont Street." They met occasionally in years to come. "Bob might be driving with Lenny and I in the back seat. He'd pick up just where he left off. He always was very demonstrative and outgoing." She paused and said, "Later I heard some talk about his homosexuality, but I always thought he liked women too much."

Although Bernstein always emphasized the impression Serge Koussevitzky made upon him, Koussevitzky was not the first conductor to catch his interest. At the first concert Bernstein, at fourteen, ever attended, a Boston Pops concert for the benefit of Temple Mishkan

Tefila, the man in the spotlight was Arthur Fiedler. Immediately, Fiedler was his ideal. Bernstein said later that he had "all sorts of fantasies" about becoming just like Fiedler and being music director of just such an orchestra, fantasies that apparently disappeared soon afterwards when Bernstein wangled an opportunity to meet Fiedler—perhaps backstage, after a concert—and was brusquely put in his place.

Rossini's Overture to *The Barber of Seville* was on the program and made such an impression that for a time overtures were his musical passion. He explained, "The lights go out, there's that silence in the audience, the conductor appears out of nowhere . . . and there's the overture—that wonderful piece that gets you ready, that sets the mood, that starts your musical blood going." Ravel's *Boléro* was on the same program. "I remember . . . being so thrilled with [it] at that concert that I saved up for two or three months so I could buy a piano arrangement . . ." From the start his instinctive musical sympathies were with the Russian repertoire. When he first heard Prokofiev's *Classical* Symphony on the radio, he rolled on the floor, and Stravinsky's *Le Sacre du printemps* transported him into a new world. He immediately began reading and listening to all the contemporary music he could find and writing sonatinas in what he believed to be "the modern idiom." He described Debussy's *L'Après-midi d'un faune* as "a lazy, hazy sort of piece, full of warm, stretchy sort of feelings, sometimes very delicate, and sometimes quite passionate . . . You can almost see, and smell, and feel a delicious summer afternoon as you listen to it. It's like looking at a painting, only with your ears instead of your eyes." Once he had discovered the Boston Symphony Orchestra, he and a group of friends, Harold Shapero, Marcella Weiner, Mildred Spiegel and others, would buy the cheapest balcony seats and, since there was open seating, make a dash up the steps as soon as the doors were open to get the best ones. It was from this vantage point that Leonard Bernstein watched the tiny figure of Koussevitzky making his way across the stage and, at the end of a concert, turning to acknowledge the plaudits of the audience. One day, when Mildred was sitting next to Lenny, Koussevitzky was given a standing ovation. Mildred stood up, then turned in surprise: Lenny was still in his seat. "Why aren't you standing?" she said. He replied, "I'm so jealous."

Rocking the Cradle

For short-lived is the day
And downhill is the road . . .

— GOETHE, "AN SCHWAGER KRONOS"

Edwin Geller, a young freshman from Cleveland, arrived at Harvard University in Cambridge in the autumn of 1935 and inspected his rooms in the Wigglesworth dormitory on campus. There were three bedrooms adjoining a common living room, and he devoutly hoped that he would get some quiet roommates. Returning later that day, he found workmen struggling up the stairs with an upright piano. The instrument was going into the bedroom next to his own: fate had sent him Leonard Bernstein.

Day students were, then as now, accepted at Harvard, and Bernstein could easily have chosen to go back and forth to Newton and spared his father's bank account. But at the time they were hardly part of the Harvard scene; and if Bernstein was going to be there, he intended to be in the thick of things. He ensconced himself in the Harvard Yard and enrolled as a music major.

In those days the music program, led by such distinguished tutors as Walter Piston, Edward Burlingame Hill and A. Tillman Merritt, was comparatively small, with about thirty undergraduates and twenty graduate students, and its emphasis was not on performance. A degree in music was designed to produce future teachers, musicologists and composers and to create that desirable ornament of civilized life the man of culture. Those who came wanting to be performers were not exactly dismissed, but they were encouraged to do their performing elsewhere; music at Harvard, quipped one graduate, "was meant to be seen and not heard."

The choice could only have been made by his father. Jerome Lipson remembered walking home with Bernstein in Sharon one day when the conversation turned to their future careers. Bernstein declared he intended to become a concert pianist. Lipson asked, "Where are you going from here?" and Bernstein said, "I'm going to the Curtis Institute in Philadelphia." Lipson asked what that was, and Bernstein replied, "That's the best school there is." Bernstein sounded so confident that Lipson was astounded to discover that he had enrolled at Harvard instead. At the end of his freshman year Bernstein did indeed try to enter Curtis. He went for an audition in the summer of 1936 and told Mildred that the judge had been favorably impressed. He was accepted. But the fact that he returned to Harvard in the autumn of 1936 shows that he was again overruled. In years to come, Bernstein would advise friends with musically gifted offspring not to let them specialize too soon and would extol the virtues of a well-rounded education. At the time, however, Harvard was second-best so far as he was concerned, and he was obviously trying to leave it. His consolation was characteristic. William A. Whitcraft, Jr., a classmate of Lenny's, recalled that they first met in September 1935 in the Harvard Student Union common room, where they teamed up with some other classmates, Charlie French and Bud Minkler, and entertained an appreciative crowd of listeners on two grand pianos, eight hands flailing away. "For the next three years Lenny and I often played piano duets in the Eliot House common room," Whitcraft recalled. "While Lenny coached me in Bach (the Two- and Three-Part Inventions), I exposed him to boogie-woogie. I must say, he absorbed any and all kinds of music and was instantly able to repeat anything I played . . ."

Edwin Geller, having recovered from the shock of rooming with Bernstein, accepted his fate. That included the inevitable midnight serenades. "We knew it would do no good to complain," he said. Besides, "everyone thought he was a genius and recognized it. Often in the evenings or after dinner he would go into the freshman Union Hall and perform for hours. There was nothing he couldn't play. You could test him: popular, Gilbert and Sullivan, jazz, the classics—he could do it all, and sing it too."

Bernstein took the absolute minimum in music courses—only those required for a music major—and as many in philosophy and languages as he could schedule. Disenchantment soon set in when he discovered that the composers of the nineteenth century, and particularly those of the romantic movement, were anathema at Harvard. To express admiration for Tchaikovsky "was an outrageous heresy; Tchaikovsky was located one pigeonhole beneath Contempt at the time, as was Verdi. The fashion dictated pre-Beethoven and post-Wagner . . ." he wrote. Fortunately for Bernstein it was perfectly correct to admire contemporary composers: Stravinsky and Hindemith, Malipiero and Prokofiev. Quite soon, he found other diversions. Mildred said, "Every day at Harvard he'd go to Briggs & Briggs music store and buy records. 'Listen to this'—he'd play the record while I listened on the phone. He hardly ever went to class." Robert Lubell, who also went to Harvard, agreed. "Yes, he didn't study. I was the grind. I had to work my way through and he would fake it. At college, when he had to write an essay, he was ill prepared and would tear his hair out, and then decide to write on a completely unrelated subject and get an A. I remember he studied Italian one semester. He panicked before the exam and sat up all night studying. The next day he sat for the exam and did brilliantly." (Bernstein made the dean's list in 1936 and won a scholarship for his junior year, 1937–38.)

When he did come to class, he was wonderful and maddening. Harold Shapero said that Bernstein "decided to show up" around Christmastime at the course in harmony and counterpoint being taught by A. Tillman Merritt. "He brought some crazy modern piece that he had been working on, which I remember not being too attractive anyway, and he played it for the instructor, and this is supposed to be a sixteenth-century counterpoint class in the style of Palestrina. The piece was a dissonant, noisy thing, and this is the first work he had done all year in the course. So the instructor said very politely, 'Well, Leonard, you know this isn't really what we're doing in this class,' and Lenny wasn't fazed a bit. Lenny smacked it on the piano with a big thwack and said, 'Well, I like it.' "

Alan Evans, who took the same course, recalled that it was in two parts. The first was musical analysis: "We would be given passages from various composers (although about 90 percent was Bach) and we had to identify each chord with its appropriate number: I for tonic, V for dominant, etc. The object was to learn how the masters handled harmonic progression, key modulation, etc." Once the principles were understood, analysis was not difficult, just time-consuming.

The second part of the course, composition, was more demanding. Students would be asked to write a four-part harmony; they were given one of the parts and then had to add the other three voices. "Even though the majority of the class had some piano background and was used to playing (and hearing) chords, it was not easy to do." It soon became clear that Bernstein was a whiz at this. "Twice that I can recall, [Merritt] asked Leonard to play his homework and it was far superior to the rest." It was soon evident that Bernstein had enormous talent. He was unfortunately so sure of himself that he was very difficult to like, Evans said. He described a class in which the discussion had to do with the way Bach had written a complex modulation. "Leonard raised his hand to say that he felt one chord had been notated incorrectly. One note in the chord was a G-sharp and Leonard thought it should be A-flat." (Although on the piano there is no difference, if it were being played on a string instrument there would be a subtle distinction and the note would sound slightly higher.) "But we are talking about how Bach notated a chord! Professor Merritt was very calm and patient and pointed out all the reasons . . . why the notation was correct. Leonard used up all the class time insisting that he 'heard' an A-flat, and Bach was wrong."

However, Bernstein really outdid himself during the three-hour final exam. Like the course itself, it was in two parts, analysis and composition, the latter with the same kind of four-part-harmony problem the class had been struggling with all year. "After the first hour," Evans remembered, "I . . . was starting to cope with the composition. Suddenly there was a loud rattling noise in the back of the room. Everyone's concentration was broken as we turned to see what was going on. Leonard was sitting in the back . . . holding up a *New York Times* and shaking it, until everyone was looking at him. Then he folded up the *Times,* carried his exam to the front, turned it in, waved his hand and walked out."

The incident indicated that Bernstein had adopted one of his father's most exasperating traits, that of speaking as the voice of authority, whatever the issue. When challenged he would go on arguing even though his position had become untenable. The choreographer Zachary

Solov recalled that he met Bernstein at a dance festival after World War II, by which time the didactic side of Bernstein's nature had become pronounced. Solov said, "I had just come back from India and taught Melissa Hayden an Indian folk dance I had learned, and we performed it. I even had an authentic costume for her. Bernstein watched us and said, 'Your rhythms and beat pattern are all wrong.' He knew what it had to be, an irregular rhythm, and mine was regular. We fought and drank and carried on all night. It didn't bother me. How could I be wrong? I'd just come from there."

Whenever he felt unappreciated, Bernstein could always return to his piano which, Raphael Silverman, later to become the famous violist Raphael Hillyer, said, "was a wreck, with missing ivories and keys not working. It was hard to believe someone serious about performing could use something like that." Gebhard had finally accepted him as a pupil; "he improved his tone, gave him polish and introduced him to the romantic repertoire," Mildred said. Thanks to Gebhard and Miss Coates, the number of works Bernstein could actually perform had grown considerably since the *Malagueña* days. His repertoire now included the Prelude and Fugue in F Minor by Bach; the *Waldstein* Sonata and the Sonata in D Minor by Beethoven; the Rhapsody in G Minor by Brahms; numerous Chopin nocturnes, rondos, polonaises and preludes; works of Liszt; the Grieg Concerto; some Schubert impromptus; the *Novelette* in E Major by Schumann; the *Seguidilla* by Albéniz; *The Juggler* by Ernst Toch; the *Danse Nègre* by Cyril Scott; *La Cathédrale engloutie* and *Poissons d'or* by Debussy, and the *Cracovienne fantastique* by Paderewski. During his first year at Harvard he was working on Liszt's *Consolation* No. 6, Ravel's Concerto in G Major and Gershwin's *Rhapsody in Blue*.

Just after graduating from Boston Latin School he had performed the Concerto in G Minor by Joseph Wagner, who was conductor of the Boston Public School Symphony, and had acquitted himself honorably. The Boston *Post* wrote that the music itself was "of pleasing richness" and the young soloist had been enthusiastically applauded. Bernstein was soon making solo appearances with this orchestra and also the Massachusetts State Symphony, conducted by Alexander Thiede, with whom he performed the Ravel concerto. He gained the attention of the critic from the *Christian Science Monitor*. While the Ravel "is a thankless piece of writing," the critic wrote, "apparently Mr. Bernstein possesses unlimited technique. Although still in his teens he plays with an authority and ease which betoken an unusual talent. His tone is crisp and his finger work clean and clear cut . . ."

Bernstein performed Chopin and Liszt at the Temple Mishkan Tefila and appeared regularly at recitals of Gebhard's pupils, playing Debussy, Liszt and Ravel and, in the summer of 1938, his own composition Music for Two Pianos No. 1. (Mildred Spiegel played the second piano.) He made what may be his first public appearance as a composer-pianist performing one of his own piano works, Music for the Dance, on a State Symphony program later in 1938. By the time he reached his senior year at Harvard Bernstein was being praised for his "authority, ease, fluency and verve" and called one of the outstanding young pianists in the Boston area.

Bernstein was still playing around town to earn money. Hillyer said, "He'd go out evenings and play waltzes at dance parties of Boston society. I don't know how they learned about him, but he was a gifted improviser and in demand. One time I went along with him for variety and he shared the fifty-dollar fee with me, which I thought very generous." Lubell said that Bernstein's favorite form of relaxation was playing jazz and listening to modern music. "When he first found Copland's El Salón México he couldn't play the record often enough," Lubell said. Then one day, on his usual pilgrimage to Briggs & Briggs, Bernstein discovered a recording of Copland playing his Piano Variations. Bernstein recalled that he "went crazy" about the piece. "A new world of music had opened to me in this work—extreme, prophetic, clangorous, fiercely dissonant, intoxicating." Since he could not afford the sheet music, Bernstein persuaded his professor of philosophy, David Prall, to buy it for him, and then wrote a paper on the work for one of Prall's courses, on aesthetics. Bernstein took it to Gebhard, whose response was that if Bernstein would teach it to him, "then, by Jove, I'll teach it back to you." Gebhard was as good as his word, and Bernstein played Copland's Piano Variations constantly after that, even though, he said wryly, it was guaranteed to "empty rooms."

Bernstein had formed a mental image of Copland as "a cross between Walt Whitman and an Old Testament prophet," perhaps even a Moses, because of the driving, uncompromising quality of his music. A graduate friend, I. B. Cohen, had managed to get tickets to a performance by the dancer Anna Sokolow, with whom Cohen and Bernstein were entranced. On November 14, 1937, they went to the Guild Theatre on Broadway with the poet Muriel Rukeyser and found their seats in the front row of the balcony. Bernstein discovered that he was seated beside "an odd-looking man in his thirties, a pair of glasses resting on his great hooked nose and a mouth filled with teeth . . ." Muriel

Rukeyser leaned across to introduce them: it was Aaron Copland. By the end of the performance Bernstein had learned that it was Copland's birthday and he was being invited to a party being held in Copland's loft, his working quarters, above a candy factory on Sixty-third Street. (The loft was later demolished to make way for Lincoln Center.) That was Bernstein's first introduction to the New York scene; prominent figures like Virgil Thomson, Paul Bowles, Edwin Denby, Victor Kraft and Rudy Burckhardt were all there. Soon Copland learned that his Piano Variations was Bernstein's absolutely favorite piece and dared him to play it. So of course Bernstein did. Then he went on to play part of the Ravel concerto until he was interrupted. "I remember distinctly Paul Bowles, sprawled out on some sort of studio-bed that everybody was sitting on, saying in that rather perfumed drawl of his, 'Oh Lenny, ne Ravelons plus.' "

Aaron Copland in 1938

They became friends immediately. Bernstein would visit Copland whenever he went to New York. "I remember I was writing a violin sonata during those Harvard days, and a two-piano piece, and a four-hand piece, and a string quartet. I even completed a trio. I would show Aaron the bits and pieces and he would say, 'All this has to go . . . this is just pure Scriabin. You've got to get that out of your head and start fresh . . . This is good . . . Take these two bars and start from there.' " Bernstein was studying advanced harmony and fugue with Piston and orchestration with Hill, but felt the courses were too remote and theoretical. His practical training as a composer, he said, came from Copland.

Bernstein and Copland also played a great many four-hand arrangements of the latter's works. "I learned such works as *Billy the Kid* and *An Outdoor Overture*—later, the Piano Sonata and Third Symphony—that way before they were ever performed publicly, and the scores to *Quiet City, Of Mice and Men,* and *Our Town,* before Hollywood got them." To have gained the friendship of someone like Copland was an enormous coup. Hillyer said, "I remember Bernstein's excitement at meeting him. He was going around in a state of euphoria."

The truth was, Bernstein at that period was "young, happy, radiant, extraordinarily endowed and irresistibly attaching," as Henry James said of the English poet Rupert Brooke. His skin would always look ravaged as a result of adolescent acne, but this minor imperfection was more than offset by classic good looks: straight nose, beautifully modeled mouth, rounded chin and dark brows perfectly positioned over deep-set hazel eyes. His head was large and his shoulders broad—conducting would develop them even further—making him seem much bigger than his modest height of five foot eight; all his life, people would be surprised at how short he actually was. Formidably intelligent, good-humored, personable, generous, gifted: like Brooke, Bernstein seemed one of life's darlings, and he was at pains to advance that impression. But the self-confidence his classmates had so much resented concealed a frenzied ambition. Bernstein "wanted to be famous," as Mildred said, who knew him as well as anyone. Obviously, part of the reason had to do with his father's opposition and his fear of ending up at the Samuel Bernstein Hair Company. But more than that seemed to be at stake; he seemed almost petrified by the possibility that he might not succeed and pestered Copland for reassurance. Copland would "always giggle first—the infectious giggle is his most common reaction to anything," Bernstein wrote, "—then, with an attempt at sternness, glower, 'Stop complaining. You are destined for success.' " Bernstein, lacking family connections, knew that his career in music depended upon his finding the right mentor, the famous composer or conductor who would give him special opportunities, introduce him to important people and elevate him to stardom. Fundamentally decent, Bernstein always tried to like that person for himself alone. Perhaps he did not know how much that person's attractiveness had to do with a basic empathy and how much with the potential role he might play: how useful he was going to be.

Musicians attach great importance to dates of passage—births, marriages and deaths, first performances and other momentous events, just as they can remember with phenomenal accuracy what works they heard on a program years before. Somehow they always know when something of vital significance is taking place, and burnish the memory forever afterwards. And so the dates of when he first met Aaron, when they first played *Billy the Kid,* when they were at Tanglewood together were enshrined in Bernstein's imagination; but no date was revered more than that of Aaron's birthday, November 14. If he had thought November 14, 1937, would turn out to be memorable, he was right.

After an uneven first attempt to perform the *Rhapsody in Blue,* the music of George Gershwin became one of Bernstein's major interests, and he would make a name for himself as an interpreter of that work and also *An American in Paris.* There are some curious similarities between the two men's lives. As Bernstein noted, Gershwin's was "one steady push to cross the tracks, both musically and socially—an effort guided and sustained by ambition, a profound learning capacity, and an enormous reservoir of sensibilities," which he could just as easily have said of himself. Like Gershwin, Bernstein would come to be undervalued for the spontaneous and natural gift he had of writing "popular" music. Like Gershwin, Bernstein would try to cross the tracks into classical writing even though, as composers like Ned Rorem have pointed out, such divisions are entirely arbitrary. Like Gershwin, Bernstein would suffer the fate of having his best pieces dissected and found structurally inadequate. And, as he did with *Rhapsody in Blue,* Bernstein would argue that such criticism was negligible, because "each of those inefficiently connected episodes is in itself melodically inspired, harmonically truthful, rhythmically authentic."

When Bernstein arrived at Harvard, Gershwin was still in his thirties and at the height of his powers; his masterpiece, *Porgy and Bess,* had just been performed in Boston and New York to great acclaim. In the summer of 1937, he died of a brain tumor. He was thirty-nine.

By chance Bernstein was working that summer as a swimming and music counselor at a boys' camp, Camp Onota, on Lake Onota near Pittsfield, Massachusetts, in the Berkshires. He said later:

> One of my duties was to play piano music for Sunday lunch when the parents came to visit. The Sunday morning when I heard on the radio that Gershwin had died, I was absolutely devastated. I tried to get out of playing but the director said I had to go through with it.
>
> I came into the dining room where all the parents were sitting . . . and instead of playing "Tea for Two" or whatever, I held up my hand, or played a chord, or something to get them quiet. Then I announced that Gershwin had died, that he had been an idol of mine, and that I was going to play his second Prelude as a memorial. They all put down their silverware and listened as I played this very slow, very sad music. As the last notes wafted away I rose from the piano and left the hall in silence.
>
> That was the first inkling I ever had of the power of music, of its possibilities for control. It was a great turning point for me. Perhaps the most theatrical thing in the world is a room full of hushed people, and the more people . . . are silent, the more dramatic it is.

Finding himself surrounded by youngsters, Bernstein set about organizing them with his usual zest. He formed a rhythm band playing triangles, tambourines and cymbals, and a photograph of the band shows seven campers, instruments held aloft like zoological specimens, seated on the steps of an open porch as Bernstein, arms raised, in shorts and with "Onota" emblazoned across his chest, prepares to lead them. He also acted as musical director for *The Pirates of Penzance,* following his Gilbert and Sullivan triumphs in Sharon. He is listed on the program as "Len" Bernstein. One of three or four mock advertisements also on the program has a sketch of a formally dressed pianist and grand piano and the comment, "When I sat down at the piano they all laughed, [*sic*] someone had taken away the chair. Lenny Bernstein."

Bernstein had managed to fill most of the roles but was desperate to find a Pirate King—"It needs a bass voice, and there was no such thing as a bass voice at Camp Onota." Then a friend of the dramatics counselor appeared, a gangly young man with a lopsided grin named Adolph Green, and Bernstein pressed him into service. Green had a reputation even then for his phenomenal musical ability. Hillyer said, "He knew a great deal of the classical literature and could improvise words to some of the classical movements in an amazing way." Bernstein decided to put Green's knowledge to an immediate test. Surely Green remembered this work by Shostakovich, Bernstein asked, pounding out "a series of stirring dissonances of his own invention." Green had to confess he had never heard of the piece. He immediately became one of Bernstein's nearest and dearest. It would be the start of a lifelong collaboration.

Bernstein was a first-rate swimmer and a strong squash player. Robert Lubell recalled that they played three times a week but that Bernstein would often have attacks of wheezing afterwards, the result of his persistent asthma. In one of the harmless embroideries of truth in which Bernstein sometimes indulged, he told a magazine in later years that he had been captain of the baseball team as a youngster. However, a camper who knew him at Camp Onota wrote that, although Bernstein was a marvel as a drama and music counselor and "would introduce many musical hits, on the baseball field he was hitless and never could advance the runner from first to second." Shortly after meeting Adolph Green Bernstein and Lubell went to visit him in New York, where Green was performing with a group called the Revuers at the Village Vanguard, a nightclub in Greenwich Village. Lubell said, "We took a trip on the Eastern Steamship Line—you could embark from Boston at five in the afternoon and arrive at eight the next morning—on New Year's Eve. There was a terrific storm that night, the ship was heaving and we were singing a duet in the dining room. Finally the crew had to tie the piano down. We were three sheets to the wind, singing 'The Music Goes 'Round and 'Round.' " In New York, they stayed at the Lincoln Hotel near Times Square and went to the Village Vanguard partly to hear Billie Holiday, who was one of Bernstein's favorites. "He smoked incessantly, of course. It was the smart thing to do."

Exactly when Bernstein became interested in conducting is an interesting question. He said, "It never entered my mind the whole time I was at Harvard." But it is clear that he was considering it a year after his arrival. After returning from his audition at Curtis in the summer of 1936, Bernstein told Beatrice Gordon that he was determined to concentrate on his piano studies. Then he mentioned that he had heard there would be auditions for the post of assistant conductor of the Harvard Orchestra and intended to apply. The test piece may have been

Mozart's Symphony No. 40 in G Minor, because, Mildred wrote, he took the piano version out of the library and, while she played the piece, practiced conducting it. (He did not get the job.) Just why he should be taking an interest in conducting when he was ostensibly set on a career as a concert pianist and be trying to enter Curtis is not clear, but he was obviously fired with a new enthusiasm. Then he met Dimitri Mitropoulos.

Mitropoulos, who was Bernstein's senior by two decades, was born in Athens. His first ambition had been to take holy orders, but he gave up this plan when he learned that he would not be able to take his most precious possession, a small harmonium, into a monastery. He turned to music and had soon developed into a brilliant pianist, graduating from the conservatory and then the University of Athens, where he composed an opera based on a play by Maeterlinck. He had talents in that direction but soon moved into conducting. He studied with Erich Kleiber and was appointed permanent conductor of the Athens Symphony in 1924. He was one of the first conductors to conduct without a score (his memory was so faultless that he could cite not only every page but even the rehearsal numbers) and caused a sensation when he both played the piano and conducted from the keyboard. He never used a baton, preferring to rely on foot stampings, head shakings, shoulder jigglings, finger clickings and ecstatic gyrations. On the podium he was brilliant, magnetic; offstage he struck most people as gentle and self-effacing. At the height of his fame he lived in squalid rooms in down-at-heel hotels and would receive frequent visitors asking for money with a nod towards a huge glass jar full of dollar bills standing on a chest of drawers. The famous impresario Sol Hurok is said to have witnessed such a scene and stared in disbelief. He not only helped impecunious students but advanced the careers of young composers and became known for his interpretations of the twelve-tone school.

After seeing Mitropoulos conduct in Europe, Koussevitzky invited the forty-year-old conductor to make his American debut in Boston in 1936. Mitropoulos paid a return visit early in 1937. His first performance was at Sanders Theatre on the Harvard University campus on January 14. As it happened, Bernstein was on vacation. He and Mildred had season tickets, so they went. Among the works on the program were Respighi's Toccata for Piano and Orchestra, which Mitropoulos, true to form, conducted from the keyboard, and his own arrangement for orchestral strings of a Beethoven quartet, Op. 131 in C-sharp Minor. Hillyer, who heard it at the same time, said, "It was like being carried into some celestial region." A day or so later Bernstein heard that Mitropoulos would be attending a tea given by the Harvard Hellenistic Society at Phillips Brooks House.

There are several versions of what followed. The most detailed was given by Bernstein some years afterward. He said that a casual acquaintance had told him about the tea, but that he had no intention of going. However, he did return to campus early to study for exams. His mother drove him back and, as luck would have it, she made a wrong turn, ran out of gas, and he found himself right outside Phillips Brooks House. Since he was there he thought he might as well go in. This version is contradicted by Robert Lubell, who recalled that Bernstein was not invited but said he was going to crash the party. It is also contradicted by the late Jennie Bernstein, who said she drove her son back to school early because Mitropoulos wanted to meet him, and it had all been arranged. The explanation sounds like the kind of patina an ambitious son might put on the truth for his mother's sake. However, why in later years, he should disavow all intention of seeking out Mitropoulos is harder to explain. For the rest of his life he insisted he had done nothing to engineer the meeting. It was all due to the occult—to "fate."

All versions agree that once inside, Bernstein found himself in a long queue of people waiting to meet the maestro. "He had these unbelievable electric blue eyes and bald head," Bernstein said later. Mitropoulos took his hand and he was immediately struck by the "incredible hypnotic quality of this man." At the end of the formalities Mitropoulos invited Bernstein to play. With much trepidation he launched into a Chopin nocturne and then the final movement of his own Sonatina. A conversation followed and Bernstein was invited to the week's rehearsals at the Boston Symphony Orchestra.

In a short story, "The Occult," written for his English composition course at Harvard a year later, Bernstein put only the lightest fictional gloss on what had taken place. Arriving at Symphony Hall, the conductor, whom Bernstein named Eros Mavro, drops the scores in his lap and begins to rehearse. "Mavro, in his . . . excitement, broke two chairs by dropping down on them . . . in order to signify a sudden diminuendo . . . The first time, he went right through the cane seat. The concertmaster rushed to his rescue. The second time . . . Mavro pulled himself up still conducting . . . Carl began to feel a great and awful love for this man." They go out to lunch, and at a certain point the Mavro-Mitropoulos figure offers the student an oyster on a fork. An oyster was, of course, *trayf* in Bernstein's world, presenting the lure of the forbidden. In other words, the narrator knew well enough what direction the relationship was taking. He had, after all, called the man Eros.

David Diamond, who was a close friend of Mitropoulos's, was certain that he and Bernstein never had an affair. Others, including Leonard Burkat, thought it very likely. Kiki Speyer Fouré, who was later practically engaged to Bernstein, was sure of it. She said, "Mitropoulos seduced him, without question." As for Bernstein, being young, emotionally susceptible and open to flattery, he would naturally be full of hope at the opportunities seemingly presented. The wife of a famous international musician, who knew both men, said, "You don't get there unless you do go to bed. Whoring is part of the business. So whether he seduced Mitropoulos, or vice versa, makes no difference. If Bernstein did, that's what he had to do. That was the gate that opened."

If Bernstein expected there would be a price to pay, the question is only implied in the story of Eros and Carl. For Carl the issue appears to be that of being courted by a famous man and his euphoria that his dream of being called a "genius-boy" is coming true, along with his admiration for Mavro and his desire to be just like him. Whether this was Bernstein's introduction to homosexuality is not known, but the emotional atmosphere of his short story gives a clue to his feelings. Here was a famous man, powerfully handsome and magnetic, with the physique of a Greek god, for whom such relationships were acceptable, normal and natural. To see someone so at ease with his feelings and making no secret of them, who was (after all) from a strongly religious background—it is not hard to imagine the reasons why, under the spell of the moment, a young man in that situation could see a physical relationship from a new perspective, as something hallowed, sacred even. Remorse would come soon enough, and at that point he could argue that he had had no choice. It had all been engineered by forces outside his conscious control.

When Mitropoulos left Boston, he gave Bernstein his photograph and some curiously pointed advice—"Do not sleep in too soft a bed" was what Bernstein remembered—and promised to write. More than a year passed and Bernstein received no word. Meantime, Mitropoulos succeeded Eugene Ormandy as conductor of the Minneapolis Symphony. In the story Carl summoned up his courage and wrote to Eros. A few days later he received a reply: "I want you—I dared not believe it before. Come to me . . ." In real life Bernstein went to Minneapolis for a week in April 1938 and stayed with Mitropoulos. What happened after that might have been predicted. The wife of the famous instrumentalist said,

"The Greeks are like the Russians, totally amoral. I learned you simply mustn't trust them or they will break your heart."

By the time Bernstein graduated from Harvard in 1939, Mildred Spiegel believed, he was in a genuine dilemma. On the one hand, he said, "the pendulum was swinging back and forth," and he did not know which sex he might eventually choose. On the other hand, he very much wanted marriage and children. Another friend, Leonard Altman, remarked on Bernstein's ability to compartmentalize his life and the paradoxical nature of his responses. "He was more than split into two people; sometimes he was a whole orchestra."

Something of the same vacillation was at work in Bernstein's response to the political movements of his day. In the 1930s most young intellectuals accepted the Marxist belief that the Depression, as Noel Annan wrote, "was the final stage of capitalism destroying itself through its own contradictions." The role of American composers in building a brave new world was to create a uniquely American contribution, based on the New England heritage of hymns, dances and folk songs and on the rich and exploitable vein of Negro rhythmic patterns and tone colors. Writing about the subject in 1939 for his doctoral thesis, Bernstein thought that composers like Gershwin, Ives, Sessions, Harris and, in particular, Copland were successfully fusing such influences to make a genuinely indigenous contribution. Finding one's source of inspiration in humble, universal folk themes, whatever the origin, was as it should be, because, he wrote, "a composer functions for the sake of society."

If there had been any doubt of the importance of a social agendum for music, American composers only had to read the daily headlines. The 1930s had been marked by fierce battles as the unions struggled to prevail. Even though many barriers had been surmounted by 1937, there were citadels as yet unconquered. In particular the group called Little Steel—National, Republic, Inland, Bethlehem and Youngstown Sheet and Tube—was holding out against sitdown strikes, and Roosevelt was turning a blind eye to their strike-breaking tactics. Jennie Bernstein had worked in a mill and no doubt had described to her son some of the strikes she witnessed in Lawrence. Yet, as a classmate, Thomas A. Goldman, recalled, no one could remember Bernstein as having been politically active. One never saw him, for instance, at the Harvard Student Union, an umbrella group for all sorts of liberal leanings, or one of the Popular Front organizations that Communists were setting up with the rise of Hitler. Goldman said he went to several open meetings of the John Reed Society, a long-established forum for Marxists, but Bernstein never appeared. Bernstein's attitude seemed to mirror the cagey approach taken by Copland to the Composers Collective, organized under Communist party auspices early in the 1930s with the aim of encouraging composers to write songs for use on parades and picket lines and choral music dealing with socially significant themes. Copland, the secretary's minutes recorded in 1935, came to a meeting "for five minutes . . ." However, the music itself was another matter. One of the leading lights of the Composers Collective was its secretary, Marc Blitzstein. Bernstein soon became his champion.

Marc Blitzstein, thirty-two in 1937 and making his name as an American composer, had written an up-to-the-moment Brechtian opera called *The Cradle Will Rock,* about an assembly-line foreman who challenges the rule of a stereotypical steel mill owner and brings about a successful strike for higher wages. It was the quintessential proletarian theme, with a plot that struck many people as hopelessly clichéd, but Blitzstein had written an engaging score, fresh, witty, and impassioned, and it aroused enormous interest. Orson Welles, then making his name as director of one of the Works Progress Administration's Federal Theatre Projects, wanted to direct it for his Mercury Theatre company. John Houseman agreed to produce it. Almost at once the project was attacked by congressional critics, who charged that public funds were being used to further left-wing propaganda. Finally WPA officials halted the production and the president of Actors' Equity enjoined its cast from performing in an unauthorized play.

The evening the play was to open, the cast walked out of the theater in which the play was to have been performed, followed by an audience of about a thousand. They went to the Venice Theatre at Fifty-ninth Street and Seventh Avenue. The composer, at the piano, took his place on the stage and members of the cast sat in the audience. Then *The Cradle Will Rock* began. It opened with a song by a prostitute, "For two days out of seven / Two dollar bills I'm given . . ." Houseman wrote, "It was almost impossible, at this distance in time, to convey the throat-catching, sickeningly exciting quality of that moment or to describe the emotions of gratitude and love with which we saw and heard that slim green figure." The play was an overnight success.

In the spring of his senior year, Bernstein went to talk to a young man in the class below his, Harold W. Williams, with a proposal. Would he like to join Bernstein in mounting a production of *The Cra-*

Virgil Thomson in 1935 or 1936

dle Will Rock? Williams wrote, "When Lenny first gave me the play to read, I thought it was pure trash and wanted nothing to do with it. Lenny asked me to withhold judgment until I could hear the music. Then he took me up to his room and played the score through, singing each part himself as he came to it. I was sold, and I agreed to handle all the business aspects of the production . . . Lenny would do the direction and play the piano. Another . . . friend, Ed Fox, signed on to do the lighting and what little stage managing was required. I got so caught up in what we were doing . . . that I asked Lenny to give me a part. He agreed to try me out for a relatively small part, that of a druggist . . . but exploded in laughter at my tryout. It was decided by all concerned that I should stick to . . . business . . .

"When I knew Lenny he was already a phenomenon. A genius, without airs and graces. Not quite a regular guy but not beyond the pale. There was no inkling that he had homosexual tendencies. Of course in those days we didn't accept homosexuals as we do today. They were labeled 'faggots' and 'fairies.' " (Or called "musical.") "I knew a couple of guys like that, but they certainly weren't friends of Lenny's. He used to date often. A lot of us would go to Wellesley to find dates."

As for *The Cradle Will Rock*, Bernstein and Williams determined it would cost about thirty-five dollars to rent lights, print programs and tickets and take out a small ad in the *Crimson*. "You know, thirty-five dollars seemed an awful lot of money in those days, and we had some difficulty raising it. But I don't ever recall talking to Lenny about money. He didn't want to deal with it. That's why he came to me.

"Lenny had decided to give the play substantially as it had been done in New York, although the cast would be seated on stage instead of in the audience, and they could get up and move about as they played their parts. Memory dims but I don't recall rehearsals being tense. In fact, there was a very collegial atmosphere, with great respect for Lenny." Bernstein had, that same spring of 1939, composed and conducted the music for a performance of *The Birds* by Aristophanes sponsored by the Harvard Classical Club, and had caused a great stir. "We all thought he was so far superior and so greatly talented that nobody could stand in his way."

Williams worked at getting publicity, but the advance sale was disappointing. The performance in Sanders Theatre was slated to begin at 8:30 p.m. By 8:15 there was hardly anyone in the audience. But about five minutes later crowds of people began to appear and, Williams said, "they overwhelmed our ability to sell tickets. I sent word to Lenny to hold the start, and we sold out the house."

Bernstein gave the crucial role of the prostitute, who opens the show (singing, "So I'm just searchin' along the street, / For on those five days it's nice to eat. / Jesus, Jesus, who said let's eat?"), to his sister, Shirley, then just fifteen. It was a great joke on Sam, always ready to label any woman a whore, to have his adolescent daughter appearing in public as one. In case Sam might miss the joke, Shirley took the stage name of Mann, a reference to the White Slave Traffic, or Mann, Act of 1910, which made it illegal to transport a woman across state lines for "immoral purposes." Shirley Bernstein said, "My parents knew nothing about the kind of girl I was playing until the curtain went up." They did not seem to mind, she said later. Just the same it was an inspired piece of casting, since she projected exactly the kind of fear, vulnerability and premature disillusionment the part required. Williams wrote, "I finished up my financial chores before the end of the first scene and wandered into the back of the auditorium. I could sense the electricity in the air. It seemed as if no one was breathing. Then all of a sudden the scene ended, the stage blacked out and the theatre erupted in a roar . . ."

On opening night Williams had so much money in his pockets that the company threw a cast party. They gathered in an Italian restaurant on Harvard Square and ate and drank the night away. Lenny played the piano; so did Marc Blitzstein himself.

Blitzstein remembered:

Lenny did my part—at the piano, and announcing to the audience. And he did it so much better than I did that I was covered with jealousy. That's what attracted me to him.

He reminded me so much of myself at his age. We are, if there is such a thing, musical brothers. We think alike, we act alike. Lenny was dynamic, he was electric, he was everywhere at once.

I remember that one day we were lying on the banks of the Charles River, looking up at the sky. Lenny was saying he didn't know *what* to be. There was some talk of being a doctor, of going into music, even of going into his father's business.

None of this seemed out of bounds. He had . . . no sense of limitation . . . One didn't know from which springboard he would dive, but one knew there would be a hell of a splash.

Wrong Note Rag

Heart and brain within me surging
Chafe at your loit'ring . . .

— GOETHE, "AN SCHWAGER KRONOS"

The Harvard performance of *The Cradle Will Rock* had been given, Eliot
Norton wrote in the Boston *Globe,* "with fire, ardor, intelligence and
altogether too much conviction for comfort," and the actors and musicians were "the most talented student cast this department has ever
seen." Moses Smith, writing in the *Transcript,* thought "Mr. Bernstein
had the professional touch at the piano" and noted he played the entire
score from memory. The production had turned a profit and attracted a
big audience. Bernstein graduated from Harvard a month later, cum
laude, which had to be considered a lesser triumph in light of his intellectual gifts. The ultimate decision of what he should do in life was
upon him.

Sam Bernstein said a few years later that he had offered his son a
hundred dollars a week to start (and he could stay home for free) as an

Adolph Green and Betty Comden

inducement to enter the beauty business. This was not altogether an untested area. Bernstein had spent the summer of his sixteenth year in the shipping room, acting as a clerk, messenger and flunky. He said, "I knew how to tie knots, wrap a package, and what 'on consignment' meant." From his father's point of view, a great deal of money had been spent, and he now wanted a return on his investment. There was the fact that he had spent his life building up a business that he expected his son to continue, and there was also the fact that family members on both sides had worked, at one time or another, for the Samuel Bernstein Hair Company. Sam looked to his own, always, and they had not let him down—until now.

Bernstein said later that he turned his father down "flatly," but given his nature and the pressures upon him, it seems more likely that he temporized. He asked for the chance to try to find work in New York that summer. He must have said he would come home if he did not succeed; at any rate, his father gave him an allowance of twenty-five dollars a week. Bernstein may have known already, but certainly discovered soon, that he would not be eligible for admission to the musicians' union until he had lived in New York for six months. Until then he was probably unemployable.

Bernstein and his friend Adolph Green took an apartment at 61 East Ninth Street that was very cheap, very hot and full of roaches, but it did have a Steinway grand piano. Green spent his evenings performing at the Village Vanguard; Bernstein was looking for a job. Writing to Helen Coates on July 8, he complained that he had been looking for three whole days and had not found anything yet. A couple of weeks later he had been all over town but had still found nothing. He had met Davidson Taylor at CBS, who, while genuinely sympathetic, had nothing to offer. The interview had been engineered by Copland, who was the great consolation of that summer. At night, while Green worked, Bernstein composed on the Steinway, although not as far into the wee hours as he would have liked, the neighbors having succeeded in doing what no one else in his life had managed to do. He took everything he wrote to Aaron for criticism. That summer he began the first sketches for what would become his First Symphony, the *Jeremiah.*

His pianistic studies were receding into the background. As he told Helen Coates, he had somewhat neglected to practice when he was composing and rehearsing for *The Birds.* By the end of July Bernstein was mulling over his future as a conductor. He put it in a typically oblique way. Others were pressing the idea upon him: Copland, William Schuman, Roy Harris, etc. He would say that until these friends made the suggestion he had not known a baton from a barge pole, or some such. However, the advantages of being a conductor as well as a pianist and composer had been obvious to him since meeting Mitropoulos, if not since his abortive attempt to enter Curtis in 1936. The pianist Eugene Istomin, who knew him in those years, said, "I think he knew he had a brilliant future ahead of him as a composer and conductor but not as a pianist."

In July Bernstein thought his influential friends would be able to conjure up a fellowship to Juilliard for the autumn, but this proved overly optimistic. By September he was back in Sharon. "I finished the summer of '39 with no job and went back home in defeat with $4 left in my pocket." On the way home he discovered a clarinet in a pawn shop. It cost four dollars, so he bought it and "for a while it comforted me." His effort to find work had failed and a klezmer's fate awaited him, if he could even find a job as humble as that, which seemed unlikely. "I was tootling my clarinet and crying. It was the beginning of the end, as far as I was concerned."

Bernstein's sole hope at that point was Mitropoulos, but since their meeting in the spring of 1938 he had heard nothing further and had evidently abandoned hope from that direction. Leonard Burkat, Bernstein's friend since Boston Latin days, recalled that his future wife's older sister and her husband had gone to Palestine that summer. Then Britain and France declared war on Germany, and the couple took the first ship leaving Haifa for Boston and New York. "The next stop was Piraeus," Burkat said, "and a tall, skinny Greek got on this overcrowded ship. My sister-in-law was the only one who recognized Dimitri Mitropoulos. She and he spent the next ten or twelve days talking."

Mitropoulos was bound for New York and decided to disembark in Boston, as he could arrive sooner by taking the train. They all got off the boat at Commonwealth Pier together, and Burkat went to meet them. Mitropoulos said he knew someone else named Leonard. When it turned out that they both knew the same person, Mitropoulos asked where Bernstein was, and was told that he was looking for work in New York—Burkat did not know he had just returned. Mitropoulos said, "Get in touch with him and ask him to call me at the Hotel Biltmore in New York. I have an idea for him." Robert Lubell recalled driving Bernstein back to New York—a seven-hour trip by car in those days— "and when we got to Mitropoulos, I was just the chauffeur," he said. Bernstein stated his dilemma, and that is when Mitropoulos is supposed to have predicted that Bernstein was born to be a conductor. Mitropoulos was offering to help him get admitted to Curtis, even though it was already too late to apply, and there must have been at least a hint that Mitropoulos promised him a future job as an assistant conductor of the Minneapolis Symphony. This was all the ammunition Bernstein needed. Fritz Reiner agreed to give the young man a special audition for his new conducting class, and Sam Bernstein agreed to let him try.

Copland was renting a house in Woodstock just then, so he invited Bernstein to "come up in my loneliness and despair," Bernstein said. He took with him some scores, Beethoven's Seventh and Rimsky-Korsakov's *Scheherazade*. "I remember sitting on the train to Woodstock with these scores in front of me, trying to memorize them for an upcoming audition with Reiner in Philadelphia and saying, 'Oh my God, this

Dimitri Mitropoulos in his younger years

Bernstein with Aaron Copland in Woodstock, circa 1940

Fritz Reiner conducting the Curtis Institute of Music student orchestra
at a dress rehersal

Isabelle Vengerova in the 1950s

is terrible.' " His state of mind did not improve once he arrived, because Copland lived with two or three cats, to which Bernstein was highly allergic; it was hay fever season as well. By the time he arrived for his audition, sneezing and with eyes running and swollen, he could barely read the scores in front of him. "And in that state I was ushered into the room of this lone little man with tiny green eyes. I was quaking in my boots, and he asked me, 'Did you ever conduct?' 'No,' I said. 'You play the piano?' 'Yes.' 'Go to the piano. Do you know what that is?' 'No.' 'Do you think you can play it?' "

"Mean!" The word spoke volumes as Bernstein went on to describe how he had played through a symphonic score that seemed completely new until, halfway through, he recognized "Gaudeamus igitur" from some high-school doggerel and realized he was playing Brahms's *Academic Festival* Overture. Reiner somewhat grudgingly told him that he

Bernstein at Curtis, third from left, with, from left, Waldemar
Dabrowski, Leo Luskin, Hershy Kay, Albert Falkove and
Constant Vauclain, 1940. Dr. Randall Thompson is seated at
the piano, and the girl in profile is Annette Elkanova,
whom Bernstein wanted to marry at one time.

Wanda Landowska in the 1920s

Efrem Zimbalist, circa 1939

The Curtis Institute of Music, Philadelphia, Pennsylvania, in the 1920s

read well and then quizzed him on the score: " 'What is the second clar-inet playing in his last bar?' and I didn't know. 'Name the percussion section.' How did I know? I'd never seen this thing in my life. But he suddenly said, 'You are in the class.' He became my next hero. But mean! He never smiled."

Bernstein decided to also major in piano and was assigned to Madame Isabelle Vengerova, who according to the pianist Gary Graffman was not very tall but "extremely wide, and she sailed around her studio like an overstuffed battleship in search of the enemy, can-non loaded and ready to fire. . . ." Bernstein had been turned down as a student of Rudolf Serkin, which was probably just as well. Graffman recalled the thrilling liberties Serkin allowed his students, "angular arm-flailing, exciting foot-stamping and even occasional humming—although their humming never reached the Olympian heights of the Schnabel students, who practically sang a duet along with their Schubert sonatas." Vengerova was ever alert to stamp out this kind of artistic license, which Bernstein already possessed to a dangerous degree.

Vengerova had been born of a prominent family in Kiev and, after leaving Russia, became a prominent member of the circle of emigrés liv-ing in New York. She was, Graffman said, wedded to the "Russian school of playing" and bent her energies toward producing beautiful sound and legato. "To achieve this, she was quite dogmatic in her teach-ing about hand positions . . . and extremely slow practicing, hands sep-arately, with accents every so many notes . . ." She terrified some students: "Shouts, screams, threats, curses and stampings were the norm, and on special occasions even the crashing of furniture could be detected." Graffman took it philosophically and so, apparently, did Bernstein: she "turned out to be equally tyrannical and brutal and fab-ulous," he said. Vengerova realized he was playing with such abandon that he had stopped hearing himself, and it was affecting his perfor-mance. "She taught me how to listen to myself, which is the greatest gift any teacher can give to a student."

Bernstein's training from Fritz Reiner would be equally valuable, although of a rather different kind. Originally from Budapest, Reiner had a distinguished career as a conductor before emigrating to the United States in the early 1920s. He had conducted the Cincinnati Symphony Orchestra for nine years and was conductor of the Pittsburgh Symphony Orchestra when Bernstein went to Curtis, as well as head of that institute's orchestral department. By then in his fifties, Reiner had a reputation as a technician par excellence, with an encyclopedic knowledge of the literature and a beat so minuscule that, some musicians claimed, he was "the laziest conductor they had ever known." Despite his phenomenal skills, Reiner's cutting humor made him generally disliked, and with his "machine-shop" exactitudes he was rarely capable of the poetic responsiveness to a score that was characteristic of Koussevitzky. However, for a student who was desperately trying to make up for lost time, both in a knowledge of literature and technique, Reiner provided the necessary corrective. Bernstein said, "Reiner was an intellectual conductor who demanded certain standards of knowledge that were absolutely basic, minimal (and these minimal standards were maximal, I can tell you)." He also said, "What I got were standards! You didn't walk up onto that box until you really knew what you were doing, or what the composer meant." He learned to look at a score from the conductor's point of view rather than from the performer's or the composer's, as he had done until then. He said, "If I'm dealing with a new score . . . I usually go through it as I would through a thriller, a detective story . . . to see what's going to happen . . . Then, when I have its basic form in my mind, I start all over again . . . analyzing it in detail . . . After analyzing the structure and the relationship of each component . . . you go back for the details. It's endless. And the better the score the more endless it is . . ." In February 1940, Bernstein was the only conducting student to get an A from Reiner.

Once he was in Philadelphia Bernstein kept in touch with everyone, including Helen Coates, who sent him brownies. He told Mildred that he had found a delicatessen in Philadelphia that sold halvah, to which they were both addicted. With his usual uncanny ability to put himself in the middle of "the action," he had rented a second-floor room at the corner of South Twenty-second and Pine streets directly above a soda fountain that was a local student meeting place. He was euphoric and determined to work hard. This would be needed, since Vengerova had asked him to return in a week's time with a Beethoven sonata and the Chopin C-Minor Etude, and he claimed not to have seen either of them before. The room's charms were minimal, but at least he had a Steinway.

The grand piano came courtesy of Curtis, which was located nearby at 1726 Locust Street. The conservatory was founded in 1924 with an endowment from Mary Curtis Bok, of the Curtis Publishing Company family, and anyone who could pass the audition was given free admission. Bernstein received a tiny weekly allowance from his father, supplemented by gifts from the ever-generous Mitropoulos. (During his second year at Curtis he taught a music course at the Meadowbrook School in Meadowbrook, Pennsylvania, on Wednesday afternoons and received a grand total of seventy-five dollars.) The whole purpose of the institute, in contrast to Harvard's, was to train future virtuosi, and never mind about such peripheral subjects as a general education.

Its faculty was enormously distinguished, and included Renée Longy Miquelle (solfège classes), the new director, the composer Randall Thompson, Wanda Landowska, Leopold Auer and Efrem Zimbalist, as well as Vengerova and Serkin, while the student orchestra rehearsed under Reiner and Stokowski. Equally talented students passed through its doors: the composers Gian Carlo Menotti and Samuel Barber, the pianist Jorge Bolet and many others. While at Curtis Bernstein fellow students included younger pianists such as Graffman and Istomin, not to mention the multitalented Lukas Foss, with whom he was competing more or less directly.

Annette Elkanova, a brilliantly gifted pianist from Atlantic City who went to study with Vengerova at the age of thirteen, said, "I was shipped off to Philadelphia away from all my friends. I lived with an uncle and aunt and younger cousin, and you never saw a more miserable person in your life. I had formed a mental picture of [Vengerova as] this elegant, cultured woman, and instead she was heavy and wore a black dress down to her ankles and had a thick accent. One time in my first year I was playing and she was saying something that sounded like 'Fourth! Fourth!' and I finally discovered she was trying to say 'Forte!'

"At Curtis they had practicing studios in a building across the street. I was working on a modern piece one day and Leonard opened the door and walked in. He had just graduated from Harvard, and was nice looking, young, enthusiastic and quite thin. He often needed a shave. I used to do imitations, and once at a party I opened my collar to indicate no tie, ruffled my hair and—that was my friend.

"We got along well. Both of us lived in center city and usually ended up having lunch. If he had wanted to, he could have practiced and been a great concert pianist, but he had no aspirations in that direction by the time I knew him. He had no other thought than to be a composer and conductor.

"He had a room near mine and I'd say, 'Come on, let's rehearse.' He taught me the love duet from *Tristan und Isolde*. It was probably extremely funny but he was enamored of Wagner at that point. We both smoked like fiends, and the ashtray on the piano would be full of cigarette butts. I think he was serious about me for a time; he asked me to marry him several times. We were going to move to San Francisco and live on Telegraph Hill.

"He had this fantastic ability to sight-read. He could read it as if he had practiced for weeks. This is one reason why he was so disliked. A lot of people thought he thought too much of himself, that he thought he knew more than anybody else. Of course, he had absolutely no tact. One time in a score-reading class something was put in front of him and he read it beautifully. Presumably, he did not know what it was. Everyone in the class thought he was lying, because it was the *Leonore* Overture [No. 3]. But I believed him, because there were surprising gaps in his musical knowledge. He knew every piece of modern music. He could play *L'Histoire du soldat* upside down and backwards, but he wouldn't know the most obvious things."

In one sense Bernstein desperately needed the Curtis experience; in another, it was too late and he knew it. Had he enrolled when he wanted to, at the age of eighteen or nineteen, he would have fitted in better with his fellow students. As it was, none of them had any kind of degree, let alone one from Harvard, and most of them were in "short pants," as he explained. When he demonstrated his usual trick of faultless sight-reading, instead of acknowledging his gifts with awe, as most of his Harvard classmates had done, these students were convinced he was cheating. The issue was not helped by his sententious, "big shot" airs, in his own phrase. By then Bernstein was used to easy success, and the antagonism depressed him; they were "still totally immersed in hammering out the Étude in thirds faster than the nearest competitor," he complained. "Philosophy, history, aesthetics—all irrelevant." While others struggled and squirmed before Reiner's rapier wit, Bernstein concentrated on making a friend out of him and succeeded to a surprising extent. So perhaps it was true, as Bernstein claimed, that another conducting student came to school one morning waving a gun and announcing his intention of killing Thompson, Reiner and Bernstein. Supposedly he was easily disarmed by Thompson, the police were called and he was removed before any harm was done. If one is to believe Bernstein, the incident brought about a thawing of the atmosphere. His fellow students became his admirers; for his part, he realized that his Harvard experience, with its theoretical approach to music, had been just as limited as the conservatory atmosphere at Curtis now seemed to him.

There was also the fact that war had been declared. At Harvard, as he said, "our great enterprise was antifascism . . . There were refugees all around us, and great ones: Thomas Mann, Hindemith, Einstein,

Shirley Rhoads Perle in the 1960s with, from left, Abraham Friedman, Bernstein's lawyer; Michael Wager; and Bernstein

Schoenberg. There was constant excitement in the air, the excitement of a huge and glorious struggle. At Harvard we had all-night bull sessions; we marched, we demonstrated; I played the piano for strikers, for Spain, for blacks, for one cause after another . . ." But after September 1939 and Hitler's invasion of Poland, he felt, with Auden, that "waves of anger and fear / Circulate over the bright / And darkened lands of the earth, / Obsessing our private lives . . ." He had struggled so hard to earn the right to be called a musician, and now all that he had accomplished seemed about to be swept away.

One consolation was his friendship with Shirley Gabis, later Shirley Rhoads Perle. They met when she was living with her mother in an apartment around the corner from his room over the soda fountain. "When I met him," she said, "he was an incredibly vibrant young man and one only saw the beginnings of the excessive behavior that would develop later. It seemed like a pardonable effusiveness." Shirley was just fifteen, in high school and herself a talented pianist, and the gap in their age, along with a certain resemblance to Shirley Bernstein, made her seem like a natural substitute for his sister. At any rate he was a constant visitor to their house. Once he played Copland's Piano Variations with such violence, stamping his feet, that the chandelier in the apartment downstairs crashed to the floor and the landlord made them leave. They saw each other constantly and had what seems to have been a close friendship that was almost a romance. Much later in their lives, when they were in a car together, he turned to a companion and said, "You should have seen her when she was young," and kissed her in a very orgiastic way. "Leonard Bernstein was like a star in a constant state of explosion," she said recently. "Not everyone likes that. It's an acquired taste." She laughed. "His seductiveness worked with me to a certain point." What made her hesitate was the realization that he temporized in close relationships. She never knew whether he was telling the truth or only what he thought she wanted to hear.

In keeping with his gift for cultivating the right people, Bernstein had made friends with Thomas D. ("Tod") Perry, Jr., then heading the Curtis concert office, which booked concerts by Curtis students for schools, women's clubs and the like. (Perry later became manager of the Boston

With Serge Koussevitzky, Tanglewood, 1941

Symphony Orchestra.) Bernstein was studying orchestration with Thompson, at least nominally, and since that office was across the hall from Perry's, he would stop in for a chat. Perry booked Bernstein for engagements, and he recalled Bernstein once lending him his tailcoat in which to conduct a concert. Bernstein performed relatively little during his first year at Curtis. He gave his first performance on March 29, 1940, accompanying six double bass players at the piano in works by Galliard, Mozart, Bottesini and Koussevitzky. Early that same year, he learned that Mitropoulos wanted him to be pianist and assistant conductor of the Minneapolis Symphony. He would be given the chance to play as a soloist and even have his work performed. There were a few formalities to be completed, and Bernstein waited anxiously for word through March and April, confidently expecting that this first year at Curtis would be his last. Finally, on April 19, 1940, he received a telegram. It said in part: "It is not wise to stop studying for a doubtful season for you here. Am very awfully sorry—Dimitri." A few days later, Mitropoulos wrote to say that his plans had been opposed by the union, which objected to having a student as assistant conductor when there were undoubtedly better-qualified candidates to be found. Bernstein was in despair. He wrote to David Diamond, who could be counted on to sympathize since he was supporting himself as a violinist while struggling to become a full-time composer. David would understand when he explained that his whole year had been focused on the goal of going to Minneapolis: "every move, every note studied, person loved, hope ignored, was a direct preparation for next year." Then Bernstein made the provocative statement that tailoring his life single-mindedly toward this objective had even included "the sexual life which I have abandoned." He does not elaborate, but there are two possible explanations: either he had taken a vow of monasticism in order to concentrate on his objective, or, conceivably, that year he had made the decision to abandon his heterosexual pursuits for the good of his career. The second interpretation is suggested by a letter he sent to Diamond two months later when, as in times past, Mitropoulos had failed to write. "It cannot be that *the thing* [italics mine] is over . . ."

Tanglewood, 1940

Forth! Stumble your way
Over stock and stone of the path
Through the portals of life

— GOETHE, "AN SCHWAGER KRONOS"

Later in life Bernstein was being interviewed about one of his favorite subjects, the conductors who had influenced him. The famous mane of hair, through which he liked to run his hands, was almost white, and scantier than in the early days of his fame, when photographers would show him in profile so as to dramatize the way the luxuriant black waves sprang from his forehead and tapered to an elegant point at the nape of his neck. The penetrating eyes had narrowed, and there were furrows and frown lines on his once serene brow. His nose seemed thicker, and "something about the mouth / Distracts the stray look with alarm and pity," as W. H. Auden wrote. But his hands, in continuous movement, were as expressive as ever, and his mobile features registered the same rapidly shifting moods; at times, he could look strangely vulnerable.

He was describing again the days when, as an undergraduate at Harvard, he had attended concerts of the Boston Symphony Orchestra. He described being seated in the second balcony and seeing, far below, the figure of the conductor, Serge Koussevitzky, appear on stage. "He wasn't a real person: he was a god, or a high priest . . ." Then, in March 1940, when Bernstein accompanied the double bass players in a program that included Koussevitzky's compositions, the great man himself came to hear the performance. Koussevitzky "remembered him," Bernstein told Mildred that day, so they had evidently met before, although in years to come Bernstein would forget that. This, no doubt, was when he learned that Koussevitzky planned to open a music school at Tanglewood, the new summer home of the Boston Symphony Orchestra outside Lenox in the Berkshires. Koussevitzky agreed to audition him, so Bernstein collected some letters of introduction and went to Boston to be interviewed in the greenroom at Symphony Hall. Others have described in detail being interviewed by Koussevitzky, an event Bernstein hardly remembered. Richard Bales, who would be one of Bernstein's classmates, said, "I already had preconceived ideas about Koussevitzky because his malapropisms were famous and people would say he was more interesting than the tsar. He was sitting with his back to me, writing, when I went in. He stood up, held out his hand and said, 'Baleth?' and then, 'Thit down.' So I did. I told him why I wanted to study at Tanglewood and he solemnly said, 'I vill accept you.' It was a foregone conclusion, of course. They needed all the students they could get." Not realizing his chances were equally good, Bernstein was almost rigid with fright and recalled only Koussevitzky's concluding words, " 'But of course I *vill* take you in my class.' It was just like that. A great shock. A wonderful shock." "Vatch that boy," Koussevitzky would later tell music critics. "Vatch him. You vill see vhat vill happen."

That summer of 1940 would be a pivotal moment in his life. Many, if not all of, the key figures who would play important roles in his life had already made their appearance. But of all his mentors it was Koussevitzky who would open up a new world of undreamed-of possibilities, and with whom Bernstein would forge the closest links. Koussevitzky, with his neat, impeccable figure, his dandy's cape, white suits and bow ties, his seigneurial life style, his musical dash and flair, his dedication to his art and farsighted concept of the path American music must take, Koussevitzky was the idol and model. He symbolized the rarified heights Bernstein wanted to scale, and his vast power and influence were the prizes Bernstein longed to win.

As for Tanglewood itself, no setting could have been more idyllic, or better suited to foster and encourage the talents of the group of young men and women who would arrive there that first summer to enroll at the Berkshire Music Center. The two-hundred-acre estate to which they came, with its impeccable lawns, extensive terraces, formal gardens and spacious summer house, was ideally situated, with a view overlooking a magnificent lake, known as the Stockbridge Bowl. The countryside was verdant and unspoiled, but that particular area of the Berkshire Mountains in southwestern Massachusetts was hardly unknown. Wealthy New York and Boston families had discovered it as early as the 1850s and had built homes on so vast a scale that one of them might require as many as a hundred servants. Writers soon followed. Edith Wharton stayed for several years and was called "the Lady of Lenox" by Henry James. Henry Wadsworth Longfellow was a faithful summer visitor. While out picnicking on Monument Mountain, Nathaniel Hawthorne and Oliver Wendell Holmes took shelter from the rain and met Herman Melville, then unknown and living nearby in Pittsfield. Hawthorne and his family actually lived in a small red cottage on the Tanglewood estate, then owned by a Boston banker, William A. Tappan; and he wrote some of his most famous books there, including *The House of the Seven Gables*. He gave Tanglewood its name and added to its luster some years later with *Tanglewood Tales*.

Serge Alexandrovich Koussevitzky was born on July 26, 1874, in Vyshny Volochek in the north Russian province of Tver, the son of an impoverished Jewish violin teacher. He entered the conservatory of the Moscow Philharmonic Society at the age of fourteen and, as a young man, became a double-bass virtuoso. His first love, however, was conducting—he had led his hometown's orchestra when he was barely twelve—and in 1905, when he married Nathalie Konstantinovna Ushkova, the daughter of Konstantin Ushkov, a Russian tea merchant, Koussevitzky was able to indulge in his great love. In 1909, helped by Nathalie's millions, he founded the Koussevitzky Orchestra, which became known in Moscow and St. Petersburg for its performances of Bach, Tchaikovsky, Beethoven, Rimsky-Korsakov and others. After the Russian Revolution the Koussevitzkys emigrated to Paris, where new Koussevitzky concerts began. Performances with other orchestras in London, Madrid, Barcelona, Berlin, Warsaw and Rome added to his growing reputation. He was invited to succeed Pierre Monteux at the Boston Symphony Orchestra in 1924, and his first appearance in Symphony Hall in the fall of that year was an event.

What distinguished Koussevitzky from other conductors of the period was his conviction that music was not a static art but continually evolving, and that it was the conductor's duty to encourage young composers. He had demonstrated the direction of his thought as early as 1909, when he and his wife had founded a publishing firm in Moscow in which all the profits went to Russian composers. Later he established a foundation at the Library of Congress to commission new works and, during his twenty-five years with the Boston Symphony, he established it as one of the foremost interpreters of the works of Stravinsky, Sibelius, Respighi, Hindemith and Shostakovich and for performing works by young unknowns like Copland, Piston, Harris, Barber and Schuman. Koussevitzky once said, "The music flows through me to the orchestra and from them to the public." It was the artist's obligation "to seek to cause music to penetrate into the living consciousness of the people and to break down the artificial barriers between the initiated and the non-initiated . . ."

Koussevitzky's demanding rehearsal style—he was known to repeat a phrase interminably before continuing to the next—became legendary. He liked to say, "Gentlemen, you are awfully not togedder," and "You play all the time the wrong notes not in time." Or he might ask, "What is this? I make it just like I vant a key and you give me something nothing." On one occasion when the orchestra seemed perversely determined to deny Koussevitzky the effect he wanted, he declared, "If I vill not have, I vill resign." When this announcement failed to persuade, he added, "I vill not resign. *You* vill resign!" Another story, perhaps apocryphal, involves a musician who repeatedly played the wrong notes. "Ged out, ged out, you're fired!" Koussevitzky yelled. On his way out, the offender had to pass by the maestro and launched a broadside of his own. "Nuts to you!" he said. Koussevitzky replied haughtily, "It's too late to abologize." He also had a sense of humor. Lukas Foss, who was also in Bernstein's class, said, "I remember once he stopped; I think it was Beethoven's Funeral March from the *Eroica,* and he said, 'Maybe it's a funeral march, but, gentlemen, you're not the corpses.' "

On July 8, 1940, three hundred men and women, most in their early twenties, arrived for the first six-week session of the Berkshire Music Center to study with a surprisingly distinguished group of teachers. Aaron Copland and Paul Hindemith, a refugee from Nazi Germany, taught composition, and Gregor Piatigorsky, chamber music. Herbert Graf directed the opera department, assisted by the young Boris Goldovsky. The chairman of Harvard's music department and famous conductor of its glee club, G. Wallace Woodworth, had charge of the choral program along with Hugh Ross, director of the Schola Cantorum. Players from the Boston Symphony Orchestra, headed by the concert-master, Richard Burgin, were also giving lessons. Tuition was one hundred dollars, and dormitory accommodations cost an additional twelve to fifteen dollars a week. Hot lunches were served every day from an old bus that pulled into Tanglewood each noon, and prices were modest.

Koussevitzky explained to a reporter that he was establishing a center because it was urgently needed. He said, "Perhaps you do not know how difficult it has been in the past to find American-trained first-desk men. . . . When first I came to America I asked, 'Where are the young American musicians? The composers, the conductors, the players?' And they said to me that there weren't any. I would not believe . . . and after a while I found out that there was a Copland, a Piston and others. So I sent for them. I said to Piston, 'Why do you not compose for orchestra?' and he replied, 'Why? No one will play such work.' I said that if he'd compose a good thing, I would play it . . . It was my great joy to give these men the hearings they deserved . . ."

Koussevitzky taught two classes in conducting, a large class for the general enrollment and an advanced class for a handpicked group that included Richard Bales, Lukas Foss, Thor Johnson, Gaylord Browne and Leonard Bernstein. Bales, who had studied at Eastman and Juilliard and would become conductor of the National Gallery Orchestra in Washington, D.C., said, "I remember my very first lesson in his studio, his 'laboratory,' as he called it. He made you go through the whole procedure of coming up to the podium, and just as I was about to start, he stopped me. 'Vait! Do not conduct until you have looked every man in the eye, and if he will not look back, fire him. He is no good. You must gip-notize the orchestra.' Then he would raise his hands very slowly, and you wondered how on earth they found the beat." Foss recalled, "His stick technique was not as precise and effortless as it might have been, but who cares? I mean, he did wonderful things."

For Bernstein, those sessions at Tanglewood were an unparalleled opportunity, because at Curtis he had been given almost no opportunity to actually conduct an orchestra. At Tanglewood, he was conducting constantly. The week he arrived Bernstein received a choice assignment, to conduct Randall Thompson's Second Symphony, "the first time I had conducted before an audience," he said in 1980, inaccurately. He recalled that the symphony's scherzo was "in seven-four time. It seemed very difficult, and I remember sitting in the bushes learning this piece and then coming to rehearsal with Koussevitzky. It was a huge thing to do for your first student concert, and when I came to the scherzo I was trying to teach it to the orchestra while Koussevitzky was sitting there in his cape looking majestic. Then he said, 'No, *Kinder,* what Lenny is trying to tell you is three plus four,' missing the syncopation entirely. [Jazz] was one thing he couldn't teach me about."

Bernstein conducted the Thompson symphony at the center's first orchestral concert and was given a passing grade: "His talent was obvious and, although he seemed unable to obtain complete hold on his players, his musical intentions were correct and inspiring," the Boston *Evening Transcript* reported. That summer Bernstein would go on to conduct Haydn's Sinfonia Concertante, Brahms's Second Piano Concerto, the Bach Double Concerto, Brahms's Variations on a Theme of Haydn, a prelude and toccata by Gardner Read, *An Outdoor Overture* by Copland, and the second and fourth movements of Rimsky-Korsakov's *Scheherazade.* He also performed Stravinsky's *L'Histoire du soldat* but substituted a comic text he had prepared for the occasion, *L'Histoire d'un élève. Newsweek* subsequently published a photograph of a smartly dressed Bernstein, arms raised, eyes glued to the score, conducting the work with a student orchestra, but he was not identified.

André Speyer, son of the Boston Symphony Orchestra's famous English horn player, Louis Speyer, was only fifteen when he went to Tanglewood that first summer. "I was a symphony brat, so I was automatically admitted." He remembered the opening exercises: "We went up the hill to the grounds not knowing anybody, of course, and Koussevitzky gave a romantic speech about the fact that, regardless of the war, the arts must continue. A few days later I was hearing the chatter about this wonderful young conductor, and my reaction was, Who cares?! Then I heard that in his first week at Tanglewood, he got the score of a new Roy Harris symphony one day and started rehearsing it the next. By, I think, Friday night, the student orchestra gave its first concert and we were absolutely astounded. He danced and gyrated and did everything in the world, but my God! You sat there. What he had done in four days! We couldn't believe it."

That first year, girls stayed at the Lenox School, and boys went to the Cranwell Jesuit School. There Bernstein shared one enormous room with five others: the violist Hillyer, the composer Harold Shapero, the clarinetist David Glazer, Henry Portnoi, who played the double bass, and the cellist Jesse Ehrlich. There was no piano in the room, "which was a good thing," Hillyer said: when they all began playing the racket was indescribable. Through it all, Bernstein went on studying his scores. Hillyer said, "Bernstein came to Koussevitzky with very little training, and his movements were instinctive, but not organized. Koussevitzky had this theory that the audience should not be able to see the conductor's hands, so Bernstein would stand in front of a mirror trying to cut his movements down."

Harold Shapero was studying composition with Hindemith. "All of Hindemith's pupils had to learn a second instrument," Hillyer remembered, "so Shapero, who was a pianist like Lenny, chose the trumpet and decided to practice it at two-thirty in the morning. It was like being beaten up. I am sure we tried to shut him up. Lenny was as bothered as anyone."

The Boston Symphony Orchestra, which had performed elsewhere in Lenox in the years preceding 1940, had recently acquired a new, wedge-shaped music shed at Tanglewood designed by Eliel Saarinen. Some five thousand people could sit under its roof, and thousands more could hear and see the concert from the lawns beyond. That was the center of concert activity; classes and social gatherings took place in the twenty-room, gabled Victorian mansion that had been built for the Tappan family, set in formal gardens with reflecting pools.

Bernstein wrote excited letters to Helen Coates, his Boston music teacher, and his family in Newton: "I have never seen such a beautiful setup in my life . . ." He was working all the time. "I don't think I slept a night that first summer . . . Up all night and then nine o'clock rehearsal. In between you were coaching and studying . . ." One can imagine those students of 1940 on the lawn some summer morning, wandering among the groves of trees that framed the distant views, as they heard Mendelssohn, Beethoven and Brahms coming across the clumps of delphiniums, from under the umbrella pines, along the gravel paths and as far away as the canopied porch of the main house. An atmosphere of ceremony, almost a court etiquette, prevailed. The concept that Tanglewood was a temple dedicated to Orpheus was exemplified by the bearing and demeanor of its creator. Year after year Koussevitzky would make his ceremonial entrance through the main gate in a limousine driven by a liveried chauffeur and accompanied by two state troopers. A valet would adjust his costume, the car door would open and the great man would step forth. "Koussevitzky had arrived; Tanglewood could begin," Speyer said. Evening performances called for formal attire; hats and gloves were worn at garden parties and, when going to class, girls wore skirts, and boys, jackets and ties. At lunchtime Bernstein, sitting on the lawn with a tray of food, might be alone in having removed his jacket and opened the top button of his shirt. One might also find him lounging bare-chested beside the lake while Copland, in stockinged feet but otherwise clothed, sat nearby. Bernstein would declare, "Tanglewood is my life. It's the place [where] I've spent my happiest hours . . ."

After dark students went to a local hangout, perhaps the Log Cabin, which served hamburgers and beers, and Bernstein and Copland pounded out jazz on "a horrible upright piano that hadn't been tuned for years," Speyer said. Hillyer recalled that, one night, Harris brought along an unfinished manuscript of a new symphony. Bernstein, whose ability to sight-read from orchestral scores was already a legend, promptly sat down and played it. Reaching the end of the manuscript, he improvised a brilliant ending to the score in the composer's style. "Harris was furious," Hillyer said.

Vera Tilson, who would become a choral conductor, said, "I was sixteen and almost the youngest person at Tanglewood. My father was Nickolai Kassman, a violinist with the Boston Symphony Orchestra, and he went to Bernstein and said, 'Look after my little girl.' Shortly after I got there, Bernstein came up to me and said, 'I am supposed to look after you. Are you all right?' I remember him very well. No one could forget him. He was so magnetic, and the center of attention wherever he went. His warmth and enthusiasm were impressive."

They all went out on parties, and she found herself more and more attracted. "I was mad about him; everyone was. He was sexuality incarnate. Everything about him blazed in some way. He was much too much for me to deal with at the age of sixteen, and I took care never to sit beside him in a car. At that time he liked anything that was moving."

Hillyer remembered going out with Bernstein on double dates when the foursome would usually end up "in someone's bedroom," he said. Bernstein was attracted to one of Hillyer's sisters and used to go to Hanover, New Hampshire, where the family lived, to visit her. Hillyer said, "My mother took to him like a second son. He had hay fever and she would rush around giving him some bitter-tasting nosedrops. I remember her dosing him with some of it and saying, 'Lenny, what big nostrils you have!'

Shirley Bernstein on the hood of the family car

"We went on outings into the countryside. Once we passed a play-ground full of children and Lenny insisted on stopping and talking to the kids. He immediately began organizing them into group games, just like a camp counselor. The remarkable thing is that they did exactly what he told them. He was hypnotic.

"He was brash only in the sense of being a very spontaneous person. He had tremendous energy, and he wasn't shy about putting himself into the middle of things. In official portraits he is always front row cen-ter." His sister, Shirley, who would spend many future summers at Tan-glewood, said, "I have such a memory of walking across the grounds with our arms around each other's waists. So many people have told me since we were so powerful. It's hard to believe, but too many people have said the same thing. How united we were; how confident." "I think peo-ple were jealous of his success," Hillyer concluded. "That wasn't his fault. He was just being his dazzling self."

In years to come Bernstein would say Koussevitzky became his sur-rogate father, a claim that is supported by those who saw them together. Foss went to have his hair cut in Lenox one day and the barber happened to mention that he also cut Koussevitzky's hair. "Koussevitzky apparently said to him, 'There are two students I have that I really believe in. One is Dionysian and the other is Apollonian.' To this day, Lenny and I are wondering which one is the Dionysian and which is the Apollonian." Bales said, "Koussevitzky liked Bernstein better than the rest of us put together."

Before long Koussevitzky was calling Bernstein Lenny, and then Lenyushka. After barely a month Koussevitzky was proposing that Bernstein study with him in Boston that autumn as a special pupil. Koussevitzky said he had a natural, a magnificent gift and that all he needed was three years' training. He had a brilliant future before him; that is, as long as he could evade the dreaded draft, which was imminent, Bernstein told Helen Coates. Bernstein was due to return to Curtis for a second year but was delighted to give up that idea. By the end of August he had composed a carefully phrased letter to Reiner. While making sure to let Reiner know about his triumphs that summer, he was quick to ascribe them to Reiner, who had achieved the superhuman feat of teaching Bernstein how to conduct without access to an orchestra. Other honeyed phrases followed, calculated to soothe what might be wounded sensibilities at the news that Bernstein did not intend to return.

At the same time Bernstein was writing mawkish letters of thanks to his new idol for the opportunities he had received and all that he had learned. Bernstein, back in Boston, was soon summoned to Lenox, where the great man was still at Seranak, his summer home. What transpired during that pivotal meeting is not described in the surviving correspondence. However it is clear that, by the end of September, Bernstein believed Koussevitzky's plan for him included being groomed as an assistant conductor of the Boston Symphony Orchestra. There he would make his sensational debut. A phenomenal career, fame, riches . . . all were within his reach, and it had all happened in the course of a single summer. In his dreams Bernstein was conducting the Boston Symphony Orchestra. The program: all his own music—symphonies, concerti, cantatas, operas . . . Quite soon after that he began to affect all-white suits with bow ties, to wear an overcoat slung carelessly over his shoulders the way Koussevitzky did, and to imitate the way he walked.

After the summer of 1940 and the realization that he had won yet another famous and influential conductor to his side, Bernstein veered between wild hope and the fear that Koussevitzky might renege on his promise just as Mitropoulos had done. The dream did, indeed, fail to materialize but the obstacle came from an unexpected quarter: Fritz Reiner. Reiner said later that he had objected to the very idea of having Bernstein go to Tanglewood. "I said, 'Lenny, by all means go to Tanglewood, it's near your home. But don't come back here; the two schools don't mix.' He cried. He wrote me a letter eight pages long . . ." Bernstein's version is that Reiner was furious when he found out that his prize pupil did not intend to return. The director of Curtis, Randall Thompson, had to tell Koussevitzky that Bernstein's scholarship there was for two years and that he was expected to return. Koussevitzky urged Bernstein by telegram to do just that. No doubt there was a tear-stained letter at that point, written by a thoroughly frightened young man faced with the prospect of losing two powerful advocates at a single stroke.

By the late autumn of 1940 Bernstein was ensconced in a new room on Walnut Street and back at class. His room was bigger and contained a double bed as well as several period pieces, but it was dark, and the single window looked down over a dismal alley. His father apparently had refused to support him any further, because he had obtained a student loan of forty dollars a month plus free lunches. He was resigned if not reconciled. With his usual energy he was looking for ways to supplement his income: in addition to the modest music course he was giving, he had been hired to conduct an amateur chorus and was lecturing at the Youth Arts Forum, an organization of apparently leftist inclinations, since it invited the artist Rockwell Kent to speak at its coming festival. Bernstein spoke of organizing and conducting an all-black symphony orchestra, but nothing came of it.

That year of 1940–41, he appeared with the Youth Arts Forum performing a Copland piano trio, *Vitebsk.* He also conducted his amateur chorus in American folk songs. His most important appearance was with Annette Elkanova, playing the Stravinsky Concerto for Two Solo Pianos at the second anniversary concert of the Twentieth Century Music Group on December 3, 1940, a concert that was broadcast on NBC two months later. He often appeared that year with Annette in two-piano performances, although not in the starring role. At a recital by pupils of Vengerova in the spring of 1941 he played second piano for two movements from Prokofiev's Piano Concerto No. 3; she took first. There were some solo appearances with Alexander Thiede conducting the Women's Symphony Orchestra of Boston; Bernstein performed a piece by Joseph Wagner and Beethoven's Piano Concerto No. 1. One critic thought his interpretation of the Wagner piece less than persuasive but praised his "remarkably sensitive conception" in the Beethoven: "His phrasing, his dynamic control, his rhythmic bounce and his interpretive faculties were vastly impressive." He was, the critic concluded, "a pianist with an original and refreshing outlook." In the late spring of 1941 Bernstein returned to Harvard, following the success of *The Birds* and *The Cradle Will Rock,* to compose original music for Aristophanes' *Peace.*

Bernstein wrote regularly to Helen Coates, who responded with warm little urgings to pay more attention to his personal appearance, since a good impression made such a difference. She was also reflecting on the tremendous progress he had made since the days when he could come to her for a lesson, bringing his first tentative arrangements of Russian and Hebrew melodies. She was consistently encouraging, but he seemed to be in a mood of despair. True to what would be a lifelong pattern, when depressed he fell ill, complaining of a bad cold and a general what's-the-use, morning-after feeling. He was often alone in his room at night, something he took care to avoid in future years. He had dawdled in his bath for an hour that January evening in 1941, just to have something to do, he wrote, and then puzzled over a cryptogram. He felt thoroughly bored and out of sorts.

David Diamond said, "The first time I met [Lenny] he sat down at the piano and sight-read my *Psalm* for orchestra from the score. We were at the apartment of an architect and set designer, at a wonderful party, with all kinds of people there, including Paul and Jane Bowles. He was playing Edgar Varèse and *Le Sacre du printemps* and everyone was asking, 'Who is this fantastic piano player? Where is he studying?' " Bernstein had just produced *The Cradle Will Rock,* "and all he could talk about was Blitzstein and Walter Piston and being invited to go to Mitropoulos's rehearsals. And his father would come up to me and say, 'Do you ever think he'll make any money?' " He found Sam Bernstein "aggressive and boorish. He always had his nose in the Talmud and was holier than thou, waving his finger at you self-righteously. Not what I call a man to like, but I adored Lenny's mother. She was warm and giving, and treated very badly by her husband." As a pianist Bernstein was astonishing, but Diamond quickly recognized that he had talents as a composer, and remembered seeing him at work on his First Symphony, the *Jeremiah.* They began to collaborate. Diamond needed a pianist to record one of his early piano pieces and sent it to Bernstein with the kindly intention of offering him a job. In his usual fashion, Bernstein took the opportunity to lecture Diamond—a far more established composer, with numerous chamber works, concerti and a first symphony to his credit—about the shortcomings of his composition. Diamond replied hotly and Bernstein wrote back in an injured tone, hoping his friend would feel better soon.

Fortunately, there was a second summer at Tanglewood to look forward to. On Saturday, May 3, 1941, Bernstein graduated from Curtis with a conducting diploma, along with two others, Walter Hendl and Max Goberman. Annette Elkanova won her piano diploma; Bernstein did not.

Of all the girls in his life at that period, the one Bernstein came closest to marrying was Jacqueline, called Kiki, Speyer. Kiki, the sister of André and the daughter of Louis Speyer, was just twenty-one that summer of 1941. Her parents had a house quite close to Copland's, and Kiki Speyer was working for Hindemith—she remembers teaching his students how to pronounce the words of Gregorian motets. She was slim, and showed her natural French flair in exquisitely chosen clothes; she had a dark, husky voice and was strikingly beautiful, with an almond-shaped face and luxuriant black hair. She happened to go to a student orchestral rehearsal at which Bernstein was conducting; once backstage, he asked to be introduced. They saw each other constantly. Koussevitzky was rehearsing Beethoven's Missa Solemnis that year and they were both in the chorus. They were also both involved in a production of Gershwin's *Porgy and Bess*—Bernstein was coaching in the opera department. She played "one of the dancing girls, so Leonard insisted I bare my midriff and paint myself black, and Koussevitzky said, 'There's Kiki, naked!' "

She continued: "We always knew we were going to get married. There used to be an orchard at Tanglewood that had our favorite apple tree. We would climb up into the tree and talk about the names we were going to give our children. We had decided that our son's name would be Jeremy, which is of course derived from Jeremiah, and when he had a daughter he called her Jamie. We were passionately in love and used to drive around in the back of Aaron's car necking like mad. But we never went to bed; don't forget, when I was a girl you did not have sexual intercourse before marriage. Physically he was absolutely beautiful, but he was something of a rough diamond. No table manners, and he would swear and say 'Fuck you,' and at times he was terribly Yiddish. After rehearsing the Missa Solemnis that first year we would go to a hamburger joint with Aaron and his boyfriend. On our way back home one night we started to argue in the middle of the street in Lenox. He had been very insolent to the conductor of our chorus, G. Wallace Woodworth, and I was reproaching him. Leonard said, 'I have had it. You are not going to tell me what I am going to do.' He began to make a scene, and windows were opening. So I hauled off and socked him. 'Now will you shut up?' I said, and he did.

"I went to school and was told I was going to be a musician and played the piano until Leonard came along. My father would make us play reductions of symphonic scores, and he was wonderful and I was awful. I got so discouraged that I stopped playing. He had the ability to make you feel totally inadequate, and he did it deliberately. He had such a time getting out of the inside of his head. He was a very difficult person to be with, because he was so brilliant. He was always testing you. He got away with everything, because of his extraordinary personality, enthusiasm, buoyancy, warmth, talent and charm and knowledge. I still have the feeling that things are mucked up in my life because of him.

Among those in Koussevitzky's first conducting class are Richard Bales, fifth from left; Bernstein, seventh from left; and Lukas Foss, standing to the left beside Koussevitzky (center, in unbuttoned jacket and bow tie).

"People don't realize that Leonard was quite a secretive person. He didn't talk about what was closest to him. He rarely confided in me, and only following a dramatic clash, and then I'd get some sort of truth. So I never asked questions. I knew I wouldn't get an answer. I sort of felt my way around. Everyone skipped, or missed, or didn't see, the anguished personality that was Leonard and his need to be accepted for himself.

"Leonard probably confided in Aaron Copland more than anyone else for years. Copland was a superb man, gentle, kind and understanding, with a sheltering way about him. He'd calm the waters. You could tell him anything. He was the only one with a car in those days, and so he used to drive us everywhere. We had a favorite owl that used to sit under a telephone pole, and if I was wrought up, Aaron would stop beneath it on the way home and wait for it to hoot. Leonard and I—I always called him that, and he called me Kee—had a very deep, musical relationship above all. It was our language. We sang to each other more than we talked, very often. We had a password in Missa Solemnis, a very joyous part of the Mass, that we shared together.

"I had a problem with him in that he could never be alone. He always had to be on show. I'd plead with him, 'Leonard, can we just go out with Aaron and Victor Kraft tonight?' We'd go out to the car and he is meeting people en route and inviting everyone. We'd leave as four and end up as twenty. The only good thing was that I would sit next to him. Otherwise he was likely to forget about me and go home without me. He'd be so contrite the next day."

That summer she was taken to Sharon to meet his parents and spent a weekend with them. "I didn't like his father. I thought he was uncouth and vulgar, throwing his weight around because he had made money. He was a blank wall. I remember one time my father tried to make him understand that Lenny *had* to be a musician. He spent hours talking to Sam, but Sam couldn't understand. His mother must have been in her early forties when I knew her. She was a divine woman. Shirley, his sister, speaks like Leonard. She is very attractive, with slit green eyes like Leonard's, dark hair, very bright, with a sparkling intelligence. I never saw her with a boyfriend." Shirley Bernstein thought that the daily battles of her parents were the reason why she could never bring herself to get married. "I broke so many engagements!" she said. "Or I fell in love with married men, who were safe. I regretted it very much, because I wanted children." She also thought that the unhappiness at home drew her closer to her older brother than she would otherwise have been. "First of all, I was his mascot." She was five years old then.

Jennie Bernstein in the 1940s

Jacqueline "Kiki" Speyer at Tanglewood, 1942

With Kiki Speyer at Tanglewood, 1941

"He and his friend would be in the attic trying to distill pure alcohol with vials and tubes when I was about four and mother would say, 'I have to go out. Take Shirley with you,' and he would agree reluctantly. He was very protective of me. I remember that Burtie was born in the middle of the night. Our parents weren't home and he put a blanket around me and held me tight."

That Leonard was very close to his sister was made abundantly clear to Kiki Speyer. The night she arrived, a Thursday, she and Shirley shared a room with twin beds. The next morning, Leonard was in the other bed with his sister, saying, "We've been cuddling for years," and inviting her to climb in. She was angry and confused. Shirley Bernstein said, "There were ways we had of being together that were unique. I always looked for that kind of intimacy with others. It precluded sex, but I know why people would think so, because we were hand in hand or with our arms around each other's waists. I used to hear these incest rumors and my reaction was, 'What are they talking about? Are they insane?' "

That was the start of Kiki Speyer's weekend with the Bernsteins, and things went from bad to worse. "Leonard's grandmother—they called her 'the old bubbe'—had just been in the U.S. for a few months and was staying there. We sat down on Friday night and there was the blessing. The old bubbe asked who I was and what did I want to drink. I asked for milk. She turned to her son and said, 'Sam, what does the shiksa want?' and started to scream. Then I lit a cigarette with the candelabra, and that was the end.

"On Saturday morning there was no one in the house. An uncle had died, so Leonard's parents left, but they left the old bubbe. I went into the kitchen to open the door of the refrigerator, but she was right behind me. She slammed it shut, because it was the Sabbath, and a light had gone on in the refrigerator, and you can't light any lights on the Sabbath. So I lit the stove to have a cup of coffee, but that was the same problem. I tried to play the piano, but she slammed the lid shut. So I packed up and left."

Those were, as Bernstein said, feverish days. Reiner's despotism on the podium was justly renowned, but Koussevitzky was no less autocratic: "I can see my beloved master Koussevitzky, a high priest at his altar, raging through an endless rehearsal, indefatigable. I can hear him now: 'I vill not stop to vork until it vill not be more beautiful.' 'Ve vill play again hundred times until it vill not be in tune!' '*Kinder,* you must *sof-*

Bernstein and Koussevitzky in 1944

fer, soffer for die musical art!' . . ." Bernstein's own attitude towards his fellow musicians, once he had his own orchestra, was much more collegial and democratic. However, the basic message "All excellent things are as difficult as they are rare," as Spinoza wrote, appealed to the perfectionism that was a marked aspect of his personality. One of the things he said he admired about Toscanini, for instance, was the way he would slap his own face, call himself names and refuse to be satisfied by anything he had done. He learned from Koussevitzky "that a musician's life was dedicated to his work and his art above all, and that if he or she was not willing to make that kind of commitment, he might as well be

With Copland at Tanglewood

And lunching on the grass, uncharacteristically alone

With Lukas Foss being pursued by the photographer
Ruth Orkin at Tanglewood

dead," Leonard Burkat said. This did not mean that Bernstein did not, on occasion, become exasperated with Koussevitzky. During one of those early summers, Bernstein shared a concert with him. Jerome Lipson recalled, "We started at ten o'clock rehearsing with Koussevitzky. Twenty minutes before the rehearsal was to end, Koussevitzky turned to Lenny and said, 'Now, mein dear, the rest of the time is all yours.' Lenny raised hell and they gave him something like an hour's overtime."

Bernstein's great success of the 1941 summer was conducting William Schuman's *American Festival Overture* on the same program with Koussevitzky conducting Liszt's *Faust Symphony*. Koussevitzky kissed him and the audience went wild. He got two more bows than Koussevitzky did, he told Mildred. That summer was triumphant for another reason: he won a competition to conduct the Boston Pops Orchestra at the Esplanade before an audience of twenty-two thousand and acquitted himself very creditably with the prelude to Wagner's *Die Meistersinger.* Conductor Harry Ellis Dickson, who was there, said there was general admiration. "I don't think he needed lessons," he said. "He was a natural." Bernstein's victory was complete when Arthur Fiedler, who remembered dismissing Bernstein when they met four years before, apologized handsomely.

Burkat, who wrote extensively about music, said shortly before he died, "Among the thousands of articles I never wrote is the way repertoire gets handed down from teacher to pupil, who then makes it his own. Bernstein had a repertoire of pieces that were his Mitropoulos pieces, his Reiner pieces, his Koussevitzky pieces . . ." Bernstein recalled that Mitropoulos specialized in performing the Ravel Piano Concerto in G Major, and this became a part of his repertoire, as did Schumann's Symphony No. 2, Ravel's *Rhapsodie espagnole,* and Mitropoulos's own arrangement of the Beethoven Op. 131 quartet, which he and Hillyer had so much admired. Following Koussevitzky's lead, Bernstein would become known for his performances of Stravinsky, Prokofiev, Hindemith, Bartók, Copland, Piston, Ives, Harris and Schuman; one of his favorites was almost Koussevitzky's signature piece, Tchaikovsky's Fifth Symphony. Conducting that work, Bernstein would find himself making the same shifts of tempi that his mentor had, observing the *accelerandi* that were not in the original score but had been added by Koussevitzky, and taking liberties with the *ritardandi,* just as Koussevitzky had done. As Koussevitzky would have urged, "De l'audace, et encore de l'audace!"

Perhaps the greatest compliment of the summer was the invitation to spend the weekend with Mr. and Mrs. Fritz Reiner in Rambleside, their handsome white brick house set in forty acres of gardens and wooded paths near Westport, Connecticut. Bernstein asked if he could bring Kiki and Shirley, and the three of them drove up in a car with Dimitri Markevitch, brother of Igor, the Russian-born pianist, composer and conductor. They arrived and were invited to take a swim in the handsome pool. Arthur Judson, the orchestra manager and agent, who would play an important role in Bernstein's life, was standing in the pool up to his waist. "Mrs. Reiner said, would we please not splash Mr. Judson; 'He's been there for an hour like that and he won't go any further.' So of course the first thing Leonard does is dive into the pool and splash Judson all over," Kiki Speyer said. "Judson stormed out. Shirley turned to Mrs. Reiner and said, 'Don't ever tell him not to do something.' "

The winter of 1941–42 Bernstein was trying to survive by giving occasional recitals and by teaching the piano. (He opened a studio on Huntington Avenue in Boston, but hardly anyone came.) He spent most of his time with Kiki and her parents. She said, "He was living on practically nothing and I know my mother fed him. Then he got a job in a

David Diamond, 1939

hotel bar and had some pocket money." Their relationship continued to deepen, and she began to take instruction in the Jewish faith. "By 1942, Koussevitzky wanted Leonard to succeed him. He sat us both down and said, '*Kinder,* you must get married.' I was hearing the same message from my parents." The day before Koussevitzky was to have made the announcement, they made a date to meet. Bernstein never appeared. "The next day I went looking for him at Tanglewood and saw him with a very tall instrumentalist, who, Leonard said, 'went off on an overnight climbing expedition.' Leonard needed a shave and his friend looked very strange. So I dragged him off to a rehearsal, with the friend shambling along behind us. After the rehearsal, Leonard said, 'I have to talk to you. The fact is, I've seduced this boy.' I said, 'What the hell are you talking about?' and he replied, 'I am in love with him.' I said, 'What happens to us?' and he said, 'You will have to tell Koussevitzky.'

"I went to see Koussevitzky and tried to explain what had happened, and Koussevitzky said, 'Vat you mean?' and I said, 'Because he is a ped-erast,' and Koussevitzky replied, 'Vat is a pederast?' and I had to tell him. So then he went to Leonard and said, 'Vat it is I hear? Kiki tells me you are a little bit pederastical.' " Kiki Speyer believed Koussevitzky supported the match because he thought his Lenyushka needed some-one like herself to "manage" him. "He was sure I could control him, but he was wrong," she said. In years to come Bernstein would actively pros-elytize for the advantages of homosexuality. The conductor Antonio de Almeida said that, at about that time, Bernstein tried "for days to talk me into homosexuality. When I said it wasn't for me, he asked how did I know, and told me I might like it. I wasn't convinced." Some time dur-ing the early years of Tanglewood, a girl whose mother had a summer house in Lenox and took in lodgers recalled coming home unexpectedly at midday to go to her room. She opened the door and found Leonard Bernstein and Aaron Copland in her bed. She said, "I was just eighteen. I'll never forget that day. It was so traumatic. I didn't know what to do. I told my mother and she told me to say nothing about it."

Bernstein's immediate goals at that period were to get an orchestra of his own and stay out of World War II. The summer of 1941 he had received his draft notice and did not know whether it would be wiser to volunteer and join the Army as a musician, or hope he could be some-how deferred. For that to happen he needed work as a conductor. Kous-sevitzky's papers show that he did his very best for his brilliant young protégé. He was so concerned about him, given the anti-Semitism of the age, that he urged him to Anglicize his name (while in Russia, Kousse-vitzky had converted to Christianity), but Bernstein refused. Kousse-vitzky wrote to every organization he could think of, both governmental and philanthropic, and even to Mary Curtis Bok, asking for help in keeping Leonard out of the war. He wrote to New York's Mayor Fiorello La Guardia when he learned there was a vacancy for assistant conductor of the New York City Symphony, saying that he thought Leonard would be ideal for the position. Months later a reply came saying that Bern-stein's name had been placed on a list. Bernstein did not get the job, and his future remained uncertain. Bernstein, who had received a temporary deferment on the basis of asthma and allergies, went to the U.S. Army medical examiner in the summer of 1943. Koussevitzky wrote the examiner a letter on Leonard's behalf. His pupil was a "born genius"—

he was asking for a deferment without actually saying so. The examiner put Bernstein in class IV where, Bernstein told Koussevitzky, there was no chance of his ever being conscripted. Nothing could interfere with his career now, the examiner had told him.

As in so many areas of his life, the issue of whether or not to take part in the war tormented and fragmented him. Being Democratic, pro-Zionist and antifascist, the Bernstein family's position could be assumed at that point and may have been formed a decade before when American Jewry rallied to stage mass demonstrations in Madison Square Garden and elsewhere in an attempt to stop the Nazi persecution of German Jews. By 1939 even people like the author Ben Hecht, by his own admission an "indifferent Jew," were taking sides: "The German mass murder of Jews," he wrote, "had brought my Jewishness to the surface." There is no doubt of the sincerity of Bernstein's convictions. The issue to him had to be which came first, his career or his fight for a cause. There is no firm evidence here about his father's position. As a Russian Jew who had emigrated to escape from the same fate, he might have been expected to encourage his son to avoid the war at all costs. On the other hand, he was a fervent Zionist, supporting the causes of his adopted country, and hardly a convert to his son's belief in the burning importance of a musical career.

Bernstein might have taken heart from Hitler's invasion of Russia in 1941, after which, Koussevitzky told him, "Lenyushka, this is the end from Hitler." Besides, Koussevitzky believed an artist should be spared a soldier's death since his mission was to exhort and inspire. As it turned out, Bernstein's health gave him a legitimate excuse and he was free to claim, then and later, that he was desperately disappointed.

It is conceivable that Sam Bernstein never knew about his son's attempts to avoid being drafted. In 1943 he described the moment when his son Leonard learned he had been turned down. "Lenny was on the couch, face down, crying as though his heart would break," Sam said. On the other hand, this may have been a prudent social lie, since Sam Bernstein is also supposed to have said, "Thanks be to God my son won't have to go to war."

After Tanglewood closed for the duration of the war in the summer of 1942, and following his break with Kiki Speyer, Bernstein moved to New York. The city had seemed like a hopeless challenge when he was there in the summer of 1939. He remembered buying the cheapest seats in Lewisohn Stadium, and "if anybody had told me I'd conduct there some day, I would have laughed in his face." Bernstein had stayed in

Boston while he waited for Koussevitzky to produce a solution. In fact, Koussevitzky had invited him to perform as soloist in a new piano concerto by Carlos Chávez, but unfortunately the BSO was nonunion at the time. Bernstein was by then a member of the musicians' union and could not get the necessary waiver. So he turned hopefully to his friends in New York. Green, who had launched on his famous partnership with Betty Comden, had been cast in a new musical by the popular song lyricist Irving Caesar. The play, *My Dear Public,* had previewed in Boston, and Bernstein was invited. At the cast party he naturally commandeered the piano. Caesar said, "He looked the closest thing to Gershwin and he played the closest thing to Gershwin. When I sang some of my songs, he accompanied me, picking up the chords, just as George used to do. I told him, 'If you ever get to New York, for heaven's sake drop in.' " Bernstein took him up on the offer, and when Caesar learned he was out of work, he recommended him to Herman Starr of Harms, Inc., a musical publishing house that was a subsidiary of Warner Bros. Harms had given Gershwin and Kern their start. Bernstein was hired for twenty-five dollars a week to listen to records by jazz musicians and transcribe the improvisations. He arranged pieces, as he put it, "for four hands on two pianos, eight hands on two pianos, two hands on eight pianos . . ." He also wrote some boring popular music. "The popular song in the twentieth century is a more or less stale and stereotyped melody set over a 4/4 accompaniment, plunged usually into a ternary form (strain and repetition, release, and strain)," as he observed in his B.A. thesis. He gave himself a new name: Lenny Amber.

Dorothy Lang, who would have her own career as a singer and composer, was working as a receptionist at Warner Bros. in those days and was used to seeing all kinds of famous men and women pass by her desk. She also noticed this "kid" who came in all the time. He seemed so handsome and friendly, so she asked who he was and was told, "He's going to be another Gershwin." Everyone was talking about him and, whenever she saw him by chance at a concert or in a restaurant, she would turn to her companion and say, "There's that wonderful boy!"

Paid with Interest

Fair, grand, boundless
Open stands before us the world . . .

— GOETHE, "AN SCHWAGER KRONOS"

Bernstein had moved into a basement flat at 15 West Fifty-second Street, paying eight dollars a week rent. After graduating from Harvard, studying with some of the best piano teachers money could buy and learning from three world-famous conductors, the best he could do was a menial klezmer's job. Meanwhile he was hunting for something worthier of his talents. Inez Ross, then one of the moving forces behind the New Opera Company, recalled that Bernstein came into her office in about 1942 looking for work. He said he would like to conduct an opera for them. She said that the group was only giving four operas and that the conductors had already been chosen.

She said, "He sat there, with his bowler in his lap and said, very earnestly, 'I'm a *very good* conductor.' " Although his attempts to further his career through the efforts of Reiner, Mitropoulos and even

Edwin Denby, Aaron Copland and Bernstein
discussing the production of Copland's
Second Hurricane in 1941

With Copland working on
The Second Hurricane score

Koussevitzky had failed, Bernstein was far from being defeated. It had been a stroke of luck to meet Adolph Green. It was an equal coup to have befriended Marc Blitzstein, a force in musical theater, not to mention Aaron Copland. They all knew everything about what might be called the politics of music: how to join the right organizations, live in the right neighborhoods, be seen in the right places and exchange judicious favors with the right people. And from Copland's point of view it was an advantage to have the allegiance of a musician of Bernstein's talents, whose admiration for his work was unfeigned and who was articulate in its praise. Speaking of Copland's Piano Sonata, Henry Simon wrote, "This is a highly individualistic work, reiterative, percussive, economical, dissonant and emotional in a shadowy way . . . Leonard Bernstein, who played it . . . expressed a deep affection for the work and somehow left the impression that anyone who disagreed was a bit of a philistine."

During Bernstein's year in Boston Copland had obviously taken trouble to help him find work. When he decided to present his opera for high-school audiences, *The Second Hurricane,* in Boston under the auspices of the Institute of Modern Art, he gave the plum position of conductor to Bernstein. The work was considered successful enough to merit a repeat performance. Bernstein made appearances as a pianist at the Institute of Modern Art and also with the League of Composers in New York, in which Copland had been an important influence almost since its formation in 1923. Thanks to his Copland and Blitzstein connections, Bernstein was invited as an "assisting artist" on a program of works of young American composers sponsored by the League of Composers, performing with Harold Shapero in the latter's Four-Hand Piano Sonata. When Marc Blitzstein produced Music at Work, a program of new music to aid Russian War Relief at the Alvin Theatre, Bernstein appeared with Copland performing a movement from Copland's new work for two pianos, originally titled *Birthday Piece (on Cuban Themes)* and later changed to *Danzón Cubano.* The same work was on the program when the League of Composers celebrated its twentieth anniversary at New York's Town Hall late in 1942. Piston, Darius Milhaud, Frederick Jacobi, Bohuslav Martinů and Louis Gruenberg wrote pieces for the occasion. Copland even found commissions for him. The late Hans Heinsheimer, former head of G. Schirmer, the musical publishing house that published Copland's work, said, *"El Salón México* was one of Copland's most successful pieces. One day I said to him, 'We should have a piano arrangement of this,' and he said, 'I know just the man. He's a poor musician and needs money badly.' It was Leonard Bernstein. We arranged to pay him twenty-five dollars and it's still in print."

Bernstein found his way onto a program being presented by the then new Museum of Modern Art, conducting an evening of music in honor of Federico García Lorca, the famous Spanish poet who had been ambushed and murdered in 1936. One of the works on the program was by Silvestre Revueltas, a Mexican composer who had fought on the Loyalist side in the Spanish Civil War and recently died. The other was a stage piece, *The Wind Remains,* based on a surrealist libretto by García Lorca and with music by Paul Bowles. Bowles, who would become something of a cult figure, was almost as multifaceted as Bernstein, making a reputation as a composer for the theater and also as a critic before turning to fiction. He seemed to have an uncanny gift for ingratiating himself with the right circles. After becoming the darling of the Gertrude Stein set in Paris he moved back to New York, his birthplace, where he and his wife, Jane, became close friends of Virgil Thomson and Copland and were protégés of Peggy Guggenheim and also of A. Everett ("Chick") Austin, Jr., the imaginative and influential director of the Wadsworth Atheneum in Hartford. The worlds of art, music and literature were small and intertwined in the New York of the early 1940s. To be championed by one or two influential members was to meet everyone who counted, and Bernstein was becoming skilled in the art of making the right connections.

Bernstein was making his first steps into the field of narrating and commenting, following the lead of Blitzstein and Copland, and appeared as a "commentator and pianist" at a Town Hall performance of Scarlatti, Chopin, Brahms and Ravel, with Thomson acting as master of ceremonies. The most exciting event of this year was his appearance as pianist in a program of Copland's music followed by a panel discussion at Town Hall. Copland himself was scheduled to perform his Piano Sonata but was in Hollywood working on a new film score and could not get away, so Bernstein was called to substitute on a day's notice. He bought a set of tails, played the sonata and answered questions from the audience with style and wit, to judge from the reviews the next day. Thomson, who was one of the panelists, actually stood on the stage and talked about him, Leonard Bernstein, for a full five minutes, he told Helen Coates. It was a stroke of luck that his father could be there to witness his son's success.

To add to his triumphs in 1943, Bernstein finally got to conduct members of the Boston Symphony Orchestra. The union problem had been solved and he was one of six conductors (the others were Goldovsky,

Woodworth, Bernard Zighera, Edgar Curtis and Richard Burgin) who performed in a series of chamber music programs in Boston and Cambridge in July and August. He received some good press notices, and one critic was aware of the extent to which the pupil was attempting to emulate the master. "As conductor, Mr. Bernstein showed himself an apt pupil of his master, Koussevitzky. Almost too apt, in fact. Not only does he act like him, he even contrives to look like him. It is positively spooky."

Besides appearing as a conductor, pianist and commentator, Bernstein made his debut as a composer, along with Lukas Foss, at a League of Composers concert at the Museum of Modern Art in the spring of 1943. The work was Sonata for Clarinet and Piano, which had received its premiere in Boston the year before. It was dedicated to David Jerome Oppenheim, a young clarinetist four years Bernstein's junior, whom he had met at Tanglewood and who would go on to have a distinguished career as a performer, record executive, television producer and dean of the School of the Arts at New York University. At that moment Oppenheim, who was in the Army Reserve Corps, was about to be placed on active service, and performing Bernstein's new work would be one of his last professional appearances before being shipped overseas.

The Sonata for Clarinet and Piano was the first work Bernstein thought worth promoting, although some earlier works for the piano showed considerable promise. In fact Bernstein would vandalize some of those early pieces—the Piano Trio and Music for Two Pianos, both from 1937—when he was looking for material for his musical *On the Town* some years later. The Boston *Globe* thought the sonata contained some "jazzy, rocking rhythms" and some interesting ideas, although the piano part was better realized than the writing for clarinet. Paul Bowles, reviewing for the New York *Herald Tribune* just two weeks before Bernstein was to perform his own work, was more sanguine. The sonata had something in short supply in contemporary music, to wit, "meaty, logical harmony. It was also alive, tough and integrated. The idiom was a happy combination of elements from both east and west of the Rhine . . . Through most of this . . . ran a quite personal element: a tender, sharp, singing quality which would appear to be Mr. Bernstein's most effective means of making himself articulate."

Ned Rorem was one of the people who met Bernstein when he was still living on West Fifty-second Street. He said, "It was just east of Fifth, and radically different in those days. Then it was brownstones and bars, including Tony's and the Onyx Club. In those days Billie Holiday was singing in both of them. There was also a gay bar on Fifty-second, called the Dizzy Club, and the Faisan d'Or was just around the corner on Sixth Avenue. I was studying at Curtis and living with Shirley Rhoads Perle and her mother, and they suggested that if I was going to New York, I had to look up Lenny.

"At the time Bernstein was living with a girl, Edys Merrill. Though poor, he already had the brash self-assurance that would solidify when he became rich and famous. And he was five and a half years older than me. When one is just nineteen, that is a large gap. He was smart-aleck and Jewish while I was a reticent Wasp. But we were both interested in 'modern' music, so we hit it off. He was rehearsing his Clarinet Sonata with David Oppenheim. There was a lot of drinking and I ended up spending the night. In fact, it became a habit to crash in Lenny's pad whenever I came up from Philadelphia for weekends. I didn't know what to think of Edys.

"The following week or month, I rang the bell, and the Revuers were there, rehearsing: Betty Comden and Adolph Green and Judy Holliday. All this loud, extrovert singing! Later that night, at their show at Café Society downtown, I remember Judy Holliday swilling straight gin and I was very impressed and decided to do the same.

"I stayed over with Lenny again and we slept on a mattress on the floor. Edys came in at two a.m. and saw us. She despised me. Was she in love with him? He was not with her. We went to the Faisan d'Or for breakfast next morning. Lenny had to give a piano lesson to a priest at ten, and I watched him slug down a couple of scotches to get him through the lesson. Never in my wildest dreams of alcoholism did I start that early, or use booze to see me through something.

"When I told him once that Shirley [Perle] had called him the best pianist in the world, he showed me some of his pianistic tricks. Lenny had one of the quickest minds in the world. His need, his essence was to be master of all trades, and he succeeded. Which is why only the ignorant say: 'What could he have done if he had specialized!' Bernstein was anxious all of his life to be thought intellectual, and he was not intellectual in the usual sense. He was a doer. My feelings toward him always blew hot and cold, because he was such a combination of qualities: madly competitive with everyone, mean, sweet, vulgar, tactful, rude and generous. If he felt someone didn't like him, he would expend a great deal of energy on being liked. Anybody—that includes everyone in the audience.

"After I moved to New York I started working for Virgil Thomson as a copyist. Bernstein introduced me to Copland, saying that Aaron loved young composers. Later I studied with Copland at Tanglewood.

It was a healthy growing place at that time, and those were the happiest days of my life."

The rapidity with which Bernstein was making inroads into New York's musical life was astounding, though not perhaps unexpected, given that his invariable method of relaxation was playing games calling for advanced tactical skills. Since he was working for a music publisher, it was logical that he should submit his sonata for publication, and it was soon accepted. However, his claim that he received advance royalties of twenty-five dollars a week, which would have doubled his income, sounds somewhat inflated. The next step in making his mark as a composer was to have a symphony to his credit, which might facilitate his appearance as conductor of a symphony orchestra. *Lamentation,* written three years before, was for voice and orchestra. He had also sketched out the first movement and it seemed as if the main outlines for *Jeremiah,* his Symphony No. 1, were in place. He was spurred to action by the discovery that the New England Conservatory of Music was sponsoring a competition and Koussevitzky was to be the chief judge. All the omens looked favorable, and he tore into the project, finishing the piano score in the space of ten days. The next step was to orchestrate the work, a traditionally time-consuming process which could take weeks, but he was up against a deadline. So he ingeniously pressed his sister and some friends into service. While Shirley contributed the time signatures and Bernstein wrote out the instrumentation in pencil, another friend produced a finished copy in ink and someone else kept pots of coffee on the boil. It took three days and nights, working around the clock. Even so, it was too late to mail the manuscript to meet the competition deadline of December 31, 1942. True to form, Bernstein got on a train for Boston and delivered his work in person, just two hours before midnight. After all that, it was a great disappointment that Koussevitzky did not care for the work and it did not win a prize.

The biblical Jeremiah, son of a priestly family, preached in Jerusalem from 628 to 586 B.C. under Josiah and his successors. He lived during a transitional period when the old Assyrian empire, of which Israel was a part, was crumbling and being replaced by the neo-Babylonian empire; there were periodic invasions of his country. His preachings centered around the sins of idolatry and false worship and predicted that Jerusalem and its temple would be destroyed unless there was a real commitment to reform and a return to the spirit of religion, not merely adherence to its rituals. Tradition has it that he was by temperament introspective and reticent, but felt compelled to condemn what he considered to be the evils

Conducting in the 1950s

of the age. He made some powerful enemies and was imprisoned several times. Jeremiah's message contained a new emphasis on the importance of a personal relationship with God, and his confessions contain dialogue with the Deity that question His judgment and even accuse God of having betrayed him.

The symphony's first movement, "Prophecy," sets a mood of somber introspection. It is followed by "Profanation," a scherzo depicting the destruction of the temple at Jerusalem, using thematic material partly drawn from the music of the Sabbath service that accompanied the reading of the Haftarah. "It has a curious wailing insistent quality," Donald Steinfirst wrote, "with strongly marked but very clearly stated rhythms especially well written for brass." The final movement, "Lamentation," with its mezzo-soprano solo, is a setting of lines from the book of Lamentations and describes the aftermath: "Jerusalem hath grievously sinned. How doth the city sit solitary . . . a widow."

The *Jeremiah* Symphony was dedicated to Samuel Bernstein and, as a further mark of respect, used the Ashkenazic pronunciation of Hebrew in use in Eastern Europe rather than the Sephardic common to Portugal, Spain and southern France. Clearly, Bernstein meant his father to be flattered by a comparison with the prophet famous for taking courageous and unpopular positions despite the personal risk. However, there is a suggestion that Jeremiah, the prophet who held God directly accountable, also refers to the composer himself. His symphony, he said, was about a crisis in faith. "I wouldn't say that it's God up there watching over me, as much as me down here looking up to find Him—I guess you would call that a chief concern of my life."

The chain of events that would cause Bernstein to be transformed overnight from an unknown to a nationally known conductor and bring about his debut at Carnegie Hall on November 14, 1943, is still unclear. Any young American conductor had to get hired by a New York agent, specifically *the* agent in this case, Arthur Judson, the man Bernstein had splashed in Reiner's pool. At that point Judson was America's preeminent musical "salesman" (self-described), not only manager of the New York Philharmonic but creator of Columbia Artists Management, the most powerful music agency. Judson managed almost all the major conductors in the United States (Arturo Toscanini was a rare exception) as well as numerous singers, composers and instrumentalists.

Richard Bales, who was struggling to establish himself as a conductor at the same time as Bernstein, claimed it was well known that any young conductor who wanted to be represented by Judson had to pass money under the table in addition to the usual hefty 15 or 20 percent commission on his income. Philip Hart, author of *Orpheus in the New World,* who knew Judson, confirmed the rumor. "I do know about one young American conductor in the mid- or early 1930s," he said. "His father owned a popular German restaurant in New York, and the gossip in the music business was that Poppa financed the boy's career. I've heard from another conductor that his father and Judson [agreed on] a price tag . . . It's promotion, and promotion costs money." Bales said, "I knew I could not become a big-time conductor because I did not have enough money behind me." Milton Goldin, author of a book on the music business, believed that without Judson's backing Bernstein could not have risen to prominence. He wrote, "Men such as Bernstein and Isaac Stern got to where they wanted to go by making certain they first identified and then pursued the powerhouses of the music business."

Reiner and Mitropoulos were both managed by Judson; Koussevitzky was independent. The story is told that Judson went to Paris

Artur Rodzinski

looking for a successor for Pierre Monteux in Boston and that the announcement that Koussevitzky would succeed him came before Monteux had even resigned. It was said, perhaps unfairly, that Nathalie Koussevitzky's fortune had bought the job for her husband. In any event, once he was established in Boston, Koussevitzky was wealthy enough not to need Judson again and kept a certain distance from him. Who persuaded Judson to take on Bernstein is an open question. Reiner would certainly have put in a word. On the other hand, one cannot believe that he would have supported Bernstein's candidacy financially, whereas Koussevitzky might have. The mystery will probably never be solved. There is only a letter from Bernstein to Olga Naumoff, Nathalie's niece and Koussevitzky's secretary, who after Nathalie's death became his wife in 1947. In it Bernstein makes a casual reference to "the Judson office," so she must have known that he was being represented by Judson. The letter is undated but appears to have been written in late 1942 or early 1943. Bernstein also remarks that Judson was considering having him "conduct" the New York Philharmonic the following year. No doubt the optimistic description referred to a job as assistant conductor under Artur Rodzinski, who would, in September 1943, be making his debut as music director.

The issue is particularly interesting in the light of the position of young American conductors at that time. Ever since the mid–nineteenth century, Joseph Horowitz wrote, America had suffered from a cultural inferiority complex. "To this inverse chauvinism, pitting American composers against such Continental luminaries as Wagner and Brahms, were added disadvantages specific to music." The British legacy, which had provided so much in the way of poetry, drama and art, was meager in musical terms, whereas the American frontier experience hardly seemed translatable into symphonies and operas. Pressures to import European culture lock, stock and barrel came from immigrants with German backgrounds who wanted their music performed by Europeans, exactly as they remembered it. But times were gradually changing. With the help of the radio and the phonograph, and aided by a new interest in music appreciation, a whole new audience had developed in the 1930s and 1940s, eager to experience a broader range of styles and less biased against home-grown talent. From Bernstein's viewpoint his debut could not have been better timed. He was about to take center stage just as the ranks of his competitors had been blocked, on the European side, and drafted, on the American. Even given the right financial incentives it is doubtful whether Judson would have troubled to further Bernstein's interests before the war. Gary Graffman commented wryly that Judson treated his young artists with "a passionate lack of commitment." This did not happen in Bernstein's case. As Goldin observed, "an emerging Jewish middle-class of concertgoers in America and terrible revelations about the Holocaust influenced Judson. He knew trends when he observed them, and he grasped that Bernstein could be turned into a cultural hero."

Besides identifying the pivotal figure in the music business, Bernstein, in pursuit of a job as assistant conductor of the New York Philharmonic, needed to ingratiate himself with Rodzinski, its new conductor. That would be easier. In her frank memoir, *Our Two Lives,* Rodzinski's widow, Halina, charted the stormy course of the Rodzinski-Judson relationship, which had often been antagonistic (it would be severed forever a few years later) but which was enjoying a brief reconciliation as a result of Rodzinski's appointment. No doubt Judson had informed his music director that his assistant conductor for the coming year could be found at Tanglewood. No doubt Rodzinski found it simple to defer to Judson on what would have been, for him, a minor issue.

Celebrating a Koussevitzky birthday, Tanglewood, 1942

Although Tanglewood remained closed for the duration of the war, its spirit was being kept alive in the summer of 1943. Koussevitzky had moved its operations to the Lenox Library, where he presented a series of concerts in which his prize pupil figured prominently. Martin Feinstein, who later worked with Sol Hurok, produced Bernstein's *Mass* and is now general manager of the Washington Opera Society, recalled that he was stationed at Fort Monmouth, New Jersey, that summer. He had a weekend pass, so he decided to hitchhike to Tanglewood and heard one of Bernstein's library concerts. "He was doing a Brahms piano quartet with some Boston Symphony Orchestra musicians and I was overwhelmed. I predicted, 'This man is going to have a career.'"

Bernstein appeared with Koussevitzky in a lecture and recital in which the latter talked about the mission of the artist. Bernstein played Bach, Copland, Chopin and Liszt. As an encore, he launched into some boogie-woogie; "he is the most exciting white boogie-woogie player I have heard," a critic said. Bernstein was also at the keyboard for a recital with Jennie Tourel. Tourel, who had recently arrived in the States, grew up in Paris and had made her debut as Carmen at the Opéra-Comique a decade before. It was the start of a long friendship. As it happened, Bernstein had just written a lighthearted group of songs for children called *I Hate Music,* the jazzy tunes and irreverent tone of which did not appeal to Koussevitzky. Tourel, however, liked the cycle and sang it as an encore after a lengthy program of Handel, Bach, Milhaud, Wagner and Rachmaninoff. The date was August 25, Bernstein's twenty-fifth birthday.

Bernstein had broken his engagement with Kiki, but they were still on good terms, and he was staying with her and her parents that summer. She remembered that Koussevitzky telephoned one day and asked her to drive Bernstein out to the farm in Stockbridge where the Rodzinskis went in the summer and were raising goats. Rodzinski was following the precepts of the Moral Re-Armament movement, which had begun in Britain as the Oxford Group, and to which he had become a recent convert. The MRA, as it was called, advocated "living in love with one's fellows instead of in fear, and following the advice of God which was free for the asking . . ." This is perhaps why in years to come Bernstein would quip that Rodzinski had asked God whom he should appoint and that God told him, "Take Bernstein." The reality of the situation was, of course, that the Deity in question was living in New York. Bernstein was told that he had to have a personal interview with Judson. Bruno Zirato, Judson's assistant at the Philharmonic, cautioned him that he had better not make another faux pas, no doubt to put him in a properly receptive frame of mind. Kiki went with him. They stayed in the Pennsylvania Hotel, in one room with twin beds. She said, "He went out for a pack of cigarettes at six o'clock one evening and came back at two the next morning. He had been with Comden and Green down at that dump in the Village where they played. That night he kept wanting to tell me what homosexual relations were like, and I didn't want to hear." The situation seemed so hopeless that she rushed into a new relationship. She said, "I married a man I didn't care for just to get away from Leonard."

Bernstein wrote an excited letter to Koussevitzky after his Judson interview. Koussevitzky had advised him to ask for $12,000 a year, but that seemed too daring. Instead he agreed to serve for one year, effectively twenty-eight weeks, at a salary of $125 a week. There was to be no contract. The announcement was made in the *New York Times* on Sep-

Arthur Judson, right, during his thirty-four years at the New York
Philharmonic, with Dimitri Mitropoulos in the 1950s

tember 9, 1943. Bernstein sent a copy to Helen Coates with a jubilant "Here we go!" scrawled in the margin. A new photograph was taken, in three-quarter face, his thick hair neatly waved; he looked dreamily handsome. The "refugee from a college campus," as one newspaper described him, began to be mentioned in newspapers and magazines and appeared at tea parties honoring the new music director and his pretty blond wife.

He took apartment 503, a $100-a-month studio above Carnegie Hall, and threw himself into his new task. The choice of quarters was a prudent one, since he was required to be on hand immediately should Rodzinski be unable to conduct, with a suit of tails, a cutaway and a clean shirt at the ready. "And in order to . . . do that, I have to study every work on every program. I really ought to know them better than anybody, I guess, because I'd have to conduct them without rehearsal." It was his job to listen to everyone who wanted to be auditioned and turn him or her down tactfully if necessary ("It's hard to do if you're tired," he said). The most demanding part of his job came as the result of a new Rodzinski policy. In the interests of encouraging performances of new works, Rodzinski decided to hold a series of rehearsals of the scores of promising composers. Works would be given a single reading, and an informal jury of performers, composers, conductors and critics would be invited to attend and nominate the best manuscripts. These scores would later be given full-dress performances by the Philharmonic (which was then called the Philharmonic-Symphony Society). The enormous task of selecting likely manuscripts and returning the rejected ones was given to Bernstein. He also performed some of them. After conducting two sittings, a total of five hours, he said it was "absolute agony."

Bernstein was determined to become indispensable and was so successful that he began to get on his music director's nerves. Halina Rodzinski wrote, "When people crowded into the Green Room to congratulate the artists after a performance, Lenny would edge himself into the situation, by letting no one misunderstand . . . who he was. This irritated Artur. In time, Artur had Zirato forbid Lenny to enter the Green Room." Zirato, who had a gift for diplomacy, no doubt found some way to cushion the news. The Roman-born assistant manager had a varied life as a newspaper man and music agent before becoming personal assistant to Arturo Toscanini during his tenure as music director of the New York Philharmonic; after Toscanini left, Zirato stayed on, and was there for thirty years. His son, Bruno Zirato, Jr., recalled that they lived in an apartment opposite Carnegie Hall and Bernstein often invited himself for dinner. "He'd wander over around seven o'clock and say, 'I'm hungry!' " He added, "Bernstein would have some crazy, wonderful parties in his cubicle in Carnegie Hall. He loved musical quiz games, in which he'd start and stop a symphony and you would have to guess. His sister, Shirley, was tremendously good at them. Lenny was a heavy drinker even then. He drank a lot of Scotch, and it had very little effect on him."

As André Gide said of Oscar Wilde, success seemed to run ahead of Bernstein and he had only to collect it. He was already expecting Saturday, November 13, to be a memorable date. Jennie Tourel was to make her Town Hall debut that day and would sing his *I Hate Music* cycle, not just as an encore but as part of her program along with Mozart, Debussy, Rameau and Rimsky-Korsakov. It was an exciting week for other reasons. Negotiations had just been completed with Reiner for the premiere of *Jeremiah* with the Pittsburgh Symphony early in the new year. The Sonata for Clarinet and Piano had just been published and was soon to be recorded by Bernstein and David Oppenheim. Most exciting of all, he had been asked to compose music for a new ballet by Ballet Theatre that would involve three sailors and a girl in a bar.

His mother, father and twelve-year-old brother, Burty (Shirley was at college), were coming from Brookline, to which they had recently moved, and staying at the Hotel Barbizon. (They were returning to Boston on Sunday at one p.m.) No doubt Bernstein planned to show them around Carnegie Hall and put the best possible face on his new position, although he knew how anonymous it was in fact. Young assistant conductors are perennial understudies, hoping for the last-minute substitution that almost never comes, and the possibility that Bernstein would ever conduct seemed remote. Rodzinski was in excellent health and had taken the further precaution, in his contract, of giving himself a two-week break after every month of concerts so as to stay in shape. In the interim, guest conductors had been hired. Among them was Bruno Walter, whose ten-day engagement included a series of concerts that would end on November 14 with a Sunday matinée, which would, as usual, be broadcast over the Columbia Broadcasting System. Walter was in his sixties and leading an active life as a guest conductor. (He would succeed Rodzinski as principal conductor of the New York Philharmonic four years later.) The week was memorable for another reason: Kiki Speyer was getting married on November 13. With his tendency to vacillate, Bernstein was probably feeling considerable regret and a wave of affection for his lost love, now that it was safe.

Bernstein took his parents to Walter's concert on Thursday because, his father said later, Lenny wanted them to see a great man at work. After listening to the concert Sam Bernstein turned to his son and said, "I would give ten years of my life, Lenny, if you could be up there." Bernstein answered crossly, "Don't be silly, Papa, don't talk such nonsense. Why, it will be years yet before I ever do anything like that!"

Jennie Tourel's reputation—it was said that the only debut that could be compared with hers was that of Kirsten Flagstad—had preceded her, and the house was packed. Virgil Thomson was admiring. "The voice is a mezzo-soprano of wide range, warm in timbre and unbelievably flexible," he wrote. "Miss Tourel is a mistress of a wider range of coloration in all ranges and at all volumes than any other singer I have ever heard." Her perfect pitch, her legato skips, her command of language and her musicianship were so exceptional that "her work belongs clearly with that of the great virtuosos of music." It was a magnificent debut and her composers Bernstein and Diamond (she also sang one of his songs) were swept along in the triumph of the moment. Everyone, including Tourel's pianist, Erich Itor Kahn, adjourned to her apartment for a party. Bernstein remembered thinking that his career had reached its absolute zenith and spent the evening drinking, playing the piano and singing with toneless vigor—he was developing, by general accord, one of the world's worst voices.

Just when he learned Bruno Walter was ill and would not be able to conduct his final concert is subject to conflicting accounts. In later years Bernstein liked to say that he did not discover he was going to be on stage until the morning of the concert when the phone rang and he, tired and bleary-eyed . . . etc. Reports at the time of the debut generally paint a different picture. Walter apparently told management as early as Friday that he had come down with the flu, had an upset stomach and did not want to conduct on Sunday. Bernstein knew by Saturday, if not before, that he would probably have to take over.

Just why Bernstein should have been asked to conduct at that particular moment is a tantalizing question. Rodzinski's position is fairly well clarified by his widow's account: he could have substituted but did not want to. He was luxuriating in the first of his two-week periods off and probably thought it was a management ploy to disrupt the agreement he had carefully arranged. Management should make other arrangements. Why not ask Bernstein? That was what he had been

Bruno Walter

Bernstein, shortly after his debut in 1943, with Artur Rodzinski, far right, the young Eugene Istomin, left, and Leonard Pennario, in uniform

hired for. Bruno Zirato, Jr., recalled that Walter had informed his father of his illness after the afternoon concert on Friday. Zirato said, "I don't know whether my father tried to get a famous conductor to replace him. But I do know he called Lenny on Saturday before the Tourel concert and told him to be prepared." Harry Beall, a former partner of Judson's, said, "I presume Judson engineered Bernstein's debut. As manager of the New York Philharmonic, he could have asked anyone in the world to substitute, but chose not to. It was going out on the radio as well, so a deliberate decision had to have been made." Meanwhile Dorle Soria, who was in charge of public relations for the New York Philharmonic, called to tell Olin Downes, the music critic of the *New York Times,* that Bernstein was to replace Walter. "He said he never worked on Sunday but finally agreed to attend as a personal favor to me."

Some accounts say that Bernstein caroused until the small hours on Sunday morning, one that Bernstein himself contradicted: " 'I had an idea,' said Mr. Bernstein, running his hand wearily through his hair, 'that I might have to do the concert. So I drank coffee at midnight, studied until 2 o'clock—not all night the way the newspapers said—and so I couldn't sleep. When I knew I had to do it, I was scared out of my wits. It took me an hour to collect myself, to find "that inner strength without which one would sink." ' " Among the telephone calls he made next morning was one to his father at the Barbizon. "Papa, cancel your reservations for home. Dr. Walter is sick and I'm going to conduct this afternoon. But I haven't rehearsed, and I wonder, should I go on, or not?" Samuel Bernstein recalled. "Should you go on?" he retorted. "You're a Bernstein, ain't you? I come to America, give you a good name, a good country where you have opportunity, and you ask me should you go on! Did a Bernstein ever turn back?"

The program was Schumann's *Manfred* Overture, Theme, Variations and Finale by Miklós Rózsa, the Hungarian-born composer best known for his film scores, Richard Strauss's *Don Quixote* (with Joseph Schuster playing solo cello and William Lincer, solo viola) and Wagner's Prelude to *Die Meistersinger.* Although there was no chance of an orchestra rehearsal, management must have thought none was really needed, because Walter had already prepared and performed the program. If necessary, the players could survive with only minimal help from a substitute conductor. Just the same, first-chair members were called in to go over some fine points with Bernstein, and Walter himself favored him with an hour's coaching. "I found Mr. Walter sitting up, wrapped in blankets, and he obligingly showed me just how he did it," Bernstein said. Adding to the afternoon's demands was the live radio broadcast. That, as Halina Rodzinski wrote, placed extra stress on the conductor, who had to ensure that each piece was precisely timed to accommodate the commercials from the sponsor, the U.S. Rubber Company. The radio programs were important since they covered the orchestra's yearly deficit and there were additional fees for the conductor and instrumentalists.

Bernstein said later, "I was so shaky that I went to the corner drugstore . . . for coffee. The druggist knew me. He said, 'You look terrible—what's the matter?' " Bernstein told him he had to conduct that afternoon, and the druggist gave him a phenobarbitol and a Benzedrine to take just before he went on stage, one to calm his nerves and the other to energize him. Bernstein put the pills in his pocket, intending to swallow them. That afternoon, he was waiting in the wings, nauseous with fright, when Zirato went on stage to announce the change of conductor. The audience responded with a unanimous groan of disapproval. To the defiant, risk-taking aspect of his nature, this kind of challenge acted as a stimulant; it galvanized him. He threw the pills onto the floor and strode out to the podium.

He knew the program well. He had performed the Wagner prelude and had made a particular study of Strauss's *Don Quixote* because he liked the Cervantes novel so much. As for the *Manfred* Overture, named for the hero of Byron's tragic poem, its tone of daring fate to do its worst exactly matched his mood of the moment. It begins with three chords by the full orchestra. Bernstein said, "It was like a great electric shock . . . ZUM—zai—zam! Pause. In that pause I knew everything was going to be all right. The orchestra was really with me, giving me everything it had."

The violinist Jacques Margolies was playing in the orchestra that afternoon. He said, "We were there a few minutes early. I was young, but that orchestra was really seasoned. The idea was, he'd follow us, only it didn't work out that way. You just couldn't believe a young man could create that kind of music. Here were players in their fifties and sixties with long experience. And here this little snot-nose comes in and creates a more exciting performance. We were supposed to have gone over it with Bruno Walter, we had rehearsed it with him and performed it with him, and this had nothing to do with Bruno Walter. The orchestra stood up and cheered. We were open-mouthed. That man was the most extraordinary musician I have met in my life."

Bernstein often said he remembered nothing, from the start of *Manfred* until the end of the concert. What the audience saw was a slim, erect figure in a well-tailored dark gray double-breasted suit (he did not have the correct morning wear for the occasion), throwing himself into the task of leading the orchestra through a demanding program. He was at the beginning of his career, but his style, energetic and fluent, was already well developed. He was using a score but seemed entirely familiar with it and gave his cues—he did not use a baton—with authority and control. But from the audience's point of view it was his passionate conviction that held their attention. In the andante passages, his movements seemed strikingly eloquent and languorous. As the music gained in momentum, so his movements reflected the emotions being expressed. His arms and shoulders exploded in a fury, shaping the attack, the mood, delineating the colors and leading inexorably to the ecstatic climax of the work. He seemed to be totally uninhibited and spontaneous, outside of himself. He said, "Things come to me in a kind of inarticulate flash—I don't understand it. It's like an atavistic memory—as though I'd done these things in another lifetime, say, seventy years ago." In identifying with the music, he lost himself, as if he were back in his father's charismatic element, joining the faithful as they sang, shouted, rocked, stamped and leapt in the dance of exaltation. All great music, he said later, must contain a quality of rightness and inevitability. Experiencing it had to make one feel that "something is right in the world. There is something that checks throughout, that follows its own law consistently: something we can trust, that will never let us down." It was, he said, his definition of God.

Wilde once said, "Work never seems to me a reality, but a way of getting rid of reality." Bernstein would describe time and again how slowly he returned to the real world of the concert hall, the stamping and screaming, the standing ovations and the repeated calls back to the podium. "The next thing I remember is my mother and father walking into the dressing room and my father was ecstatic and baffled." Sam still wanted to know the point of the exercise: Lenny was bound to end up in a hotel lobby behind the potted palms, making background noise like any other klezmer. Others realized the significance of what had happened. The Rodzinskis drove in from the Berkshires and missed the radio broadcast, but arrived full of compliments just the same. Rodzinski said that he, too, had made his debut by substituting for someone, in his case, for Stokowski with the Philadelphia Orchestra. (By an amazing coincidence, *Don Quixote* was also on that program.)

Koussevitzky, in Boston, sent a telegram, which Bernstein received at intermission: "Listening now. Wonderful." The management of the New York Philharmonic let it be known that Mr. Bernstein was the youngest man ever to direct a Philharmonic subscription concert, and would receive many more opportunities to demonstrate his gifts. Shortly thereafter, Judson "called him into the office, showed him a sheaf of contracts and said: 'All you've got to do is to keep those dates.' " As for the hero of the hour, chance had once again favored his well-prepared mind. He went off with his family and had "four scotches and the best steak I've had in years." About a week after that, having finally been convinced that his boy was a success, Sam Bernstein was ready to say how pleased he was. He told his son, "Lenny, I spent $12,000 on you. But . . . you paid me back every cent—with interest!"

All-American Boy

And when peak calls to peak
Ever th' eternal soul
Summons us forth through the ages to be.

— GOETHE, "AN SCHWAGER KRONOS"

Thanks to the foresight of the public relations manager at the New York Philharmonic, the news of Bernstein's debut appeared on the front page of the *New York Times,* along with an inside photograph of him being congratulated by members of the orchestra. An editorial followed, commenting on the phenomenon of the young unknown who steps into the breach, a stereotypical event that happened rarely enough in real life. It took "something approaching genius" to achieve such a feat, the newspaper noted. "It's a good American success story . . ." Or, as the *Daily News* put it more prosaically, it was "one of those opportunities that are like a shoestring catch in center field. Make it, and you're a hero. Muff it and you're a dope . . . He made it."

He was called the "white-haired boy of symphonists," the "Orson Welles of music," the concert hall's answer to Frank Sinatra, even "our musical Dick Tracy," this slight, boyish figure with perceptive, hazel-green eyes underneath strongly marked brows. Bernstein had realized that, as Dwight Macdonald wrote, "the masses put an absurdly high value on the personal genius, the charisma, of the performer, but they also demand a secret rebate: he must play the game—*their* game—must distort his personality to suit their taste." Joseph Horowitz has described how in an epoch marked by the struggles of immigrants in a polyglot culture to construct an orthodox image of what an American was, foreigners like Toscanini and Vladimir Horowitz were remade to satisfy the public's requirement that they be "regular guys." Bernstein knew almost immediately how to present himself to conform to the right image of a homegrown American genius: baseball-loving, steak-eating, jazz-playing, someone who read the funnies and lived in a wholesome suburb just like everybody else.

Those who knew him remarked on his ability to cloak his true feelings. "I don't think he ever said what he really thought," said the conductor Maurice Peress, who came to know him well. "He was very smooth, very careful to choose his words. It was a great compliment to his self-control. What he really felt had to be something else." That ability to discipline his responses, framing his comments slowly and thoughtfully, in quiet, well-modulated tones, was a marked quality of his persona in early adulthood. The triumph of this painstaking facade was that, to the world at large, he seemed so frank, youthful and enthusiastic. He conformed exactly to the picture of the boy next door drawn in countless films by Jimmy Stewart or Ronald Reagan, the boy who throws your newspaper onto the porch, serves at the soda fountain and becomes captain of the baseball team, the myth of small-town America reflected in its films, books and magazines, its radio programs and comic strips.

This ability to mirror others' expectations encompassed a display of emotions that might be completely assumed so that, as with any great actor, it was difficult to see where artifice ended and reality began. The *New Yorker* commented, "The bones of his face are arranged so theatrically that in shifting light he gives the impression, without moving a muscle, of being an entire cast of characters; it is hard to find two photographs of him that are clearly of the same man." He could, for instance, put on a convincing show of motion sickness on a train and display elaborate grief as the boat on which he was departing left the dock—waving tearful farewells to complete strangers. The tenor

Paul Sperry, a good friend of his, recalled seeing *La Bohème* with Bernstein and his wife, Felicia, at La Scala, and watching with awe the tears streaming down Bernstein's face during Act IV. Afterwards, Felicia explained with resignation: "He always cries at that spot in *La Bohème.*"

Given the facade, it is possible to see the appeal that music performance had for him. On the podium he could let down his guard; indeed, given his Hasidic heritage, an abandoned display of feeling was almost required. With the help of music he could come to terms with all those feelings he could not afford to express, for, as he said, "this probably saved my life as far as unreleased or repressed hostility goes. Because I can do things in the performance of music . . . that if I did on an ordinary street would land me in jail. In other words, I can fume and rage and storm at a hundred men in an orchestra and *mmmmmmm*ake them play this or that chord, and get rid of all kinds of tensions and hostilities. By the time I come to the end of Beethoven's Fifth, I'm a new man."

One criticism that would be made of Bernstein was that he feigned feelings in conducting as in everything else. It seems truer to say that music remained his exorcism, an emotional release that was heightened by the fantasy that he had become the composer in the moment of creation. "I always know when such a thing has happened because it takes me so long to come back. It takes four or five minutes to know what city I'm in, who the orchestra is, who are the people making all that noise behind me, *who am I?*"

Bernstein's chameleonlike awareness of the kind of response required of him gave him the necessary flexibility to be on easy terms with a wide range of people and contributed to his almost magnetic allure. He was, everyone said, the kind of person who was so good at listening that one immediately felt he cared. He had this in common with Lord Beaverbrook, the British newspaper magnate, who, the historian A. J. P. Taylor said, had "a gift for making you feel when you were with him that you were the most important person in the world. I knew he forgot about me the moment I left the room but it was magical all the same." One could partly explain his gift by seeing him as an "animator," one of those people who "liberate their contemporaries by their vitality, exuberance and spontaneity . . ." He was so full of ideas and he had such a zest for life, such an ability to make things happen, such a sense of fun. He might decide to lighten the atmosphere at orchestra rehearsals with kooky plays on words: "No," he would say, "not *rallentando,* just relaxo." Once he ran through a passage from Mozart's Requiem with an obviously nervous soprano. He asked, "First timesies?" and the singer confessed it was. He replied, "Marvellusio! Couragiosa!"

He dominated at parties as much as before and could be sure of gathering a crowd as he, in faultless evening dress, belted out popular songs with his usual barroom gusto. Nowadays the crowd might contain his delighted father, yelling away with the best of them. Bernstein's memory, if anything, improved. Returning one time from a performance of a popular musical, he sat down at his hostess's piano and proceeded to play all seventeen of the songs from the show with hardly a mistake. His prowess with the *Times* crossword puzzle was legendary. André Speyer said, "One of my more hateful moments with Bernstein came about one time when I was in my room practicing. He walked in, stretched out on my bed and did the crossword puzzle and double acrostic in five minutes—with a fountain pen. I have never been able to do a word puzzle since." The pianist Leon Fleisher remembered playing word games with Bernstein at the dinner table at which each word had to begin with the last letter of the previous word and fit a predetermined category. "You'd have to say your word within three beats, and as the game went on, the beat would increase." Besides being complex and subtle, Bernstein was fearless. "He often used the expression 'the edge of the abyss,' " Fleisher recalled. "An artist's life is a risk. You're taking chances all the time, and sometimes you don't succeed. I remember a performance of Tchaikovsky's *Pathétique* which he stretched out to the last nanosecond, and he said, 'I really went to the edge that time.' He showed his orchestra how to risk and return safely."

With all of his gambling and risk-taking, his standards for himself and others remained perfectionistic. Once when he found a rare mistake in the *Times* crossword puzzle he sent a letter of protest. He was still ruthless with himself if he made a mistake. Although a tendency to be late, to put things off, had begun to manifest itself, once he had begun to prepare a performance he worked tirelessly and with an exaggerated attention to detail that was sometimes the despair of performers and singers. Among the contradictory elements of his character was a tendency to hypochondria—"he was always imagining he had something," a friend said—and, on the other hand, a daredevil refusal to take the slightest care of his health. If, for instance, he had pneumonia and had to finish a concert or recording, he stoically went on working. If necessary, he could live without sleep and on black coffee and as much Benzedrine as it took. He drank with the same abandon, and chain-smoked Viceroys (he always had several cartons on hand) despite his lifelong asthma. He used to boast that he had been warned to stop smoking in his twenties, with the prediction that he would be dead by the time he was thirty. He would prove them all wrong. Bravado and braggadocio existed side by side in his character with a tendency toward periodic depressions, anxiety and continuing doubts about his self-worth, doubts perhaps intensified by the uncertainties intrinsic to his choice of career. As Leonard Altman said, "There was no security except the applause he received all his life." Dimitri Mitropoulos remarked to David Diamond, once Bernstein was launched on his brilliant career, "He's a genius boy, but he wants success and he is going to pay a high price."

Marc Blitzstein wrote to tell his sister that Leonard Bernstein's success was the "talk of the music world." He continued, "I'm happy about it, because I think he deserves it all. A fine kid." Within three days of his debut at Carnegie Hall, eight crews of photographers had taken approximately one hundred and ten pictures of Bernstein, and he had been interviewed by reporters from *Life, Time, Newsweek, Pic, Look, Vogue, PM, Pix, Harper's Bazaar,* the *Times,* the *Herald Tribune,* the *Jewish Forward,* the *Jewish Day,* the *News,* the *Post* and *The New Yorker.* They learned that he did not wear a hat, kept his hair trimmed, worked in a sleeveless pullover or a red-and-black checked lumber jacket and cooked his own breakfast. He was writing a series of antifascist songs, the least he could do for the war effort. "How can I be blind to the problems of my people?"

The New York Philharmonic, which would see legions of anonymous assistant conductors come and go without once mounting the podium, had managed to fit Bernstein on one of its programs barely two weeks after his debut. He conducted *Three Jewish Poems* by Ernest Bloch and acquitted himself well in what was a "purely atmospheric work," as Paul Bowles said dismissively. Hardly two weeks after that he had another stroke of luck. The guest conductor, Howard Barlow, came down with influenza and told management in time to give Bernstein at least one rehearsal. After he had taken the Philharmonic through Brahms, Delius and Beethoven it was evident, most critics said, that here was no fluke performer but a musician of commanding gifts. They praised his readiness and fluency, his responsiveness to the music and his rhythmic understanding. During the 1943–44 season Bernstein would conduct the Philharmonic eleven times, sharing concerts with, or substituting for, Barlow, Walter and Rodzinski, and he would return the following year in the elevated position of guest conductor. Meantime Judson and Zirato were booking concert dates for him in Chicago, Rochester, Cincinnati, Detroit, Pittsburgh, San Francisco and Montreal.

Now that he no longer needed a symphony to launch him as a conductor, fate again conspired to shower him with opportunities. When Rodzinski himself came down with influenza and had to cancel early in 1944, for once Mr. Bernstein was otherwise engaged: he had gone to Pittsburgh, where Reiner had offered him the opportunity to conduct *Jeremiah* with the Pittsburgh Symphony. Koussevitzky then invited him to make his long-sought debut with the Boston Symphony. Bernstein would also conduct the New York Philharmonic in *Jeremiah* that spring. It was an incredible season; the symphony would win the New York Music Critics Circle Award for 1944.

The symphony's premiere in Pittsburgh on Friday evening, January 28, 1944, must have fulfilled Bernstein's every fantasy. Critics vied with each other to find enough words of praise. It was "a significant and intellectual contribution to contemporary symphonic writing." The work revealed a "passionate glow, an unusual profundity of poetic thought and a clear manner of expression and presentation"; "we have rarely heard music of modern vintage of such honest and absorbing emotion": these were some of the comments. On the same program Bernstein conducted Stravinsky's *Firebird* Suite, which one critic thought he had shaped and clarified with such luminous intensity that "the nerves could have borne very little more." Bernstein looked to be very much in the mold of his mentor Dr. Reiner: "his cues are clean, his demands from the orchestra are within reason, his careful molding of phrase and line, admirable . . ." Another thought his style of conducting rather more energetic. It was "unlike any I have seen, an indescribable combination of supplication, command, yearning, and gesture. Some day he will destroy himself on the podium," the critic predicted. Orchestra members were so admiring that they refused to stand for bows along with the conductor but left the stage to him and his soloist, Jennie Tourel.

He was in Pittsburgh with his sister Shirley, who had left Mount Holyoke in order to act as his secretary. She sat in the conductor's box at the concerts, gave him a rub-down at intermission and packed his collars and toilet articles. They went to Boston a month later for his appearance on the same podium with the beaming Koussevitzky. Next day, Bernstein asked his sister how the concert had gone. She said it was good, but "you snorted and heaved again and you promised you wouldn't." Bernstein clapped his hand to his forehead. "Oh Lord, did I? How am I going to break myself?"

Boston critics continued to see clear resemblances between the conducting styles of the pupil and *their* maestro: "Imagine . . . Koussevitzky at the beginning of his career, perhaps, and you will be able to catch the essential quality of it. The same intensity, the same orchestral technique, the same ability to make an orchestra sound . . . even some of the same gestures . . ." Reception to the symphony was more guarded: "It will not disparage Mr. Bernstein's creative gifts to say that the *Jeremiah* . . . is remarkable more for what it promises in the future than for the achievement it represents." But all were agreed that the evening had seen the debut of a remarkable figure. "It was Leonard Bernstein day at the symphony yesterday, no doubt about it." Warren Storey Smith, writing in the Boston *Post,* was willing to "quote Schumann's famous salutation to Chopin: 'Hats off, gentlemen, a genius!' " One of the dissenting voices came from Virgil Thomson, after the New York premiere. He thought that while its creator was a brilliant master of orchestration, *Jeremiah* was not composed with skill or originality. It lacked "contrapuntal coherence, melodic distinction, contrapuntal progress, harmonic logic and concentration of thought." On the other hand, Thomson thought Bernstein had genius as an executant and interpreter and was confidently predicting great things.

Within weeks Bernstein would be making yet another debut in New York, this time as composer for the ballet. He had been working for about a year with Jerome Robbins, a young dancer who had grown up in Weehawken, New Jersey, and joined Ballet Theatre in 1940. Robbins was ambitious to make his name as a choreographer and had a scenario for a ballet about three sailors on shore leave in New York, at a time when soldiers and sailors in uniform were ubiquitous in big cities. The scenario began: "Three sailors explode on stage. They are out on shore leave, looking for excitement, women, drink, any kind of fun they can stir up. Right now they are fresh, full of animal exuberance . . . They dance down the street with typical sailor movements, the brassy walk, the inoffensive vulgarity, the feeling of being all steamed up and ready to go . . ." They meet a girl, start fighting over her and lose her while they are arguing. Time passes, they meet another girl and chase after her. That was all there was to the plot, but Robbins had clear ideas about the characterizations and style and spent months looking for a composer. He showed the idea to a composer in Philadelphia named Vincent Persichetti, who did not think it was right for him but gave him Bernstein's address. Robbins went looking for him on Fifty-second Street and found "an empty lot"— the building had been demolished. However, his collaborator Oliver

Smith knew Bernstein through Paul Bowles, for whom he had designed sets. The three men met and began work. Robbins was out of town much of the time touring. Bernstein would write something, record it on the piano, usually with Aaron Copland, and send it to Robbins.

Halina Rodzinski recalled taking the same train to Hartford with Bernstein during an orchestra tour. "While I read or counted the telephone poles leaping past, I noticed Lenny take a pad of staved paper from his briefcase, then draw notes. I pretended not to watch, but was amazed at the speed with which he covered sheet after sheet, rarely pausing or making an erasure." Bernstein said, "You have no idea how exciting it is to hear in one's head the music that comes out in these black dots." It was the music for *Fancy Free.* That year, ideas were coming to him from every direction. He was having lunch one day at the Russian Tea Room, talking about nothing in particular, when "the opening tune of *Fancy Free . . .* came to me—just like that." He jotted it on a napkin, took it back to his studio and wrote the whole first movement.

Although Koussevitzky would reproach Bernstein for abandoning high art for what seemed to him like commercialism, the fact is that American composers were writing for the theater almost as a matter of course. Blitzstein said, "There's no future for the American composer in writing music for Carnegie Hall. His hope lies in writing music that is intimate, entertaining, accessible—that reaches an audience directly, like a ballet or a theatrical score." The concept that music ought to be for Everyman (Copland, after all, wrote his *Fanfare for the Common Man* in 1943) would have had enormous appeal for Bernstein even if he had not been caught up in leftist causes at Harvard. Apart from ideological considerations, it was, as the United States recovered from the worst depression in its history, the only practical thing to do. In Britain in the 1930s, famous British artists like Graham Sutherland and Henry Moore were designing advertisements and posters for Shell and London Transport and were grateful for the work; their advanced concepts influenced a whole generation of commercial artists. Salvador Dalí, living in Paris, was designing dresses and hats for Schiaparelli—but then, the European tradition was far different, and Ravel, Milhaud, Poulenc, Honegger and Auric had all written for the theater. Copland was writing for theater and film in the twenties and thirties; Virgil Thomson had written for ballet and numerous films; Paul Bowles composed for the Federal Theatre and Group Theatre; and Roy Harris, who had written several symphonies, had written another for Tommy Dorsey's swing band. Even if Bernstein had had no natural aptitude, he would have looked in that direction because, in contrast to works for the concert hall (which took an enormous amount of time and effort and paid very little), a ballet score was almost easy and paid a great deal better. Besides, as he also said, "Compare for a moment the excitement that is generated by the approach of a new Rodgers and Hammerstein show, the table talk, excitement at breakfast—'Oh boy, a new Rodgers and Hammerstein show!'—compared with the announcement that next week a new string quartet by me or somebody else is going to be given its premiere. 'Oh boy, a new quartet by—!' Can you picture it?"

The ballet opened on April 18, 1944, in the old Metropolitan Opera House between Thirty-ninth and Fortieth streets on Broadway, around the corner from Times Square. When conductor Bernstein raised his baton and jukebox music responded, the audience gasped; from then on they were enthralled. Robbins had devised a solo for the first sailor, Harold Lang, that involved flying splits and dancing on everything, including a bar: the kind of virtuoso athletics that Gene Kelly would perfect in *Singin' in the Rain*. Then John Kriza followed with dances that depended on sly characterization and individuality of style, and Robbins came third, "looking more like Massine than ever," one critic noted. Oliver Smith had designed the perfect set, a bar and a lamp-post silhouetted against a New York skyline by night. Henry Simon wrote, "Mr. Robbins has invested this little incident with such ingratiating toughness, such a distinctly American accent and such infectious high spirits that the audience is constantly either snickering, applauding or laughing outright." As for Mr. Bernstein, "conducting in the pit was itself a fancy bit of choreography."

The Bernstein music demonstrated equal form, skill and imagination. It was full of complex rhythms and romping, jazzy themes, "expertly scored and always skillfully attuned to the doings on stage," another critic wrote. One critic thought that the work owed too much to Copland and that the composer "unwisely added to the excitement by constantly accelerating the tempo," producing a blatant effect. Almost everyone else was wildly enthusiastic. The dancers took over twenty curtain calls, and Robbins found himself besieged with offers. Extra performances were scheduled at once, and Bernstein realized he had discovered yet another avenue for his talents. He later noted that he made enough money from the run of six weeks to keep him for the year.

When he was not conducting *Fancy Free,* Bernstein spent months traveling, which was probably just as well. Rodzinski, who had an enviable reputation as a conductor, was known to be unpredictable and difficult—he always conducted with a gun in his back pocket. The insecurity, if not paranoia, this would seem to symbolize was, Bernstein claimed, projected on him that year. It was, after all, Rodzinski's debut season at the Philharmonic, but his lowly assistant conductor was getting all the press attention and gallivanting off to conduct and write new music. Meanwhile, he was neglecting his work at the Philharmonic, Rodzinski declared. Bernstein subsequently denied it, but it was probably true. Matters came to a head one day when Bernstein discovered that he was not feeling well during an orchestra rehearsal and went to lie down. Later that day he felt better, so he went out to have a haircut and then took his new dog for a walk. Rodzinski caught him at the barber shop and someone else saw him walking the dog. Rodzinski was outraged. Bernstein was advised to apologize but when he attempted to do so, the maestro took him by the throat. It might be wise, Judson thought, for Bernstein to disappear for a while.

Having been given license to do exactly what he planned, i.e., build a national reputation as a conductor, Bernstein took to the road with enthusiasm. Early in May he hurried to Boston to conduct the Boston Pops in Beethoven, Chopin and Tchaikovsky as well as perform the Ravel Piano Concerto in G. He asked Kiki's father, Louis Speyer, to conduct the orchestra while he played. He was interviewed in Koussevitzky's room ("You know, just being in this room is an inspiration") and talked about the success of his new ballet. "I conduct every night— I just dashed for a train after the performance last night and barely made the sleeper . . . I'm pretty tired—but . . . of course, I'm excited . . ."

Bernstein was, a Chicago critic commented when he made his debut at the Ravinia Park Pavilion with the Chicago Symphony Orchestra that summer, "one of those young and fortunate beings into whose lap the deities, who determine the destinies of artists, have poured all possible tokens of success." Faced with a thoroughly expert orchestra, Bernstein tackled his program of Beethoven's *Egmont* Overture and Violin Concerto (played by Joseph Szigeti) and Sibelius's First Symphony with sensitivity, sound preparation and an impetuosity that was just kept under control. Claudia Cassidy of the Chicago *Daily Tribune* wrote, "The eye and the ear inevitably gravitated to the slight young figure on the podium, a dark young man with a sensitive, sensuous face . . . hands that gyrate so convulsively they scarcely could hold a baton if they tried, and eyes that somehow manage to be agonized, supplicant and truculent without losing their place in the score." Her first impression, that he was "dynamic, emotional, yet under complete control," was confirmed when he returned a couple of days later to perform his favorite piece, the Ravel concerto. He had "eloquence and fire and a basic honesty" that kept him in focus, and his appeal for the audience seemed to be irresistible. Over four thousand people came to hear him, the largest crowd of the season.

The crowd was even larger, over ten thousand, when Bernstein made his debut at Lewisohn Stadium in the summer of 1944, that same outdoor arena in which he had sat, five summers earlier, in the cheapest seats. His choice of the Ravel concerto was judged unfortunate, because it was too delicate a work to be relayed by the stadium's primitive amplification system and often drowned out altogether by the planes overhead. The most successful piece on the program was Tchaikovsky's *Romeo and Juliet*, which was "well suited to his flair for the dramatic" and which he conducted with intensity and vigor. Then it was on to Les Concerts Symphoniques in Montreal, where he conducted Sibelius, Tchaikovsky and Gershwin out of doors and went sightseeing with Shirley the rest of the time. Photographs show her, wide-eyed, seated on the grass close to her brother or stepping down from a horse and carriage. Bernstein's next stop was the Hollywood Bowl, where he appeared with Oscar Levant, the concert pianist and great friend of George Gershwin, who played *Rhapsody in Blue.* Meanwhile he somehow found time to be on a composers' committee that included Copland, Piston, Schuman, Hanson, Harris and Barber, planning a testimonial dinner in honor of Koussevitzky, who was celebrating his twentieth year as conductor of the Boston Symphony. He helped sponsor a new youth orchestra, along with Bruno Walter and Yehudi Menuhin. He appeared with Paul Robeson at the Metropolitan Opera House in a benefit concert for the Joint Anti-Fascist Refugee Committee, an organization that had helped many to escape from Franco's Spain, including Marshal Tito. Bernstein played works of Brahms, Liszt and Ravel, and a new work of his own, *Seven Anniversaries,* pianistic character sketches of people who were close to him: Koussevitzky, Shirley, Copland, Bowles, Schuman, Nathalie Koussevitzky, who had just died, and Alfred Eisner, a former roommate at Harvard, who had died of cancer. It would establish a pattern of graceful musical tributes to friends and family. Bernstein's Carnegie Hall performance of *Jeremiah* with the New York Philharmonic in the spring of 1944 was a benefit for Red Mogen Dovid, Palestine's first-aid agency.

Bernstein's philanthropic activities increased after the United States Junior Chamber of Commerce named him one of the ten outstanding young men of 1944 along with Nelson A. Rockefeller, then assistant secretary of state. He began to say in interviews that musicians ought to be more involved in politics. He had made campaign speeches for Franklin Delano Roosevelt in the autumn of 1944 and within a year was on ten political committees at least. He was one of some two hundred "leaders" who signed a statement in support of Truman's proposed national health program. He became New York chairman (Jascha Heifetz was national chairman) of a committee to send used musical instruments for the Jewish colonies in Palestine; and served on another, to improve the wages of the girls who worked in New York's department stores. He conducted a performance of new Russian music at Carnegie Hall to benefit the "war orphans of Stalingrad" and accepted the position of chairman of the first annual George Gershwin Memorial Contest. (The prize was $1,000 and a premiere at the Metropolitan Opera House with Bernstein conducting.) In the late autumn of 1945, he took a leading role in organizing the first conference on American and Soviet cultural exchange, along with Koussevitzky, Copland and Blitzstein. He signed a contract as conductor for Victor Red Seal recordings, the "Victor Recording Family," as the press release coyly expressed it. He became a panelist on a new radio quiz show, "So You Think You Know Music?" on WOR-Mutual, along with Vaughn Monroe and Vernon Duke.

Then there was *On the Town,* the musical that Bernstein somehow managed to write in 1944 and that opened in December of that year. It was his first formal collaboration with his good friends Comden and Green, who had gone far since the days when they were performing as the Revuers. Nightclub work was, Betty Comden wrote, the ultimate apprenticeship; it made writing for the theater look easy. "The aim of the performer is to make the nightclub patron put down his drink, stop ogling his companion, turn around to see where the noise is coming from, and change his attitude from one of mild surprise and resentment . . . to one of hilarious and devoted attention." They wrote their own material because they could not afford to hire anyone else, but soon discovered a natural gift for satire. They were now so well known they were being booked into the city's most sophisticated night spots and had appeared on coast-to-coast radio and even television. The original five had shrunk to two—Judy Holliday and two other cast members had gone off to Hollywood. So did Comden and Green: they made cameo appearances in a film called *Greenwich Village.* There they ran into their old friend Lenny, appearing at the Hollywood Bowl, and now a conducting and composing sensation, as they knew he would be. Soon they were discussing the idea of writing a musical comedy. Once they joined forces with Robbins and Smith the conversation focused on three sailors on twenty-four-hour shore leave in New York. They take a subway ride, one of them falls for Miss Turnstiles, the subway's girl of the month, and all three go on a search for her. "With the other two sailors picking off girls en route, *On the Town* sings and dances, joshes and handsprings its way from Central Park to the Museum of Natural History, from Carnegie Hall to Times Square, from a flock of night spots to Coney Island."

On the Town may seem naive and too picture-postcard-pretty for contemporary tastes but, as Comden and Green wrote, it mirrored the uncertainty of the war years and the "poignancy of young people trying to cram a lifetime of experiences into a day." They continued: "The 'Future,' of course (which was to begin as soon as everyone came home and we could all pick up where we had left off), meant some kind of marvelous expansion of life as it was before the '30's, before the Depression, combining the latest technological advances with the old pioneer spirit, and the sweetest, most sentimental moral traditions of the 19th century—home, family, success—all the desired rewards of individual get-up-and-go, with a dash of the more recently enlightened humanitarian principles of the New Deal." The mood of the times had been reflected by *Oklahoma!*, the famous 1943 Rodgers and Hammerstein production, which revealed the longing for that "open-vista-ed America of old." Last but not least, *On the Town* was, like *Fancy Free*, a celebration of all that was wonderful about the city of New York, where "there were nine daily newspapers, you could buy a hot dog for a nickel, adventure in the streets may have been raffish but not necessarily fatal . . . And you could buy an orchestra seat for a show . . . say, *On the Town*, for $4.85," Comden and Green wrote.

Work began in the summer of 1944, and Smith and Paul Feigay, the producers, began looking for a director. They took their opening scenes to the Theater Guild, but "Lawrence Langner fell asleep during the audition. Elia Kazan turned it down . . ." They asked themselves whom they would like to have if money were no object and unanimously agreed upon George Abbott. To their delight he accepted immediately. Bernstein then resumed what would become a typical pattern of sneaking moments to compose whenever he could. Adolph Green had to have his tonsils removed, and Bernstein was having an operation for a deviated septum in the hope of clearing up his constant colds. Why not time

Bernstein composing, circa 1947

The subway scene from *On the Town*, 1944: As sailors, from left, are Cris
Alexander, Adolph Green and John Battles. Bernstein's sister
Shirley can be seen in a minor role at far right.

their visits to coincide and stay in adjoining rooms? They cheerfully entered Doctor's Hospital, and while Green scribbled in one room Bernstein belted out new songs in his horrible baritone and beat the rhythms on the wall. What with Betty Comden rushing back and forth, games of gin rummy and music far into the night, one nurse was driven to remark of Bernstein that "he may be God's gift to music, but I'd hate to tell you where he gives me a pain."

The producers had raised a small amount of "front" money, some $25,000, and now needed the balance. Once Abbott joined their venture the remaining $100,000 came within a day. Then they had the good luck to sell the idea for a movie to MGM. (It was made a few years later with Gene Kelly and Frank Sinatra and contained so much rewritten music that Bernstein asked to have his name removed.) Writing for musical comedy was harder than writing for a symphony, Bernstein

Sono Osato, right, as Ivy, and Susan Steell as Madame Dilly in
On the Town

said. "If you are writing for a symphony you are your own boss. If you are writing a musical comedy, you are subject to dozens of strictures . . . You finish a piece and the choreographer calls up and says, 'I will have to have six more measures of this. I can't get the ballerina off the stage.' You do a song in a certain key for a certain member of the cast. When the show opens you find that, with the audience reaction to spur her on, the singer can hit two notes higher than she can in rehearsal. The song actually sounds better in a higher key so you do it over."

The play opened at the Colonial Theatre in Boston—sister Shirley, using the last name "Burton," had a part in the chorus. Bernstein called the Boston run "the worst ten days of my life . . . when we spent our time 'fixing' the show, living mostly on coffee." But then it went to New York and was hailed as "the freshest and most engaging musical show to come this way since the golden day of *Oklahoma.*" *On the Town* ran for 463 performances and confirmed Bernstein's growing reputation. It was also immensely profitable, earning him $100,000: all that for five weeks' work.

In later years Bernstein would expound an elaborate theory to describe the way he believed he wrote music. In those early years he made no attempt to analyze or even identify the kind of moment at which an idea came to him, when he was lying down, or at the piano, or walking along the street, or on a train, or having lunch in the Russian Tea Room. It was all part of the great and marvelous good luck of being a musician. He said, "I wish I could convey to you the excitement and insane joy of it, which nothing else touches—not making love, not that wonderful glass of orange juice in the morning; nothing! Nothing touches the extraordinary, jubilant sensation . . . It's madness and it's marvellous."

Soon after the success of *On the Town,* interviewers began to call him a "genius" and a "swoon boy." Hundreds of teenagers flocked around the stage door waiting for him to appear and, when he conducted in the stadium at the City College of New York, he had to have his car brought inside the gate to avoid being mobbed. He had his own fan club in Brooklyn. This new matinée idol, the "Sinatra of the Symphony," was being besieged by offers of marriage as well as by a French lady who had written him a nine-page letter, in French, asking to take care of him. She would not take no for an answer and had been hounding him for months. He shrugged off the idea that he was a genius with the modest comment that he had some talent and people should let it go at that.

He objected to being mistaken for Frank Sinatra because he had had all the buttons torn off his coat by autograph hunters.

He had already perfected the art of the interview and, at the same time, was refining his performance technique. After the phenomenal success of his New York Philharmonic debut he seemed to have concluded that one must put on a show at all costs, playing to the gallery if necessary, but always giving the audience what it wanted. Eugene Istomin had known him at Curtis and made his own debut with the New York Philharmonic just a week after Bernstein's, in November 1943. Istomin said, "I had won the third Leventritt competition, and performing with the Philharmonic over nationwide radio was my reward. I was just seventeen and having stomach cramps with fright before the performance. Bernstein had led the rehearsals, and I knew he loved my playing—after first hearing me at Curtis, he said, 'You're an oasis in the desert!' Anyway, I had chosen my own piano and practiced on it, but when I got on stage the stagehands had moved in the wrong piano and it threw me. Bernstein came backstage afterwards and reproached me. 'Why didn't you play the way you could play?' he said." If the soloist did not make an immediate impression, Bernstein was not pleased. Istomin added that, "Years later when we were appearing together, he felt I did not play my best until the final movement, and that for him didn't count. He said the critics weren't there and therefore it hadn't happened."

None of this cynical awareness of the uses of journalism escaped his mentors, who made their displeasure known. That Bernstein should allow *Harper's Bazaar*—a fashion magazine!—to take photographs and his name to appear in the gossip columns of Walter Winchell and Dorothy Kilgallen . . . well, it was clear he lacked the sense of decorum the role of conductor required. For his part Bernstein poked sly fun at the notion that a conductor was descended from Mount Olympus, an idea that went out with the Gay Nineties. His determination to democratize the symphony began then. He disliked the whole idea of being on a pedestal, preferring to persuade and cajole. He questioned the uniform—a cutaway—and the custom of waving a baton and the convention that dictated a conductor memorize every score, an evident reference to Mitropoulos. Life was too short. "There's no logical, and certainly no musical, reason for creating a mental hazard by leaving it [the score] in the dressing room."

After traveling something like fifty thousand miles and giving eighty-nine concerts, he was becoming versed in the art of guest conducting. He knew he would have to run a certain gauntlet every time he arrived. He described a few of an orchestra's tricks: playing a wrong note to see whether he would notice, talking loudly while another section was rehearsing, "forgetting" to make an entrance. He also knew that he was younger than most of the men he was conducting and that this was perhaps the biggest hurdle of all. But the experience could also be immensely rewarding. He had just finished a three-day recording session of his *Jeremiah* for Victor Red Seal with the St. Louis Symphony Orchestra. "When it was completed the members of the orchestra rose and beat on their instruments in a thrilling ovation. I just stood on the podium and cried."

"Music I Heard with You"

See by the roadside a tavern's
Wide open door,
Friendly sign!

— GOETHE, "AN SCHWAGER KRONOS"

Bernstein left the cramped studio apartment in Carnegie Hall and moved several times in the next few years before settling at the Osborne, an apartment building on the northwest corner of Fifty-seventh Street and Seventh Avenue diagonally across from Carnegie Hall. For a while he had an apartment in Greenwich Village and also a seventeenth-floor penthouse on Broadway in the garment district, above an office building, where he became known as "the songwriter and piano player who lives upstairs." He smiled at the office girls and bookkeepers as he rode up and down on the elevators and was judged good-looking in spite of his large nose. The penthouse contained a spacious living room with a large record library and a handsome grand piano with a photograph of Koussevitzky prominently displayed.

His ménage now included Helen Coates, his former music teacher. Shirley Bernstein had given up trying to be her brother's amanuensis, and in July 1944 he appealed to Miss Coates. His former music teacher promptly resigned from her position at Dana Hall School in Wellesley, Massachusetts, went looking for an apartment, had rented one within two days and was ready for work.

Finding herself in the position of employee to a former student did not trouble her in the least. Since it was obvious that Lenny needed a competent stenographer, she showed her dedication by taking a typing course. "I did those first letters . . . over and over to make them perfect." She arrived around noon each day, sent photos to fans, opened the mail, catalogued scores, made and broke appointments, kept scrapbooks, sent clothes to the dry cleaner's, cooked dinner if necessary and was ready with a glass of wine to help her employer sleep. She also traveled with him. Now that her protégé had made such a brilliant start, she was prepared to do whatever it took to further his career and defend him against the world. "It would be aggravating to have someone poking along or taking too much time for coffee breaks or suddenly leaving. If there is anything of importance to do, I return to my desk after dinner. You don't keep hours when you love what you are doing." In setting herself up as the person who dealt with trivia, Coates quickly assumed a powerful position since Bernstein hated having to handle money, and she was good at that. He also hated having to say no, and she was good at that too. Stephen Sondheim once invented a game for Bernstein that involved a recording of Helen Coates's shrill voice saying "No" at intervals. In years to come, no one spoke to Leonard Bernstein without going through Helen Coates.

The city of New York had assumed ownership through foreclosure of a famous old building on Fifty-fifth Street, the Mecca Temple. It was notoriously ramshackle, but it contained ideal spaces for rehearsals, offices, practice rooms and storage, and it did have a two-thousand-seat auditorium. Thanks to the efforts of Mayor Fiorello La Guardia, the temple was refurbished and opened as a center for music, drama, ballet and opera. The city would provide a subsidy—it was about ten thousand dollars, or just enough to pay real-estate taxes—and the center would operate as a nonprofit institution with the goals of bringing the arts to a wide audience at low prices and of emphasizing the work of contemporary artists. Leopold

Stokowski was appointed in 1944 to form an orchestra, which he did with his usual panache and to general acclaim. However, he also became musical director of the Hollywood Bowl and was soon absorbed by the larger possibilities this position offered. He resigned at the end of the 1944–45 season. The New York City Symphony, largely a pickup group, was below size and poorly paid, and the position of conductor was unpaid. But it was an orchestra and Bernstein's, if he wanted it. He took it.

In September 1945, Bernstein announced that he would be conducting a series of twelve Monday and Tuesday concerts, opening with Copland's *An Outdoor Overture,* Shostakovich's First Symphony and Brahms's Second Symphony. He would not program his own works because he had only written *Jeremiah* and *Fancy Free* and "I've gotten to the point where I feel I am boring everyone stiff with them." He was auditioning musicians in his penthouse apartment during an elevator strike, but the musicians came anyway, lugging their heavy instruments up seventeen flights and back down again. The jobs were being hotly competed for even though they only paid five hundred dollars for the season. André Speyer recalled being at lunch one day in New York when Bernstein walked in. There were other musicians within earshot, so Bernstein leaned over and whispered, "There's an opening for second horn at City Center. Do you want it?" Speyer certainly did. The oboist Ralph Gomberg, who was at Curtis with Bernstein and would go on to play with the Boston Symphony Orchestra, recalled that he was doing work around Hollywood in those days. It was not very satisfying for a classically trained musician, and he was thinking of going into real estate with a friend. He heard a rumor and decided to call Bernstein long distance. "I understand you need an oboist," he said. "I'm available." Bernstein replied, "You're hired." The season was short, but musicians played for opera and ballet at City Center as well and could eke out a living. From the start the well-being of his musicians was uppermost in Bernstein's mind. He thought it was disgraceful that the orchestra was paid so little and had such a short season. He wanted a twenty-four-week season, a recording contract and a radio sponsor, in the cause of getting better working conditions. He called the orchestra his "kids" even though, as Irving Kolodin pointed out in an article, the average age of the musicians was thirty and Bernstein was then twenty-seven. At breaks, Bernstein began a custom that would carry through for the rest of his conducting career. Anyone in the orchestra could come and consult him about anything, including his personal problems. He began to proselytize for better wages. "We get no concessions. We are the youngest, poorest orchestra in the world and the biggest stink I can make is not a big enough stink for me."

Barely a month later Bernstein gave his first performance, and Olin Downes of the *New York Times* was most admiring. The orchestra was materially better than it had been the season before, he wrote—a compliment indeed—and Bernstein conducted a concert of "exceptional brilliancy." Two weeks later, he returned with a program of Haydn and Hindemith and Tchaikovsky's rarely heard Concert Fantasy for Piano and Orchestra, with Leo Smit as pianist. Downes praised an "innate resourcefulness and vitalizing temperament" and thought the orchestra had improved immensely in just two weeks, in rhythm, precision of attack, balance and intonation. *Vogue* included a reference to the "emergence" of Bernstein and his New York City Symphony in its "People Are Talking About" section. The egalitarian nature of the venture appealed to Bernstein (most ticket prices were less than two dollars), as well as the chance to mount new or seldom-heard works, from Milhaud's Concerto for Two Pianos to works of Shostakovich, Copland and Harris, Benjamin Britten's Violin Concerto and Stravinsky's opera-oratorio, *Oedipus Rex*. His programming was audacious, his musicians talented and his work full of fire and conviction, but the budget remained an intractable obstacle—money was so short, Bernstein had to act as his own manager. While making a speech appealing for private funds, he asserted heatedly that his orchestra received no municipal subsidy of any kind and then had to make a lame retraction the next day. The year he arrived, the City Center had a deficit of $34,000 and all its arts organizations were struggling. It was, as the tabloids liked to quip, "Do Re Mi—But No Dough."

As reviews continued to appear, most critics agreed that Bernstein had an exceptional flair for interpreting modern music but that his work with the classics was uneven. *Music News* wrote: "While he does the classics exactly and clearly, there isn't a bit of sparkle in his interpretations. Bernstein also tends to drag the Andantes and Adagios beyond the bearable, thus substituting slowness for real feeling." Just as many reviewers grumbled that his tempi were too fast, but most complaints centered around the physical aspects of his conducting. Virgil Thomson wrote that Bernstein "shagged, shimmied, and believe it or not, *bumped*." In those days, Thomson was Bernstein's severest critic. After reviewing a performance of the City Symphony Thomson wrote that, for the past two years, Bernstein had turned away from objective music-making and embraced a career of "sheer vainglory." He added, "With every season his personal performance becomes more ostentatious, and his musical one less convincing. There was a time when he used to forget occasionally and let the music speak. Nowadays he keeps it always, like the touring Italian bandmasters of forty years ago, a vehicle for the waving about of hair, for the twisting of shoulder and torso, for the miming by facial expressions of uncontrolled emotional states." Privately he said he thought Bernstein would probably "come out all right eventually," but, "he does require lots of slapping down."

People like Oscar Levant began to quip that Bernstein was a hopeless egotist: "I think a lot of Bernstein—but not as much as he does." The best joke on the subject came about one summer after World War II when Bernstein was teaching student conductors at Tanglewood. A group of choral students and G. Wallace Woodworth were sitting on the lawn watching him rehearse. Woodworth had just observed that Bernstein would be a brilliant conductor if he would just stop waving his arms around. They were still laughing about that when Bernstein himself appeared to chat. Speaking of the young man he had just been coaching, Bernstein said, "You know, this guy is a great conductor, if I can just keep him from bouncing all over the stage!"

Since the New York City Center season was so brief, Bernstein, in theory, had plenty of free time to compose and announced he was working on a new ballet with Jerome Robbins and a piano concerto and also starting work on a musical version of Maxwell Anderson's play *Winterset*. He was, as usual, traveling constantly as a guest conductor. When, some time in 1945, his photograph appeared in a full-page advertisement by the Detroit Symphony Orchestra announcing its guest artists, and he was called one of "America's Great Conductors" along with George Szell, Eugene Goossens and Erich Leinsdorf, he might have been forgiven for believing that an appointment to a major symphony orchestra—one that paid—was imminent. In those days he was constantly being rumored as under consideration for positions that were becoming available, in Washington, Houston, Detroit and elsewhere; but nothing happened.

The most profound disappointment of that period would be the decision by the board of trustees of the Boston Symphony Orchestra not to accept him as a successor to Koussevitzky even though Koussevitzky had campaigned hard on his behalf. The reasons seem clear enough in retrospect. Opinion is divided about whether anti-Semitism played a role, as Bernstein always believed. The fact that he was an American, and young, undoubtedly did. It would have seemed to the trustees of that staid institution that a youth who played boogie-woogie, who danced on tables in restaurants, as Bernstein had been seen to do at Tanglewood, and had a hit musical on Broadway did not project the right image. They wanted a European, someone with an established reputation, and found him in Charles Munch. (Munch was Bernstein's senior by more than twenty-five years.) Bernstein also may have hoped he had a chance to succeed Reiner in Pittsburgh after his former mentor stepped down in 1948, and his hopes would have been further lifted when he was invited, as one of several guest conductors, to be in residence for seven weeks, during which he would take the orchestra on tour. Nothing came of that, either.

Bernstein was repeatedly being passed over in favor of Europeans, who were carrying off the prize American trophies. William Steinberg, a German, eventually took over the Pittsburgh Symphony; Paul Paray, a Frenchman, went to Detroit. When Rodzinski left the New York Philharmonic in 1947, Bernstein might have been considered to replace him, but Bruno Walter was appointed instead. Again in 1949, when Walter left, the men chosen to conduct during an interregnum were Stokowski and Mitropoulos, and at the end of a year the verdict went to the malleable Mitropoulos rather than the defiant Stokowski, who had already crossed swords with Judson more than once. Roger Englander, a television producer who would work closely with Bernstein, recalled being at Tanglewood with him in the postwar years and finding his friend in despair because he was getting so old (he was almost thirty) and "he hadn't accomplished enough."

Bernstein later claimed that Judson offered to get him the New York Philharmonic before he was thirty. Judson said, "You'll go to Los Angeles next year . . . You'll make your repertoire. Then I'll move you to Cleveland for two years. Then you'll be ready for the Philharmonic." This happened shortly after Bernstein's debut in 1943, and, he said many years later, he turned the offer down. He did not want to be tied to one orchestra in one city. He wanted to "see the world" and "be free to compose." Interestingly, Bernstein did not question Judson's ability to dictate the leadership of America's orchestras and move him around like a pawn on a chessboard. Bernstein knew he could do this. The point of the anecdote was to demonstrate his independence, his inner confidence, his bravery even, at rejecting such an offer. The story is unconvincing, however, because there is too much evidence that Bernstein was angling for an important orchestra. (The New York City Symphony, being young and struggling, did not fill that bill.) Bernstein did not describe the terms, but no doubt Judson's offer came with a high price attached and Bernstein could not pay. In the future, he would wait on the sidelines while choice appointments went to candidates he must have felt were less gifted than himself. As has been noted, it did not do to flout Judson.

The most likely opportunity during those postwar years was in Rochester. José Iturbi had resigned as director of the Rochester Philharmonic Orchestra and the trustees were looking for a replacement. Bernstein often went there to conduct and took the orchestra on tour. Bettina Bachmann recalled, "My father and mother, Mr. and Mrs. Alfred Hart, were on the orchestra board, and I was raised in the Eastman Theatre," the hall in which the orchestra performed. "If we went to the orchestra on Thursday nights we didn't have to do our homework." She was very familiar with the orchestra's history and inner politics. "In those days we were all in our twenties. I was married to a businessman and had a baby. We would give parties after the concert. I had a chafing-dish recipe for chicken hash from the Plaza Hotel that I used to make a lot. It consisted of chicken cut into neat cubes with a lovely sauce, and it was Lenny's favorite dish. I well remember the first time he came to our house. He burst through the door, propelled like a rocket. We had a xylophone in the living room and he raced over to it and picked up the hammers and was improvising jazz within minutes.

"After our hot buffet supper we would play 'The Game' (charades). Lenny's team invariably came up with unheard-of words—original, funny and often unmentionable. We were forever running to the dictionary. There was drinking and smoking and peals of laughter." She and Bernstein were the same age and used to "pal around," Bachmann said. "He liked women. He was demonstrative and affectionate—full of hugs and kisses, hence my late husband did not like him *at all*. He thought he had a crush on me. Sometimes I thought so too."

Bernstein was being mentioned as the next conductor of the Rochester Philharmonic. So was Erich Leinsdorf, the Viennese conductor at the Metropolitan and the San Francisco Opera, who had also conducted in Rochester during the interim period. Then the trustees announced their decision: Leinsdorf would take charge in the autumn of 1947.

Bachmann said Bernstein always believed he was rejected because it was rumored he was a homosexual. "Sadly, he was right," she said. "In

Rochester they would worry if he liked boys. It was very square and perhaps the most provincial society in the U.S." No doubt this was true, but it is interesting to note that Leinsdorf's autobiography makes a point of mentioning that Rochester came with "Arthur Judson's blessing."

The incident has two curious sequels. Noel Farrand, composer, pianist and sometime record producer, recalled that as a freshman composer at the Eastman School of Music he had season tickets to the Rochester Philharmonic and heard many great conductors, including Thomas Beecham, Albert Coates, Goossens and Iturbi. On February 27, 1947, he was sitting in the front row when Bernstein gave a concert that included a performance of Tchaikovsky's Fifth Symphony. (Isaac Stern was on the same program and performed Bach's Violin Concerto in E Major.) Farrand said, "He was conducting without a score, which was the fashion in those days, and when he got to the slow section he signaled the resumption of the allegro section four bars too soon. He crouched over and turned scarlet. He was mortified.

"To make a long story short, I went to Hillside, New York, in 1953 to visit Lenny with a student of his, now a conductor and married, and we had a very relaxed afternoon playing Scrabble in the meadow. At dinner, I was relaxed enough to mention having seen him conduct in Rochester six years before and the mistake. He looked at me and his face darkened. 'I have never conducted the Fifth Symphony of Tchaikovsky in America.' His sister Shirley said, 'It sounds like he's right, Lenny,' but he refused to listen. He continued, 'Furthermore, they had to beg me to play it.'"

Noel Farrand's memory is accurate, since a review of the concert he remembered exists, published by the Rochester *Democrat and Chronicle* on February 28, 1947. Obviously the incident was too painful and Bernstein simply blocked it out. The sequel is harder to understand. Bettina Bachmann wrote that Bernstein visited the college of her granddaughter, Jessica Gordon, to give a lecture. "Jessica . . . told her friends with great pride that her grandmother was a friend of Bernstein's," said Bachmann. "She gathered all her courage together, introduced herself and told him who she was, reminding him that he was often at my house. He responded for all the world to hear, 'No, you're wrong. I never was in Rochester.'"

While Bernstein was performing as guest conductor in Rochester, a young student, Byron Bray, came to visit him. Bray, who was in college in North Carolina in 1946, had heard a Bernstein broadcast of a new work by Marc Blitzstein, the *Airborne* Symphony, performed by the

NBC Symphony Orchestra, of which Arturo Toscanini was music director. Bray, who would go on to become an executive with Columbia Artists Management, recalled that the radio reception was not good, so he wrote to Bernstein requesting a copy of the text. Helen Coates responded with two, one of them personally autographed by Bernstein. Some time later Bray learned that Bernstein was to perform the work again in New York, and a teacher at his college offered to pay his fare so that he could be at the concert.

He attended and went backstage afterwards. "I was shabbily dressed, perhaps, but Helen Coates was so nice. She said, 'Oh, you are the boy from North Carolina. Come with me. Mr. Bernstein wants to meet you.' I went into his dressing room. He was very young, so handsome and so very friendly. He kept his focus on me and introduced me to Blitzstein and Robert Shaw (who had conducted the chorus for the symphony). Helen Coates asked me how long I was going to be in town and invited me to a repeat performance the next day, but I already had bought a ticket to another concert. She seemed genuinely friendly and encouraged me to keep in touch." Bray was given autographed photographs of Bernstein, expressed his thanks and left.

"I started off down the street. In seconds, Bernstein, in tails, had caught up with me. 'You've come so far to see me,' he said. 'Byron Bray, my name is Leonard Bernstein but I want you to call me Lenny.' " Bray was invited to dinner with Bernstein and David Oppenheim. They all sat in his car, a station wagon, eating apples, and Bray borrowed Bernstein's handkerchief and thought, "I'll never use this handkerchief again." Some time after that Bray received his invitation to stay with Bernstein in Rochester. "I wasn't in love with him or even much attracted. I felt so lonely in college and such a freak. I was terrified to know what he would think if he knew what I was. So I was floored when he wrote to me, 'You make me wish we could be together.' At one time I had a lot of his letters. He asked me if I had kept them and then he stopped writing. So I sent them all back, but I memorized them first."

They remained good friends all their lives, but their relationship was not typical of that which Bernstein had with many young men at that time. Antonio de Almeida said, "They all went to bed with each other, but it was all very casual. Like a Turkish bath. Anyone who showed up." The transient nature of such relationships was also remarked on by Maurice Peress, who said, "I don't know if Bernstein could love a man that way. They were just *boys*." David Diamond said, "Mitropoulos thought Bernstein was very indiscreet, carrying on with boys the way he did. He used to say to me, 'Isn't Lenny silly with all these boy-girls he finds? We Greeks like real men.'" One of Bernstein's most intractable contradictions was the special contempt he reserved for the kinds of homosexuals he seemed to pursue. In her biography of him Joan Peyser quotes Tennessee Williams recalling a luncheon he attended with Bernstein one day in 1945, given "by a pair of very effete American queens. Bernstein was very hard on them and I was embarrassed by the way he insulted them." After lunch, Bernstein told Williams that "when the revolution came, they would be stood up against a wall and shot." Perhaps the best comment on the subject came from Shirley Rhoads Perle. She said, "We had a long ride back from Tanglewood to his house ten years ago and I said I thought he required men sexually and women emotionally."

While acting as conductor and manager of the New York City Symphony, Bernstein demonstrated his usual enterprise by getting soloists who were friends of his, like Jennie Tourel and Joseph Szigeti, to perform without fee. He also managed to persuade the famous Chilean pianist Claudio Arrau to appear. One of Arrau's guests for his performance of the Brahms Concerto No. 1 on the evening of February 6, 1946, was a young Chilean, Felicia Montealegre y Cohn. Felicia, who always used her mother's maiden name of Montealegre, was the oldest of three daughters of an intercultural marriage. Her mother, Clemencia, was Costa Rican and Catholic. Her father, Roy Cohn, an American, was the son of a Jewish father and an Episcopalian mother. Her great-grandfather the Reverend Dr. E. Cohn had founded Temple Emmanu-El in San Francisco. Felicia Montealegre was born in Costa Rica, but her parents moved to Santiago, Chile, when she was two months old. Her father became head of the American Smelting and Refining Company. She grew up in a multilingual, cosmopolitan household full of servants, was educated in a convent school run by British nuns and had arrived in New York a few months before, in 1945, ostensibly to study the piano, "because that's what my parents had sent me to do.

"After the stately, organized life of Chile, to me a Bohemian existence of no responsibilities was pure heaven. I had never gone about by myself in a city at night. My biggest thrill was putting the nickel in the lighted slot of the subway turnstile. When it fell through, you could see Jefferson's head magnified in a little glass window. Then I was free to go anywhere. At that age, nothing . . . seems impossible . . ."

Performing with Jennie Tourel

Felicia Montealegre had made up her mind to live in the United States since the age of twelve or thirteen. Since her father was American, she was able to decide which citizenship she would choose. At twenty-one, she went straight to the American embassy in Santiago and took an oath of allegiance to the United States. Two years later, she emigrated and never returned to Chile to live.

She was taking lessons under the benevolent eye of Arrau, a family friend. The composer John McLennan, who knew Arrau and his wife, said, "I got the feeling they were rather in the position of being guardians for Felicia. Arrau was a pianist of the old school, extraordinarily dignified and quite unbalanced. I remember that he did a Town Hall performance of a Beethoven piano sonata that was brilliant, but he was so angry with his performance that he disappeared for ten days. He could also be charming, and of course he was a superb musician. His wife, Betty, was one of the most beautiful women I have ever seen." The Arraus lived in a small, rather suburban house in Forest Hills, Queens, with a separate studio for him, and it was to this house that Bernstein went after his City Center performance with Arrau that February evening in 1946. It was, by chance, Felicia Montealegre's birthday.

She said later that, shortly after she arrived in the States, a friend of hers suggested that the man she ought to marry was Leonard Bernstein. Felicia Montealegre dismissed the idea; she was more interested in having a career. But that evening, after seeing him perform, she became convinced that she would marry him. She told Arrau and her other friends, and they laughed. She replied, "You'll see."

All this happened before the party began. They met and she was "bowled over—completely bowled over. It was such a mixture of things. It's very rare that people see and meet someone with whom they feel they are destined to share a life . . . The incredible thing was that he felt the same way about me as soon as we were introduced." That night, he took her home.

The actress Jane White, who met Felicia Montealegre almost upon her arrival, recalled that she lived in a basement apartment close to Washington Square in Greenwich Village with its own entrance and one relatively spacious room, with a Pullman kitchen and possibly a fireplace. They shared the same ambition and met at acting lessons at the New School for Social Research on Twelfth Street, where Herbert Berghof was teaching an introductory course. Jane White said, "About forty people went there once a week from six to ten at night. Most of them were dilettantes, stuttering and shy, all mixed up together, thinking this course will solve the problems of their lives. It turned out that only two of us would become professionals, and we recognized each other immediately."

In those days, Felicia Montealegre's hair was brown with red and gold highlights. She was, by general agreement, beautiful in a delicate, porcelain way, like a piece of cloisonné, with wide-spaced eyes, a tiny nose and a perfect figure; but what was unforgettable about her was her air of repose and the way she could relax into graceful but unselfconscious attitudes, like a great dancer. Jane White said, "She was very direct. She looked you right in the eye and talked to you, not at you. She told you things about herself. She seemed virtually alone in the city, and I used to stay overnight with her sometimes. Was she really chic and well turned out, or was it that I thought her elegant because I was dowdy myself? Whatever she wore looked wonderful. She would choose clothes that were not unfeminine, but unbusy. She didn't go in for froufrou."

Dr. Anna Lou De Havenon, who was married to William Kapell, a brilliant pianist who often performed with Bernstein, met Felicia Montealegre in those years and thought she was "a lovely woman. Physically, she was beautiful and elegant in a chic kind of way, the kind of woman who is out of style today. One felt she was quietly forceful, someone of integrity." That impression was shared by Elizabeth ("Candy") Finkler, who would work closely in television with Bernstein. She said, "Felicia was so private that when she came out with direct things, and she could be marvelously direct, she took one by surprise. She had the world's greatest handshake, bar none. You knew you had had your hand shaken!" Dan Gustin, acting general manager of the Boston Symphony Orchestra, who also became a good friend, said, "Whenever you were in the room with Felicia you automatically sat up straighter, because she had the most wonderful posture. You'd feel her presence. She didn't say much, because Lenny talked enough for three."

The artist Daniel Schwartz, who would give her painting lessons, said, "I was crazy about her. She was an extraordinary person, very tiny, very feminine, with beautiful features. Not a British accent, but a bit Continental, someone who has been to fancy schools: the slightly mannered kind of European woman. An actress, who knew how to project. I was surprised that someone like that could be as open, frank and friendly as she was." Stephen Sondheim had much the same reaction. "She had exquisite taste," he said. "She was a class act."

Earl Hammond, who would go on to have a career in radio and television, also knew her in the 1940s. He said, "I was in a play called *A Lamp at Midnight,* about the life of Galileo. I am on stage rehearsing one night and up walks this great-looking girl in a red cape, with a high collar. She looked like the queen in *Snow White.* Wow! I started to date her. She was rather a good actress. She was serious about her art. She studied and worked; she was self-confident. She was not cold and distant, but warm and a lot of fun—a funny, funny girl. And she was a pretty good cook, not just Chilean food. She could make a steak dinner on her two-burner stove. She smoked a great deal—a pack of Pall Malls a day—but she drank very little. I remember one time I took her a bottle of Scotch and five months later it was still there."

Felicia's mother came to visit her, "a very charming, very wealthy, upper-class, convent-educated woman," Hammond recalled. "I speak Spanish well, but my vocabulary is limited. I would speak it with Mrs. Cohn and she liked that. While she was staying with Felicia I brought two red roses with a card that said, 'Dos rosas por dos rosas.' Mrs. Cohn just went to pieces."

They had an affair, but Montealegre was still dating other men, including a television producer. One evening Hammond became incensed about the whole situation and stormed off to his apartment a few blocks away. "At about one in the morning, there was a knock on my door. 'What is the matter, you foolish boy? Don't you know I love you?' It was Montealegre.

"I don't remember how it ended, but there was no trauma or shock. The people she went with were those who could help her in her career, and the only thing I could do for her in those days was hold her back."

The attraction between Felicia Montealegre and Leonard Bernstein may have been instantaneous, but the courtship was not to be smooth. Almost as soon as they met, Bernstein had to leave to conduct in Rochester. She had no telephone. "He'd send me a telegram saying, 'Phone me.' Then I'd rush out, call him up and get Helen Coates, his secretary, who'd say he couldn't be disturbed. She'd never believe me when I said he'd told me to call. And I was very proud. So it was nip-and-tuck for a while."

They dated at intervals through 1946. Jane White said, "I remember one time when we got into her convertible couch-bed in our p.j.'s and she complained about the situation. She was not secure in the relationship. She'd be turned on by him—and then there would be this hiatus. She'd think it was over because she hadn't heard from him and then he would be back in her life.

"I don't remember any reference in those talks to the subject of homosexuality. I was ridiculously innocent, and it was all very sotto voce. Either Felicia did not know that Lenny had those leanings or she might not have wanted to talk about it. There is no question she was very much in love, and very distressed about these ups and downs." Bethel Leslie, another actress who knew Felicia Montealegre in those days, said, "She was enormously respectful of and very impressed by Lenny and not at all intimidated, and awfully good for him. There was a large part of him that was very much the small boy in those days, and she was the grown-up, responsible one. As for their being madly in love, I would have thought they were each in love with *what* the other person was, but not *who*. It's a common problem."

In the meantime Bernstein kept up his usual pace. He made his debut in Europe early in May conducting the Czech Philharmonic in Prague, then returned to New York two weeks later to conduct Blitzstein's *Airborne* Symphony with the NBC Symphony. In July he went to London to conduct the premiere of *Fancy Free* at Covent Garden. It was a great success, he wrote Koussevitzky from the Hyde Park Hotel in Knightsbridge. He also gave a concert with the London Philharmonic at the Royal Albert Hall, where the critics had not been kind, their British sensibilities offended by what seemed to be an outrageously affected conducting style. Bernstein did not mention the poor reviews to Koussevitzky but complained about the program, which he had not chosen, and the performance by Eileen Joyce of Grieg's Piano Concerto, which he said was bad.

Because of his European commitments Bernstein missed the first week of the reopened Tanglewood—he was now Koussevitzky's assistant, teaching conducting. The big event that summer was to be the American premiere of *Peter Grimes,* Benjamin Britten's new opera, which had been commissioned by the Koussevitzky Foundation. However, when he arrived at Tanglewood his old mentor was upset. Bernstein was planning to conduct the Boston Symphony Orchestra for three weeks during its 1946–47 season while Koussevitzky enjoyed a winter holiday in Florida. He had asked for, and received, Koussevitzky's permission to appear in Boston with the Rochester Philharmonic that winter. Bernstein then booked a Boston appearance for his City Center orchestra as well. That, it seemed, was too much for Koussevitzky. The reason for Koussevitzky's objection is not clear, unless he felt that by appearing with two rival orchestras in a single season, Bernstein was competing more or less directly with him personally.

That summer and autumn, there is a hint that Koussevitzky had begun to feel, in Virgil Thomson's phrase, that his protégé needed some "slapping down." When Bernstein sent him a list of programs planned for the three-week series of concerts that included his Broadway music, Koussevitzky wrote a stern letter in reply. Did Bernstein actually think that this kind of music was worthy of the Boston Symphony Orchestra?

There were difficulties of another kind. David Diamond, a close friend of those years, was having serious emotional problems. Diamond recalled that he was out of work in the autumn of 1946 and that Allela, the girl he had been living with, had committed suicide. Diamond recalled that he took an overdose of sleeping pills and then, realizing that he did not want to die after all, called Mitropoulos in Minneapolis at six in the morning. Within minutes Mitropoulos had phoned the police, who broke down the door of the unconscious Diamond's loft apartment and got him to the hospital. Diamond said, "The moment it happened Lenny said, 'The time has come. You have got to get yourself to an analyst.' I said, 'Where is the money coming from?' and Lenny called everyone he knew who had money, including Bette Davis, whom he had met in Hollywood, and raised what I needed." Bernstein also approached Koussevitzky for a contribution to the fund and received one hundred dollars.

Spontaneous acts of kindness were typical of Bernstein. Dr. Bertram Slaff recalled that while he was an intern at St. Louis City Hospital in the 1940s, Bernstein came to town to spend two weeks as guest conductor of the St. Louis Symphony. Dr. Slaff had met Bernstein casually, so he invited him to dinner at a restaurant during his stay and was accepted. Since, as an intern, Dr. Slaff received only $32.50 a month, he wrote to his father for $100 to cover the cost of the meal, and it was sent. Dr. Slaff wrote, "Leonard brought William Inge, then drama critic of the St. Louis *Star-Times,* later the well-known playwright, and another individual, and I brought a friend. We had a most enjoyable and festive dinner." He is sure the subject of the starvation wages paid to young interns never arose, but when the check was presented, Bernstein "grabbed it out of my hand." Bernstein said he had suspected a family loan and insisted on paying. He had a hit show, *On the Town,* running on Broadway and did not know what to do with all the money.

That summer Bernstein was doing his best to maintain his special relationship with Koussevitzky while rehearsing *Peter Grimes,* which would become one of Britten's most performed works. John McLennan said, "[Peter] Pears and Britten have written since that it was a shockingly bad performance but it was nothing of the kind. The company was made up of young but brilliant players and singers, and Bernstein got an absolutely sizzling performance, rough but highly charged."

Roger Englander, then an undergraduate at the University of Chicago, who worked on the *Peter Grimes* production, thought Britten's music significant for another reason: he would detect themes from the

At Tanglewood, with sister Shirley,
in the late 1940s

Dining at Tanglewood in the 1940s: Seymour Lipkin stands behind
Bernstein, Copland is seated on his left and Lukas Foss, at right,
drinks from a straw.

opera's Sea Interludes in Bernstein's later *West Side Story*. He said, "I had been an opera stage director and had pretensions of becoming a writer, and Bernstein and I were going to make an opera out of James M. Cain's novel *Serenade*. The main character is a baritone who sings Escamillo, and Bernstein's idea for the opening, that the orchestra would strike up the Toreador song, I thought was brilliant. We discussed it for the whole summer but never got very far." When Englander discovered that Bernstein was coming to Chicago to conduct, he organized a program about the role of the composer in dance. Antony Tudor and Ruth Page took part and Bernstein gave a lecture-demonstration. It was a huge success and a forerunner of the kind of programming on which Englander and Bernstein would collaborate so eminently.

Hardly was Tanglewood launched once more than Bernstein was back in Europe for the Italian premiere of his "Sinfonia *Geremia*," given at the Ninth Festival of International Contemporary Music at the Teatro la Fenice in Venice. He flew back to New York, where a new season was beginning at City Center that would include a performance of Copland's Piano Concerto. He was also putting the finishing touches on a new ballet.

If Bernstein's music for *Fancy Free* and *On the Town* had been designed to illustrate animal high spirits and an irresistible optimism, *Facsimile* can be said to be the forerunner of compositions that would, in years to come, be bedeviled by the contrast between dream and reality, between the outward facade and a spiritual vacuum. The ballet, which dealt with the fleeting relationships between a woman and two men, was about people, Walter Terry wrote, "who attempt to conceal (or compensate for) their inner emptiness with a veneer of trivial but desperate action." As before Bernstein worked with Robbins, Smith and Ballet Theatre (Nora Kaye played the leading role), and the critical notices were respectful. While it was clear that Robbins had enlarged his repertoire by this foray into psychological drama, as a study of aimlessness and frustration it was depressing, and Bernstein's score, insofar as it added to the mood, only depressed people further. A word or two was said about the role the principal dancer was forced to endure. At one point her male partners tossed her "back and forth like a shuttlecock until she fell sobbing to the floor," *Time* magazine wrote.

Facsimile had, in short, made a respectable debut but was not the brilliant success Bernstein had come to expect, and at that point he turned his thoughts to Hollywood. Bernstein had been in and out of Los Angeles for two or three years, looking for the kind of film work that

Copland had exploited so successfully. Thanks to his influential friends, he met the right people almost at once. When he went to the Civic Auditorium in San Francisco to give a series of summer promenade concerts in 1945, he was guest of honor at a dinner party attended by Ethel Barrymore, Somerset Maugham and Joan Fontaine. That same summer, Virgil Thomson told Marian Chase Dunham, Fontaine was doing "a wonderful imitation of him sitting at a piano and monopolizing a party." Various rumors circulated in the gossip columns, that Bernstein was being considered for a role as Rimsky-Korsakov in a film, or George Gershwin in a film, or Tchaikovsky in a film. None of these appears to have had the slightest foundation in fact. But more concrete proposals soon appeared. Irene Diamond, who was working for Warner Bros.— she says her claim to fame is that she discovered the play on which *Casablanca* was based—met Bernstein through Blitzstein in the early 1940s and was very much impressed by him. "He was young, very beautiful and tremendously alive. He had all sorts of interests and total passion and commitment to music." When Diamond learned of a plan to make a movie about Liszt, she suggested Bernstein and he came to Hollywood to make a screen test. "He was starstruck," she said. "I have to say he wasn't bad—he was so articulate, he couldn't be bad at anything." He was not an immediate hit, either, and the plan was dropped.

Still another idea was being launched. Lester Cowan, film producer, had bought the rights to an English short story about a concert pianist with Mary Pickford and planned to film it. Cowan was looking for someone to write the score and approached Bernstein. The year of 1946 had been a banner year for Felicia Montealegre. She had graduated from student to professional actress, making her debut in *If Five Years Pass* by García Lorca at the Provincetown Playhouse. She then appeared on Broadway in an ingénue role in *Swan Song* by Ben Hecht and Charles MacArthur. She was anxious to work in television and films and eager to establish herself on the West Coast. So she went out to Hollywood for a month with Lenny late in 1946.

Cowan's wife, Ann Ronell, who had been a friend of Gershwin's and was herself a composer of note, said, "As I recall he appeared unexpectedly with Felicia. We had a house we called our ranch, four houses built around a swimming pool in the San Fernando Valley, with forty acres and horses. Each of the houses had a different function. One was for us, one for the servants, one was for partying and the fourth was a guest house. They were already there when I got back from the studio. I remember seeing them playing with a puppy and remarking to Lenny

Irene Diamond, on the set during the filming of *The Fugitive Kind* in 1959,
with Norman Mailer and Marlon Brando

At Tanglewood, from left, Claudio Spies, Lukas Foss, Harold Shapero, Esther
Shapero, Verna Fine, Irving Fine and Bernstein, 1940s

The young conductor in the mid-1940s

on how lovely [Felicia] was. Well, he had fallen for her of course. They were crazy about one another."

Helen Coates was afraid that Bernstein would not have time to write a film score since he was already committed to an orchestra tour early in the new year. Ronell said, "Lenny was there to investigate the potential for the idea. He had never done anything like that before, but my husband thought he could do it. We had lots of luncheons and dinners and horseback riding. Felicia was a darling, the perfect guest. They wanted to drive to Mexico, so we gave them a car and an introduction to Ben Hecht, and I think they stopped off to see him. We had a Ping-Pong table in our entertainment house, and we moved in a Baldwin piano just for Lenny that had belonged to José Iturbi."

Bernstein had been saying for some time that he ought to "settle down." He was once interviewed by a reporter for the Vancouver *News Herald* and told her he "figured" he needed a wife, but added, "I meet lots of nice girls, but to find one you could bear to live with, that's a problem—a rather awe-inspiring thought." By the time Bernstein met Felicia Montealegre he was almost thirty and had developed a fairly clear pattern of falling for one girl after another and backing off once the girl's interest had been aroused. Rather than tell the girl the bad news he would try to pass her off on a friend, or let her find out slowly by fading away, as with Beatrice Gordon, or, as in the case of Kiki Speyer, let her discover him in a situation that made his message embarrassingly clear—bruising her feelings the way his heroine had been physically manhandled in *Facsimile*. The girls he felt safest with were those who, like Annette Elkanova and Elaine Newman, were pledged to others, or who, like Mildred Spiegel, were not making any emotional demands. Yet, as Annette Elkanova observed, "Leonard had a very strong sense of Jewish ethics and old-fashioned Jewish ideas about marriage and children." His early religious training, that a boy's first obligation was to father children, had taken firm root in his mind. Apart from that, he genuinely loved children and had a natural rapport with them. He startled an interviewer once by confessing in a charming way that he had gone into a children's clothing store to buy a gift and had been so entranced by the baby clothes that he stayed for an hour.

Ann Ronell believed that Bernstein telephoned Koussevitzky while he and Felicia were in Mexico and Koussevitzky told him to announce his engagement, advising him that the Boston Symphony Orchestra position would be barred to him unless he did marry. This seems to be a misapprehension, since Bernstein's letter to Koussevitzky announcing his engagement makes it clear that the subject was being raised for the first time. Bernstein must have known that marrying would improve his career chances. It would also be fair to say that, for Felicia, marriage to a phenomenally successful musician with Broadway and Hollywood connections would do wonders for her career as an actress. To marry was prudent, but they also loved each other and had taken the measure of each other's strengths and limitations. When their engagement was announced at the Cowan ranch on New Year's Eve, 1946, among the few who disapproved were Claudio Arrau and his wife. John McLennan said, "They were upset because, once when they were together, Lenny told them he didn't know whether he could marry Felicia because she would never know who he was in bed with, man, woman or child." The comment was made in Felicia's presence and she took it with calm.

The Elegant Construction

And a welcome is waiting for you
Where a maiden looks out from the door.

— GOETHE, "AN SCHWAGER KRONOS"

The wedding date was set for June. Bernstein had agreed to take part in the Lester Cowan–Mary Pickford production—according to the press, he would write the score, play the piano, conduct the orchestra and even act in it—but no more was heard about that particular project. Felicia Montealegre stayed on in Hollywood to try her luck while her fiancé went off on another of his ebullient conducting tours. In January 1947 he was in New York, Boston and Chicago. In February he appeared at Carnegie Hall with the Boston Symphony Orchestra, the first time Koussevitzky had allowed his orchestra to perform in New York with anyone but himself; then he went to Boston for three weeks. He conducted the Rochester Philharmonic in Hartford; Poughkeepsie, New York; and Pottsville, Pennsylvania. In March he was conducting the New York City Symphony in a George Gershwin memorial concert at the Brooklyn Academy. That month he announced his second European tour, to Czecho-slovakia, Belgium, Holland, Austria and England, and his first visit to Palestine.

In the spring of 1947, Bernstein and his sister, Shirley, sailed on the SS *America* from Pier 61, on the Hudson River at Twenty-first Street, along with almost a thousand passengers bound for Cobh, Southampton and Cherbourg. The great liner had returned to peacetime service just six months before, and since it was leaving on the same day as the Cunard liner *Queen Elizabeth* and the Panama Railroad liner *Cristobal,* several newspapers sent reporters to the docks to describe the festive pandemo-nium: almost four thousand passengers were embarking. Among those sailing with the Bernsteins were the Countess of Jersey, the former Vir-ginia Cherrill, a minor film star; the pianist Alexander Brailowsky; the European director of Tiffany's; and the chairman of the United States Tar-iff Commission, who gave several interviews. On arrival Bernstein planned to fly directly to Tel Aviv, where he had four concerts; others would follow in Jerusalem, Rehoboth and Haifa. His father, Sam, ardent Zionist, was seizing the opportunity to visit Palestine and planned to join them. Bernstein was also to appear at the second International Music Festival in Prague to conduct the Vienna Philharmonic, the opening of a concert at a world film festival in Brussels and concerts in Scheve-ningen, Holland.

His appearances as guest conductor of the young and leaderless Palestine Symphony Orchestra were perhaps the biggest triumphs of his career to date. He had planned to open his series in Tel Aviv with the local premiere of his *Jeremiah* Symphony, but the score was lost some-where between Rome and Tel Aviv and a replacement did not arrive in time for the first concert. Bernstein conducted Mozart's "Linz" Sym-phony, followed by his old faithful the Ravel Piano Concerto in G, which he conducted from the keyboard. It looked magically adroit, but he was so familiar with the score by now it was said "he could be roused from a sound sleep and led onto the stage in his pajamas and give an acceptable performance."

The enthusiasm of Tel Aviv audiences for Bernstein and his musi-cians, who were all refugees from Europe, was astonishing. Newspapers described his reception as second only to that given to Toscanini. Audi-ences were entranced, Clifton Daniel wrote in the *New York Times,* "by his combined qualities of being young, handsome, talented and Jew-ish." When he went to Jerusalem, sixteen hundred people crowded into the auditorium, standing in the aisles and passageways. He received wave after wave of screaming applause. "I found myself weeping on the forty-third bow," he said.

Israel was then fighting for its independence, and in May 1947 the United Nations in New York was debating the future of the new state. Meanwhile the British were in charge and there was constant terrorism. While Bernstein was there two members of a terrorist army drove a van loaded with explosives into a British police encampment, killing and wounding several men. Then five others, posing as British police officers, kidnapped a British businessman from the hotel in which Bernstein was staying and freed him only after learning that he was Jewish. Bernstein subsequently wrote, "I gave a downbeat at this morning's rehearsal. It coincided with a perfectly timed explosion outside the hall. We picked ourselves up and calmly resumed our labors. We've had four incidents in two days: a kidnaping at this hotel, a train demolished, a police station blown up, a military truck bombed. But the café-sitters don't put down their newspapers, the children continue to jump rope, the Arab goatherd in the square adjusts another milking bag, and I give the next downbeat . . ." Bernstein had made another instant personal triumph; the orchestra appealed to him and he to it. True, it needed the benefit of its own conductor and some concentrated coaching, but he did not see why it should not make a tour of the United States. "It could become the greatest orchestra in the world . . ."

Bernstein followed his triumph with other successful appearances in Europe and demonstrated his continuing ability to rise to a challenge once he reached the Dutch holiday resort of Scheveningen, where he was to conduct the Residentie Orchestra in the Kurhaus, a concert hall. Upon arrival he learned that there was a railway strike in France and that Nathan Milstein, who was to have performed with him, was stranded in Paris. Bernstein stepped in with his Ravel concerto and astonished the critics. This man had to be "one of the most brilliant musical personalities of this age," *De Nederlander* wrote. The fact that he had performed in Milstein's place "indicates an unheard-of musical facility and an unlimited self confidence . . ." Dutch audiences were not normally demonstrative, but this one jumped to its collective feet, yelling and stamping, and the conductor responded with blown kisses. Daniel Schorr, the radio commentator, was then working for the world service of the Netherlands Radio and went to interview Bernstein a few months later when he returned to Scheveningen. "We ended up downstairs where there was a restaurant with a piano, having drinks. Bernstein overwhelmed you with his sense of virtuosity," Schorr said. "All of

these talents seemed out of control. He babbled on and on. He p
the galleries. I was trying to impress him and realized he was trying t
impress me. We were undying friends for a whole week . . ."

In Palestine, there were bombs; in Holland, he lost his soloist and,
he said, the hotel at which he was staying had a cat and he had a bad
attack of asthma until the manager removed it. In Paris it was so hot that
he conducted a rehearsal naked to the waist, but, as the musicians said,
"Tout va à Paris." As an eligible bachelor in Tel Aviv, and finding him-

With his fiancée, Felicia Montealegre y Cohn

self surrounded by lovely young girls with their ambitious mothers, he took a photograph out of his pocket, waved it over his head and announced, "This is the lady I am engaged to!" Since he was not returning to New York until June, he should have been making plans to get married. But, although he told Henri Bernstein, the French playwright, that his fiancée would keep her maiden name because it sounded better for an ingénue than Bernstein, there was no wedding date. Helen Coates gave an interview to the New York *World Telegram* during her employer's absence. She made a passing reference to the legions of bobby soxers who dogged his footsteps. But there was no one important in his life, she said. "With Lenny, his music comes first and it always will. If he ever does marry, his wife will just have to recognize that from the beginning."

"If he ever does marry . . ."

The first concert at Tanglewood that year was on July 24. Ann Ronell said, "We had a house near Tanglewood and I remember Felicia calling me and saying that Lenny was going there and hadn't invited her. In fact she told me he hadn't even been in contact with her, and I think his sister, Shirley, must have told her when he was planning to arrive. I told her to go anyway."

Exactly what took place that summer is not known. Felicia Montealegre was introduced around as his fiancée and, on the surface, everything looked ideal; they were even staying together in a rustic cottage on the Blantyre estate near Lee, something that was considered quite shocking for an unmarried couple. Leonard Burkat said, "We all loved her. She was bright, sweet and attractive." Kiki Speyer also recalled meeting her at about that time after one of Bernstein's concerts. "I went to the greenroom with my parents and husband, and saw behind Leonard a terrifically attractive girl wearing a black beret who glared at me." However, at the end of the season the engagement was over, and all that can be gleaned is the fact that Felicia Montealegre thought her fiancé was not paying enough attention to her. By that she might have meant he was paying too much attention to someone else. Perhaps he even staged another embarrassing confrontation for her benefit.

The year of his engagement was the same year Bernstein learned he had lost both the Boston Symphony Orchestra and the Rochester Philharmonic. That year he would also decide to give up the New York City Symphony. (He resigned in the spring of 1948.) Despite all of his efforts to measure every word, cultivate the right people, appear on the right platforms, perform the right repertoire, project the right image, despite his Broadway triumphs and all the money, reviews and applause, doors were still being slammed in his face. He felt himself in a strait jacket. "I had become a very-well-behaviorized chimpanzee," he said a year later, and that feeling of being programmed by others could have turned into resentment against doing what his parents wanted and his father's Hasidic beliefs required, i.e., have a son of his own. As his sister had observed, to demand that Lenny behave in a certain way was to invite immediate rebellion. But then an inner voice could have told him he should be ashamed of himself. He ought to want a home, family and children. A part of him felt loneliness acutely and longed for the intimacy and connectedness of marriage. If he felt torn, defiant and guilty, and if he were beginning to feel pursued by Felicia, then the easiest solution was to back away. However, that he wanted someone in his life seems clear. Kiki Speyer recalled that Bernstein came to her flat in Boston to ask her to leave her husband and marry him. She replied that she would get a divorce if he would come to Reno with her for six weeks, but, as she suspected, he was not really in earnest.

Other girlfriends reached the same conclusion. Ellen Adler, daughter of the actress Stella Adler, who would later marry Bernstein's friend David Oppenheim, said, "I had a big crush on Lenny. My mother was very active in the creation of the state of Israel and on the American Committee for a Free Palestine. I came home from school one afternoon and found him at a meeting in our apartment. He was the most incredibly seductive man who ever lived. Otherwise he would have been murdered, because he sometimes made unbelievable gaffes. We used to say he had foot-and-mouth disease. Anyway, his charm was so enormous, and he was stupendously handsome—no one could resist him. He created an intimacy with each person, a tremendous intimacy, and he remembered everything about you; it was etched on his mind." He and Adler saw a great deal of each other in New York and later in Paris. She was quite sure she was one in a crowd—"he proposed to absolutely every woman he ever met," she said jokingly. Yet he made sure one would not take him seriously by openly discussing his sexual dilemma. On the one hand he would say he had been told he "probably" was not a homosexual. On the other hand, she recalled going back to her Paris hotel one evening with the son of a famous Frenchman of letters in a taxi. "François got out first and there was something about the way Lenny said goodnight to him . . ." And then she knew.

Bernstein's repugnant feelings about homosexuality had been apparently inherited from his "ghetto past," and the same applied to women and procreation, to judge from a poem he wrote that summer

Performing Gershwin's *Rhapsody in Blue* with the Israel Philharmonic
beside the walls of Beersheba

beside Lake Mah-kee-nak in Stockbridge. It was a meditation on the origins of life in the primordial ooze, "the scaly and scummy, / The poisonous green without breath": all that was pulpy and slimy and slippery and rotting. That revolting stew, however, was "the seed of the marriage / Of liquid and solid events." No one could escape from this shameful business, unless into the sterile and lifeless, "the crisp and the clean / The fine oxidation, the rust, / The spermless, the painless . . ." One hears all-too-faithful echoes of Sam's obsession with filth and his misogynistic conviction that behind a beautiful facade lurked the soul of a whore, someone who contaminated everything she touched.

That, for Bernstein, considerable self-loathing was also involved is hinted at in another poem of the same period in which he writes: "Open, slow, ashamed, consumed with fear, / The elegant construction rots away." It would be a time of depression and introspection in the care of a psychoanalyst; "my lovers come to know the facts / in terms of secret, awkward acts." He was dissatisfied and angry, in a bleak mood. Even conducting had lost its charms. What's the point of it? he asked an interviewer. "You rush from town to town just in time to rehearse and perform, then you rush to the next place. When it sounds good, that's swell. When it sounds lousy, they still cheer and you get rave reviews. It's a stupid business."

He would soon be thirty years old and no longer a wunderkind. After the rebuffs he had experienced it was a relief to be appointed conductor, for the 1948–49 season, of the Israel Philharmonic, renamed in honor of the newly established state of Israel. The reception that accompanied his first visit had not gone unnoticed. Bernstein had only to appear to be given exalted status, and he was delighted to reciprocate, even though it meant putting himself at personal risk. His two-month visit to Israel in the autumn of 1948 coincided with civil war between Jews and Arabs, the latter being greatly aided by the neighboring Arab countries. Bernstein arrived at the airport in Shannon, Ireland, just as a United Nations mediator, Count Bernadotte, who was attempting to bring about a cease-fire, was assassinated by Jewish extremists. Bernstein was forced to spend three days in Paris waiting for the borders to reopen.

Bernstein traveled throughout the country, performing within range of Arab guns. His most celebrated concert took place in the southern city of Beersheba, held in the open air under towering cliffs before an audience of several thousand troops. Bernstein played Beethoven's Piano Concerto No. 2, his stool precariously balanced on a heap of stones. When they shifted, Bernstein would have to go on "playing in a sort of half-crouch while someone got behind me and jacked up the stool again." One month after the Israeli army had opened the narrow, twisting road to Jerusalem, orchestra members filed into armored buses, and, traveling with guards equipped with Sten guns, made their way to Jerusalem. There Bernstein conducted a program of Brahms and played Gershwin's *Rhapsody in Blue* to the cheers of several thousand more soldiers. It was the kind of challenge he loved; he gave forty concerts in sixty days.

Despite his repeated announcements that he intended to concentrate on composing Bernstein continued his conducting marathons. A few days after he returned from Europe he was rehearsing the Boston Symphony in a program of Beethoven, Schumann, Debussy and Stravinsky. Wherever he went he disarmed and amused his musicians. "Be-ba-bomba," he said, waving his arms as he rehearsed the San Francisco Symphony in a performance of Bartók's Music for Strings, Percussion and Celesta. "That's the way it should go—THEN, um-cha, um-cha, um-cha! Let's try that Hungarian spot again." Or he would say, "It is possible that some of you were truck drivers before you embraced another—ah—art. In that case you will understand what I mean when I say to you to hit each eighth note like a ten-ton truck." Or he might say, "What gentleman in the woodwinds was out to lunch a moment ago?" or "Fiddles are not rotary saws, gentlemen."

If musicians were easy marks for his teasing charm, the same could not be said of reviewers, who were by no means as unanimous as they had been a few years before. While the *New York Times* might judge his performance of three fragments from Alban Berg's *Wozzeck* "incandescent" and "unforgettable" and call him an "interpreter in excelsis" of modern music, another reviewer might write, "His treatment of Beethoven's Eighth Symphony was an attempt to oversell himself as a baton virtuoso; it was hysterical, misshapen, thoughtlessly planned and coarse and strained in sound. The trouble with Bernstein is that you cannot depend on him to use his best abilities or to retain reasonable self command. When he is good he is very good; when he is bad he is haywire." The trouble with Bernstein was that he was now supposed to show a new maturity, and "I am afraid that he has not yet made the transition," another critic wrote.

When he was in New York guests came to dinner constantly. Kiki Speyer said, "All during these years Leonard was astonished, amazed and blinded by all these famous people who were attracted to him. I remember having dinner with Leonard in the Russian Tea Room with Orson Welles and I don't think I opened my mouth all evening. I barely knew who Orson Welles was." The after-concert visit to the Russian Tea Room, usually in a private dining room, became obligatory, surrounded by the usual boisterous crowd. There he might drink a double scotch or two and order blinis. After that he might go to Reuben's for a sandwich of raw beef with a side order of chopped onion, or a midnight film, or to a party where he would pound out boogie-woogie until forcibly removed. Some would have liked to eject him for his habit of chattering, grunting and groaning all the way through a performance. At the opening night of one play the man in front of him became so exasperated that he threatened to turn up at Bernstein's next concert with a fluegelhorn. He was going to bed later than ever and sleeping fitfully. In the daytime, in obedience to his belief that composers must not be distracted, the curtains would be drawn and he wrote by artificial light. A certain tendency to whistle in the dark rather like Voltaire's hero became manifest at about this time. He said of the Ravel Concerto in G, "That's the one piece I play better than anybody in the world." Or he would boast, "No one can handle the sonnet form like me and Millay." That a core of vulnerability lay not far below the surface was demonstrated by an incident that occurred after *Time* magazine called him brash. He collared the offending author at a party and demanded to know what he meant when he said he was brash. How dared he call him brash?

Bernstein continued to be active in politics. Along with Aaron Copland, who was to be attacked in the 1950s for his supposed Communist sympathies, Bernstein was taking a considerable chance by openly supporting those who were protesting the Senator Joseph McCarthy witch hunt. Since Bernstein had taken great care to steer his career around obstacles during these formative years, the fact that he would do so was an indication of his concern. Like all fair-minded people, he was not so much pro-Stalin as pro–free speech, and horrified by the developing climate of paranoia and suspicion. During the war, it had been patriotic to give concerts for Russian relief and perform the work of Russian composers; and, following the lead of Copland and Koussevitzky, when Bernstein was asked to give a benefit concert or lend his name to a cause he was always generous. Now it was suddenly unfashionable to help Russia or admire Prokofiev, Rimsky-Korsakov and Shostakovich. Like Copland and Koussevitzky, Bernstein was constitutionally incapable of honing his artistic judgments to fit the political whim of the moment.

As early as 1947 Bernstein was being labeled a Communist sympathizer because, an inflammatory article in the New York *World-Telegram* declared, he was a member of an American-Soviet council which supported Russian-inspired opposition to the government in Greece and plotted its overthrow. He joined Betty Comden, Judy Holliday and Dorothy Parker to protest the decision to fire four famous broadcasters, Orson Welles among them, solely because of their political views. He took part, along with Copland, Diamond, Roy Harris, Roger Sessions, Walter Piston and Randall Thompson, in a Town Hall concert dedicated to the work of the German composer Hanns Eisler, who was being forced to leave the country simply because his brother Gerhard was a prominent Communist. And, in the autumn of 1947, Bernstein joined a committee of film stars who had organized to express their opposition to the hearings then being conducted by the House Un-American Activities Committee on "subversive activity" by Communists in Hollywood. Such hearings were immoral, the committee said. "Any attempt to curb freedom of expression and to set arbitrary standards of Americanism is in itself disloyal to both the spirit and the letter of our Constitution . . ."

As soon as Bernstein learned that Shostakovich would attend the Cultural and Scientific Conference for World Peace to be held in the Waldorf Astoria in the spring of 1949, he agreed to allow his name to be used as one of the sponsors. The group sponsoring the event was labeled a "Communist front" by the House Un-American Activities Committee in 1950. A year after that Copland's name was on the committee's list of Americans who, it claimed, had been "affiliated with from five to ten Communist-front organizations." The list also included Judy Holliday, Lillian Hellman, Paul Robeson, Albert Einstein, Thomas Mann and Frank Lloyd Wright. Copland was subsequently called to testify before McCarthy's committee, and his *Lincoln Portrait* was dropped from Eisenhower's inaugural concert because a congressman objected. As for Bernstein, his photograph was published in *Life* magazine under the headline "Dupes and Fellow Travelers Dress Up Communist Fronts."

The increasing public criticism, professional disappointments and his own mood of dissatisfaction were bringing about a shift in his thinking. He was beginning to think of guest conducting as a means to an end, the important goal being to make a name for himself as a serious composer. That would put a stop to the complaint that he could do a little bit of everything and nothing well. He began to talk about taking one or two years off and to say that he might never return to conducting. He and Jerome Robbins were discussing a new ballet based on the Hebrew legend of the Dybbuk, which would not actually be completed for another two decades. He had written some new songs, including a successful song cycle for Jennie Tourel taken from an old French cookbook, called *La Bonne Cuisine.* He was telling people, "I'm the logical man to write the Great American Opera." And he was beginning to ask his friends, "Would you like me just as well if I were a composer and not a conductor?"

Given the handicaps to the composer in himself, the introvert with a strong inner life who needs plenty of time alone, as he described it, that he managed to compose at all during this period is a tribute to his remarkable ability to concentrate. His Second Symphony, *The Age of Anxiety,* was written over a two-year period on trains, ships and planes, in hotel lobbies and restaurants around the world. "I wrote the jazz movement in Tel Aviv, seven variations in Taos, New Mexico, and seven other variations in Massachusetts. The finale I wrote on a Pittsburgh orchestra tour [during which] we gave a concert a night for a whole month, each one in a different city."

The symphony for orchestra and solo piano would be described as a "meditation" on the Auden poem, which Bernstein felt "compelled" to express in music after he had read it. The period in Taos to which he referred came about through his friendship with the British poet Stephen Spender. Spender said, "I suppose I told him that Frieda Lawrence had lent me the D. H. Lawrence Ranch in Taos and he wanted to come with me and work on the Auden poem. I said no, because I couldn't see it working out. He offered to drive me there anyway if he could stay for a few days. I remember there was a lot of discussion about whether his kid brother, Burtie, could come with us, and I finally agreed because I couldn't drive and Burtie would spell him out. We left from New York in July and it took us three or four days. We stayed in Santa Fe and I can't remember where else. It was a brand-new Buick convertible, but the tires were of poor quality and we had three blowouts, which was quite frightening."

Bernstein subsequently wrote about the trip to Taos and gave a supposedly verbatim account of a discussion about the meaning of music, poetry and meaning itself, which he said took place after Spender made an offhand remark comparing some mountains in the scenery to a work of Beethoven's. Spender recalled that much of the conversation was a great deal more prosaic. "I remember he told me about his career and perhaps how much money he was earning. I seem to remember $250,000 a year, but that may have come later. He had financial advice and was looking for ways to lose money, buying farms with hens that never laid an egg, barren oil wells and so on." Spender found him a delightful companion, generous and genuinely friendly and amusing, particularly if one could get him alone. He took a tolerant view of Bernstein's growing reputation as a tiresome show-off. "He was mad about Ben Britten. All the way across America he sang the music from *Peter Grimes*. Of course, Britten hated him. Britten once told me the only person he had ever hit was Bernstein, in a taxi I think. Auden, too, disliked him. I think he thought him vulgar.

"I always got on extremely well with him, but I was aware that there was something very public about him, so that it was difficult to have a personal relationship. People who are surrounded by others tend to lose most of their friends, either because they give up competing or because the friendliest thing you can do for them is to leave them alone.

Discussing his *Age of Anxiety* symphony with W. H. Auden,
January 1950

"He may have had the idea in the back of his mind that he and I would do an opera together. But by that time he already belonged to musical comedy, and I didn't belong to that sort of world—I rather wish I had."

Spender planned to be in Taos for about six weeks. His visit to the "upper ranch," as it was called, had been arranged by Walter Berns, later a professor of government at Georgetown University, and his friend William Goyen. Berns knew both Spender and Lawrence well and was staying nearby. The Lawrence house was on top of a mountain two thousand meters above Taos and accessible only by a dirt track. Berns said of Frieda Lawrence, "Oh boy, she was wonderful! She remained a very alive human being up to the very end. A great reader of everything. She lacked real critical skills and tended to divide writers into those who had 'zut' and those who didn't. Her family originally came from Silesia and her father was an aristocrat who had lost all his money. She was a cousin of the Red Baron and used to say, 'My ancestors were Polish kings.' She told some wonderful stories. She would pad around in her bare feet and scrub clothes. You didn't wear much up there." Frieda Lawrence asked everyone to sign her guest book, and Bernstein signed it "Citizen of the World," which "she thought was bizarre," Berns said.

At first Bernstein dazzled everyone with his pianistic facility. But then, Spender said, "after about three days he was almost ill. He just couldn't bear it, he was so bored. So he gave up and drove back to New York." Walter Berns subsequently ran across Bernstein again in Rome about a year later. Bernstein was performing Mahler's *Resurrection* Symphony and Berns was invited to rehearsals and the performance. At dinner one night Bernstein said he was going on to Naples and invited Berns to accompany him. "He was obviously propositioning me," Berns said. He declined.

The Age of Anxiety was given its premiere performance in the spring of 1949 by the Boston Symphony with Koussevitzky conducting and repeated in Tanglewood that summer. Bernstein played the piano. Early in 1950 Bernstein conducted the New York Philharmonic at Carnegie Hall in a performance of the work with Lukas Foss at the piano just a week before Jerome Robbins unveiled his new ballet set to the same music, performed by the New York City Ballet at City Center.

The lengthy poem, written during the war years, is about the search for faith. Bernstein took as his point of departure a scene involving three men and a girl in a Third Avenue bar who are engaged in a "symposium on the stages of man." There are fourteen variations on a theme, the first seven called "The Seven Ages" and the second, "The Seven Stages," during which the group engages in every conceivable kind of partnership but without success.

In the second part of the symphony the same group is in a taxi bound for a nightcap in the girl's apartment. A masque follows in which the four, still arguing, dance, drink and wrangle. At the end of the poem they go their separate ways, but not before recognizing the emptiness of their lives and their need for faith. The symphony ends with "a sort of tinsel, bourgeois evocation of some distant plush paradise," Olin Downes wrote. Bernstein later explained that the ironic ending was deliberate. "My original idea . . . was to produce a mockery of faith, a phony faith." He rewrote the ending some years later because, he decided, "I meant every note."

The composer was delighted with the result and not above pressing comparative strangers into becoming an impromptu audience. The late Andor Foldes, the renowned concert pianist, recalled that he and his wife met Bernstein by chance on Fifty-seventh Street and Bernstein insisted they accompany him to his apartment to hear a tape recording of the new work. Foldes thought it was an extremely interesting piece and was listening to it intently. After standing silently for some time

Bernstein disappeared and returned with a long, wide, crimson-red silk scarf. "He swung it around his neck, then took it off again, choreographing dramatic movements" and performing "a virtual dance for an audience of two." Foldes and his wife were perhaps unaware that the music had also been written for ballet and that Bernstein's innocent desire to tell his story in dance came from an ancient heritage. To them, it looked like evidence of an egotism so complete that Bernstein would not allow anything else to take center stage, even his own music.

The work was greeted enthusiastically by reviewers at its Boston and Tanglewood premieres. Jay C. Rosenfeld, the influential critic of the Berkshire *Evening Eagle,* wrote, "It might be difficult to pick an individual prominent in the cultural life of our country who more nearly typifies the spirit of youth today than Leonard Bernstein." And his *Age of Anxiety* was a young man's work with a tremendously vital appeal. "Even in its most meditative and introspective moments it has the soberness of youth . . . It is vigorous and ebullient . . ." Speaking of the middle movement, which uses only piano and a group of percussion instruments, Cyrus Durgin of the Boston *Globe* called it "the finest single movement in an American idiom and feeling that ever I have heard." He continued, "It is a triumph of rhythmic interplay, subtle and unexpected accents, in short, a marvelous distillation of the whole style, technique and mood of jazz." Olin Downes was less enthusiastic. While admiring the workmanship and style—which owed something to Schoenberg but was essentially Stravinskian neoclassicism—he felt that the score was "a triumph of superficiality." That did not mean that he was calling the composer's sincerity into question. "But just what is sincerity? Is not the glitter of this score, its restlessness, its unease, its obvious artificiality, precisely the sincere expression by a young musician of today, of today's 'anxiety'?" Although he allowed himself to be photographed looking over the score with Bernstein, Auden declined to add anything to the debate. He said, "It really has nothing to do with me. Any connections with my book are rather distant."

Felicia Montealegre had made great strides in her chosen career and was one of ten television actresses featured in *Life* magazine in May 1952. She got her first television role as a tubercular Italian girl, earning $20, and quickly graduated to fees of $750 to $1,000 per performance. She was, she said, usually cast as "a strange one . . . I'm ill, a psychopath, on parole or underfed . . ." Her best-known role in those years would be as

Nora in Ibsen's *A Doll's House.* After her break with Bernstein she fell in love with Richard Hart, a brilliant young actor who, Jane White said, "was extraordinarily handsome, dark, slim and brooding, of average height, with a rich, deep voice." The physical resemblance to Bernstein seemed more than a coincidence, and Shirley Bernstein thought that Montealegre was still emotionally attached to her brother. She said, "When she and Lenny weren't seeing each other she and I were close friends. We went to the movies together and played four-hand piano, even after she started living with Dick Hart. Occasionally I would hear a certain yearning in her voice, and it was very clear that Lenny was the love of her life. Then I took a trip to Europe with him and he'd been writing to me about her. I said, 'You are making a terrible mistake here. You have got to play out the string.' He told me he had written her a letter and hadn't even known where she lived. So he sent it to an old address, it was forwarded and she finally answered it."

On their return to New York from Europe in January of 1951, Shirley and Lenny were met at the boat by Felicia and there was "an enormous reunion." They went to a friend's for a drink, and while she was at the party Montealegre called her answering service. She learned that Hart had had a heart attack and was in the hospital. "She flew out of there," Shirley Bernstein said. Some time later that evening Shirley suggested to her brother that he go and sit with Montealegre during the crisis, which he did. Hart died later that night at the age of thirty-six. Jane White remembered going to a party to cheer up Montealegre with about twenty other women friends. Everyone knew she was devastated. "She's by herself, mourning like a widow the death of Richard Hart."

That was the successful reconciliation that led to their marriage, but there appears to have been at least one other, two years earlier. An item in Dorothy Kilgallen's column in the spring of 1949 reported they were seeing a great deal of each other. Some months after that, in January 1950, Bernstein was hinting that he would like to "settle down." The wedding was called off less than a week later, on January 12. A year after that Bernstein announced that he would stop conducting that spring for an indefinite period. "I'm worn out," he said. "I've been conducting almost continuously for seven years. Now I feel I have to give myself a chance to find out about the importance of composing." He was going to retreat to a farm in New Hampshire, or an apartment in New York, or an island in the West Indies. He decided on Cuernavaca, Mexico, and by the end of May he had finished the first act of a new opera.

Bernstein might have continued to vacillate for several more years had it not been for an event that would throw him into emotional turmoil. He had been in close touch with Koussevitzky while preparing the Israel Philharmonic's first American tour early in 1951. They had crossed the country together on the tour, alternating as conductors. When they reached Denver, Colorado, Koussevitzky, now seventy-six years old, had a heavy cold and a fever and was hospitalized for a few days. He rallied and insisted on continuing to San Francisco, performing, Olga Koussevitzky said, "by sheer force of will."

Koussevitzky was suffering from a chronic blood disease, polycythemia rubra vera, characterized by an overproduction of blood cells. By the spring of 1951 he felt well enough to work and was planning to conduct his first opera at Tanglewood that summer, Tchaikovsky's *Queen of Spades,* which he had conducted in Russia years before. Bernstein drove to Mexico by way of Phoenix, where the Koussevitzkys had a home, in order to discuss the work. Bernstein later wrote in a letter to Olga, "He knew something was ending, because he was subtly and quietly assigning charges to me—dreams to be realized, responsibilities to be shouldered . . ." Early in May the Koussevitzkys flew to Boston and Koussevitzky had a series of conferences about *The Queen of Spades,* but he began to feel weak again and was hospitalized at the New England Medical Center. Over the next few weeks he was in and out of hospital. During one of his stays at home he slipped on a rug and fell, hitting his head and opening a gash in his forehead. He went back to hospital and Bernstein flew back to be at his bedside. Bernstein liked to say that Koussevitzky died in his arms. In actual fact he visited Koussevitzky earlier in the day on June 4, 1951, and left him in good spirits. At eleven that evening Koussevitzky had a cerebral hemorrhage and died.

Two funeral services took place, one in Boston on June 7 and another at the Congregational Church on the Hill in Lenox a day later. The small white clapboard church was simply decorated and jammed with family and friends. At the end of the service they filed from the church down a graveled path a few yards to the open grave under the shade of a large maple. Olga Naumoff Koussevitzky, heavily veiled and in black, carried a lighted candle, escorted by Bernstein, who had been one of the honorary pallbearers in Boston. Verna Fine said, "I remember he didn't have a suit to wear. So he borrowed a charcoal gray winter suit from my husband. Russian Orthodox funerals can take five hours, and it was about a hundred degrees that day. I can still see poor Lenny with the sweat running down his neck." Kiki Speyer, who by then was divorced from her first husband, had married Roger Picard and had a baby boy, was at the Lenox funeral with her parents. She said, "When I got to the cemetery and Leonard saw me, he threw himself into my arms. We were crying our eyes out. My mother thought I was going to divorce again."

That summer, Bethel Leslie and Felicia Montealegre were traveling in Europe. Leslie said, "I think he tracked her down in Florence with me. I was with her when she bought her wedding dress." Montealegre returned to the States and drove up to Tanglewood with Bernstein. She said that he formally proposed over a dinner in Milbrook, New York.

All this took place a few weeks after the death of Koussevitzky, and they set the wedding date for September 9. Plans were to have been kept secret until their families could be notified. However, at a faculty dinner in Tanglewood given by Olga Koussevitzky (Bernstein attended as head of the conducting department), the butler brought in a tray of wineglasses, all of them filled save one. The empty glass suddenly snapped apart. A guest said nervously, "It's a sign from Koussy." "If it *is* a sign," his widow replied, "it must be a signal for me to tell you the news," and she announced the engagement.

Since by then Bernstein had abandoned his conducting ambitions and was concentrating on composing for the theater, there can be no doubt that his marriage was a genuine emotional commitment, not just a calculated career move. Those close to him knew he had been wrestling for years with the problems posed by his ambivalent sexuality. Shirley Bernstein said, "He had had a lot of therapy by then, to accomplish one thing or another. He wanted to be at peace with himself, either as a homosexual or a heterosexual." Noel Farrand, who shared similar problems, recalled a conversation on that topic at about that time. "He told me that where sex was concerned he had always been very adaptable, but he had decided that homosexuality was a curse. He was so tense and emphatic about it. He felt marriage had saved him from a homosexual life style. He suggested I follow his example, and it was very good advice. Had I not done so, I'd be dead." Shirley Bernstein also recalled getting a letter from her brother shortly before his marriage that included a reference to the "darker impulses" that were ultimately so unsatisfying. At issue was the effect on a sensitive child of the paternal indoctrination that sex was a dirty, furtive business, certainly not to be connected with nice girls, that homosexuality was to be condemned—along with the evidence of his own eyes that marriage was a lifelong ordeal. Given that every avenue for sexual expression was seemingly closed to him, it is not surprising that his subsequent accommodation to sexuality should take some unexpected twists and turns. He himself suspected that defiance was part of the equation. His sister recalled her brother saying, "Am I still rebelling against my father and his values?" She said, "You know, Aaron Copland made up a term for him. He called him a B.H.: a bluff homosexual. 'You are not one of us,' he said."

If it is true that one loves in others what one feels lacking in oneself, then Bernstein's attraction to Felicia Montealegre is easy to understand. She was a flawless example of a completely cultured human being, fluent in languages, at ease in any social circle, always perfectly dressed and with a well-schooled ability to present an unruffled facade. Shirley Bernstein said, "Felicia used to say that she did not have a natural maternal instinct; she balanced Lenny, who was so very doting with children. She was also not demonstrative in the way she wanted to be. She had all the feelings . . . She was full of feelings, but they were not easy to express. She was really hobbled by her upbringing and she knew it." She welcomed the ways in which his impulsive, gregarious nature, his eager interest in people and new situations, complemented her own. If he lacked any sense of life's limitations, the corollary was his tendency to go to extremes, lose perspective. She always knew as if by instinct the median point; she had a sense of the fitness of things. And, when necessary, she was able to make the difficult decisions from which he shrank.

They shared common interests, goals and beliefs. Both of them feared failure most, but they had different ways of showing it: while he tended to agonize publicly, she seldom voiced her private doubts, and only after weighing the consequences. Ultimately, he lived for his art; for her, the goal was to make an art out of life. She seemed to have the inner composure he felt most lacking in himself. He wrote, "In stillness, every human being is great . . . he is a poet, and most like an angel." His desire for marriage and his past hesitancy before it also demonstrate that he felt such a commitment to be irrevocable. Speaking of his father, he wrote, "The total manifestations of God are to be understood as Wisdom, or *Chachmah,* but . . . this cannot exist except in the dual form of male and female; and so *Chachmah* is the Father, and *Binah,* or Understanding, is the Mother. But the two are not separate—that is the mystical necessity; they are indivisible . . ."

The White Suit

Quaff your fill, clear and cool
Give me, too, maiden, of thy foaming bowl
Let me worship thy glowing youth.

—GOETHE, "AN SCHWAGER KRONOS"

Their joint bereavement had brought them together. As if to underscore that point, Bernstein chose to wear one of Koussevitzky's white suits at his wedding—it had to be radically altered, since he was much broader across the shoulders—and even his shirt, tie, socks and shoes. From that point on he also wore Koussevitzky's cufflinks, which he kissed before every performance, and his cape, or an exact copy of it (information on that point is conflicting). There is a photograph of the just-married couple standing on a well-manicured lawn beside a clipped hedge in Brookline. His arm is around her waist, and she, in a full-skirted, three-quarter-length white dress with a portrait neckline displaying an elaborate necklace, carries a bouquet of yellow roses. Her veil has been thrown back. She looks ecstatic and understandably elated. If he had felt himself to be alone in a vast and hostile universe, disconnected and adrift, as he wrote in his poem "Letter to Myself," this was a step towards connectedness.

When Koussevitzky called his Lenyushka "myself, reincarnated," he could not have said anything that more perfectly matched Bernstein's fantasies. Wearing his clothes, stepping into his shoes—it was the fulfillment of his adolescent dream to enter the ranks of the rarely privileged, the gods of his world. But to become Koussevitzky also required living to serve music, as Koussevitzky had done. One had to take his exalted view that a conductor must cherish, foster and encourage the muse, must mediate for the masses as if he were a *rebbe*. As Koussevitzky said, "The music flows through me to the orchestra and from them to the public . . ." Koussevitzky believed that the most exalted role of all belonged to the composer, the person who communed with the divine and returned with a message. "This reach, this leap, aspiration, thrust—this is what Koussevitzky held most sacred . . ." With Koussevitzky's death Bernstein scrutinized his own motives to see whether they could be made to fit that exalted ideal, and rededicated himself with a passion.

They had acknowledged their need for each other, but the doubts remained. The night before the wedding, Shirley Bernstein recalled, both of them were in such a state of panic that she and her brother Burtie, just out of college, went out and bought a bagful of joke props: "whoopie" cushions, exploding cigarettes, fake spoons and tumblers, and inflicted them on the prospective bride and groom. Felicia Montealegre said later that she had a headache and went upstairs to lie down. When she asked for an aspirin, the fiendish pair inflicted another joke prop on her, an undrinkable glass of water. She said, "It was the last straw. I wanted to fling it at them and say, 'This is a houseful of loonies, madmen, monsters!' " His sister said, "They were exasperated but they had to laugh and it did distract them."

Her brother was unable to sleep, so Shirley Bernstein sat up all night with him. As for his bride, although she had voluntarily renounced her Catholicism at the age of eighteen, her decision to convert to Judaism for the wedding was a serious step, and one her mother found hard to accept. Sam and Jennie Bernstein were not altogether pleased, either; they had wanted a good Jewish wife for their son, and here was this Catholic foreigner with her curious family and distant ways. The question of religion continued to be a delicate subject, and when, after the birth of their first daughter, Bernstein caught his mother-in-law slipping a golden crucifix on a chain around the baby's neck, he was not amused.

After the ceremony they headed straight for Cuernavaca in his Buick convertible. His sister said, "They told me that some time during the drive they decided they had made a terrible mistake and had one bad night en route." But their new union demonstrated its resilience shortly afterwards when both sets of parents decided to visit them for a week and arrived simultaneously. Shirley Bernstein said, "Somehow they survived."

They remained in Cuernavaca for several months. Although Bernstein had successfully launched another symphony, ever since *Fancy Free* he had been convinced that the future of American music lay in the theater—and as he told himself in an imaginary conversation, "nobody, with the possible exception of some other composers and some critics who live by denouncing or flattering new works, will be any the sorrier if you or any of your symphonic colleagues never writes a symphony again." The symphonic form, as it developed in Europe, had reached its apogee with Mahler, and nothing more could be done with it. However, if one examined the American tradition, one could see that the musical comedy scores of the day had direct parallels to the singspiels from which the operas of Mozart and Haydn had been developed. "This is a period we must pass through before we can arrive at a real American symphonic form, or a real American style of whatever kind of concert music . . . But the musical language it will speak must first be created in our theater . . ." His new goal would be to write an American opera, one that was accessible to a wide audience but serious in intent. If he could do that, "I shall be a happy man."

Bernstein's most recent attempt at "singspiel" had been incidental music for a production of J. M. Barrie's *Peter Pan,* starring Jean Arthur, that opened in New York in the spring of 1950. He contributed some seven songs and about ten minutes of music, which was well reviewed. Yet, despite a string of successes, the verdict on the eventual worth of Bernstein's music was uncertain. Aaron Copland spoke for the majority when he wrote that the music had such immediate emotional appeal that it was difficult to know how long it would last. At its best Bernstein's music had immense rhythmic invention, tremendous dramatic power and an "irresistible elan." At worst, it was "conductor's music, eclectic in style and facile in inspiration." The lukewarm assessment, made in 1949, must have spurred Bernstein to show what he could do if he took the time to do it. Seen in this context, *Trouble in Tahiti,* which absorbed most of his free time in those honeymoon months, was to be an opening salvo.

John Tyers and Alice Ghostley (below) play the roles of Sam and Dinah in the original production of *Trouble in Tahiti*, which opened at the Playhouse in New York in April 1955 and closed after forty-nine performances.

Bernstein's operetta—it is only forty-five minutes long—describes a contemporary marriage in a comfortable suburb, the one portrayed in every detergent advertisement of the times. The white house with its picket fence, the kitchen gadgets, the tiled bathrooms, the latest books, the chromium streamlining on the family car, the vapidity and gloss that symbolized ideals of suburbia in the 1950s, are sketched in a few deft songs. Bernstein underlined the irony of the situation with a three-voice ensemble reminiscent of the Andrews Sisters, who, in close harmony, assure the listener that this is the best of all possible worlds. But the couple are miserable. They bicker constantly, talking across rather than to each other, giving vent to their frustrations. His frustration is the gulf between the model he has tried to emulate, that of the godly man whose life is dedicated to self-improvement, but who will never succeed in the battle of life, and that of the man of affairs successfully climbing the corporate ladder. Meanwhile his wife fusses and whines, buys a hat, sees a psychiatrist, goes to a frivolous movie and, like her husband, cannot be bothered to see her son perform in a school play. As Irving Kolodin observed, "Two emptier, duller people never lived; and if they did knock their heads together nothing would result but a muffled thud."

To make sure no one missed the point, Bernstein named the husband Sam and, in a minor concession to his mother's feelings, called the wife Dinah, presumably for his paternal grandmother. It is a savage indictment and perhaps a cry of outrage from a son who was held up to exacting personal standards while his father felt free to demonstrate all the petty and mean-spirited behavior of which he was capable. Here Bernstein is questioning not just his parents' marriage but the whole basis of their lives. One does not know how Sam and Jennie Bernstein reacted to this assessment but there is an indication that this was a family in which people routinely rode roughshod over each others' feelings, while the one being pilloried was supposed not to mind. John Gruen, who wrote about them, recalled that Bernstein once drove a car onto his foot and refused to remove it. Gruen said, "I was used as a clown sometimes to make them laugh, and I wasn't always ready to be the butt of the joke." So in this case, no doubt, the elder Bernsteins, their failings ridiculed, were expected to keep smiling.

Like *Facsimile's*, *Trouble in Tahiti's* main theme is a spiritual vacuum. However, rather than paint its somber message in musical terms, Bernstein had hit upon the more effective solution of satirizing the facade itself. That was the music Irving Kolodin found most successful, "crisp and flavorsome, even witty." Passages designed to bring to life the personal drama of the main characters were inventive, if not actually moving, with a wistful quality of their own. But as for the composer's attempt to characterize, "it is here, to me, that Bernstein is on the thinnest of thin ice." The operetta ends with "a return to the idiot trio, who are now bleating away about a silver moon kissing the windows and kissing the walls of the little white house, shining its promise of 'lovely tomorrows just like today.' "

As a work of art it was flawed but as a commentary on the confused and contradictory values of his upbringing it was brilliant. What was the point of getting rich if the result was to be the sterile acceptance of the values of a debased culture? How could a man claim to follow a godly path when his life was in ruins? The opera ends without a solution for the main characters. But the fact that it was written at a moment when Bernstein was taking the fateful step into marriage shows that he was groping towards an acceptance of himself as a flawed human being. He and Felicia would tolerate each other's imperfections and find that happy solution, that path between conformism and outcast status, which his own parents had so conspicuously failed to find. Within a year, he would be photographed standing at the doorway of a pretty white house behind a white picket fence, beside his shining wife in her checked gingham dress.

They were very happy in Mexico, playing tennis, swimming, riding horses, going to bullfights and playing with their dogs. Felicia intended to continue with her career, but for the moment there was something of a lull. "And I can tell you this," Lenny told a reporter a day before their marriage, evidently having changed his mind, "from now on my bride will be Mrs. Bernstein and will forget she was Miss Montealegre"—but in fact she continued to use her maiden name. Soon after they arrived Lenny found out by chance that Felicia did not know what a past participle was. He immediately sat down and drummed grammar into her ears until she "burst into tears." It appears to have been one of their few unhappy moments. They were entertaining a stream of visitors, including brother Burtie and the publicist Constance Hope, who said, "My husband and I drove to Cuernavaca in December. We had lunch in town, then telephoned Lenny. He said, 'Why didn't you come and have lunch here?' I explained that his phone had been busy.

"He said, 'You know why it's been busy? We're pregnant!'

"I went into a shop and bought some hand-knit booties, then we drove to their house. Lenny and Felicia were sitting there in white bathing suits. They were beautiful . . . like the spirit of youth. They looked at the booties and started to cry. The present made the baby real."

A summons from Boston cut their stay short. Charles Munch, conductor of the Boston Symphony, had just had a heart attack. Would Bernstein substitute? He would. They packed up and returned for a series of concerts to close the season. He particularly distinguished himself during an all-Beethoven program that included a performance of the Piano Concerto No. 4 by Arthur Rubinstein. Rudolph Elie of the Boston *Herald* was struck by the beauty of sound coming from the string section. "Obeying, with that curious intuition developed by a string orchestra, every least inflexion of rhythm, dynamic shading and nuance of phrase demanded by the conductor, its flight to the last bar was absolutely magical." As conductor, Bernstein was in his "most maturely eloquent vein," Elie wrote.

Some of Bernstein's time in Cuernavaca had been taken up with plans for the following summer. He had been appointed professor of music at Brandeis University and was working with his friend the composer Irving Fine, who was chairman of the newly established School of the Creative Arts, to develop the university's first arts festival. It was the kind of challenge that Bernstein loved and would provide the ideal forum for his latest attempt at "singspiel." He was also able to examine, through lectures and seminars, some of the questions that were uppermost in his mind at that time, such as, "How does the concert hall relate to society in America? Do we need it? Do we want it?"; "Are we living in an age of experimentalism?"; "What is happening in our musical theater?"; and "How grand can our opera become?"

Brandeis University was to hold other arts festivals, but for sheer brilliance and inventive flair its first attempt would be hard to equal. To add to the challenge, when the idea of the festival was first broached by Fine and Copland, the university, then only three years old, lacked an auditorium in which to hold the events. An open-air amphitheater, with a vast stage and orchestra pit, was finished just hours before Bernstein raised his baton for opening night. There are photographs of Bernstein and his wife in the rain at the dedication ceremonies; she is wearing something dark and straight cut, with a tiny white hat and flowers at the neckline.

A concert performance of Kurt Weill's *Threepenny Opera,* in a marvelous new translation by Marc Blitzstein, opened that week. It was an instant success and moved to off-Broadway, where it was fully staged and would have an eight-year run at the Theater de Lys. This was followed by the premiere of Bernstein's *Trouble in Tahiti* and a new production of Stravinsky's *Les Noces,* choreographed and danced by Merce Cunningham. There was also a performance of some *musique concrète* by Pierre Schaeffer, a French electronics engineer, who had put together a tape of such sounds as a girl laughing in a certain key, the thud of something dropping to the floor and Beethoven's *Eroica* played backwards. (Bernstein explained he had decided to program an extract from the forty-minute work rather than the whole thing for fear "the audience would run screaming from the hall.") There were an art exhibition, a jazz festival and poetry readings by Karl Shapiro, William Carlos Williams and Peter Viereck. Bernstein was everywhere, acting as moderator of the discussions, directing and conducting as well as being a composer, demonstrating the protean talents that would be displayed to such advantage in years to come. Bernstein's association with Brandeis, fruitful as it was, would be brief. He was involved in teaching and directing the arts festival only for a few years in the early 1950s.

On September 8, 1952, one day short of their first anniversary, Felicia gave birth to a baby girl. Sam Bernstein had said, "Let's hope it's a boy," which Felicia very much resented. She wanted to name the baby Nina, a proper girl's name. Her husband originally agreed, but "then Lenny telephoned me at the hospital early the next morning and said, 'It's a frightful mistake—don't sign the papers.' He rushed over and we began hurling names at each other again. He kept saying, 'Jamie,' and I kept saying, 'No.' Finally I said, 'All right.' "

The magical universe that was Tanglewood was, apart from his wife and child, foremost in Bernstein's mind during the years following Koussevitzky's death, and his speeches to the students there show the importance he attached to his role. Eleven years earlier he, too, sat on the grass listening to the great man exhort, encourage and inspire. He wanted them to remember Koussevitzky's vision, his ideals and ethical standards, and to bear in mind that their reason for coming to Tanglewood was not to learn technique alone but to understand the meaning behind the music.

Since the death of Koussevitzky the man who had come closest to the title of "Mr. Tanglewood" was Bernstein. Just as Koussevitzky had, Bernstein would make his grand entrance: driving his Cadillac convertible through the main gates and down a winding path to the big shed, nattily dressed in white or pale blue denim trousers and a white shirt, a white tennis sweater slung over his shoulders, with the arms knotted in front. Room at his classes was at a premium; fifty to a hundred students might appear. Leonard Marcus, who would become a well-known editor, was among them. He recalled that in 1952 the young Lorin Maazel was one of three student conductors who were active there. "I still remember him conducting the student orchestra in Britten's *Young Person's Guide to the Orchestra*. During the postmortem the following day, Bernstein pointed out an aspect of Maazel's conducting that wasn't absolutely necessary to get a certain effect. As we were leaving class, Maazel, who had been a child prodigy, said, 'Who does he think he is, telling me what to do? I've been conducting longer than he has.'"

Very few conducting students made similar objections. Most of them felt, as Marcus did, that he was "handsome, charming and brilliant. He taught me more than music. One of the people who has influenced my life. He taught me that, no matter what happens, you can always find joy in life as long as you have music."

They clustered around when Bernstein joined forces with Boris Goldovsky, head of the opera department, and the class would become a free-for-all. There was Goldovsky bellowing out the arias of Don José, and there was Bernstein bellowing Carmen's arias back at him, both of them hideously out of tune. It was up to the aspiring opera conductor to follow their erratic path and bring in the orchestra (represented by a pianist) at the right moment. All that, Goldovsky said, was training for the real world.

They would applaud when, as one of his students recalled, Bernstein demonstrated his phenomenal ear. The student said, "One of the things I conducted here was the Beethoven Violin Concerto. Of the five hundred measures there were only two I felt unsure of. Bernstein listened to it all, said, 'Wonderful—but there are two measures . . .' They were exactly the measures I'd been worried about."

Bernstein was occasionally bested in turn. During the early 1950s, a pianist named Zita Carno came to his class. Carno, who would go on to perform with the Los Angeles Philharmonic, became a legend within a few days of her arrival. "Every day or two one of us would come to her with an orchestral score by Schoenberg or Webern or Richard Strauss," wrote Marcia Kraus, who would become a cellist with the Portland Symphony and eventually a composer. Carno, "casting a withering eye at the music and the purveyor, would then sit down at whatever piano was handy and play it without hesitation. Her prowess, which she took matter-of-factly, had us all agog, including Bernstein, [who] deferred to her comments during rehearsals of the student orchestra. We would be playing through a movement and suddenly Zita would call out, 'Lenny, two measures before L the second trombone played a B and it should be a B-flat.' Bernstein would stop conducting, look around at her (Zita didn't have a score because she already 'knew' that piece) and then tell the second trombonist that he must have misread the note. The trombonist would confirm his mistake and mark his part. Nobody but Zita with her golden ears had heard the error. Not even Bernstein. Zita would sit with arms folded across her chest, . . . waiting for the next lapse from the printed score . . ."

Those six weeks at Tanglewood, Marcia Kraus wrote, were the most extraordinary of her youth, and the high point was Bernstein's conducting of Stravinsky's *Petrouchka.* "I had never before played the piece . . . so this work, one of the masterpieces of twentieth-century music, is indelibly stamped upon my memory with Bernstein's image. Lenny, before our eyes, became the hapless puppet. His hands went limp and his head lolled to one side, as he mimed the spirit of the work. It was not so much what he said as how he looked that gave us the key to how we should play . . . I've no idea how we sounded, but I know we gave our all. Our efforts were epitomized at one rehearsal by the boy playing the famous trumpet solo in the dance of the Ballerina. This solo, which lasts twenty-five measures without a rest, ending in eight rapid high G's, is a well-known test of a trumpeter's ability. The boy playing it had repeated it several times at Bernstein's behest and suddenly fell backwards off the riser . . ." The conductor discovered to his chagrin that he had fainted for lack of oxygen.

Felicia Bernstein soon returned to her acting career. Just a month after Jamie's arrival she appeared in a "Kraft Television Theatre" production of *Divine Drudge,* a play by Vicki Baum and John Golden. They were, Bernstein told Irving Fine, beginning to settle into their new nine-room duplex apartment in the Osborne on West Fifty-seventh Street, the one in which they would spend the next ten years. The handsome twelve-storey American Renaissance–style structure dated from the 1890s and had long been known as the "residential Carnegie Hall" because of its advantageous location opposite that building. The Osborne had been a favorite haunt of actors, actresses, artists, musicians and singers because its internal walls were up to four feet thick, making noisy rehearsals practicable propositions. Its Italianate lobby was famous: an ornate marble floor, mosaic-encrusted walls, stained-glass windows, dozens of archways and bas-reliefs. Its apartments were high-ceilinged, with fire-places and graceful proportions. A month after moving, he and Felicia were spending every spare second trying to furnish the place with cur-tains, carpets and objects of all sorts. After trying to do without a nurse for two weeks in the interests of economy, they had re-engaged the nurse in desperation. The apartment was wonderful, but everyone already knew where they were, and it was like living on the sidewalk. The baby was crying, the dog was at the vet's with an intestinal ailment, he was rapidly approaching bankruptcy and simply did not know how he was ever going to write.

Helen Coates also took an apartment in the Osborne; it doubled as her office. It was very convenient and turned out to be a tactful way of delineating her new duties, which up to that moment had involved every aspect of his life. Now Felicia was taking over the household affairs, and Helen managed to be gracious about it. She could tell that it would be a perfect marriage, she said, because Felicia was the least possessive of women and knew that his work would always come first.

The role Felicia Bernstein mapped out for herself began at once; she even took along barbering equipment on her honeymoon, teach-ing herself to cut Lenny's hair so that not a single strand would be out of place. There is evidence that he was soon using her as a sounding board for career choices, because when La Scala first offered him a chance to conduct Cherubini's *Medea* in 1953, he turned it down on his wife's advice. She did not think it would be a good career move (wrongly, as it turned out). She was prepared to listen endlessly. Jane White recalled one visit to the Osborne. "I called Felicia up and said I had written a play. She was very excited. I asked, 'Do you have an evening and can I come and read it to you?' " They were both there when she arrived, but Bernstein soon fled. "Felicia, however, listened for hours and made some very constructive remarks. Nothing ever came of the play, but I appreciated her kindness." She would be the caregiver, the confidante Bernstein could trust, his mainstay and champion. At an early stage, Felicia Bernstein also became the voice of caution in her husband's life. Verna Fine said, "I always remember one summer, it was 1952 or 1953, that Charles Munch was staying in one of these fancy hotels near Tanglewood and Lenny was going on and on, criticizing him. Felicia—she had a thick British accent—replied, 'Lenny, stop it. Don't be so vulgar.' I can still hear her voice in my ear. She made him live up to a certain ideal of behavior." Tod Perry's description of Felicia's influence was that she "gentled" him. Mary

In Pisa, where Felicia and Bernstein visited David Diamond
following Bernstein's successful performance of *Medea;* and
below with David Diamond in Florence, 1955

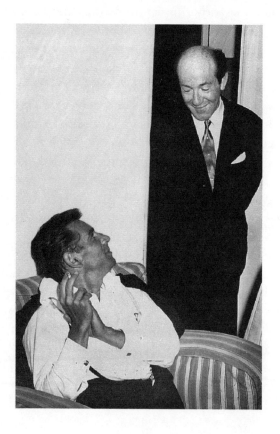

Triumphant in 1953, after becoming the first
American conductor ever to appear at La Scala,
Milan, when he conducted Cherubini's *Medea*.
Maria Callas sang the title role.

Rodgers, who would work with Bernstein extensively, said, " 'curbed'
is more like it."

As for Bernstein it was clear that, in the early days, he accepted his
wife's "gentling" as in his best interests and obviously adored her. They
spent some time in Milan—Bernstein had been asked to take over *Medea*
for the second time and had consented. It was his first opera, he was the
first American to conduct at La Scala, his prima donna was Maria Callas,
and the reviews were spectacular: he was "absolutely predestined" to
music, a critic wrote in late 1953. But in terms of his private life the
stay in Milan was remarkable for a revealing series of photographs. In
them, the brilliant young conductor is shown twirling his wife, in faultless evening dress, around the floor, both arms locked around her, looking as if he can hardly believe his luck.

They both had wanted to be parents. Noel Farrand recalled that during his talks with Bernstein in which the latter called homosexuality a

The successful team in *Wonderful Town* with the composer at the piano: from
left, Betty Comden, Rosalind Russell, Adolph Green, producer George
Abbott and conductor Lehman Engel

curse, he also said, "When I am sitting with that baby, it's worth everything." People were struck by his unusual response to babies and children. Ellice F. S. Patnaik, now an engineer and musician by avocation,
said, "One time when I was about five years old I was coming back from
Chicago to New York on the train with my mother. She liked to ride in
the club car, and I was rambling around and sat down beside a man who
had a practice keyboard in his lap. My mother came over to retrieve me,
but he said, 'No, let her stay.' He started telling me stories and reading
me *Winnie the Pooh,* and I spent almost the whole two-day trip with him.
I remember our last lunch together. He was wearing a navy-blue suit
and I was eating vanilla ice cream. My mother said, 'Be careful of that
ice cream,' and of course I dropped a blob on his beautiful suit. I can
still see the mess I made. When we got to New York, 'Uncle Len'
walked off into a flood of flashbulbs, and that's when my mother realized who he was."

· · ·

Celebrating their triumph with Comden and Green
at the Theatre Guild party after the successful
opening of *Wonderful Town*, 1953

Rosalind Russell being manhandled by an enthusiastic group of Brazilian
cadets in *Wonderful Town*

With five weeks to go until rehearsals, Comden and Green were called in by their old friend George Abbott to write some new lyrics for a musical. The book, written by Joseph Fields and Jerome Chodorov, was based on their successful comedy *My Sister Eileen,* which had enjoyed a lengthy run on Broadway a decade before. This in turn was based on the memoirs of Ruth McKenney about two girls from Ohio who arrive in Greenwich Village in the 1930s in pursuit of fame and fortune.

Abbott had cast Rosalind Russell as Ruth, the responsible older sister from Columbus, the leading role that was originally played by Shirley Booth. Ruth wants to be a writer but is continually being upstaged by her personable younger sister, Eileen. They take an apartment below the sidewalk on Christopher Street that rocks with blasting from midnight until six a.m. and through which—the door is never locked—wander an eclectic assortment of lovable characters, including a conga line of Brazilian naval cadets whose antics land Eileen in jail.

Bernstein was asked to write some new music, and Comden and Green were waiting in his studio opposite Carnegie Hall for him to arrive one day (he was late, as usual), feeling depressed about the assignment. Green said later:

> *Eileen* seemed so awfully Thirties-bound, sort of a post-depression play, full of over-exploited plot lines and passé references. We were discussing it all when suddenly Lenny stands in the doorway.
>
> "The Thirties!" he said. "My God, those were the years! The excitement there was around! The political awareness! The optimism! Franklin Delano! Fiorello! Real personalities! And the wonderful fashions. Glorious! Hey, and the songs! What beat! Remember the songs?" And he rushed to the piano and began to belt out five nostalgic hits. And then he suddenly stopped and said, "Say, I've got a great idea for a *Sister Eileen* tune." And then and there we started working on the show. I don't think we left that studio all month.

Fields and Chodorov had rewritten their comedy and set it in the present day, but, once galvanized by Bernstein, the team of Comden and Green realized that *Eileen*'s fragile charm depended entirely on its ability to fashion a portrait of the Greenwich Village everyone wanted to remember, even if it had never existed. That meant a radical revision, and even Bernstein, in his rush of enthusiasm, had not grasped how much work would be involved. At first he thought he could resurrect some of the material in his files. One of the pieces he tried to insert was a short jazz work, *Prelude, Fugue and Riffs,* that he had written for Woody Herman but that was not completed until after the band had disbanded. Bernstein thought it might be usable as a ballet, but the tone was wrong and it was dropped. He had been intrigued by the challenge of making the score an integral part of the drama, not just an interruption for some set numbers. Comden and Green liked the idea of weaving literary themes into their lyrics. One of the most hilarious involves Ruth's blundering attempts to introduce *Moby-Dick* as a conversational gambit. This song was judged far too esoteric and was almost thrown out. They also had fun with three episodes designed to demonstrate Ruth's versatility as a writer; she appears as heroine of a Hemingwayesque African big-game-hunting episode, then as a shantytown character from Steinbeck and finally as a grande dame out of the high-style drawing rooms of John O'Hara.

None of the creators was quite sure how to write for Rosalind Russell, who had gone to Hollywood after an undistinguished start on Broadway and stayed away for twenty years. It was evident, however, after the pre-Broadway tryouts in Boston, New Haven and Philadelphia, that Russell was ideal. Brooks Atkinson of the *New York Times* wrote that she gave a "memorably versatile comic performance. She is tall, willowy and gawky; she is droll, sardonic and incredulous." He and other critics thought there had not been such "an uproarious and original musical carnival" since *Guys and Dolls.*

Wonderful Town was the third and last statement in a group of works about the innocent who arrives in the city to find there is happiness, fulfillment and warm camaraderie beneath the gruff exterior, the kind of portrait of themselves New Yorkers liked. But the shift in decade was significant; Bernstein, Comden and Green all knew that this romantic view of life in the big city was no longer tenable, if it had ever been. Shortly after the musical began its run at the Winter Garden, Ed Sullivan, the television personality, who was then a columnist for the *Daily News,* opened his attack. He had learned that a left-wing publication, the *National Guardian,* had bought a block of tickets for resale. These profits would be used to "disseminate ideas hostile to the interests of America." Sullivan called on Rosalind Russell to "step out of this April 8 job for the Kremlin. And reveal who, in the show's management, set it up as leftist sucker bait." That a lighthearted piece of escapism should be singled out for such bullying tactics was bad enough, but the show's producer added insult to injury by cancelling the offending performance. Elmer Rice, an officer of the American Civil Liberties Union, noted that the producer's action "raises the amazing possibility that theatergoers must now pass political tests set up by the producers . . ." For Bernstein it was all beginning to sound familiar. At about that time the New York *Journal-American,* ever alert to subversive artistic statements, noted that Bernstein's "lengthy Communist-front record" was well known by the House Un-American Activities Committee.

Bernstein wrote a number of agreeable songs, including "Ohio," "A Little Bit in Love," "A Quiet Girl," "My Darlin' Eileen" and "It's Love." The success of the production—*Show Business* reported in the spring of 1953 that there were "123 very happy investors"—ought to have made him thoroughly pleased with himself. But, as the *New Yorker* noted, his tunes, although gay and appropriate, were unlikely to be "great favorites with the juke-box set." This comment may have inspired Bernstein's next mock dialogue with himself, this one with a professional manager who was trying to sell his music. The manager complained that Bernstein's new show had been playing for five months and lacked a single hit. The self-reproach had a certain validity. The songs were catchy, amusing and clever, but they were not being played on radio, television or even Muzak. It would be like him to set his artistic goals on the creation of a complex intermeshing of mood, theme and dialogue and then berate himself because he had not written any Tin Pan Alley hits. He was displaying a trait that would become marked, that is, chronic dissatisfaction with his own compositions. That trait would have the positive result of keeping him at work on less-than-successful ventures and substituting to some extent for the waning of inspiration as he grew older. But its negative aspect was to rob him of that delight in his work that had been the major motivation a decade before. Instead of the artist's joy of creation there was "a devil at his back, prodding him with a pitchfork." From now on, whatever he did would contain a flaw in his eyes. So would whatever choices he was making in career terms. As he said at the end of 1953, "When you're conducting, you itch to compose, and when you're composing, you itch to conduct."

"Wow, I'm Famous!"

Downhill now and away
See the sun is low
While there's day, while there's time . . .

— GOETHE, "AN SCHWAGER KRONOS"

He had promised himself that he would take on the Hollywood challenge but wanted it on his own terms, that is, to compose for a film that had artistic integrity and the right message. He found it in *On the Waterfront*.

Budd Schulberg, writer of the scenario, wrote that the film was based on a report about conditions on the New York waterfront where "guys who said no to industrial feudalism were getting clobbered and killed." The reporter who brought the facts to light won a Pulitzer Prize, but it took four years for Schulberg to get the necessary financing, since the subject was considered far too gritty and realistic for a commercial film. Bernstein arrived at a late stage, after the film, starring Marlon Brando, Lee J. Cobb, Karl Malden, Rod Steiger and Eva

Practicing for a performance, early 1950s

Marie Saint, had been completed. As soon as he had viewed it, he offered to write the score.

He wrote, "It has often been said that the best dramatic background music for a motion picture is that which is not heard. At least, not consciously heard . . ." Setting the mood was probably the most difficult work he had ever tried to do. Intellectually, he could accept the concept that wherever music and dialogue, or even music and background noise, were in conflict, music had to go. Emotionally it was harder: "I found myself pleading for a beloved G-flat . . ." The score was a great success and, as a symphonic suite, was often played during Bernstein's lifetime. Some critics thought they heard a new element in his music, "a curiously piercing purity that seemed to burst from a hot core of originality," in *Time*'s overheated phrases. The film received twelve Academy Award nominations, including one for best musical score. It would receive eight Oscars, equaling the former record-holder, *Gone With the Wind,* but none for its music. Bernstein's work was passed over in favor of the score for *The High and the Mighty* by Dimitri Tiomkin, by general agreement highly derivative and not to be compared with that of *On the Waterfront*. That disappointment may account for the fact that Bernstein never wrote another film score. It could also be that he found the role of the film composer too recessive.

Bernstein soon returned to his favorite milieu, collaborating with Lillian Hellman on *The Lark,* a play about Joan of Arc by Jean Anouilh that she had adapted. He wrote incidental music for a mixed-voice chorus and countertenor, showing the versatility and suppleness of his imagination by composing in medieval polyphony. It was a minor exercise, but it served to cement his friendship with Hellman during the anti-Communist purges of the 1950s. They both wanted to make an artistic statement on behalf of human freedoms and thought they had found just the right vehicle, Voltaire's *Candide.* Hellman said she had reread the novel since childhood, for its humor and because it attacked "all rigid thinking . . . all isms." Bernstein voiced similar sentiments. "Puritanical snobbery, phony moralism, inquisitorial attacks on the individual, brave-new-world optimism, essential superiority—aren't these all charges leveled against American society by our best thinkers? And they are also charges made by Voltaire against his own society."

Voltaire, the iconoclastic French poet and philosopher who has been called the father of the French Revolution, was the leading voice for tolerance and freedom in the eighteenth century. *Candide, or The Optimist* is a picaresque novel written in protest against a philosophy which the author himself had once espoused. His early views had been influenced by the German philosopher Gottfried Wilhelm Leibniz and the English poet Alexander Pope, who were proponents of the theory of providentialism and of an all-embracing, hierarchical universe. For, as Pope thought, "God sends not ill, if rightly understood." However, that all was for the best in the best of all possible worlds was being used to justify the grossest excesses of the age. If there were no wars, man would not appreciate peace; therefore he should submit to the horrors of war. As Tom Donnelly wrote, " 'Optimism' is thus equated with a callous acceptance of evil . . ."

One of the scenes in *Candide* is based on an actual event, the great earthquake of Lisbon in 1775, which caused the deaths of tens of thousands of people. This event served to convince Voltaire of the imperfections of "optimism," since it could not account for the random violence of fate. In his eyes, the only true evil was to deny this reality. A man had better avoid abstractions as he would the plague, come to terms with life, accept his human limitations and confine himself to the practical considerations of work, home and family: in short, cultivate his garden.

Lillian Hellman, 1930s

As a way to dramatize what they thought about political intolerance, *Candide* was an ambitious choice for Hellman and Bernstein. But
it contained some practical difficulties. Candide's travails—he suffers
through thirty blows of fate before he comes to his senses—make a single repetitive point that would have to be handled with just the right
touch if it was not to become tedious. A great deal of judicious cutting
was needed and one might question whether the theater was the best
medium for a narrative that seemed better suited to film.

Another challenge had to do with the style itself. Voltaire's clarity,
simplicity and wit, Lytton Strachey wrote, reached the summit of their
perfection in *Candide.* His prose "reminds one of a pirouette . . . executed with all the grace, all the ease, all the latent strength of a consummate dancer"; his novel was "the final embodiment of the most
characteristic qualities of French genius." Finally there was the challenge of the message itself, which, while rejecting simplistic solutions,
was not exactly pessimistic, either. Voltaire held out a ray of hope since

man still had free will and therefore choices. To convey the underlying seriousness of purpose, to demonstrate that Voltaire's diatribe concealed a genuine concern, a humanist's view, required a skill equal to his own.

Bernstein and Hellman began work on their *Candide* early in 1954. "We're having a fling at this thing," Bernstein told a reporter, as excited as he always was at the start of anything new. "It was her idea, but there's nothing official about it yet." He was working on the violin-and-orchestra piece that would become the Serenade for Solo Violin, String Orchestra, Harp and Percussion, based on Plato's *Symposium;* it had been commissioned by the Koussevitzky Foundation and would have its first performance in the autumn of 1954 at the Venice Festival. He was also at work on a book of imaginary conversations between "real people," as he described it. "It's an amusing way to say some things of stature without sounding like a fool." That, unfortunately, was already five years overdue. The original title had been *Conversations at Thirty* and was now being called *Conversations at Thirty-five.* Since he was then in his thirty-sixth year, he joked that by the time it was finished, the book would be *Conversations at Seventy.*

Bernstein interrupted his collaboration with Hellman to write for *On the Waterfront* but was back working on the project by early summer and had contributed some frothy melodies in the style of Verdi, he told David Diamond. He was on leave from Tanglewood, and he, Felicia and Jamie were living in the Ratclin house at Lambert's Cove in Martha's Vineyard, Massachusetts, one of their favorite vacation places. John La Touche was writing the lyrics, and Bernstein had some guardedly optimistic things to say about those when he reported on his progress to Diamond. Hellman's script was developing in an offbeat, unexpected way; it was obviously not going to be commercial. The *Symposium* piece was bound to be dismissed by Italian critics because it was not in the fashionable twelve-tone style but lush, melodic and romantic. By November, La Touche had left and Hellman and Bernstein had decided to do their own lyrics. It was a great relief. Bernstein was about to make a mad dash for the finish and thought he could have a new operetta in two months. He also told Diamond that they were expecting another baby.

Bernstein's prediction that he could dispatch *Candide* as brilliantly as he had *Wonderful Town* was, for once, wide of the mark. Two years later, in May of 1956, he and Hellman were still working on *Candide* at Vineyard Haven. This time they had the capable assistance of Richard Wilbur, a young poet who had never written lyrics but who had written a much-admired translation of *The Misanthrope* by Molière. Meanwhile, Bernstein was also writing a new musical that he had told Diamond about, based on the Romeo and Juliet theme, with Robbins, Arthur Laurents and a clever young kid named Steve Sondheim. The double exercise was proving quite a challenge, even for him. While the versions came and went (even Dorothy Parker and James Agee contributed to the cause), Wilbur and Bernstein sat and struggled.

Given Bernstein's reputation for procrastination in later years, Wilbur thought his collaborator was capable of doing some "remarkably concentrated, quick" work, particularly for concerts he was about to conduct. It was true that he had trouble coming up with music and tended to put off the evil day. "He never had as much melodic invention as he wanted to have," Wilbur said, "and kept producing pieces of music he had already written for people's anniversaries. For instance, the schottische, 'Bon Voyage,' had originally been written for his son Alexander's birthday. The pilgrims' chorus . . . was written originally for Lillian's birthday.

"I once wrote a lyric that everyone, including the director, Tony [Tyrone] Guthrie, liked, and gave it to Bernstein to set. A couple of days later he came back saying he had no idea how to do it, and could we go back to a piece of music he had written earlier and fit some words to that? Tony Guthrie said to him, 'Lenny, we know you weren't working yesterday. We know you were waterskiing all day at Piggy Warburg's. Now will you please sit down and write this music?' And so he did."

On another occasion they had disagreed about something and were at a stalemate. Wilbur said, "Neither of us was very good at knock-down quarreling, so we were sitting there sort of unhappy and mute." Wilbur began to whistle the aria "Pace, pace" from *La forza del destino*. Bernstein recognized it, went over to the piano and started to play it. "It was so attractively self-forgetful . . . of him that we immediately stopped quarreling and made up our brief difference."

During one of *Candide*'s intermediate stages Irving Fine wrote to tell his wife that he had had dinner with Bernstein and listened to Hellman talking about the work in progress and "finally heard a few things from *Candide*. Hellman is a very impressive, one might almost say austere woman. She takes the *Candide* book very seriously. Judging from the few excerpts I heard from Lenny's music she takes it far more seriously than he does. The numbers I heard were a curious kind of Americanized Gilbert and Sullivan. Well done, and very deft in their treatment of words, but not particularly original." As for Bernstein, though he was calling *Candide* an operetta, there is no doubt he was trying to write in the grand manner, a work in which pathos and tragedy would be closely allied underneath a highly polished surface. He said, "It's the very hardest work I've done for the theater. I hope it will be my best. I think the hardest should be the best, don't you?"

Candide made its debut in Boston in the autumn of 1956 and arrived at the Martin Beck Theatre in New York at the end of the year. It had a distinguished cast. Max Adrian, who had appeared with the Old Vic as well as in a string of clever British revues, played Dr. Pangloss. Robert Rounseville, who had had a tremendous success in the film version of *The Tales of Hoffmann,* was Candide. Barbara Cook, famous for her roles in *Oklahoma!* and *Carousel,* played Cunégonde, the heroine. Besides Tyrone Guthrie, its distinguished director, there was Oliver Smith, Bernstein's reliable collaborator, who designed the sets.

By the time it was produced, *Candide* had developed far from Hellman's original conception of a play with music, like her version of *The Lark.* Wilbur said, "The music got bigger and bigger and the scenes got to be 'numbers.' " As for the political comment, there is a story, perhaps apocryphal, that the Federal Bureau of Investigation had infiltrated the orchestra so successfully that there were more FBI agents than musicians. Wilbur could not verify that but said, "I can see why the story might arise. The swats we took at McCarthy did alarm our producers." *Candide* may have begun in order to draw a meaningful parallel, but it was "one from which the show drew back." Wilbur had originally written an Inquisition scene which carried the bulk of Hellman's message, but it was dropped in the final version. So were even relatively mild comments which the producers thought would wound some section or other of the audience. Wilbur quoted the line "a bloody North African riot," written for the song "Quiet," as one example. There was also a nonsense line in Spanish that Felicia Bernstein had contributed to "I am easily assimilated" which, when translated, meant "I am busting out with a hernia." The producers feared that the sensibilities of some Spaniard would be bruised.

Their concerns, Wilbur thought, stemmed from the amount of money invested. He had a dim memory that the wigs alone cost $8,000 and the total was $300,000, very high for those days. *Candide* was judged "overproduced," and during the Boston tryouts everyone was apprehensive. Wilbur said, "People who were believed to know Broadway said that if we got five favorable reviews out of seven *Candide* would run for a year. As it happened, we got six out of seven," but the show was a financial failure.

Wilbur believed the problem with *Candide* was fundamental. "If one looks for faults, the inherent fault is that it's a one-joke novel that goes on for thirty chapters. On the stage what one sees, on the one hand, is the repetition of a single joke, and one feels that the changes brought about in Candide and Cunégonde are artificially imposed by the expediencies of the stage. Their experiences, in short, are not sufficient to make them wise. This inherent weakness is nobody's fault."

In the crucial final scene Candide has decided to take the advice of an old gardener, forget about philosophizing and cultivate his own plot of land. Wilbur said, "It's extremely hard to write a big finale which will leave the audience knuckling away tears when the message is 'Don't be so silly' and 'Hold yourself back.' " That was another of *Candide*'s handicaps. Given these limitations, Bernstein contributed one of his best songs, "Make Our Garden Grow," which has had an enduring appeal. Candide and Cunégonde sing, "We're neither pure nor wise nor good." Wilbur said, "I can assure you that Lenny didn't initiate those words, but he set them with fervor."

Candide closed after seventy-three performances, many of them given to empty seats. If *Candide*'s creators had retreated from drawing overt political morals, they also removed the sting from Voltaire's sexual satire. As Mary McCarthy pointed out, Voltaire has his hero banished and the romance with Cunégonde is broken off because the pair are discovered making love behind a screen. Hellman rewrote the scene to make the outbreak of war the cause of the ruptured romance. Similarly, the song Wilbur wrote about an attack of syphilis, which attempted to look on the bright side ("'Twas Love, great Love, that did the deed, / Through Nature's gentle laws, / And how should ill effects proceed / From so divine a cause?"), was also cut. "Thus, Voltaire's point about the 'old Adam,' which is both Candide's salvation and his nemesis as it drives him into and out of his scrapes, is nullified. The play suffers, in the last analysis, from a failure of nerve," Carl Rollyson, Hellman's biographer, wrote.

Robert Lewis, who directed *Candide* in London three years later, said that the failure of audiences to "get the point" was the main problem. No one had ever seen a "hybrid" quite like it before and the reaction in London was much the same as it had been in New York: "Opera fans did not go to the West End looking for operas, and for people who came expecting a musical it was too serious. It was the *Regina* syndrome," he said, referring to Blitzstein's adaptation of Hellman's *The Little Foxes,* which suffered much the same fate when it first appeared. "When I knew I would be directing *Candide* I asked for a meeting with Hellman

Barbara Cook singing her famous aria, "Glitter and Be Gay," from Bernstein's *Candide,* 1956; and Max Adrian, as Dr. Pangloss, performing the Venice gavotte

in July 1958 in Martha's Vineyard." She gave him a box of notes for proposed changes but refused to make them herself. "Hellman has said her disillusion with the theater started with *Candide,* but she conceded she was not a collaborator." He heard nothing more from *Candide's* playwright until their opening night in Liverpool, just before London, when she suddenly appeared and started giving detailed notes to each of the actors about their roles—characters they had been playing for a month—moments before they were to step out on stage. Lewis said, "My favorite reaction came from Edith Coates, who was playing the Old Lady; she just smiled sardonically and said 'Lovely!' "

By general agreement the great loss was Bernstein's music. His overture, one of his most frequently performed works, has exactly the right mocking, impish, nose-thumbing mood, full of preposterous assertion, parodying false hopes and revealing, behind the buffoonery, the occasional moment of tender melody, summing up in its vitality and headlong pace all that Voltaire's satire implied. Lewis said, "Bernstein was the perfect composer because he could write 'funny' music—'Glitter and Be Gay' is the quintessential take-off from the Jewel Song of *Faust*—and because he was not a 'show business' composer but a legitimate composer, his work still had that quality of concert music. I don't know anyone who is writing that way now." His songs were full of such sophisticated parodies, borrowing from Gilbert and Sullivan, Verdi and even Irish ballads, complete with a harp. Perhaps the funniest is his "Mazurka," a deft parody of a Viennese waltz after Franz Lehár, with much use of musical jokes: deliberate wrong notes, much crashing and bumping and a few honks thrown in for good measure. Then there is "You Were Dead, You Know," a parody of the kind of song in which hero and heroine each discover that the other is still alive: Nelson Eddy and Jeanette MacDonald could not have been any more fatuous. Finally there was the heartfelt and instantly memorable finale, "Make Our Garden Grow," in which the composer comes out from behind his many masks and makes a moving plea for tolerance and understanding.

Candide might never have been seen again but for the enthusiasm of Robert Kalfin, director of the Chelsea Theater Center of Brooklyn. Kalfin had wanted to mount a new production of *Candide* ever since he first saw it. In 1974, some eighteen years later, he suggested the project to Harold Prince, who had produced *West Side Story.* Prince at first thought the work could not be revived: there seemed to be no common meeting ground between Hellman's script, Voltaire's novel and Bernstein's music. But he was won over by Kalfin's enthusiasm and the opportunities for a new kind of knockabout staging offered by the Chelsea, a theater in the round.

Hellman was approached, but while she refused to revise her own script, she did not object to having someone else write a new version. Kalfin engaged Hugh Wheeler, who had written the book for *A Little Night Music,* a Sondheim musical that Prince had produced and directed. Wheeler, eschewing any attempt at satire or political commentary, concentrated on *Candide*'s madcap humor. He invented some new characters (Voltaire himself appears as narrator), envisioned some new scenes and went back to Bernstein for some additional music. Sondheim agreed to write more lyrics and Prince began his casting. Rather than hire prominent singers from opera or musical comedy, as had been done for the first productions, Prince deliberately looked for *ingénues,* the younger the better, because "I know that when you're talking about rape and destruction . . . and such cynicism in comic terms, that it's enormously aided by a sense that wraps the entire show—of optimism really, of ingenuousness, of vitality, of naïveté."

Without its dark undertones *Candide* was an antic romp, a cross between a circus and a funhouse, and the production was enormously aided by an ingenious, multilevel set that placed the spectators in the middle of the action. This "faster and frothier" version now had "a sort of light intellectual jump to it, like the skittering of ideas through an exceptionally agile and civilized mind." The new *Candide,* now simply billed as a "musical," moved to the Broadway Theater and played to packed houses for 741 performances.

This should have been the final version, but the composer was not entirely satisfied. In the interests of staging the orchestra had dwindled to thirteen musicians, and that included three keyboard players. A great deal of material close to his heart had been discarded. What was needed was one more version, which would restore some of this material and incorporate the best aspects of the original production while retaining the Wheeler approach. Eight years later, in 1982, the New York City Opera presented its version at the New York State Theater, with Prince again directing. Most of the critics agreed that *Candide* had been further embellished. They also thought that what once more was being called an operetta had an outstanding score. Peter G. Davis wrote, "This is probably Bernstein's grandest, wittiest, most sophisticated theater score, showing the full range of his talents: simple ballads, intricate ensembles, zany operatic parodies, a Coplandesque choral finale of heart-stopping beauty, dance sequences of ingenious rhythmic diversity, and irresistible tunes at every turn, all of it crafted with a virtuosity far beyond the capacities of most Broadway composers." When the composer arrived fashionably late just before the curtain was raised on opening night, he was given a standing ovation by the audience. He received another before the start of the final act.

There would be yet another version, this one in 1988, directed by Jonathan Miller for Scottish Opera. John Wells, a British playwright, recalled that Miller had asked him to codirect the revival, and it soon became evident that *Candide* needed to be drastically reorganized, if not completely rewritten. Wells agreed to help reshape the piece and went back to Voltaire. He was living in London and, he wrote, "immediately started running into objections from members of the Bernstein entourage . . . saying, 'Lenny wouldn't like that!' so I decided . . . to get on a plane and go and see him.

"Richard Mantle of Scottish Opera came with me, and we met Lenny in Connecticut. He was wearing jeans and cowboy boots and a blue shirt, smoking a cigarette and standing on the deck outside his studio. He was friendly but daunting. I was nervous.

"A few hours later he said he wanted to hear the script, and sat opposite me across the fireplace, sniping. He couldn't understand my accent, 'Speak more clearly,' what did a 'lit area' mean? 'A "litaria," what's that? Is that some Latin word, like "vomitorium"?'

"To cut a long story short, we got on. He was particularly happy about Candide singing the 'Cunégonde Lament' over the body of Cunégonde rather than in limbo as he receives the news, as had been the case in earlier versions. I suppose the crucial thing from my point of view was a scrap of paper he found among the drafts of music . . . it was the 'Westphalia Chorale,' which I said the moment I heard it ought to be included in the piece, and which eventually recurred three times, making a kind of frame, although we only put words to it later . . .

"I suppose that trip lasted about three days. What we had at the end of that was a clear idea of the sequence of numbers, the narrative, and what episodes in the book would be included. One I was particularly fond of, where Candide shoots a pair of monkeys he thinks are raping two ladies in South America and then discovers that the monkeys are their lovers, unfortunately went later on, cut by Jonathan Miller because he didn't feel the hand-puppet monkeys I'd bought . . . quite harmonised with the . . . set."

The Scottish Opera version went on to the Old Vic in London in 1989 and served as the definitive version for a concert performance that Bernstein himself conducted and recorded at the end of his life.

That *Candide* had a unique significance for him is clear. Bernstein told his musical advisor, Matthew Epstein, "There's more of me in that piece than anything else I have done."

The fact that Bernstein was continually trying to categorize the works that he wrote in the 1950s: *Trouble in Tahiti, Candide,* and *West Side Story,* is a clue to his aims. He did not want to write operetta, or musical comedy, or even opera, but something so new no one had a name for it. In his determination to fuse popular and high culture he became something of a proselytizer for the idea; he wrote articles and devoted a television program to the subject. What to call it, how to describe it, what elements to use, how to educate his audience, how to make the new form uniquely American, all obsessed him. However, unlike architects who were competing to invent a quintessentially American style in the mid–nineteenth century, he and other contemporary composers were hardly venturing into virgin territory. The team of Rodgers and Hammerstein had, in the postwar years, swept all before them with an astounding string of successes: *Oklahoma!, Carousel, Allegro, South Pacific* and *The King and I.* They had taken musical comedy and by means of an expert blending of dialogue, dance and song turned it into musical theater. Presumably Bernstein could argue that their goals had been more modest and "commercial" than his own. They merely aimed to please. He intended to instruct with Voltairean satire on the one hand and inspire with pity and awe by means of Shakespearean tragedy on the other. But he could hardly claim to be the first to tackle serious themes, since Rodgers and Hammerstein had already done so as far back as *Carousel.* As for fusing high and low art, Brecht and Weill had shown what could be done with *The Threepenny Opera* and *Mahagonny.* Given these formidable precursors, Bernstein took refuge in semantics. His would have more of this and less of that. His theater would succeed in such fresh and inventive ways that it became something that transcended all other forms; it would be Wagner's vision, a Total Theater. His new collaborators, Robbins and Laurents, had more modest goals. Robbins hoped that they, as "long-haired" artists, could bring a new perspective to a popular medium. Laurents hoped Bernstein would not try to do anything as grand as an opera.

. . .

West Side Story had its first performance in Washington, D.C., less than a year after *Candide,* but its origins went back eight years, and, again, it owed its existence to an idea of Jerry Robbins's. As early as January 1949 Robbins had come to Bernstein with a proposal that they make a modern-day version of *Romeo and Juliet,* using the conflict between Jews and Catholics during the Easter-Passover celebrations as a contemporary equivalent. Bernstein was immediately intrigued and especially liked the inclusion of Arthur Laurents as playwright, since he had written *Home of the Brave,* which Bernstein found immensely affecting. However, when he saw what Laurents planned to do with the subject, he dropped out, pleading a hectic conducting schedule. He did not like the book or the tone. There the matter would have rested, but Robbins approached him again six years later. Why not revive the *Romeo* idea? That summer Bernstein discussed it with Laurents in Beverly Hills and a new idea took hold, that of shifting the subject matter to Puerto Rican gang violence. And it was another New York subject, the third in a row. Bernstein said afterwards:

> It's this town that still gets me. No wonder I keep composing about it. I've lived here for so long, sometimes I don't even notice it any more—and then I open my eyes and, my god! It's so dramatic and so alive! Like the time I was coming out of the Henry Hudson Parkway. I'd been mulling over the *West Side* score and I didn't take the right exit, I think. Somehow I was under a huge causeway somewhere right by the river up around 125th street. All around me Puerto Rican kids were playing, with those typical New York City shouts and the New York raucousness. And yet the causeway backdrop was in a classic key, pillars and Roman arches. The contrast was a fascination. It really contained the theme of *West Side Story.* You know, contemporary content echoing a classic myth. Suddenly I had the inspiration for the rhumba scene. We even used that wonderful causeway in the set.

The comment is fascinating because it provides a major clue to the creative process which, for Bernstein, was a constant matter for analysis. At about that time he developed an elaborate theory to describe the way ideas came to him. In order to create he had to put himself in a properly contemplative frame of mind, which involved lying on a sofa or the floor, attempting to reach that twilight state between consciousness and sleep when images began to rise to the surface. That, he believed, was when his creative vision was clearest. The important thing was that one had to be completely relaxed, so that it all happened "while you're not looking. If you're looking, nothing will happen." He knew that it could not come from the conscious, controlling, critical part of his brain. In this discussion of how a work is created Bernstein omitted an essential element in the equation. What is clear about all of his early work is that he wrote at his best when most excited by the potential of the work and carried along by it. Once sufficiently stimulated, he could immediately go to the piano with the germ of an idea, "and you don't know what you're going to do next, and then you're doing something else next, and you can't stop doing the next thing . . ." *West Side Story* was having that exhilarating effect on him, and ideas were pouring out.

However, at first he did not have a lyricist. Comden and Green were approached and turned the idea down; "Thank God," Laurents said, "because it wasn't for them." Stephen Sondheim had auditioned for Laurents, and when they met again by chance, Laurents realized that he was the perfect choice. Sondheim, who would demonstrate his gifts as a composer, was not particularly keen, even at a relatively untested stage, to work as a mere lyricist. He was persuaded by his mentor, Oscar Hammerstein II, that *West Side Story* would be a useful exercise.

Sondheim recalled that Bernstein had already written lyrics in what he thought was an appropriate form but which struck him as excruciatingly embarrassing. He said, "The music was so rich that if the lyrics are too ripe and fruity you have overdone it." It was perhaps the difference in response to be expected from an introvert for whom the deepest feelings are always understated and an effusive, impressionable extrovert. Original documents in the Library of Congress show that Bernstein's lyrics were at once maudlin and pretentious. For instance, in the song "I Feel Pretty," in which the heroine, Maria, describes the effect of falling in love with Tony, in Bernstein's version her words are commented upon admiringly by her listeners. Sondheim went to work and in the final version, Maria's infatuation gets the sardonic retorts that provide the necessary corrective.

Sondheim rewrote as much as he dared but still feels too much of the original Bernstein hearts and flowers remained in place, because he was unsure of himself. He said, of some of the worst songs, "They still make my blood curdle." Apart from this, the collaboration was close and differences were minor. Sondheim said, "Perhaps he was a little too

Rehearsing during the tryouts: Bernstein, with Carol Lawrence at right and Stephen Sondheim at the piano

Left to right: Stephen Sondheim, Arthur Laurents, Hal Prince, Robert Griffith (seated), Bernstein and Jerome Robbins on the *West Side Story* set, 1957

picky about the lyrics. He tended to want to argue over every word. As I got more confident, I would sometimes interfere with the music." Their working styles were at variance. "I'm a slow, steady worker. I keep going day and night, mulling it over." Whereas Bernstein tended to want to work in short bursts unless there was a deadline, in which case he was virtually indefatigable. "We got our tensions out with word games. I introduced him to the *Listener* crossword puzzle and at the anagram table I drove him crazy because, to his dying day, he never beat me."

The working title had been *East Side Story* but, after Laurents shifted the original idea of a conflict between Catholics and Jews to ethnic gangs on the Upper West Side, a title change was essential. Laurents said he brought up the title of "Gangway!" as a joke, "but to my horror, they took it so seriously, it was stencilled on the back of the scenery and stayed there even after reason prevailed." In its early stages the musical achieved a certain notoriety for being turned down by everyone. No one thought such a "serious" subject (there are bodies on the floor at the end of Act One, and the hero, of course, dies at the end) would have any appeal. Walter Trenerry, then counsel and advisor to the St. James Theater in New York, jokes that his claim to fame was advising against backing *West Side Story*. Others could make the same claim. Finally Cheryl Crawford and Roger Stevens agreed to produce, but that was before *Candide* was an ostentatious flop. It was clear that *West Side Story* was going to lose money for everyone.

Laurents said, "Cheryl Crawford lied to me. We had a famous audition at a house on the East River owned by a wealthy lady named Bea Lawrence. It was before the days of air conditioning, and it was hot, the windows were open and you could hear the tugboats going up and down. I told the story, Lenny played and everybody sang. No one offered a nickel. Roger Stevens, who was there, was going abroad. He called me and said, 'Cheryl's gone cold but I will stick, no matter what.' Cheryl called and we had a meeting the following Monday, which was just six weeks before rehearsals were due to begin. She had been saying things to Jerry Robbins like 'The book is no good' and, to me, that Jerry Robbins was no good. Anyway, she said she was pulling out. There was a woman there, Sylvia Mazzola, a fund-raiser for Stevens, and I said to Cheryl, 'Does Roger agree?' and she said, 'Oh yes!' but Sylvia was sitting there silently shaking her head at me. So I said, 'Cheryl, you're an immoral woman.' "

Laurents called Stevens in Europe and got his promise to provide a temporary loan until another team of producers could be found. In desperation, they were prepared to enter *West Side Story* as part of a series of musicals planned for City Center, which meant that it would have closed after two weeks. But then Sondheim got in touch with a friend of his. While still in his twenties, Harold Prince had become famous for co-producing three successful musicals: *Pajama Game, Damn Yankees* and *New Girl in Town.* He and his partner, Robert Griffith, had never had a failure, and their past successes had earned more than $10 million. Unknown to Bernstein, Prince had already been approached informally. He said, "Lenny didn't want people to hear the score. People would always do that. Richard Rodgers wouldn't even tell his family. But Steve had played it for me and I had memorized it. When I got Steve's call for help I flew to New York from Boston and went to Lenny's at the Osborne. Arthur, Jerry and Bernstein's old music publisher were there and Lenny played the score. I had been warned by Steve not to recognize it. I couldn't help singing along, and Bernstein said, 'That's what I need. A producer who understands music.'" Apart from his bridge loan Stevens played no further role, and neither did Crawford. Prince and Griffith found the needed $300,000 within a week.

As a pivotal figure, Laurents had to shape the musical's concept, and collaboration began at the earliest possible moment, even before the actual dialogue was written. Only after these discussions did he begin writing, "to stay ahead of them," he explained. "For instance, Steve had to take diction and character from the playwright; then he and Lenny would work on the songs. As for Jerry Robbins, he is part of Antony Tudor's literary tradition of choreography and would want to know what the dance was about, so I would write him a scenario.

"Originally we had Tony and Maria meeting at a dance as the first scene, but Jerry argued we had to meet them before that, so I wrote two introductory scenes. The song 'Something's Coming' was originally a speech, but Steve and Lenny saw it as a song, and that's the way it ended up. There were pieces of dialogue that were originally intended as songs and vice versa." Ideas went back and forth. For the climactic balcony scene Bernstein had written "One Hand, One Heart," which the others liked but thought was in the wrong place. When they could not decide, Hammerstein was brought in to give his verdict. He agreed that the placement was wrong, the song was moved to a later spot, and "Tonight" took its place.

Laurents said, "All three of them fought me on 'Gee, Officer Krupke,' but I sold it to them by arguing that the song was the equivalent of the clowns in Shakespeare." That was one of their few artistic disagreements. He said, "When we opened in Washington and realized we had a surprising success we decided we needed another song, this one for the three youngest kids in the gang. Lenny and Steve instantly wrote a song called 'Kid Stuff' and we all listened to it. To show you how close the collaboration was, we all agreed at once that it could not stay. It tipped the show over into musical comedy.

"Lenny was a marvelous collaborator. He was enormously enthusiastic and generous beyond belief." Bernstein was originally listed as co-lyricist but decided that the Sondheim contribution was so major that he should receive the sole credit. He later said he had received a great education from "that young man." That kind of gesture, Laurents said, was almost unheard of in musical theater.

Robbins, who had persevered with the concept despite discouragements, was equally influential. By then he had built a distinguished reputation with *On the Town, The King and I* and *Peter Pan,* and the interdependence of choreography and music put Robbins, who was also the director, into an intense working relationship with Bernstein. Bernstein said later that the challenge of the work was to maintain the right balance between poetry and realism, which meant walking an artistic tightrope:

> The last scene of the first act is a typical West side "rumble," a free-for-all knife fight between the two rival gangs. As Jerry staged it, the fight is as good, as frightening as any I've . . . seen in a Gary Cooper Western, and yet it's choreographed to my music from beginning to end. That's where the tightrope comes in. If the "rumble" had been too balletic, we would have fallen off on one side—all you'd have is just another ballet. And if it had been too realistic, we would have fallen off on the other side— there would have been no poetry, no art. Now carry that example to every single detail in the show and you can understand why *West Side Story* was such hard work to put together . . .

By then Robbins had a reputation for being brilliant but demanding. The late Larry Kert, who played Tony, said, "rehearsals were a very painful experience. Jerry Robbins is an incredible man . . . but he is a painful man—a perfectionist who sees himself in every role, and if you come onstage and don't give him exactly what he's pictured the night before, his tolerance level is too low, so in his own kind of way he destroys you." Robbins was famous for his ability to get his own way, and Bernstein was powerless against him. The conductor Yuri Krasnopolsky said, "I know years ago from Lenny's own lips that one of the people he respected most in the world and who intimidated him most was Jerry Robbins. He was terrified of making a whisper of criticism in case Jerry should be angry." When queried, Robbins expressed surprise that Bernstein supposedly feared him and said that he had seen no sign of this when they worked together. His explanation was that perhaps Bernstein did not like being pushed to come up with material. He was, Robbins thought, something of a procrastinator, a common trait in creative people.

Sondheim recalled:

> At one point in Washington during the *West Side Story* tryout . . . Robbins took over the orchestra from Lenny and inserted some music to fit a choreographic idea that he had just created.
>
> Lenny was in the back of the theater and when he saw what was happening he started to storm down the aisle. I thought he was going to go after Jerry. But then he stopped, turned around and practically ran out of the theater. I ran after him and found him in the bar next door to the theater with five shots of whisky in front of him. He was furious and miserable and I think was probably hating himself for not standing up for his music. He just couldn't stand an ugly, screaming scene.

Another point of conflict arose during the Philadelphia performances. It had been agreed that dancers and actors would not stop for applause because, Laurents said, "we didn't want the actors to step out of character. We wanted the whole thing to go like a steamroller." However, there is a moment when a big ballet in the second act is immediately followed by a concluding sequence during which Tony and Maria, sitting on a bed in a tiny room, sing a reprise of the last eight bars of "Somewhere." Jerry Robbins said that Griffith, the producer, suggested they try a black-out following the ballet. Laurents said, "Thinking the sequence was over, the audience erupted in applause and kept clapping," while Tony and Maria tried to go on singing. At the end of "Somewhere" there was silence. Robbins agreed that the black-out should be dropped. Somehow, however, there was a black-out at the identical moment on opening night in New York. Robbins called it an accident but Bernstein plainly did not believe him at the time. Laurents recalled that

"Lenny came running up the aisle, angry as hell and saying, 'Where is he? I'll kill the son of a bitch!' "

Perhaps the failure of *Candide* had dealt a blow to Bernstein's artless belief that everything he touched must turn to gold. Krasnopolsky went to the first rehearsal of *West Side Story.* "I remember him saying, 'I think we have a show. What do you think?' I replied I thought it was a stunning ballet, but as a musical it was somber. Some days later I saw him on Fifty-seventh Street and he said to me, almost pleadingly, 'All I meant was, *with work?*' "

Apart from finding backers, casting thirty-eight people who could sing and dance was the most difficult aspect of the production. Robbins, Bernstein and Laurents all wanted youthful unknowns, and they came in their thousands from high schools, ballet companies, college choirs and nightclubs. Few of the good singers had the advanced dancing skills Robbins demanded, so they settled for dancers who could sing. The final choices were agonizing. Kenneth LeRoy, who had joined the production as an assistant stage manager, finally agreed to read for several different roles. This was narrowed to three, and he was not picked for a role, that of Bernardo, leader of the Sharks, until the last minute. Much the same experience happened to Larry Kert, who played Tony, the Romeo figure. He auditioned for so many roles that "when I first heard I had gotten a part I didn't know which one." Mickey Calin (later known as Michael Callan), who became Riff, the leader of the native-born gang, the Jets, was rejected at two auditions and given no word of the response after his third. He learned he had a role while he was on tour with another show in Valley Forge, Pennsylvania.

Carol Lawrence, who played the part of the Puerto Rican Juliet, arrived for her audition looking, she thought, in character, with plenty of jewelry and heavy makeup. Robbins told her to take a shower and come back. She was called to sing and dance twice. On the third call, the question of her age was raised. She hesitated because she was twenty-three and she knew her character was supposed to be seventeen. Then someone yelled, "She's exactly seventeen!" and everybody laughed. Laurents said he was the one who had spoken up. "By that time I knew that Carol was our girl, and I wouldn't have cared if she was seventy."

Laurents realized that his composer had written some exceptional music the first time he heard a run-through. "That was the most exciting moment for me. The thing that distinguishes American theater music is its vitality and its complex rhythms, the qualities to be found in Bernstein, and to me those qualities reach their peak in *West Side*

Story. It was the best theater music that's ever been written. He didn't think. The music just poured out of him. He somehow knew how to take the vernacular and raise it up, make it music instead of a pastiche. He had that rare quality of being able to feel each character; he was a musical dramatist." Among his innovations was the ending of the first act. "You always end with a bang and he had this little piddling out, but it was exactly right. That's Lenny. And the first time you heard that music with an orchestra, you went out of your head.

"For me it was the artistic pinnacle of his career, but it wasn't for him. The reason was cultural snobbism. Musical theater is an art form, but he couldn't believe it. He didn't trust his innate talent and his instincts."

Critics were just as admiring. Robert Evett observed that Bernstein had brought to the score a sophisticated and seemingly inexhaustible technique, far beyond that of most Broadway tunesmiths, allied to what he suspected was a missionary zeal. "Music is a cause for him, and it would be like him to use a medium as unpretentious as the musical as a means of popularizing the abstruse technical tricks of modern composition, much as C. S. Lewis uses science fiction as a vehicle for austere theological dogma."

Other critics agreed. "Bernstein's music has a wide and impressive range. It can be harsh and ominous, cheerfully antic, and really quite lovely," Wolcott Gibbs wrote. Brooks Atkinson said that he had "composed another one of his nervous, flaring scores that capture the shrill beat of life in the streets." Howard Taubman, however, questioned whether the right balance had been struck. The uncompromising theme was there, but he thought the composer had repeatedly capitulated to the Broadway requirement to prettify the emotion and blunt the social commentary. Other critics thought Robbins was a genius as a choreographer but inadequate as a director, and the acting had suffered. No one really cared about the central characters, which robbed the ending of its tragedy and pathos.

Despite these reservations *West Side Story* was a respectable success on Broadway and even more so as a cast recording, with over a million copies sold. Prince said, "The big money that *West Side* made came later from the movie and the record. Our investors are the beneficiaries of that movie sale, which was very small but with a substantial piece of the gross. When we sold it nobody wanted it. No one cared and then it turned out to be this monumental success. The ledger on *West Side* is very handsome—but not because of its life on Broadway." The movie won an Oscar for Best Picture of 1961 and a total of ten Academy Awards.

As posterity has shown, Bernstein had at last written a hit with "Maria"; in fact, with several of the songs. Raphael Hillyer recalled being in a car with him not long after the success of *West Side Story*, tuning the radio to one of the songs and hearing Bernstein declare, "Wow, I'm famous!" David Diamond had a similar anecdote. He said, "We were walking together one summer in the Piazza San Marco in Venice. There was music coming from all the outdoor cafés and, by an amazing coincidence, four bands at once struck up 'Maria.' Bernstein said, 'Listen to that!' and started taking bows. Nobody knew who he was."

The Omnipotent One

Ere old age a dismal shadow casts . . .

— GOETHE, "AN SCHWAGER KRONOS"

In the early days after Bernstein's famous debut, when he was being hailed as "a born conductor" and "the first American-born and American-trained conductor to whom the word 'great' could be applied," it was predicted that such a musician must soon be offered the post of conductor of one of the nation's leading orchestras. As it happened, it took thirteen years; but when the offer did come, it was one of the best. In the autumn of 1956 Bernstein was named co-conductor, with Mitropoulos, of the New York Philharmonic for the 1957–58 season. A year after that, in the autumn of 1958, he became its principal conductor and remained there for ten glorious years.

The appointment was totally unexpected. Bernstein had not been asked to appear as guest conductor since the 1950–51 season, the first Mitropoulos led as principal conductor. In recent years Mitropoulos had repeatedly invited Bruno Walter, George Szell and a young Italian, two years Bernstein's junior, Guido Cantelli, a protégé of Toscanini's, who was, it was rumored, being groomed to succeed Mitropoulos. It would seem that Bernstein's chances at the New York Philharmonic were as slim as they had been everywhere else.

That a musician with such an unorthodox background as a Broadway composer and teenage idol should be chosen was equally surprising. Furthermore, he was very young for such a position, being then thirty-nine and only two years older than the youngest man to have held that post, John Barbirolli, appointed in 1936. However, from another perspective that could be considered an advantage, because so many conductors were growing old. Walter and Szell, Mitropoulos's choices, were eighty and fifty-nine respectively. Fritz Reiner was sixty-eight, Charles Munch, sixty-six, and Mitropoulos himself was sixty. Such great men as Beecham, Stokowski, Boult, Ansermet and Klemperer were reaching or in their seventies. Pierre Monteux and Toscanini were in their eighties. (Toscanini died in his sleep early in 1957.) Of the promising international figures, there were Igor Markevitch at forty-five and Herbert von Karajan at age forty-nine. Only Thomas Schippers, at the age of twenty-seven, was younger than Bernstein.

If he were the right age, he was, in terms of the Philharmonic's bias, from the wrong country. It was the first time in living memory that the position of principal conductor had gone to a native-born musician. Paul Henry Lang, the distinguished musicologist, noted a year later that a young Belgian, Edouard van Remoortel, had been appointed to the position of music director of the St. Louis Symphony Orchestra. Van Remoortel was only thirty-one yet he had been summoned from Belgium to make guest appearances while he was being considered and no Americans had been asked to apply. Even though he was such a young man, he had already conducted every major Belgian orchestra and had been principal conductor of one of them. Lang wrote, "Does anyone imagine that a Belgian orchestra faced with a vacancy would import a young man from abroad without first considering all native candidates?" There was hope, Howard Taubman wrote in the *New York Times*, that Bernstein's appointment would demonstrate that "New York and the nation at large have outgrown the inferiority complex that insisted that only foreigners could be entrusted with our major musical institutions."

Given these obstacles, it is a moot point whether Bernstein could ever have achieved such exalted status in New York were it not that the orchestra was in an uproar. The precipitating factor in the crisis was an article by Taubman in the *Times,* "The Philharmonic—What's Wrong with It and Why," which was published in the spring of 1956, a few months before Bernstein's appointment. As Taubman noted, subscription sales were down and so were ticket sales, and the orchestra's yearly deficit was growing. As for Dimitri Mitropoulos, while it was true that for late-nineteenth- and some twentieth-century works he had an incomparable flair, and could conduct with "an almost feverish intensity," there were too many gaps in his repertoire. He had, perhaps, too malleable a temperament to demand the best from a notoriously unruly group of musicians. As a result the orchestra's tone was slipping. "Attacks and releases, which are the hallmarks of a smartly trained ensemble of the first rank, are often careless. The texture of chords is frequently raveled, with upper, lower and middle voices in inept balance." The New York Philharmonic, once in the forefront of American ensembles, was slipping behind the Philadelphia and Boston Symphony orchestras.

At the root of the problem, Taubman implied, was the continued employment of Arthur Judson as manager. This formidable figure who had joined the New York Philharmonic in 1922 had, by 1956, acquired a position that seemed impregnable. "A.J.," as he was called, born in Dayton, Ohio, on February 17, 1881, was a violinist who took to music management *faute de mieux.* He was six feet tall, extremely handsome and broad-shouldered and apparently such a convincing salesman for his own talents that Denison University in Ohio actually made him dean of its music conservatory at the age of nineteen. He was there for seven years, bringing a series of reforms to the school and staging a number of music festivals that attracted great interest.

He went to New York in 1907 to pursue a recital career but was unsuccessful. So he turned to journalism—he was on the staff of *Musical America*—and then to the music business as manager of the Philadelphia Orchestra. After a few years he was managing artists as a sideline and fascinated by the possibilities presented by the emerging field of radio. In 1926, with three partners and an initial investment of $75,000, he had founded what would become the Columbia Broadcasting System. Within a year Judson had pulled the young company from the brink of bankruptcy and launched his first successful program, the "La Palina Hour." He would later become the second-largest individual stockholder of the Columbia Broadcasting System; in 1938, he was sole owner of Columbia Records.

By the early 1930s Judson, by now a thriving entrepreneur, proposed that he and a group of managers set up something he called Columbia

Concerts (later, Columbia Artists Management, Inc., or CAMI). The idea was simple but ingenious. They should band together to form a countrywide network of community concerts. Local volunteer groups would raise money in advance by selling season subscriptions for a concert series. These groups would book only artists being represented by the managers; advance bookings would remove the element of risk, and the artists would have an audience; it made the business of sending artists out on tours almost easy. The Columbia Broadcasting System put up the necessary advance funds. During the 1930s the rallying call for music went to every town and hamlet and became a civic duty. NBC retaliated with a "Civic Music Service" of its own, and at the height of their success the two organizers claimed to have inaugurated two thousand community concerts.

However, as Milton Goldin pointed out in his study of the music business, *Music Makers,* the performers were as poorly paid as ever. There was the "differential," i.e., the difference between the ostensible fee paid the artist and the one he or she actually received. It was commonplace to charge the concert series a fee of, say, $400 for a performer while the person in question received only $250. Judson's ingenious explanation was that the money CBS had originally advanced to build the network was loaned not to the communities involved but to the artists. The Department of Justice began to take an interest in the Community Concerts Corporation for monopolistic practices and succeeded in breaking the Columbia Artists monopoly. After 1952 the series was open to all comers, in theory at least.

By then Judson had refined his techniques for succeeding in a cutthroat business and applied the same principles once he was president of his own division of Columbia Artists. He discovered that most managers did not bother with conductors, who went to a position and stayed there. They preferred to concentrate on performers, the providers of multiple commissions. But Judson saw that the man in charge of the conductors could "harness their orchestras to CAMI schemes," as Norman Lebrecht explained in *The Maestro Myth,* his groundbreaking study of the business aspects of the classical music world. The man who could shuffle conductors around the country controlled the artists they hired. By then CAMI was the biggest single agency in New York and Judson in a position of immense power. For example, Henri Verbrugghen, born in Brussels in 1873, had been conductor of the Minneapolis Symphony for eight years but was forced to step down because of ill health in 1931. The trustees decided they wanted another Belgian, Leon Barzin, but they had forgotten to consult with Judson. He informed them that they could have Barzin if they wished, but they would not get any soloists from Columbia Artists. Presumably, Barzin was not a client of Judson's. Quite soon, Minneapolis wanted whoever Judson wanted. The Hungarian-born Eugene Ormandy, who was a client of Judson's, was bustled onto a train, still in his evening clothes following a performance, and sent out to Minneapolis.

Leopold Stokowski and Judson were often at swords' points during the former's tenure as music director of the Philadelphia Orchestra. Judson, it is believed, used his influence with the board and Stokowski's vulnerabilities—his fondness for programming difficult modern works and his extended absences—to insinuate Ormandy into the position of co-conductor. The situation continued to deteriorate, and Stokowski was forced out, or left, depending on which version one believes, in 1938. At any rate, "Stokie was Judson's mortal enemy," Halina Rodzinski recalled. There was a photograph of Stokowski always on display in Judson's outer office. It was autographed "To the Omnipotent One."

Judson is always described as courtly and a man of immense intellectual and physical vigor. It is said that his favorite way to work off steam was chopping wood. He brought in twenty-two cords of timber at his summer home in Canada in 1943; he was then sixty-two years old. Halina Rodzinski wrote, "There was something very cold, very aloof about him, something emotionally formal and formidable. He smoked cigars, alternately wielding them like truncheons, batons, or fairy wands . . . I do remember clearly his impeccable grooming and his decorous manners, both very like the style of a sleek businessman."

Even those who feared him—when he said "Jump," the well-known Washington impresario Patrick Hayes quipped, you asked, "How high?"—or hated him conceded that Judson had a gift for spotting new talent. Antonio de Almeida said, "He was really a barroom Irishman, but he had an uncanny sense. I was in his office one day when the phone rang. He asked to be excused, saying he had to go to Carnegie Hall to hear an audition. Would I like to join him? I did. On came this violinist, wearing a double-breasted blazer and gray flannel trousers, and proceeded to play. I thought he was sensational.

"Back at his office I asked, 'You are going to take him, of course?' He said, 'No—there is a flaw in there somewhere'—and he was right. As it turned out, it was one of the great wasted talents, and he spotted it right away. He wouldn't have been there without that gift."

One of the few people to openly challenge Judson was Rodzinski. There had been bad feeling between the men for years. While Rodzinski was under a four-year contract with the Los Angeles Philharmonic in the early 1930s (a contract Judson had not helped him get, even though he was then Rodzinski's agent) Rodzinski regularly paid his hefty 20 percent commission on his salary. That commission was described as a conductor's "insurance" by *Time* magazine some years later. Despite these regular payments, Rodzinski had been marked down in Judson's mental log as a troublemaker. Halina Rodzinski recalled that when Rodzinski went to the New York Philharmonic as guest conductor, Judson vetoed every piece of music he wanted to program and was especially vehement about a concert performance of Richard Strauss's opera *Elektra.* By then it was well known that Judson was musically conservative and considered everything written since Sibelius box-office poison. Rodzinski was furious. Shortly after that, the New York Philharmonic was looking for a music director to replace Toscanini for the 1936–37 season. Rodzinski, knowing that his chances were good, waited confidently for an interview. The call never came. Instead, the trustees hired the young Englishman John Barbirolli, then thirty-seven years old, who had yet to conduct a Beethoven symphony. After some tremendous battles with the terrible-tempered Toscanini, no doubt Judson was determined to find someone more malleable.

Rodzinski kept cancelling his contract with Judson and then reluctantly opening it again. Judson had a monopoly, and without his imprimatur he could not get work. But it was not until Rodzinski became conductor of the New York Philharmonic in 1943 that he discovered how thoroughly Judson had assumed control of the inner workings of that organization during his twenty-year tenure. Rodzinski had become accustomed, as a music director in other cities, to making personal appearances at board meetings. That was no longer allowed in New York. Now Judson "enunciated and elucidated" Rodzinski's ideas to the board. "When it came to the production of a big, expensive work, an operatic or choral work, my husband correctly understood that Judson argued at cross purposes . . . To Judson money saved on an expensive oratorio . . . could be put into fees for a soloist, from which . . . a commission could be extracted." Rodzinski wanted to increase the subscriptions to help pay off the orchestra's annual deficit; Judson did not. Using the logic of an impresario, it was in Judson's interests to have as many single tickets sold at the box office as possible so that he could judge the appeal of his artists. Being privy to board decisions and fee structures, Judson could also demand the maximum fees available.

To find himself working on a daily basis with a man he had always mistrusted did not improve Rodzinski's opinion of Judson; on the contrary, the more he learned, the more indignant he became. Shortly after his tenure began he identified a number of unsatisfactory orchestra players whose continued employment, he suspected, had something to do with the under-the-table payments they were making to Judson. Rodzinski's immediate impulse was to fire them all, bringing down the wrath of the musicians' union on his head. Lacking sufficient proof, he was never able to make public the hidden motivation for the firings, a fact that Judson adroitly exploited, Rodzinski believed. Rodzinski won that particular battle but it was the end of whatever brief reconciliation the two men had had.

When Rodzinski was offered a new contract, he essentially told the board that things had to change before he would sign it. The contract he was being offered gave him first choice of what works would be played, which was something; but he had no control over the programs set by guest conductors. Most important, he had no voice in the hiring of guests and soloists, unless Judson and the board chose to consult him. Judson was a dictator, running, he said, "the worst musical racket in the world." It was unfortunate, perhaps, that Rodzinski had gained a reputation for having a violent and unpredictable temper. The trustees gave Judson a unanimous vote of confidence and Rodzinski left.

He had, however, brought to light a major issue. Virgil Thomson called his resignation "a courageous gesture" towards exposing what had been a scandal. It was one that could only get worse. Nine years later, by 1956, Judson's responsibility for the Philharmonic's problems was too obvious for even the trustees to ignore. Taubman did not assert that artists from Columbia Artists Management had been hired to the exclusion of anyone else. True, they were in the majority; but, on the other hand, that was the biggest agency. However, he did charge that many guest artists, with names like Yankoff, Deering, Gousseau, Henriot, Malcuzynski, Scarpini, Bagarotti and Gitlis, had "little or no right to solo appearances" while artists as famous as Lisa Della Casa, Victoria de los Angeles, Elisabeth Schwarzkopf and Dietrich Fischer-Dieskau had never been asked to perform with the Philharmonic. Taubman wrote, "Disaffected people, with or without axes to grind, keep insisting that the Philharmonic is being used to magnify reputations of Columbia artists." As for the repertoire, although that had broadened somewhat under Mitropoulos, there was still a host of twentieth-century composers, such as Honegger, Tippett, Ginastera, Schuman, Sessions and Ives, who had never been heard.

Taubman's article, while raising the issues, was gentlemanly. He wrote, "Let us take for granted that the Philharmonic's managers—and board—would not tolerate such a state of affairs" as a direct conflict of interest. "Would it not be better if there were an independent management in charge of the orchestra, as in Philadelphia, Boston and other cities?"

Arthur Judson's retirement was announced in September of 1956, six months after the Taubman article was published. Taubman recalled, "My article was so upsetting to the powers that be that they were threatening to run a campaign to discredit me." He was glad to see Judson resign. "He was a bad influence."

The Taubman attack was the most severe criticism the orchestra had experienced for decades. David M. Keiser, the new president of the board, accepted it gracefully—similar objections had come from Paul Henry Lang and Virgil Thomson—citing "valuable recommendations." One of the recommendations was that Mitropoulos resign and a new conductor be appointed. Taubman said that no one consulted him and the choice of Bernstein came as a surprise. "Somebody had a brilliant idea." It is clear that, had Judson still been in power, Bernstein would not have been appointed. It was his good luck that the opportunity, and Judson's departure, should have come about simultaneously. In naming him the trustees had nothing but praise: "wide knowledge of musical literature," "long identified with contemporary music," "wide cultural background," "forceful and individual personality," and so on. But it was his audience appeal that was obviously uppermost. Bernstein had been hired to sell more tickets, obtain more and better recording contracts and a longer season for musicians, program more imaginatively and so on. His chief rival for the position, Guido Cantelli, could not offer as brilliant a record in so many fields. (As it happened, he was killed in a plane crash on November 23, 1956, just a month after Bernstein's appointment was announced.)

There was another area that interested the trustees. They wanted to get the New York Philharmonic onto a television screen, and Bernstein had already demonstrated that he could use this medium as well. Some two years before, in the autumn of 1954, Bernstein had made a spectacular debut on the Ford Foundation hour, "Omnibus." He presented a series of lectures on music appreciation with such imagination and flair that they became models of their kind. For his first program, about Beethoven's Fifth Symphony, the first page of which was blown up to enormous dimensions on the studio floor, Bernstein introduced the instruments, talked about the work and launched into a discussion about the making of a masterpiece.

Going to the piano, he explored some of the versions Beethoven had attempted and the reasons why they had been rejected. As he said, "The real function of form is to take us on a varied and complicated half-hour journey of continuous symphonic progress." If the composition was to succeed, the notes that followed had to have a quality of rightness, even inevitability. Bernstein showed on camera some of Beethoven's original manuscripts, eloquent testimonials to the anguished process of discovery that the work entailed. In other hands it might have been the kind of discussion only a specialist loves. But Bernstein's gift was his ability to enliven the interest of the intelligent layman. With his jaunty use of colloquialisms ("Form is not a mold for Jell-O," he said at one point, and he likened the sound of a flute to the intrusion of "a delicate lady at a club smoker") he dispelled the notion that music could be appreciated only after advanced study. This is not to say that he thought none was needed. The paradox of modern life was that music was so omnipresent, and was competing with so many other daily intrusions, that most people had learned to tune it out. They would refuse to listen unless the experience were physically painful, a fact of life young rock-and-roll musicians were quick to take advantage of. Bernstein wanted his audiences to make a conscious effort to listen to music and learn to appreciate its richness, subtleties and rewards. He thought one of the quickest ways to make people musically literate was to revive chamber music as a family pastime, so that its concepts were no longer dry abstractions but "living truths."

At an early stage Bernstein drew some provocative parallels between music and the universal experience of being human. In a telecast on rhythm he began the program with the sound of a heart beating, which then slowly dissolved into a passage from Beethoven's Seventh. The beat was the fundamental fact of life, whether it was the pulse of blood through the veins, the steady drip of a faucet, the tick of a clock or the tap of a drummer's foot. From this simple analogy Bernstein went on to illustrate the ways in which jazz, with its rhythmical intricacy, "those syncopations and twists . . . that go on over and against the beat," gave a work its element of surprise and sophistication. Most music, he pointed out, was based on a dual concept, one that seemed intrinsic to the human condition, just as a heart expanded and contracted. "We live in a world of up and down, back and forth, day and night. In order to exhale we must first inhale; there is no third step in the process, no intermediate function. It is in and out, in and out, 1–2, 1–2." In imitation of life music was invariably structured with two beats to the bar or multiples thereof. Even bars tended to run in pairs, the first set of notes needing the second in order to complete its musical intentions. Or perhaps it might be a four-bar phrase, or an eight or even a sixteen. As he was quick to concede, the one exception was the triple beat, a theoretical concept and therefore linked to mystical thought, e.g. the Holy Trinity. Nevertheless, however complex most rhythms became, the ultimate building blocks could always be traced to the interaction of two plus two or three plus three and symmetrical combinations thereof, at least to the end of the nineteenth century. The revolution Stravinsky ushered in, he said, giving his *Rite of Spring* as an example, had to do with the composer's use of two plus three to make five- and even seven-beat bars. Bernstein then referred to Copland's *El Salón México* with its similar structure, its superb vitality and twentieth-century ingenuity. All of that, of course, stopped with the avant-garde, which was now multiplying rhythms with such complexity that the result was formlessness for most listeners. But then, contemporary music had left tonality behind as well, he said, in a postscript that was added several years later. It was clear this was a subject about which he was not going to wax eloquent.

No matter what subject he chose, whether it were Mozart, Bach, the art of conducting, jazz, the musical theater, drawing upon his encyclopedic knowledge of the literature, Bernstein had the gift of making what might have been a routine lecture stimulating and invigorating, thanks to the lucidity of his mind and the originality of his concepts. He was particularly interesting on the subject of romanticism, that great historical movement which swept Europe in the early nineteenth century, as personified by Goethe, Victor Hugo, Lamartine, Byron, Keats, Shelley and Beethoven. They were "all shouting for freedom, for the glorification of the individual spirit, freedom from formality and stylization," and he illustrated his theme by contrasting such painters as Fragonard and Goya, such poets as Milton and Edgar Allan Poe, the stylized grief of Purcell's Dido and the impassioned lament of Wagner's dying Isolde. A new spirit required a new music, a new way of imagining themes, he said, drawing a parallel between the notes of the diatonic scale, which could be said to express whole colors, and those of the chromatic scale, in which a myriad subtle half-tones and indeterminate shades sprang to life.

This new freedom extended to chords, "rich, luscious, what we have come to call romantic," he continued. Beethoven, and also Berlioz, expanded the tools of music not only with a multiplicity of musical colors and ambiguous, complex chords but with daring liberties such as syncopation and rubato that vastly enlarged their work's rhythmic reach. Finally, the orthodoxy of form was broken, the tone poem came into being and with it Richard Strauss's masterpiece *Don Juan,* "a perfect summary of everything we have been discussing, every aspect of those fine romantic freedoms: tonal, rhythmic, and formal." That work also symbolized the end of the romantic movement and ushered in the twentieth century, with its impatience with bombast and cant, its faith in science and its sterilized certainties. It was curious, just the same, to see how people still flocked to the concert hall to listen to Brahms, Schubert, Schumann and Wagner. The reason for that, he thought, was because Tchaikovsky and his contemporaries "give you what you yearn for secretly . . . The romantics give us back our moon, for instance, which science has taken away from us and made into just another airport." At heart most of us were still romantics, he concluded, obviously referring to himself.

By the time his appointment to the New York Philharmonic was announced in mid-October of 1956 Bernstein had given three immensely successful programs (the two others were on jazz, and on the art of conducting); he would give nine in all between 1954 and 1958. Two would win Emmy Awards. His success demonstrated that something musically worthwhile could be done on television, Taubman wrote. "He gave his audience an insight into the mind of a creative worker. Without resorting to the rhetorical flourishes so common to discussions of good music on the airwaves, he showed what a tremendous adventure a symphony can be."

To appear on television in the early days was no easy matter. Then, everything was live, which meant that script and music all had to be memorized, along with the moment at which, for instance, one went from piano to microphone and back again. Bernstein devoted his nights to memorizing while Felicia Bernstein and Adolph Green took turns acting as prompters. In his third program, about conducting, Bernstein's mind went blank for about forty seconds, an eternity on a television screen. He finally remembered that there was a cue sheet hidden on the piano. But his spontaneity was part of his charm. Viewers saw a young man wearing a soft, three-button collegiate suit that looked too tight and a diamond-striped tie, handsome, charming and earnest-looking. At the keyboard, picking out Beethoven's themes, he moved

Bernstein with Mitropoulos in the 1950s

rhythmically and nodded his head affirmatively. If there were a slight stiffness in his manner, it disappeared as soon as he began to conduct. He hurled himself into the music, demonstrating the intensity, brio and total lack of inhibition that had made him famous. It could not possibly have been a better advertisement for his own gifts as a conductor, or for those of his orchestra. The trustees must have realized how much the players, members of the Symphony of the Air, were benefitting. So could the New York Philharmonic.

Bernstein and Mitropoulos were scheduled to share the podium for the 1957–58 season, but that the former would soon be in complete charge was being taken for granted. It must have been galling for Mitropoulos to be replaced by a young man who had once been an acolyte, particularly since conductors expected to have long careers and he considered himself in good health. (In fact, he had a heart attack in 1959 and died a year later.) Despite the public criticisms he had to present a pleased facade and keep his feelings to himself. As for Bernstein, it was the climax of his astonishing career and more than ample compensation for past humiliations. The irony is that the conductor who had fought hardest to have him as successor, i.e., Koussevitzky, had failed, whereas fate had decreed that the one who had failed him at a crucial moment had been ousted by him. Such poetic justice being rare, Bernstein could be forgiven for some self-satisfied remarks. Several years before, he had remarked dismissively that the New York Philharmonic, while being led by Stokowski and Mitropoulos, had sunk to tenth place. Hillyer recalled that shortly after he got the appointment Bernstein said, "I am going to turn this into a great orchestra." Hillyer said, "I was shocked. It seemed a slap at Mitropoulos." Bernstein told Harold C. Schonberg, music reporter for the *New York Times,* that he planned to devote himself full-time to the orchestra. "I'm going to give it everything I have . . . I will undertake no Broadway shows for the time being. No guest-conducting dates in this country . . . The Philharmonic is *it.*"

The months of December 1956 and January 1957 were crowned with successes. He had a punishing load of concerts, ten in December and twelve in January. He was working on rehearsals for *West Side Story* and about to give a new "Omnibus" program, this one on modern music and why people hated it. Reviewing the result, Henry Mitchell commented, "To those who, living unprotected lives, would not be able to escape modern music anyway, he speeded up the process of taking it easy and enjoying it. To those who are timid and afraid, and want the warm custard of Mozart or the slop of the juke box, he said chins up, you can handle it. Use your teeth . . ."

Wonderful Town and *Fancy Free* had moved to Europe, where audiences were enthusiastic, and Robbins's ballet *The Age of Anxiety* was being given a revival at the City Center. Meanwhile, Columbia Records had just issued five Bernstein records, its entire release for January, either composed, conducted or performed by him. They included the "Omnibus" lectures on jazz and the Beethoven Fifth. There was a new recording of Handel's *Messiah,* for which Bernstein had radically arranged the sequence of numbers, eliminating some old favorites and introducing unorthodox tempi. Some critics were affronted; others praised his version as imaginative and rejuvenating. Finally there was a recording of his Serenade for Solo Violin, String Orchestra, Harp and Percussion, which had received admiring reviews when it was given its first performance by the Boston Symphony Orchestra three years before. If *The Age of Anxiety* had shown the composer's anguish and confusion, this new work showed a new maturity and calm consideration. The work, loosely based on Plato's *Symposium,* was in praise of love. The first movement explored its lyrical aspects, the second the charming, the third the amusing, the fourth the emotional and the fifth the sophisticated. Cyrus Durgin wrote, "This is music of genuine creative ideas in terms of abundant melody, and of a texture wherein the solo instrument stands out boldly against the weavings of strings and the rhythmic propulsion, the colors and . . . decorative accents . . . This is perhaps the finest and most condensed serious music that Mr. Bernstein has written. It is mature, it communicates emotionally, it has beauty of sound and a sense of structure."

Bernstein was father of a son, born on July 7, 1955, and named Alexander Serge in memory of Koussevitzky. By 1957 Jamie was a pert five-year-old. Alexander was two and already talking. "Cigarette?" he politely asked a guest, and took one out from a box on the coffee table. "Here, come let me fix your mussy hair," his mother said. Bernstein was an adoring father but sometimes too energetic. His wife said, "He plays too hard, throws them too high, squeezes them too tight." Jamie was showing signs of musical precocity. "She will listen to music by the hour or she will sit at the piano and improvise," her mother said. "She will hear a melody and shout, 'Mama, that's Mozart.' I don't encourage her. To me this is a frightening thing in a five-year-old."

The household was as frantic as ever, akin to a French farce, with phones ringing, telegrams delivered, doors opening, frequent appearances of Helen Coates, the maids, the cleaners and Lenny's tailor. When the doorbell rang, he usually jumped up, grumbling, "Why doesn't Helen open the door? Why doesn't Rosalia [the housekeeper] answer the door? Why doesn't *ANYONE* answer the door besides *DADDY?*" When he needed to compose, the interruptions became too frenzied even for him and he would retreat to a small studio two floors below. Felicia Bernstein said, "You know, it is very funny—for six years he has

At home, as photographed for *Vogue* in 1955, with the infant Alexander and daughter Jamie in the background

And with Jamie and Alexander in 1957

been going to write a piece for me, dedicated to me. Then someone comes up with a commission that changes all that. Six years I have been waiting."

After a concert it became the rule for friends to troop across the street from Carnegie Hall. Lena Horne, Harry Belafonte, Vivien Leigh, Adolph Green and Betty Comden were regular visitors, as well as Shirley and Burton Bernstein. Felicia Bernstein said, "He's like a child in many ways. He enjoys being a celebrity but his biggest pleasure is collecting other celebrities, just like a kid. He was overwhelmed when he met Greta Garbo at a party." At parties Bernstein had developed a certain routine. A friend said:

> As each guest came into the room, Lenny embraced him or her. Then he'd go back to the sofa with all of his admirers seated on the floor around him. He talked about a wide variety of subjects and obviously enjoyed the admiration from below . . . Then he started playing records . . . a Mahler symphony and something of Prokofiev and then Beethoven. But he'd never let a piece finish and he'd talk all the way through, saying some fairly clever things about each work. Then he'd go to the piano and play some real corny jazz of the 1930s and rave about Benny Goodman. Back to the phonograph and one of his own recordings. That record he'd let go all the way through . . .

Felicia Bernstein, who had lightened her hair so dramatically that she was now being described as a blond, had continued her acting career in such television dramas as *Five Minutes to Live* for "Kraft Television Theater." She said, "I think a woman has to keep her own identity. Acting lets me preserve some of mine." However, she was careful not to accept too many engagements, because "I'm an old-fashioned wife . . . I have one rule, and I keep it always: his career is much more important than mine." She hated to cook but very much enjoyed upholstering and refinishing furniture. They collected eighteenth-century English pieces, and she was working on needlepoint for a Queen Anne footstool. She wanted to correct the notion that her husband was an absentminded genius. "The only storming he does is about my forgetting to put a pad and pencil by the telephone, or the way I throw my mail all over. I'm the disorderly one. He's extremely organized—he puts his laundry in the hamper every night, goes around emptying ashtrays . . . And he never forgets an anniversary or a birthday."

Although she did not say so, there was a hint that the importance she attached to correct behavior and avoiding what the English would call "bad form" was becoming a source of tension between them. For her it would be a point of honor to be punctual, and, as she had discovered, Bernstein detested being pinned down. She was overheard asking him anxiously, "Will you be back here before the concert? Because maybe I'll cut your hair then." He was evasive: "I'll be back between one and two." He leaned over and kissed the tip of her nose. "Isn't that yellow marvelous?"

After six years of marriage she would admit that he had only one flaw: he was getting fat. He would insist on eating second helpings of everything and adored desserts. Then he would purport to be on a diet because he was using saccharin in his coffee. His concern, as he approached forty, was that he was getting old. He was determined to make time to compose and to "think deep thoughts about music." Having achieved his ambition had the paradoxical effect of making him acutely unsure of himself. A friend said, "He has a great deal of boldness, vision and imagination—when he doesn't stop to get scared. He's scared mostly of what other people may think about him. He needs to be constantly reassured, and he needs people around to tell him he's wonderful. He's a terrible worrier. He's been running around with the idea that nobody pays any serious attention to him . . . He worries that he has too much talent. He worries because he thinks the critics dislike him . . . He's busting out with genius, he makes about $100,000 a year—and he's insecure. I tell you, Lenny's a very complicated man." Bernstein was particularly irritated at the assertion that he was facile. On the contrary, he was a perfectionist. He said, "To live with myself I have to do each thing better than I've ever done any of them before." Shortly after the news came confirming his appointment as music director in the autumn of 1957, Bernstein entered the hospital with a slipped disc. Then he rang Felicia to complain that thirteen people had been in and out of his room during the past three hours. "This is rest?" he asked. He was soon bored and talked the doctors into letting him watch some operations.

Earlier that year Bernstein had written music for his alma mater, Harvard. Alan Jay Lerner was a fellow alumnus, and they collaborated on two songs for a benefit for Harvard College at Carnegie Hall in the spring of 1957. One of them was called "Lonely Men of Harvard." The theme may have begun as an outgrowth of Bernstein's feelings of alienation following his graduation, as he wrote in "Letter to Myself" in 1948. It was meant to be a lighthearted spoof (they were lonely because they were so superior), but it fell flat. Once the Harvard Glee Club began rehearsing the piece, the word was out that Bernstein had written a dud. It was too late; the song was scheduled to be one of the evening's highlights. To add to the embarrassment from Bernstein's point of view, he had been asked to read the words. One of the glee club's members recalled that when he and some friends trooped out to the bar at intermission, Bernstein was well installed, and by the time he gave his remarks he was rather the worse for wear.

He had always been a popular subject for interviewers, and following his appointment and the success of *West Side Story,* the press began to court him assiduously. Lloyd Garrison recalled that he was working as a television script writer in those days and was sent to interview Bernstein in preparation for a Mike Wallace program in 1957. Garrison, then in his twenties, went to the Bernstein apartment at the Osborne. "I knocked on the door and Bernstein said, 'Come in, the door's open.' It was three in the afternoon, but all the living room curtains were closed and there was only one light, illuminating him as he lay on the floor studying a score. He said, 'Oh, hello,' and patted the floor beside him. I walked over to the couch and sat down. Pretty soon he leapt up to sit beside me. The interview went very normally and smoothly and neither of us alluded to the incident."

If, as was said, Felicia Bernstein had urged her husband to settle down with an orchestra of his own, Bernstein's agile mind was soon spinning with ideas. He was fortunate that the bête noire of his predecessors, Arthur Judson, was no longer on hand to veto his ideas. He wanted to lengthen the season, increase salaries via new radio and recording contracts, attract new subscribers, venture into television and go on more tours overseas. Early in 1958 he showed that a new man was in charge by altering the orchestra's seating so that double-bass players were arranged on a platform across the back of the stage. It was hardly a major departure but clear enough to the naked eye to be symbolic.

He announced that, instead of a formal concert on Thursday evenings as had been the rule, he would begin a series of informal Thursday previews. Musicians would wear casual attire and the conductor would make remarks to the audience. This was welcomed as an ingenious way to give the orchestra one more performance of a program before it was reviewed by the critics.

Another departure was his announcement that he planned to give each season of programs a cohesive plan. He said, "The old norm, the idea of the well-balanced variety program—this does not any longer belong to the Philharmonic. The function of the orchestra has to be different—because it is in New York, the center of the music world. The programs should add up to something: they should have a theme running through them. Each series, cycle, block, should be a festival of a particular composer, or a particular time or . . . movement. There should always be a sense of festival about going to the Philharmonic . . . In a way my job is an educational mission . . ."

For his opening season he planned to divide the eighteen weeks into four segments for an ambitious survey of American music. The first programs would center on the first generation of serious American composers, such as George Whitefield Chadwick, Edward MacDowell and Carl Ruggles. In the second period he would play American music before the 1930s. The third would span the Depression era and World War II, and the final segment would feature music written since the war years. There would be a parallel series dealing with more classical fare, such as the six *Brandenburg* Concerti and a Vivaldi series. These ideas were welcomed by Taubman, who liked having soloists hired to fit an overall plan for the year rather than the other way around, as in the Jud-

Leaving the stage at Carnegie Hall following his opening concert as music director for the New York Philharmonic in October 1958

son era. But then Bernstein seemed to have a real feeling for how to program, which was an art in itself, Schonberg wrote. During his three seasons at the New York City Symphony during the 1940s he had presented some of the most original and stimulating concerts the city had seen. There were classics on the program, but the emphasis was on masterpieces of the twentieth century, from Stravinsky, Hindemith, Bartók and Berg to Milhaud, Shostakovich and Chavez and a host of important American composers. Taubman wrote, "Much remains to be done, but the Philharmonic is awake. It is behaving at long last as if it knows that it is functioning in the middle of the twentieth century."

For his first concert as heir apparent in January 1958—his three-year term as music director did not officially begin until the following autumn—Bernstein programmed two of the works he had conducted on that fateful November 14, 1943: Strauss's *Don Quixote* and Schumann's *Manfred* Overture. In a characteristic gesture of bravado he also doubled as soloist for a performance of Shostakovich's Piano Concerto No. 2, which was receiving its first performance outside Russia. The concerto, which the composer had written the year before for his nineteen-year-old son, made no great demands on Bernstein as pianist and struck reviewers as a minor work, "far from the bite and sparkle of Shostakovich's first piano concerto." Bernstein played it with conviction, and the packed house at Carnegie Hall thundered its approval, although whether for the work or the performer was impossible to tell. As for the Strauss tone poem, Taubman thought it was the kind of work for which Bernstein had a natural gift. The Schumann overture, too, was beautifully performed, "phrased with a sense of poise and relaxed poetry. No longer a young man in a hurry, Mr. Bernstein could allow himself to pause over a tender song. But he did not drag, and where Schumann demanded a flashing stroke, it was summoned up . . ."

In the interests of protecting his back Bernstein had begun to use a small baton, but he kept forgetting he was holding it. On at least one occasion it flew out of his hand and landed in the lap of a lady in the front row. (He kept conducting and she returned it at the next break.) Adolph Green suggested that what Lenny needed was a thong around his wrist to keep the stick from taking off, which Bernstein did not find funny. At the end of his first week, having sung himself hoarse at every rehearsal and concert, his voice was gone. "What an orchestra! What unity! What sensitivity! What vigor!" he croaked. "I am a happy man."

Maestro

Ere limbs begin to totter,
Ere the blood runs thin and slow . . .

— GOETHE, "AN SCHWAGER KRONOS"

As he approached his fortieth birthday Bernstein had reached a new echelon of success. Composer William Schuman, who met Bernstein at Harvard when the latter was just twenty and he himself only eight years older, remarked years later that it had not taken any great prescience to see that this particular youth had "star caliber." No one who could play and conduct, discourse intelligently on the art of music to his peers, attract children like the proverbial Pied Piper and write everything from symphonies to rumbas had ever been seen before. He was an authentic American demigod, a new breed of arts hero, and wherever he went in the world it was an event of importance, "a vibrant reminder that America does indeed honor the intellect, the spirit and the achievements of her artists."

That Bernstein was in demand around the world was only a slight exaggeration. Invitations were pouring in, including one from the Israel Philharmonic. The orchestra's twenty-first year of existence was to be marked with the opening of a new auditorium, the Frederick Mann, in Tel Aviv, and Bernstein was invited to give the opening concerts. The day after *West Side Story* opened on Broadway, Bernstein was to fly to Israel. The "Omnibus" series made a travelogue in honor of the occasion and subsequently showed it on nationwide television.

West Side Story's advance publicity, following its successful trials in Philadelphia and Washington, had guaranteed that its arrival in New York on September 26, 1957, at the Winter Garden Theatre would be the event of the fall season. All the agonizing hours of writing and rewriting, the false starts, the discouragements, the endless rehearsals and crises and exhaustion had been rewarded. Bernstein had the air of a man who could hardly believe his good fortune.

The travelogue begins with that scene familiar to newsreel viewers of the 1940s and 1950s in which the camera descends upon a marquee, lit up with such a blaze of lights that every other image in that shifting pattern of black and white seems unfocused, almost hallucinatory. Below the marquee crowds loom out of the darkness, fitfully illuminated by flash-bulbs, herded behind ropes to await the famous arrivals. Here is the composer, with his wife on his arm, he in black tie and she in a mink stole. He is boyish and almost crew-cut, striding towards the open doors, smil-ing, recognizing someone in the crowd, shaking a hand and tossing off a joke as he passes, his wife turning her head at the identical moment to mirror his smile. Background music: it is a Puerto Rican dance theme from *West Side Story*. Bernstein is narrating the film. He remarks that there will be just enough time to read the first reviews and have a drink in celebration before boarding a plane the following morning.

Next shot: finishing touches to the Frederick Mann Auditorium. The camera pans to reveal the seated musicians. Bernstein enters far left. A ripple of applause sweeps through the assembly. He takes time to shake hands with each of the first-chair men and blows kisses at the rest. "What can I say? Do I have to make a speech?" he says, taking off his watch. He suggests they begin with the first piece on the program, a Beethoven overture which "I have never heard in my life," he says to appreciative laughter. Photographers are crouching at the background, flashbulbs at the ready. Then, saying, "I am just guessing at this," he gives them their first downbeat with both arms, fists clenched. Nothing about his walk or his relaxed manner has prepared one for this explosion of movement, this sudden demonstration of superb physical resources. It is followed by a second, less emphatic gesture, and he casually turns his back on the players to make a complimentary remark to someone off camera while continuing to conduct with his right hand. Further along in the rehearsal the tempo suddenly shifts from languorous to animated. The musicians are caught off guard and make a ragged entrance. Bernstein claps his hands to stop them. "Oh please, take the tempo immediately. I give you a divided upbeat," he said. "Four and three and . . ." He stops them again. "Is that clear?"

Now they are sightseeing in Israel and en route to a boarding school where youngsters from seventy countries are studying music along with their courses on agriculture. On they go, to concerts in a movie house in Jerusalem and an evening of performances in their honor. A young girl sings a traditional lament while Felicia Bernstein sits transfixed. Her husband holds her, his hands wrapped around her waist, and her hands are entwined in his. Fairly soon after that he is in bed, bare chested and complaining, talking to a doctor. His "Asiatic" back has given out—"everybody breaks his back in this country," he says. He is hobbling along between his wife and a woman friend, an arm on each of their shoulders, his body bowed, frustrated and laughing at himself. As his head dips down Felicia Bernstein's hand reaches up in an affectionate, almost automatic gesture to cradle his chin.

Given his unique gifts and his rapport with children, Bernstein's success in the specialized world of children's programming was a foregone conclusion. Still, no one believed his series of Young People's Concerts would become classics of their kind. Beginning in 1958 and for the next fourteen years, Bernstein gave fifty-three concerts for children, on such subjects as: "What Does Music Mean?" "What is American Music?" "What Makes Music Symphonic?" "Who Is Gustav Mahler?" "Humor in Music," "A Toast to Vienna" and "How Musical Are You?" that established him as the precursor of a select group of performer-teachers who would demonstrate the art of explaining the arts to a wide audience. A new generation of musicians would develop, declaring that their love of music was kindled by the Young People's Concerts.

The Philharmonic had offered a series of concerts for children and students for decades, most recently under Wilfrid Pelletier (1953–57). These were given at Town Hall and Carnegie Hall and were considered successful enough, but they had never been seen on television. In fact, apart from one "See It Now" program with Edward R. Murrow in 1954, neither had the New York Philharmonic. However, the idea that a music program for children could be effective on television was in the air. Roger Englander, who would become producer of the series, went to CBS to propose a series of programs about good music for children just as, he later learned, Bernstein and William S. Paley were discussing an identical project. It was decided that television should not use special effects but simply film the same concert Bernstein was giving to an audience of three thousand children in Carnegie Hall.

Weeks before the actual concert Bernstein would send a draft of his script, handwritten. He said, "A typewriter is too noisy. I love the silence of a pencil and paper. I'm too self-conscious to dictate. I find myself mumbling when I write, because it is to be spoken, not read. Sometimes I realize that my voice has been going on for an hour." Mary Rodgers, who wrote the score for *Once Upon a Mattress*, would go over it; John Corigliano, then a very youthful composer, would deal with its musicological aspects; Ann Blumenthal would time it with a stopwatch; Jack Gottlieb would provide a cue sheet for the musicians; and Candy Finkler would chart the script changes. Corigliano said, "He did the entire script. You couldn't suggest anything to him. He'd have to change it. It's an ego thing. He wanted to make it his own. Not always better, but it was his . . . And yet . . . he's brilliant. The man's a genius. We'd make suggestions in an incomplete way, so that he could add his own flourishes. I don't mean this as a criticism. The results were the best ever." Once a script was finished, "He'd look at the positive side. He wouldn't go on tearing it apart, as he had at the beginning. He suspended judgment. He wanted to be pleased with it."

Although the series became more elaborate as the years went by and Englander assembled more than a million dollars' worth of television equipment (eventually the programs were broadcast in color) as well as a squadron of programming and engineering specialists, he continued to insist that a concert was simply being reported. Once simultaneous transmission was abandoned, Englander did not take advantage of that fact to edit the tapes before they went on the air, so that the air of spontaneity and improvisation was retained. The only concession made to television was an extra rehearsal on the day of the concert. The series became so popular that it was shown not only in the United States but Germany, Italy, Belgium, Denmark, Switzerland, Sweden, Japan, Australia and other countries—twenty-nine in all. There was a waiting list

Henry Chapin, age twelve, narrates from Benjamin Britten's *Young Person's Guide to the Orchestra* in the spring of 1961 during one of the fifty-three Young People's Concerts for which Bernstein served as music director during his years with the New York Philharmonic

Besieged by admirers following a typical Young People's Concert in 1960

of two thousand children to buy tickets to the actual performance, some of them enrolled the day they were born—the Young People's Concerts had become as exclusive as Eton. Eventually the series won every award given in the field of educational television.

Bernstein had surprisingly little to say about his success with children. "I don't talk down to them" was about the extent of it. The experience did convince him, however, that all children have a natural musical gift and that musical training ought to be an integral part of education instead of being considered a luxury. Those who worked with him thought the series had been written, more or less unconsciously, for his daughter Jamie, which would explain why, as the years went by, the subjects became more complex, such as the music of Charles Ives or a discussion of the ancient system of scales that preceded the modern tempered scale. When the series began, Jamie was only six, and so his first program centered on the meaning of music. Music might seem to be telling one story but, as Bernstein demonstrated amusingly, could be telling any number of other stories just as convincingly. What music could do was paint a picture, like a spring landscape, such as Beethoven's *Pastoral* Symphony, to give an impression of things. To explain what he meant by that, he turned to painting: Monet's famous series of the cathedral at Rouen, which he compared with actual photographs. The artist, he said, "wants you to see not so much a cathedral as light itself, and colors, as they look to him reflecting on a cathedral. This is almost like a *dream* of a cathedral . . ." Mussorgsky's *Pictures at an Exhibition* was another case in point, but even so, the pictures that went with the music were there only because the composer had chosen them and were not really part of the music. Using simple analogies and frequent trips to the piano to play snatches of music illustrating his theme, Bernstein arrived at his main point, that music was "the way it makes you feel when you hear it," sometimes feelings so mingled that they could not be described. That was what made music so unique. "It names the feelings for us, only in notes instead of words."

Bernstein's flexible, persuasive narrative was perfectly suited to making complex subjects accessible to young audiences. One of his favorite subjects was the debt symphonic music owed to the folk song, along with the ways in which the folk music of each country was unique because it echoed the special patterns of that particular language. Hungarians, for instance, almost always stressed the first syllable of every word, and that explained the strong stresses which one heard in Hungarian folk songs. By contrast the French language was smooth and flowing, with almost no abrupt emphasis, and this easy, liquid style showed itself in French folk songs. In the same way one could find, in the beautiful singing line of a Vivaldi concerto, the Italian love for melody and its habitual use of expressive vowels; Spanish music, by contrast, reflected the crisp rhythms of its language. Such familiar melodies as "Strawberry Fair" bore a corresponding resemblance to the English love for clearly enunciated, tripping speech. However, when one came to American cowboy tunes like "As I Was A-walkin' One Mornin' for Pleasure," one heard the soft, slow Western drawl in its musical patterns.

As for classical music, that was not so hard to understand. The great thing to know about a Bach fugue, for instance, was that it had a clear set of rules, "something like the printed directions you get when you buy an Erector Set": exact and rigorous, and which if followed precisely will produce the desired result, whether a fire truck or a Ferris wheel. That all changed as Mozart came along and people wanted "pretty tunes and easy accompaniments . . . And this was right in line with the times: a time of elegance and refinement, good manners, proper etiquette; a time of lace cuffs and silk suits, powdered wigs and jeweled fans for the ladies and gentlemen of the court." Referring to a Mozart piano concerto, Bernstein commented, "There's no Erector Set here; only the gorgeous melody, with a simple little accompaniment underneath—simple, but oh, how beautiful!" People also wanted gaiety, and a certain lightheartedness crept in, not only in the comic operas of Mozart but in some of Haydn's musical jokes in which surprise played a large part. "In music, composers can make these surprises in lots of different ways—by making the music loud when you expect it to be soft, or the other way around; or by suddenly stopping in the middle of a phrase; or by writing a wrong note on purpose, a note you don't expect, that doesn't belong in the music." To illustrate he got the children singing "Shave and a haircut," and the orchestra answered: "Two bits!"

The idea that music could be—ought to be—fun is a recurrent theme in Bernstein's life at this period.

He even managed to explain why a gavotte in Prokofiev's *Classical Symphony* was funny, following that with examples of broader humor, like Mozart's *A Musical Joke,* in which the instruments played "ghastly wrong notes." Then there was Copland's Music for the Theatre, in which the composer parodied not only the notes but the rhythms themselves. "This music is constantly falling down and picking itself up again, and at the very end it slips for the last time, and just stays there, with a very puzzled look on its face." Then there were all the "rude noises" played by the trombones and especially the bassoon, that "clown of the orchestra." Even parents were amused, but most of all they were grateful. One wrote, "When a six-year-old comes tearing into the kitchen and reports, 'There's beautiful music on TV,' and sits still for a full sixty minutes, you feel his head, and if it isn't hot, you write to the person responsible . . ." Bernstein said that the children's shows gave him particular satisfaction. "When you know that you're reaching children without compromise or the assistance of acrobats, marching bands, slides, and movies, but that you are getting them with hard talk, a piano, and an orchestra, it gives you a gratification that is enormous." Ellen Adler recalled taking a small boy to one of the concerts; as they left he turned to her and said, "I want him to be my daddy."

The four Young People's Concerts a year were among the most demanding television performances he gave but, at the time, they were sandwiched between more important appearances, from the Philharmonic's point of view, that of the orchestra itself. The Bernstein name had succeeded in garnering a highly desirable Sunday-afternoon appearance once a month on CBS-TV, a repeat of the Thursday-night concerts in Carnegie Hall. These were the so-called previews at which the director was free to comment on the music that was about to be heard. As the Philharmonic's 117th season opened in the autumn of 1958 Bernstein sat down at the piano and began to sing, "Where, oh where are the pea-green freshmen? . . . Safe at last in the sophomore class." It was a ditty he had learned at Harvard, and along with "America the Beautiful," "Turkey in the Straw" and "Camptown Races," it was incorporated into the Symphony No. 2 by Charles Ives, which the orchestra was about to play. Bernstein said, "How many times have you sat there and had a new piece of music thrown at you by Theocritus Schwartz or John Foster Doe and longed for something that would bring the piece closer to you?" This was particularly necessary in the case of Ives, because he was "a greatly gifted primitive, and the trouble with primitives is that they are an acquired taste, like olives." There were a few complaints afterwards, but the mood was overwhelmingly favorable. "Attaboy, Sugar," Adolph Green remarked after the performer, stripped to the waist, was being massaged by his wife. "You fought a good fight."

All this extra activity—a longer season, more recordings, a dozen or so television shows—was having the expected effect on morale at the Philharmonic. With the exception of a few grumblers, still harking back to the days of Toscanini and Mengelberg, "it's a positive honeymoon!" as one of them said, rubbing his hands. No one called him "Maestro"; he was Lenny to them all. Even the staid music critic Paul Henry Lang, who would turn out to be one of Bernstein's most vocal critics, could find no fault with Bernstein or his rehearsal style. "Bill, don't come in so soon," Bernstein instructed his trumpet player. "Now you are late . . . That's fine." Lang wrote, "This manner may seem perfectly natural to any American, but is not customary in our major orchestras . . . No one cracks a whip, no one has tantrums, and no one puts on unapproachable Olympian airs, yet the conductor's commands, which are more in the nature of casual requests, are instantly obeyed."

They were rehearsing the Violin Concerto by Roger Sessions, who was in the audience. Lang wrote, "Then a most unusual phenomenon took place. Mr. Bernstein asks the composer: 'Is there anything missing?' Mr. Sessions makes a few requests and recommendations, [and] the conductor listens attentively . . . I was present at the occasion when a very famous conductor turned his back on Ravel because the great French composer requested a different tempo in his *Boléro*." At last, a humanist had stepped onto the podium. If this was the result of hiring an American as a conductor, then the sooner other orchestra boards followed New York's example, the better.

Like Koussevitzky, Bernstein thought that the opening of a season ought to be a festive event and that men and women should wear evening dress. In that respect he was helped by the Friends of the Philharmonic, a fund-raising group, which put out the word, and also by all the big Fifth Avenue department stores, which had window displays of outfits grand enough for the occasion. He was also helped by his wife, whose delicate silhouette was ideally suited to showing off the kind of designer clothes she thought appropriate. She was photographed by the *New York Times* wearing a blue, cut-velvet evening gown by Gunther Jaeckel, strapless, with a tight bodice and full skirt sprinkled with bows. She also ordered a full-length sheath of patterned red satin from Pauline Trigère. She and her husband subsequently appeared in *Life* magazine, dancing, chatting and dining with all kinds of beautiful people on opening night, including Merle Oberon (wearing an exquisite turquoise-and-diamond necklace), Mrs. Nathan Milstein (wearing a Balenciaga), heiress-author Gloria Vanderbilt Lumet, former wife of Leopold Stokowski, and the omnipresent Elsa Maxwell, who pronounced it "the most socially important affair of the season."

Could Bernstein succeed as conductor and music director? Preliminary reports were that the overall attendance had increased by 20 percent, an astonishing jump in a single season. There were more sub-

Checking a note during rehearsal with the New York Philharmonic

scribers than at any other point in the orchestra's history. As for the critical reception, Bernstein could hardly have asked for better: "The orchestra played with a sort of tautness and responsiveness that it has shown only intermittently during the past few decades. Mr. Bernstein had evidently infused into it . . . the same spirit of enthusiasm that he imparted to his audience . . ." After a few months of regular monthly performances with the Philharmonic on television, Bernstein was being urged to appear every week. "Few people seem to realize what goes into one of these hours of television," he complained. "It takes a full month to prepare for a one-hour TV program . . . Television is a visual medium, a program has rigorous time limitations and it must have a form—a carefully developed idea." He added, "I'm doing too much as it is." The interviewer noted that the conductor was displaying "the nervous tension of one who works too hard and seldom relaxes."

By the time he became music director of the New York Philharmonic, Bernstein had been able to count upon an average yearly income of $75,000, from a variety of sources: conducting, lecturing, writing, composing and music, record and performance royalties. His income would rise sharply whenever he had a Broadway success. *On the Town* had earned him a total of $100,000 and in 1957 he was paid $30,000 for three "Omnibus" programs alone. To have gone from being a penniless composer in Greenwich Village to one of the highest-paid musicians in the country in just fifteen years was extraordinary and a testament to his ability to prosper in a notoriously penurious profession.

He liked to tell friends it was sheer chance. Leonard Marcus was looking for work around 1958 and went to Bernstein for help; he recalled Bernstein saying, "Look around you. Lightning has to strike. You have to be in the right place at the right time." Marcus said, "I remember him also saying there was so much marvelous talent around. 'You can throw a stone in Greenwich Village and hit a world-class pianist, and they are so tragic because they can't, or won't, do anything else.'" Bernstein could have shared their fate had he not realized that he had to become a conductor as well as a pianist. He had to compose for the theater as well as the concert hall. He had to teach and write if he were to piece together a living wage. Fortunately he had the facility such an approach required, and it had all succeeded beyond his wildest dreams. He was typically generous. He helped people with loans and gifts. He gave inspired presents. He always picked up the check. He looked for ways to find jobs; family members came first, but friends and "unser einers" were not far behind. Like Koussevitzky and Mitropoulos, he thought it his duty to help those less fortunate, and established a small foundation for that purpose in 1958.

He liked to have enough money so that he did not have to think about it, to let other people, Helen Coates for example, take care of the daily accounting. In later years he liked to claim that money meant nothing to him. This was misleading, because there is evidence that his business acumen was acute at an early stage. As a friend said, "For someone only interested in music, Bernstein had an awfully good bookkeeper's eye. He could read columns of figures the way the rest of us read novels." When it came to performing, "he wouldn't breathe without money." There are many examples of his readiness to strike a hard bargain. The publishing executive Arthur Shimkin recalled that he was in charge of developing a line of children's records in the autumn of 1948 and had engaged Alec Wilder to write ten "historical ballads" for children on such subjects as Columbus, the Pilgrims, Paul Revere and Jefferson. Wilder had written two and then had to break off to write a film score. He suggested that his friend Leonard Bernstein be asked to write the other eight songs.

They all met for lunch at the Algonquin. Shimkin wrote, "Alec was there when I arrived and predicted Lenny would be late, which he was. I explained the project—and he listened respectfully. I brought along

Bernstein conducting the New York Philharmonic

With Igor Stravinsky in earnest conversation during
the Festival of Stravinsky—a series of concerts and
chamber music performances with the New York
Philharmonic—in the summer of 1966

the script and small (seven-piece) score for the first one already written . . . and after some discussion of terms and payment, which were
completely satisfactory to him, he paused a long moment and said,
'There is one thing, though . . .' I asked what that might be and Alec
waited silently. Lenny finally explained that if he agreed to do them,
he'd have to write all ten of them." Shimkin was not prepared to jetti-
son work by the better-known composer. But Bernstein, realizing the
commercial importance of being the sole author, refused to compromise. Shimkin concluded, "I was in the midst of paying the luncheon
bill when Alec [stood up] and poured his glass of water on the table in
front of Lenny's place, then left the dining room. I excused myself and
joined him. Lenny remained seated—looking slightly puzzled."

Bernstein seldom lost such an argument. By 1957 his grasp of the
complexities of the music business was so complete that he actually

argued a case before the Internal Revenue Service. Organizations that were presenting concerts, a legal definition expanded to include some ballets and operas, were exempt from the usual 10 percent admissions tax if they were nonprofit. The IRS contended, however, that *Carousel* did not fit the definition of an opera and therefore the admissions tax could not be waived, in this case, for a City Center performance. Bernstein gave a dazzling lecture in miniature on musical theater and *Carousel* in particular, arguing that it had to be accepted as an opera because it was almost entirely sung. He won the case. His victory was, presumably, not altogether altruistic, since much the same argument might need to be made on behalf of *West Side Story.*

As a young composer, working on salary for a music publisher and getting his first royalties Bernstein had, as a matter of course, agreed to sell his copyright. Only a very few, very successful composers had the bargaining power to retain copyright ownership; but when Bernstein began writing, the proviso was not the one-sided bargain it later became. Before the days of the Xerox machine there was money to be made in music publishing. Composers of a certain status could negotiate work-for-hire contracts, as Wilder had done, i.e., a monthly check amounting to a regular salary. There were similar royalty arrangements that paid almost as well. In those days, an American composer who had signed with a good publisher did not need another agent because that publisher would promote the works he wrote.

Bernstein's first works, such as his Clarinet Sonata, went to Harms, which also got *Fancy Free.* Tams-Witmark published *On the Town* and *Wonderful Town.* From 1948 on, G. Schirmer became Bernstein's principal publisher and remained so for many years thereafter. Schirmer published the early version of *Candide, Trouble in Tahiti* and, the most lucrative of them all, *West Side Story.* However, by the time Bernstein moved to the New York Philharmonic, with its even greater opportunities for television performances and record contracts, it became clear that he needed specialized help. *West Side Story* was a case in point. In 1957 Schirmer published "Songs from *West Side Story.*" In 1958 there was "Selections from *West Side Story.*" After the film appeared in 1961, there was an arrangement for guitar; in 1962, for the Baldwin organ; in 1963, for accordion, and a further publication of "Highlights from *West Side Story.*" All of them were copyrighted by Schirmer. Apart from the lucrative byways which Schirmer was assiduously exploring, there were foreign sheet-music sales to Germany, Norway, Czechoslovakia, Denmark, Finland, Hungary, Japan, Roumania, Bulgaria, Spain and Sweden. There were best-selling records. All of these profits were being filtered through a complicated network in which various publishers and agents deducted their percentages before the composer received a penny. Bernstein, then being represented by Abraham Friedman, who had been Koussevitzky's lawyer and also was Copland's, probably realized too late that he had made a bad bargain in allowing G. Schirmer to own the *West Side Story* copyright.

He could, however, prevent this from happening again if he were prepared to become his own publisher and agent. Bernstein's solution was identical to that later adopted by Stephen Sondheim, i.e., he no longer sold his copyright and formed a company to license the publication and allied rights. He retained the most important right, i.e., to own his own work. Such an arrangement automatically meant a larger share of the profits for the composer and performer. Amberson Enterprises, founded in 1959 ("Amber" is the English translation of "Bernstein"), would soon expand far beyond its original purpose. That, it seems clear, was simply to prevent its musician from being exploited.

As many have observed, man's most sublime art has been supported by the sharpest of business practices, with the performer at the bottom of the pecking order, another reason for wanting to incorporate. Richard Dyer, music critic of the Boston *Globe,* believes very little attention is paid to the inner workings of the music world because "it's a very small world and very protective and power is concentrated in two or three places." The domination of the market by the biggest agency is "so complete, even its rivals won't complain because they could get shut down. The classical world has been so marginalized no one cares." In such a world, where men like Judson had enormous power and where legions of aspiring artists had no work, all kinds of hard bargains were likely to be struck, as has been suggested. Cal Stewart Kellogg, an American opera conductor who knows the international scene, said, "In Italy you have to be horizontal if you are a woman. It's a dirty rotten business." In the United States, the role homosexuals have played in the arts is too obvious to need emphasis; as in Britain it has flourished almost as a cult. The composer Benjamin Lees claimed it was a disadvantage not to be a homosexual in the music world and that careers of many heterosexuals had suffered from a form of discrimination. He claimed to know a well-known composer who had deliberately changed his sexual orientation in order to improve his career prospects. John McLennan, another composer, said he had been sexually propositioned as the price of having a work performed. He declined; the work was not performed. Another astute observer of the opera and concert world said, "There is a certain secret-society aspect to the music world. The thing that is surprising is that it should surprise anyone."

The situation was more complicated for conductors since, as the Rochester incident showed, conservative symphony boards, usually dominated by women, liked having a virile conductor in the prime of life. "The strain of sexual fantasy and sublimation in this relationship is undeniable and sometimes encouraged," Norman Lebrecht observed. For that reason, "conductors are required to maintain a facade of sexual 'normality,' " sometimes for decades, and often go to great lengths to avoid suspicion. A conductor could be placed in the theoretical position of either play-acting a role in the music world, or for his public's benefit. Given the emotional strains involved, the conductor who was genuinely bisexual would seem to have a distinct advantage.

Judson may have brought the "market mentality" to new heights, but he was hardly alone, nor was he the first. New York's reputation for blatant commercialism had been known since the mid–nineteenth century, when piano companies sent soloists like Paderewski on tours and it was an open secret that no European pianist would perform in the United States without a guarantee from a manufacturer. Certain orchestras developed ties with certain piano companies. Leinsdorf described a conversation he had with Tod Perry, manager of the Boston Symphony Orchestra, during his years as music director there. Perry delicately explained that since the Baldwin piano company had been so generous to the BSO for so many years (lending over seventy pianos every summer for use at Tanglewood), the orchestra felt under an obligation to have as guest soloists some pianists who "prefer the Baldwin." Bernstein, it should be noted, appeared in advertisements in 1958 preferring the Baldwin.

Similarly, a certain hall might be reserved for the exclusive use of one recording company and its rivals barred. In his book *Musical Chairs,* Schuyler Chapin noted that the Boston Symphony recorded with RCA and that company had a contract preventing any other company from using Symphony Hall. However, an exchange of favors under certain circumstances also takes place in the music world, and those owed are carefully noted for future reference. It transpired that Columbia had recently done RCA a favor by lending that company one of its artists for a performance with the Boston Symphony Orchestra. Now it wanted to record a Bernstein performance in Symphony Hall and the request was granted. As Judson had shown, the more exclusive contracts could be amassed, the more powerful the individual or company became and the stronger the bargaining position. Knowing when to press one's advantage and when to yield in the game of favors owed required artistry of a sort. Chapin recounts another incident that took place in Vienna during a filming of Beethoven's *Fidelio* conducted by Bernstein at the Theater an der Wien. A stagehand brought down the house curtain and it passed too close to the hot television lights. There was a fire, which was quickly extinguished. The television crew was ordered off the premises and urgent negotiations began. It goes without saying that the accident would have been covered by insurance. Chapin was far too diplomatic to use the word "bribe." He called it "a handsome monetary donation toward the upkeep of the building."

As Judson had demonstrated, after defeating the opposition the logical next step was to represent both buyer and seller, at least until it became illegal. In recent years it has become fashionable to blur the boundaries, as in the case of Matthew Epstein, who, as an agent for Columbia Artists, acted as advisor for several opera companies before joining the Welsh National Opera as its director. As of 1993, Epstein maintained an office at CAMI. Columbia Artists Management has always figured as a force in the opera world. Shortly after leaving the Metropolitan Opera, where he was general manager, Sir Rudolf Bing was hired as consultant to Columbia Artists by Ronald Wilford, president and principal shareholder, who now manages the enviable list of conductors once controlled by Judson.

David M. Rubin, chairman of the journalism department at New York University, has pointed out that in such a small world it is possible for a whole network of relationships to develop between certain prominent teachers, music schools, competitions, patrons and summer festivals. He wrote:

> To most of these musicians it is possible to affix a "brand" that reveals their musical pedigree, and their route of admission into the cylinder: some are of Curtis/Serkin/Marlboro stock . . . some are Isaac Stern protégés by way of the Juilliard . . . others were in the Tanglewood conducting program or were nurtured by Young Concert Artists, which provides management help to a select group of soloists in their early years . . . All of these musicians are usually managed by Columbia Artists . . . ICM Artists Ltd . . . or one of a dozen or so smaller firms that together constitute a third management force in the industry.

When managers of orchestras complain, it is usually about "coat-tailing," a common practice since Judson's day, in which "a highly desirable artist is used to sell other artists off a list," Rubin wrote. After engaging the pianist Emanuel Ax and cellist Yo-Yo Ma, one presenter was told he was expected to book a lesser attraction from the same agency as a kind of "luxury tax" for the privilege of engaging Ax and Ma. "Coat-tailing" as a technique is so effective that on occasion it is even used by press agents to promote the careers of lesser lights by promising or withholding access to a more important figure. And it is hard to combat, because, as one aspiring artist explained, "We always hope that we will be the ones whose careers are being given a boost next time."

Orchestra managers and presenters also complain about the grip a few big agents have on the market and the exorbitant fees being charged. Occasionally orchestras fight back. Johanna Fiedler, who was manager of the New York Chamber Symphony, said she never had to pay full price for her artists. "They reduced their fees substantially because all the artists wanted to perform in New York. After all, it's a game." Another orchestra manager who tried and failed to engage Karajan because, at each new round of negotiations with CAMI the price went up, retaliated by refusing to hire CAMI artists for the next two seasons. The larger issue, others say, is whether the big agencies are necessarily promoting the careers of those with the most talent. Kellogg said, "You might have found people once with a modicum of ability to recognize talent. Nowadays there are fewer and fewer. Music managers have business and marketing degrees. They are salesmen, peddling people."

Bernstein would make a historic tour of Europe early in his second season with the New York Philharmonic in 1959, but it was not his first tour with the orchestra. In 1958 he and his co-conductor, Mitropoulos, had made a twelve-country tour of Latin America that was even more fraught with incident than his visit to Israel during the War of Independence had been. As he arrived in La Paz, Bolivia, where a political uprising was expected, loudspeakers at the airport were warning the excited crowd not to fire off any guns, in case anyone should think that hostilities had begun. In Bogotá, they arrived two days after the government had managed to suppress a police revolt and rescue its captured members. Bayonets and machine guns were very much in evidence at the theater that evening when the government came en masse to hear the performance. Among the dignitaries was Major General Gabriel Paris, who had been kidnapped and wounded literally hours before.

The crowds cheered when they appeared, lined the sidewalks to watch their cars pass and applauded "The Star-Spangled Banner." This was considered significant, since Vice President and Mrs. Richard Nixon, making a similar goodwill tour a few days before, had met with stones being thrown. The crowds threw flowers at Bernstein instead. The musicians traveled in two specially equipped planes with their eight tons of luggage, which included Bernstein's grand piano. One of their endless stories concerned the grand piano, which a well-meaning attendant had polished from top to bottom, including the keys. The only remover that worked was whiskey. In La Paz, twelve thousand feet above sea level, the wind players and particularly Bernstein needed oxygen between numbers. In Santiago they played in an open sports arena on such a windy stage that electric heaters had to be installed at strategic intervals. Another improvised stage was constructed on the shore of Lake Maracaibo, lined with oil derricks.

The State Department was sponsoring the tour, and an official dispatch has survived describing the farcical ineptitude of the organization in charge of publicizing two concerts in Mexico City, and the desperation of the U.S. officials as they tried to surmount the hurdles and tell people about the concerts in time. Their main concern was publicity for the second concert, in the National Auditorium, which seated nine thousand. Thanks to the almost malign incompetence of the Mexican authorities, the auditorium had almost that many tickets unsold a week before the concert was to take place. The American officials took over and, literally hours after the first radio announcements and advertisements appeared, the concert was sold out.

The Mexicans had staged an elaborate reception for their arrival in Mexico City. There were buses festooned with signs welcoming the orchestra, two motorcycle policemen in handsome uniforms, two mariachi bands and pretty girls with bouquets of flowers. They were all at the airport at nine o'clock on the evening of June 12. They waited and waited. Finally, the first plane arrived three hours late, after a thirty-six-hour journey from Rio de Janeiro. The musicians lurched and staggered off, "unkempt, unshaven, tie-less and coatless," Jacob Canter, who wrote the report, observed. To add to the problems, the men were in a terrible mood, snarled at their hosts and, when their buses did not leave immediately, staged a scene. The diplomats were horrified. The second plane, with the two conductors on board, arrived seven hours late. The girls with the flowers had long since departed, as had the mariachi bands and the smartly dressed policemen. "Broken, exhausted and disheveled, the second contingent nevertheless comported itself with utmost decorum, and Mr. Bernstein and Mr. Mitropoulos even managed a smile and a wave of the hand . . ." They got to their hotel by five in the morning. That afternoon the two conductors gave a poised press conference, and Bernstein even managed to slip in a few words of Spanish, which made a good impression.

At least a half hour before the Bernstein concert on June 14, the Palace of Fine Arts was jammed to the rafters. Then, when the Philharmonic performed the *Sinfonía India* by Chávez, Mexico's best-known composer, the result was pandemonium. Next day at the National Auditorium, all nine thousand seats were full and hundreds more sat on steps or lined the sides of the auditorium. The audience was equally enthralled. Mitropoulos played an excerpt from Falla's *Sombrero de tres picos* as an encore and the audience, one newspaper said, was "thunderstruck." When they finally let him leave the stage, Mitropoulos was in tears.

Mitropoulos died less than two years after relinquishing his post as music director of the New York Philharmonic to Bernstein. Bernstein had invited him for a month-long series of concerts, but a heart attack prevented Mitropoulos from appearing. He made a quick recovery and conducted at the Salzburg Festival in the summer of 1960. In October of that year he was at the Met, conducting *Tosca* with his old verve and energy. In November he was in Milan, rehearsing Mahler's Third Symphony at La Scala, when he put his hand up to his heart. Then he toppled from the podium. Mitropoulos was one of the great exponents of Mahler's music, and in a tribute to him a few days later, Bernstein led an unscheduled performance of the "Urlicht" ("Primal Light") movement from Mahler's Second Symphony, the *Resurrection.* To die on the podium—that, Bernstein said, was the way *he* wanted to leave the world.

Then there was the affair of the Mitropoulos cross. David Diamond said, "One day Mitropoulos and I were walking on the terrace of Mrs. Selden-Goth's Florentine villa. She was his closest friend and her daughter, Trudy, was his secretary. I was going through a very bad period emotionally and religiously and thought I might become a Catholic. Dimitri was very moved by this. I noticed that he sometimes wore a very beautiful cross of black ebony." Diamond thought the cross came from the monastery where Mitropoulos often stayed; the figure of a dove was superimposed. Diamond asked Mitropoulos where he could find one just like it, and the conductor immediately insisted on giving it to him.

Knowing that Mitropoulos sometimes used the cross when he was praying, Diamond refused to take it. But when the conductor left for Milan just a week before he died, he left the cross with his secretary. Diamond said, "Several months later I was given the cross." The next time Bernstein was in Italy, in 1961 or 1962, "he saw it and wanted it. He had given me so many things and helped me so much that I said all right." From then on, whenever he walked on stage, Bernstein wore Koussevitzky's cuff links and the cross that had belonged to Mitropoulos.

For Bernstein, a fine line divided his desire to emulate and identify with those conductors who had entered his pantheon and his wish to get the better of each one, beat him at his own game. He had spent a year acting as co-conductor with Mitropoulos and had had the profound satisfaction of observing the amount of attention paid to him versus the scant attention paid to Mitropoulos. When the two of them returned from their trip to South America and were given an official welcome by the city of New York, Mitropoulos's name had been hardly mentioned. He had toppled his idol. Now the conductor was dead and Bernstein could allow himself to feel nostalgic, even sentimental. In years to come he never seemed aware that he had nursed any such rivalrous feelings, and made the ingenuous assertion that every conductor he ever met had loved him, and several had died in his arms.

Now that he had reached a pinnacle of success, fate again played into his hands. As part of the President's Special International Program for Cultural Presentations, the State Department had set up an extensive tour of Europe and the Middle East, including Russia, for the Chicago Symphony Orchestra, then being led by Fritz Reiner. It was to be the most ambitious tour so far organized under the program, which had already sent two other American orchestras to perform in the Soviet Union: the Boston Symphony in the summer of 1956 and the Philadelphia Orchestra in 1958. The ten-week tour included two weeks in Moscow plus other appearances in Milan, Athens, Berlin, Brussels, Helsinki, Paris and elsewhere. It was, in short, highly desirable, but Reiner was recalcitrant. He was seventy and having some heart problems, which may have explained why he thought "this awful tour" would leave everyone "miserably worn out." So he canceled the trip. His players subsequently laid a suit of formal attire on the floor backstage with a note attached reading "Farewell, European Tour—Thanks, Fritz." Then they stamped all over it. The musicians were furious at having to give up an average of $2,000 in extra income. The cancellation seemed inexplicable. "For the first time Chicago might have gained a reputation for something else than Prohibition Era hoodlums, gang wars and civic graft. Fritz Reiner owes Chicago an explanation," a music critic wrote. It must have given Bernstein immense satisfaction when the State Department made an announcement the following day that he and the New York Philharmonic would take over Reiner's tour. Reiner had missed a splendid opportunity and they all knew it. Musicians in New York greeted the news with "great cheering."

That spring Bernstein was, as usual, juggling concert dates, television shows and recording sessions and squeezing in interviews following rehearsals, during which someone gave him a massage while someone else worked on his scalp. The orchestra would begin its tour in August, right after its usual summer series in Lewisohn Stadium. It was to perform in mid-May for an important event: President Eisenhower would break ground for the new Lincoln Center for the Performing Arts at Sixty-fourth Street, west of Broadway, a complex of buildings that would include a new concert hall for the New York Philharmonic. Bernstein was to be master of ceremonies. Early in May, Lenny and Felicia flew to London for a few days to attend the opening of a revised *Candide* (still using the Lillian Hellman script, with Osbert Lancaster's costumes and decor).

"Philharmonic Hits New Peak," the headlines read that summer as 128 orchestra members and staff left New York on two planes bound for their first destination, Athens. A third plane followed, carrying eighteen thousand pounds of instruments and luggage. The first seven concerts, in Greece, Lebanon and Turkey, were played al fresco, and there were the predictable hazards of stiff winds and less likely ones, such as the amplified quarter-tone chanting of an Oriental café singer coming in over the concert at an outdoor stadium in Istanbul. As in South America, the tour began in triumph and continued to gather an unbroken string of superlatives as the 106 musicians staggered off plane after plane and into the flower-filled arms of their audiences. After hearing them play at the Baalbek Festival in Lebanon, the festival's music chairman said, "I want to cry. Everything now will be anticlimactic." Two days before, they had so moved the audience in Athens by their performance of Mozart's Piano Concerto in G Major (K453, No. 17), which Bernstein performed and conducted, that they demanded three encores. They had to stop because they were exhausted. As Bernstein tottered off the stage a Greek woman shouted, "A new god has come to Athens."

In Warsaw they were deluged with flowers. Bernstein managed to visit Chopin's house and went to a jazz club for the usual late-night session. As dawn arrived he wound his way back to the hotel followed by an admiring throng that would let him leave only after everyone kissed everyone. Bernstein was scheduled to perform in Vienna and Salzburg. Steve Rosenfeld, now deputy editorial page editor for the Washington *Post,* went on the trip as Bernstein's Russian interpreter. He had just graduated from the Russian Institute at Columbia University that year and already knew Bernstein, since his father, Jay, was music critic for the Berkshire *Eagle.* Rosenfeld said, "One person I was aware of that he really didn't like was Herbert von Karajan," then conductor of the Berlin Philharmonic and also director of the Vienna State Opera and the Salzburg Festival. "Bernstein thought he was vying to be the most important conductor in the world. I was instructed to go out in a rainy night in Salzburg to paper the house, so I went to the conservatory and handed out tickets. He wanted the best reviews and the best performances." Bernstein need not have worried.

He was sharing the podium with Thomas Schippers but, even so, the pressure on him to perform was relentless. The orchestra gave fifty concerts in seventy days, which, after travel, left hardly any time for the dinners, parties, conferences and interviews that were de rigueur wherever they went. Rosenfeld said, "Lenny was not a personality, he was a musician. Even when drunk and maniacal he was humming, beating his fingers, he was talking to other musicians in the orchestra about this piece and that phrase. He did not take holidays off. He always had a score to study with him. He was always singing. He always had something in his head. It was a capacity to be completely absorbed. People like that are not like you and me.

"I recall an episode during the Russian trip. We were talking to a bunch of Russian composers and a Russian woman was translating, and I am following along. In a casual way Bernstein started talking about sex, and the woman's eyes started shifting about and she didn't know where to look, and he was saying, 'Translate!' His point was that he had tried to make love to music but at a certain moment the demands of the music and the demands of the moment were in conflict, and music would win. Then he began to sing the kind of music he meant. Felicia tried to shut him up but couldn't."

For the most part Bernstein conducted himself impeccably. He drank very little, worked all the time and was a completely devoted husband to his elegant wife. She could usually be found in the background of photographs, dressed in something beautifully cut and black, with a

Bernstein rehearsing at the Tchaikovsky Conservatory in Moscow during his triumphal tour of Russia with the New York Philharmonic in 1959

Playing a blues piano in 1959

triple strand of pearls at the neckline. Bernstein's parents and sister were also on part of the trip. Sam Bernstein, who had left Russia all those years ago and never learned to speak Russian, refused to join them at first. But when his son arrived in Leningrad he received a surprise phone call from his uncle Semyon Solomon, Sam's younger brother, whom he had not seen for almost half a century. Semyon was now a retired engineer—he had been in charge of coal mines in Siberia. He and Mikhoel Zvainboim from Dnepropetrovsk, one of Bernstein's cousins, wanted to be reunited, so Sam and Jennie flew to Moscow. Rosenfeld said, "They had a most unhappy, brief stay. Neither of them were in the musical orbit. They were just a couple of little old people." After ten days together, Samuel Bernstein gave his brother all his clothes and flew home. He said that he felt no identification whatsoever with the strange country.

Bernstein's first concert in Moscow, in the Grand Hall of the

Backstage at the Tchaikovsky Conservatory in Moscow, with Boris
Pasternak, following a concert with the New York Philharmonic in 1959

Tchaikovsky Conservatory of Music, was the most frenzied reception an
American had received, critics wrote, since Van Cliburn won the
Tchaikovsky International Piano Competition in that same hall a year
earlier. Bernstein conducted and performed the Mozart piano concerto
and followed it with Shostakovich's Symphony No. 5. Rosenfeld said, "It
was considered bold and daring to play that work on that trip while the
composer was still alive. Shostakovich at that time was a very controversial character, and although his Fifth Symphony was performed, it was
played in a very conservative, nineteenth-century style. Here was this
great brash American throwing himself over the stage, and he wants con-
trasts, variations and inner tension. Nothing they had ever heard before."
Bernstein gave eighteen concerts in twenty-one days, and at the last
concert in Moscow Shostakovich himself appeared. "This caused a sensation in the hall," Rosenfeld continued. "The murmur started running
through the crowd. A group of us was sent to make sure Shostakovich

got backstage. Then Bernstein brought him onto the stage and the audience went wild. In that political context, it was a tremendous moment and very moving."

Bernstein had not dared to program any of his Broadway works since Russians officially frowned on American jazz, but he was determined to play some contemporary American pieces, including his own *Age of Anxiety*. He caused another stir by prefacing a performance of Charles Ives's *The Unanswered Question* with an explanatory lecture about the composer's theory of "accidental music" in which several themes in contrasting tempi are interwoven in unpredictable ways. This turned out to be an inspired idea, because the audience liked the piece so much they insisted upon an immediate repeat. Copland's *Billy the Kid,* which was presented without any explanation, did not fare so well. Then Bernstein gave another short talk to introduce Stravinsky's Concerto for Piano and Wind Instruments and *Sacre du printemps,* works virtually banned in Russia. Of the latter, he said that it "touched off a musical revolution five years before your own." Bernstein said, "They want to touch me, shake my hand, embrace me, even kiss me. I feel we are this much closer. Nothing else will be worth a hill of beans if we don't have peace."

Apart from Shostakovich, among Bernstein's admirers were the composer Dmitri Kabelevsky, the conductors Alexander Gauk and Kiril Kondrashin, the widow of Serge Prokofiev—and Boris Pasternak. The great poet and novelist had won the Nobel Prize in 1958 for his novel *Dr. Zhivago,* but was forced to renounce it after public pressure. (The book was banned in the Soviet Union.) He had gone into seclusion after that incident and had not been seen until he appeared, unannounced, at one of Bernstein's concerts at the end of the Russian tour. His appearance was highly flattering but not entirely unplanned. Felicia Bernstein, with Rosenfeld as interpreter, had commandeered a taxi outside their hotel and gone looking for him a few days before. They drove out of Moscow for several hours and became convinced that they were being deliberately led astray by the driver. Then, looking out of the window, Felicia Bernstein began to scream. They had entered a village of wooden huts, mud streets and chickens, and she had just seen Pasternak crossing the road. That evening the three of them returned for a dinner in the Pasternak dacha. It was a Russian meal of cabbage, tomatoes, peppers, pickled mushrooms, a roast and Georgian wine. Pasternak invited Bernstein to play the piano but received an embarrassed refusal. Rosenfeld said, "It made him weak-kneed. He wouldn't play the piano because he was so ashamed that he hadn't practiced." He finally played one lame little song from *West Side Story*.

They returned later that evening to Moscow because Bernstein was expected at a big musicians' party. Word got around that he had just dined with Pasternak and he was immediately surrounded. He moved to the piano and started playing jazz. Pretty soon he slid his chair back, still playing. Then he kicked the chair away and dropped to the floor, still playing. "He tucked himself under the piano," Rosenfeld wrote, "with hands reaching behind him and over him, really playing: all you could see was hands and they were making this fantastic music." The American musicians cheered and the Russians roared. The party went far into the night.

The Kissing Bandit

Blind in the sunset . . .

—GOETHE, "AN SCHWAGER KRONOS"

Leonard Bernstein gave his final concert in Carnegie Hall in May of 1962 with a superb performance of Brahms's Second, took an exhausting number of bows and, when the frantic applause continued, threw his baton into the audience and left the stage. Four months later he was conducting his first rehearsal in Lincoln Center's new Philharmonic (later Avery Fisher) Hall, designed in blue and gilt with terrazzo floors and walls of glass designed to display elegant concertgoers promenading the five storeys of long hallways. Predictably, the building was completed barely hours before the inaugural concert, for which Bernstein, as conductor and master of ceremonies, would be the dominant presence. The opening required such sartorial display that, Paul Henry Lang grumbled, even the working press had to don the white tie and tails worn by "dukes, virtuosos and waiters." The concertgoers, some of whom had paid as much as $250 a ticket, crowded into the halls, champagne flowed with abandon, thousands stood nine and ten deep outside to see the arrivals and millions more watched the event on the first "Live from Lincoln Center" telecast. Meanwhile Bernstein, in shirt sleeves, was studying his scores in a chaotic dressing room, its walls unfinished and light bulbs dangling from their sockets, admitting that even he was nervous. At the end of the evening he was, as usual, soaked to the skin and disheveled, but euphoric. Jennie Tourel embraced him, his wife patted his hair, Mrs. Lytle Hull, a noted patron, squeezed his hand, and all his old friends impatiently awaited their turns. Bernstein had programmed a single movement, the Gloria, from Beethoven's Missa Solemnis, and this was much criticized; the work was like an old cathedral that could not be dissected without being demolished, one critic wrote. That, however, was in keeping with Bernstein's insistence upon a properly religious fervor to mark the new enterprise. But the main emphasis that night was the social réclame of being seen to rub elbows, if not with the President himself, then at least with Mrs. Kennedy. She appeared on the arm of John D. Rockefeller III, president of Lincoln Center, her dark hair swept up in a becoming coiffure, wearing a black velvet bolero glittering with jet sequins and a bell-shaped skirt of palest pink. Bernstein, resplendent in his Koussevitzky cape, swept down upon her with open arms and planted a boisterous kiss, which was considered a definite breach of protocol. Mrs. Kennedy wore black gloves, diamond earrings and a somewhat bemused expression.

Bernstein was fortunate to have ascended the podium at a moment when John and Jacqueline Kennedy had moved to the White House. In inviting Robert Frost to participate in the inaugural ceremony, President Kennedy had signaled that he and his wife were determined to recognize excellence in the arts. About a hundred and fifty leading figures in the arts and sciences, including playwrights, artists, architects, novelists and musicians, were invited to attend his inauguration, and Bernstein was given a leading role at his gala. Finding that his influence extended as far as the White House brought out the most expansive side of Bernstein's nature. A few months after the Kennedys took up residence there, he and his wife were invited to a small private dinner. After the meal Bernstein found what looked like the most comfortable seat. It happened to be the President's indispensable rocking chair. There he sat and chattered brightly while his wife glowered and hissed at him in Spanish. She finally had to tell him in plain English to get up. On another occasion, he cheerfully criticized his President. Eugene Istomin recalled that he and the Bernsteins attended a dinner for André Malraux, then French minister of culture, and afterwards talked to Kennedy for two hours in his private quarters. Istomin said, "I had never met a President before and was practically paralyzed with awe, but he was so likable. He looked at everyone so inquiringly, as if he really wanted to know what you thought. Some time during our conversation Bernstein said, of some policy matter Kennedy was considering, 'Your problem is you don't see the forest for the trees,' and I saw Kennedy's eyelids come down like the slamming of a gate." Nevertheless Kennedy remained one of Bernstein's admirers and paid him the supreme compliment of remarking, "You're the only man I know I would never run against." It was generally agreed that Bernstein had become America's most powerful musical figure and, arguably, the most famous conductor in the world.

His ability to work punishingly long days was becoming a legend. On a typical morning he rose at six and, stylishly dressed in a navy blazer and black silk shirt, would study scores for two hours before breakfast. Then he might eat breakfast with an organization that intended to give him an award. Then he was off to morning rehearsal, where he might play Handel with a cigarette dangling from the edge of his lip, irreverently inserting snatches of flamenco between passages of the Saint John Passion Music. Such a morning might be followed by lunch with the president of the orchestra board, then a crowded afternoon in his apartment spent playing with the children, conferring about the next tour, being interviewed, discussing the latest film and turning down new offers to conduct an orchestra or write a Broadway show. The Philharmonic's manager, Carlos Moseley, said, "You have to remember that Lenny is the symbol of music throughout the length and breadth of this land. Anybody who's building a school, or wants to bring business and music together, or education and music together, or just wants to raise money—he wants Bernstein. The quantity of this sort of thing is beyond belief."

Between six and eight he would dine and dress and, as the evening performance arrived, would appear at the podium refreshed and revived. A typical Thursday-evening concert was introduced with the comment "Handel's *Passion According to Saint John* is thought of as an early and conventional work. But if it's conventional, I'll eat it. Just listen to what Handel does with the bass notes of this theme. Fabulous!" and he was off and running. Finally, at the first intermission, he would be likely to flag and would grumble about the lack of adequate rehearsals and complain that the critics had arrived a night early. But by eleven he was back in form, and Helen Coates would have to tunnel a way through the crowds so that he could make his escape through a side exit. It might be time for bed, but he was not tired. His wife said, "Lenny never does anything in moderation. If we're playing anagrams he always wants to play until dawn. If we watch the Late Show on television, then we watch the Late Late Show. If we go to the opera, we stop at a midnight movie on the way home. He always carries a pocketful of antacid pills; if he decides he must eat a raw onion sandwich, he first eats the sandwich and then the pills."

He was named Musician of the Year in 1960 and was being awarded honorary degrees from such schools as Northwestern, Hebrew Union College, Brandeis, Temple and Dartmouth. He won an Emmy for "Bernstein and the New York Philharmonic" (1960–61) and the Page One Award of New York's Newspaper Guild for 1960. He was elected to the National Institute of Arts and Letters. His yearly income was estimated at, variously, a hundred thousand and half a million dollars. He became famous for his dashing entrances on first nights, the inevitable cape slung carelessly around his shoulders, grabbing everyone within kissing range—Copland called him the Kissing Bandit—and shouting

In rehearsal with Martial Singher, Frances Bible and Felicia

endearments to the rest. He might, a newspaper commented, "have . . . been created by Madison Avenue as a cultural symbol for twentieth-century America . . . erudite, handsome, theatrical and formidably articulate." Capsule summaries appeared in the press of whatever television shows, recording sessions, overseas tours and conducting dates he was managing to squeeze in that particular week. He somehow had managed to write a book, *The Joy of Music,* which had developed from his "Omnibus" programs, and published it in 1959. It became an instant best-seller, was published in five foreign languages and showered with awards. Under his directorship the New York Philharmonic was soon playing to 98.2 percent capacity, a feat not even Toscanini had equaled. To no one's surprise, Bernstein's original contract of three years was soon extended for a further seven. It would end in May 1969.

Whenever he appeared, this formidable figure, with his mane of black hair now graying at the temples, his mouth mobile and sensuous, his eyes alert and amused, seemed to be moving in his own private spotlight. People have described the way Bernstein would enter a room and immediately galvanize it with his vitality, enthusiasm, spontaneity and wit. Once when an "Omnibus" rehearsal about American musical comedy was going badly and the whole cast seemed dispirited, Bernstein sat

The Bernsteins greeting guests following another triumphal opening with the New York Philharmonic

Bernstein greets a delegation of visitors; Felicia waits on the sidelines.
She once said, "I've spent my life waiting for Lenny."

down at the piano and played four bars of ragtime. That was all he did, but he broke the mood in a way that was impossible to describe yet immediately recognized by everyone; from then on, the rehearsal was a success. His ease of manner and his genuine interest in other people and their ideas were the subject of constant anecdotes. Moseley said, "No matter how crowded the room is, when he sees someone he knows, there's a special ray of sunshine for that person." Alison Ames, who would work closely with him in her capacity as United States director of Deutsche Grammophon, once gave a small party for him at a restaurant near Lincoln Center. They were crossing the street from Avery Fisher Hall, arm in arm: "I don't remember what was said," she recalled, but the moment was intensely private and intimate. "You felt special; he had eyes and ears for you only." An interviewer noted that he made friends of musicians, singers, technicians and offered photographers "a fraternal gulp of his scotch . . . His words, astonishingly clear, disarm and fascinate and his voice is resonant and round like that of a cello. The green-brown eyes hold your own . . ." Lillian Hellman was not alone in thinking he was a Renaissance man. "There's something absolutely inexplicable about his talent. Maybe it's what we call genius . . . In many ways his is the most remarkable mind I've ever seen."

For some it was his spontaneity, his gift for the improvised and uninhibited gesture, that was so memorable. Stephanie Barber recalled that she and her late husband, Philip, used to run a jazz club called the Music Inn near Tanglewood, to which Copland, Blitzstein and Bernstein came to listen to Mahalia Jackson. Then when the Barbers took over the Wheatleigh Inn in the 1960s, Bernstein and his family would stay there during their Tanglewood summers. Bernstein was a frequent visitor to her tiny nightclub in the basement of the inn, where she played a guitar and sang Piaf and Dietrich songs. One night, she recalled, she was wearing a new dress, very simple and low-cut, and he was smoking as usual when a spark from his cigarette jumped onto the dress and burned "the neatest little hole you have ever seen. So he said, 'Do you suppose it could happen again?' " and proceeded to burn a playful pattern of new holes. She finally had to stop him. Then there was the time that she found Joan Baez, a guest at the inn, sitting serenely beside the swimming pool, quite topless. When she objected that this was New England and not Southern California, the singer pointed to Bernstein seated nearby and said, "He said I could!" Arthur Laurents recalled that they were all staying together in a hotel in Florida once during a "dreadful revival" of *West Side Story* when Bernstein decided he wanted to learn scuba diving. He bought himself a lot of expensive equipment and then proceeded to try it out in the hotel swimming pool; they finally had to evict him. Laurents said there was a big difference between "self-conscious Hollywood behavior" and Bernstein's completely unrehearsed and artless outrageousness. He was, he said, "an enormously intelligent child."

People thought no one else in the world had quite that kind of look in his eye. Laurents called him "one of the most endearing men I have ever met," and Ken Heyman, who photographed him, thought he had "a kind of love energy. The ability to seduce anyone. After leaving a performance of the Vienna Philharmonic, I remember seeing four men wiping tears from their eyes, and one of them was a stagehand. Everybody *loved* him." Dan Gustin summed up that and similar reactions with the comment "It was a great gift to have known him."

When Koussevitzky told Bernstein in 1942 that conducting would "open to you all the gates from the world," he spoke the literal truth. His pupil's new prominence had demonstrated not only that American conductors could break the barriers excluding them from leading the nation's best orchestras but that an American could become an international figure on a par, it would be said within the decade, with only one other superstar, Herbert von Karajan. In mounting the podium in New York Bernstein had become a member of that select minority—Monteux, Klemperer, Beecham, Munch, Reiner, Walter, Koussevitzky and Toscanini—who had joined the ranks of the immortals. Each of them, in his own way, as Harold C. Schonberg wrote, personified a certain popular ideal of the conductor as a man "of commanding presence, infinite dignity, fabulous memory, vast experience and serene wisdom." Such a man "is at once a father image, the great provider and the fount of inspiration. To call him a great moral force would hardly be an overstatement. Perhaps he is half divine; certainly he works in the shadow of divinity. He has to be a strong man, and the stronger he is, the more dictatorial he is called by those he governs . . ."

That there was something inherently unfair in the tradition that gave the lion's share of the praise to the conductor when the effort had been made by the actual performers themselves was undeniable. But the conductor's role was pivotal, because he was the one who deciphered the notes, probed the work's essence, heard its ideal sounds in his ear, and because the effort of cajoling all those individuals into performing in unison really was as difficult as it seemed, requiring a kind of hypnotism.

Like William Steinberg, Bernstein had seen music as a calling. Like Georg Solti, he had sensed that he possessed the ability to instruct, cajole, charm and lead, along with the necessary authority, a trait that would become more pronounced as his confidence grew. Bernstein knew he had to win the respect of his musicians by knowing more than they did. He once said, "The conductor is a kind of sculptor whose element is time instead of marble; and in sculpturing it, he must have a superior sense of proportion and relationship." Like Koussevitzky, he knew that his power derived from the adoration of his audiences and would have been inhuman not to enjoy it, perhaps require it. He also knew that an American conductor in particular had a further obligation. As emissary for his art to the community at large, "like the missionary in darkest Africa, he must be armed with much more than the Gospel and a zeal to expound it; and, furthermore, like the politico, he must have a real flair for baby-kissing and back-slapping bonhomie as well as a cast-iron stomach for creamed chicken." That was the role that Bernstein played to perfection. He was seen as a maestro in the new tradition of personality and educator, someone who had singlehandedly taken a rarified art and made it available to the masses. Igor Markevitch once remarked that what a conductor needed most of all was *"rayonnement"*—in other words, a radiant personality. Perhaps Bernstein had that quality most of all.

How Bernstein would deal with instrumentalists was an issue that was frequently raised in his early years as conductor. The reputation of the New York Philharmonic orchestra members, for instance, as being tough and unruly, had been common currency since Toscanini's period and before: "My boy, they are bandits," Koussevitzky is supposed to have said. But many musicians besides the New York Philharmonic had "a fearsome reputation for slaughtering soft-skinned conductors," as Lebrecht characterized it, and, as was well known, Bernstein's facade was far from being impregnable. The oboist Dick White recalled playing the *Symphonie fantastique* by Berlioz with Bernstein. There is an oboe part offstage, so Bernstein had positioned him at stage left in a stairwell. White had just begun playing his part when a pair of double doors opened behind him and the wind blew his music everywhere. Bernstein was "laughing so hard he could hardly finish," White said, and the audience thought it was part of the show. In the days when Bernstein first took command, one of the principal players at the New York Philharmonic decided he did not like him and did his best to make him uncomfortable. His part called for a long solo. During a rehearsal, Bernstein walked to the back of the hall and stood there listening. The player packed up his instrument and started to walk out, because, "you left the podium so I thought the rehearsal was over."

"They expected a fight to the death, because there were so many tyrants on the podium," White said. Ed Skidmore, bass player for the National Symphony, agreed. "In my early days the musician was definitely an inferior person and the great Maestros, people like Toscanini and Reiner, had life and death control."

White continued, "Normally in a rehearsal we will read through an entire piece at tempo and then we'll go back to the beginning at a slower pace. There are conductors who will play the first six bars and stop, and start correcting. The piece never does get put back together, and we hate that.

"We like to divide conductors into two groups, those who are great in performance and those who are great in rehearsal. Sir Thomas Beecham (we all called him Tommy) was an example of the first group. He hated to rehearse, but at the performance he was as busy as an engineer, and the result was marvelous; it was always fresh. Then there is the conductor who gives a perfect rehearsal. During the performance every note is in place, but it is the dullest experience in the world because nothing happens. Bernstein covered both sides. In rehearsal he was very intent to get the right effect, but in performance he'd feel the body heat and create new effects. You never knew what was going to happen."

The essential difference between Bernstein and, say, a conductor like Reiner was never more evident than during rehearsals. What Bernstein wanted was not precision but a certain emotional effect, although he was not always able to tell his instrumentalists how to get it. Martin Mayer wrote:

> It is easy enough to compare Bernstein's inability to give specific instructions with the educational exactitudes of a Szell or an Ormandy—but the fact . . . is that a first-rate orchestral musician, once he knows what the boss wants, may be able to find a better way to do it than the boss can know. Those who heard the performance [of Verdi's *Falstaff*] will not soon forget the Metropolitan Opera Orchestra's management of the marvelous little string tune that breaks in on the trombones at the end of Ford's jealous aria, announcing the arrival of a Falstaff bedecked for his appointment with Ford's wife. Bernstein got this effect from the men with one remark, at the second orchestral rehearsal. They lumbered into the passage, playing the notes, and he stopped them. "Gentlemen," he said rather softly, "this is the *divine* moment of the work. If you f—— this up at the performance, so help me God, I'll murder you." After the uproar had ended, they played it precisely right. "That's *beautiful*," Bernstein said, and everyone glowed.

In dealing with his musicians Bernstein managed to steer a course between being "one of the boys" and being the kind of conductor who exhibited an Olympian detachment, then went into his dressing room and closed the door. Edward Skidmore, who, like White, is an unofficial historian of the National Symphony, said, "We were rehearsing a new work by Bernstein with a new manuscript, and questions were constantly coming up as mistakes occurred. I remember our former woodwind player asking about a certain note and chord. Bernstein said quickly that it was correct. At intermission the player said, 'I still don't understand it.' " Some conductors might have considered that to be an insubordinate remark. "Bernstein proceeded to tell him how it had been analyzed harmonically so that the player understood it perfectly, and thanked him. Bernstein was so pleased and delighted that someone was interested enough to ask."

Bernstein's success in improving morale at the Philharmonic became celebrated at an early stage. One musician was heard to say, "He can come out wearing pink tights as far as I am concerned." What they liked was that he was so generously pleased when they performed well. Ann Barak, who played solo viola during one of the *Candide* productions, recalled that Bernstein came to her afterward with arms outstretched. "He hugged me so hard I thought my ribs would break. He was overwhelmed. 'That's how I wanted it to sound,' he said, and I hadn't even known he was there. Ten years later he still remembered how I had played it." Then there was the occasion when, after a flutist and a bassoonist played a passage particularly beautifully, Bernstein stopped, came over to them and put a hand gently on each of their heads. Grown men who, as Ken Pasmanick, principal bassoonist of the National Symphony Orchestra, said, had been taught since childhood to bury their feelings, found themselves stirred by Bernstein's uncanny ability, not only to communicate his feelings in the consummate language of gesture, but to put them in touch with their own. Jon Deak, associate principal bass at the New York Philharmonic, said, "He was able to bring a piece to life. He could reach unemotional people on *his* terms and make them appreciate something that was even antipathetic to their own approach. If you could just listen to the way he would approach a piece of music, you couldn't remain unconvinced. I'd get almost resentful that he could do that to me." Pasmanick said, "Once my wife and I were going for a swim on an island off the coast of Maine and the whole sky was filled with the sun. It was enormous. It made me cry. And I think Bernstein filled our cultural lives in such a huge way that anything else about him gets dwarfed."

He always came to a rehearsal completely prepared, in contrast to some conductors, who were notorious for "letting an orchestra teach them the score," as someone said. Bernstein almost erred to the other extreme. As Stanley Drucker, the principal clarinetist of the New York Philharmonic, said, Bernstein would not just walk out and announce that the next piece would be by Beethoven. He would want to explain and philosophize before they played a note. Jacques Margolies said, "Toscanini would never have talked about music." Deak recalled, "*Also Sprach Zarathustra* had not been one of my favorites." Strauss's symphonic poem is based on the work by Nietzsche that proclaims the gospel of superman overcoming monstrous obstacles. At one point

Zarathustra comes out of his cave and leaps from a mountaintop to the top of the clouds. "Bernstein would tell us how Strauss's score illustrates this moment and, at the end, the hair is standing up on my head. Plus, he is showing us the technique behind this incredibly uplifting experience." One expected Bernstein to be capable of such large-scale effects, but "he was all soft colors and pastels, too," Deak continued. "He'd take it as a challenge to understand an indescribably delicate moment."

His beat was for the most part clear and concise, although occasionally in performance, Pasmanick said, he would forget "and start making love to the audience," and the instrumentalists were on their own. He was famous for his downbeat at the start of Beethoven's Fifth Symphony. Deak said he began with a violent, lurching movement. Both hands shot up over his head and shook, like Zeus shaking a thunderbolt out of the sky. "Everyone came in at the right moment. I couldn't believe it. These people imagined where the symphony had to start. The only other person who was as obscure was Karajan with Brahms's Fourth; he began by describing circles.

"I also remember coming to the end of Debussy's *L'Après-midi d'un faune.* The flute is hanging in the air and the basses have two pizzicatos. One time the ending was so ethereal, so otherworldly, and the downbeat was so feathery, that none of us came in. We thought for sure we would get fired, but he just smiled."

Bernstein often said that, when he was conducting, he had to feel as if he were the composer at the moment of creation. It is a remark that has frequently been criticized but Deak, who is also a composer, felt that what Bernstein meant was that he was trying to relive the work so as to recreate it as faithfully as possible. The meaning of the music, the phrasing and the form were all important. Deak said, "If you didn't play the whole phrase you weren't playing. I remember during a rehearsal of Tchaikovsky's *Francesca da Rimini* he got insulted. We were playing along happily when he suddenly put down his baton and said, 'You people don't understand it. This is the longest melody ever written. Let's play it that way, for heaven's sake.' He would actually be upset because you weren't playing this music as if you loved it."

No matter how many times he had played and recorded a work, Bernstein always wanted to come back to it and consider it for the first time. What was judged to be a fault by his critics—it is said there is no recognizable Bernstein style, because his interpretations changed so much—was a rare and valuable quality so far as his instrumentalists were concerned. Nathan Stutch, first cellist at the New York Philharmonic, said, "I remember we had performed and recorded Beethoven's Seventh Symphony and the next season it was again on the program to be recorded. Bernstein said, 'I have changed my mind about it. This is the way it should sound,' so we did a new recording. Then the same piece came up for the third time. 'This is really the way it should sound.' The same thing happened with Tchaikovsky's *Pathétique* Symphony. He came to a rehearsal saying, 'I have spent the whole summer rethinking the *Pathétique*. Forget what we did before.' That was a wonderful quality. It makes everything fresh. There are no worn edges." And he was demanding, a perfectionist. "Rehearsals were incredibly hard," Drucker said. "Someone counted how many times he stopped in a Schumann symphony, and it was a hundred and forty-eight times."

Bernstein's one problem was, perhaps, a defect of his qualities. Deak said, "There was a sad, almost tragic thing about his rehearsals. He would always arrive about ten minutes late. Then he would fool around for ten minutes and finally get more and more into it and not want to stop." Stutch said, "No matter how much time you gave him it was never enough. At the Philharmonic we had rehearsals on Thursday mornings from ten to twelve-thirty, two and a half hours, with a half-hour limit on overtime. By contractual agreement, a player could leave at twelve-thirty, which many of them had to do because they had other commitments. But Bernstein would keep right on rehearsing for at least another half hour, and once it went to forty minutes. One by one people would slip away, and what began as a symphony orchestra ended up as a string quartet. It was like Haydn's *Farewell* Symphony." It became such a cause célèbre that a clause was inserted into the contract saying that overtime was allowed only during a dress rehearsal and limited to half an hour. Kenneth Mirkin, a violist and a younger member of the Philharmonic, recalled that the attempt to discipline Bernstein never worked; if anything, he became more and more stubborn.

"I remember one rehearsal in which he came in ten minutes late. Then he had to go around kissing everyone and took out some joke horoscope book and read everyone's horoscopes for forty-five or fifty minutes. We didn't get started until ten minutes to eleven. Then we had to have a twenty-minute intermission at eleven-thirty. So of course by twelve-thirty he hadn't had enough rehearsal time. The personnel manager stopped us and Lenny had a fit. He went on and on about how much he had done for us. 'I've given you your TVs and your swimming pools and you shit all over me.' " (He was referring to the fact that the musicians were earning nearly double the incomes they had had when Bernstein

Going over the fine points of a score

took over in 1958.) Once during an open rehearsal the personnel manager stopped the show in the middle of a bar and the audience, not
understanding, booed him. Mirkin said, "Bernstein threw down his
baton and stormed off." In later years he would make caustic comments
about musicians who "just sit there and stare, and think of their union
rules." Stutch said, "No matter how many times it happened, it meant
we didn't love him. We'd have to stay around afterward and assure him
it was nothing personal."

The tenor Jerry Hadley, who worked with him in later years, agreed
that Bernstein could be exasperatingly demanding but that his abilities
as a conductor, including the ability to help a soloist past his own inse-
curities, outweighed his defects. "We are indoctrinated in school with
a fear of making mistakes and somehow he'd envelop everyone in an
atmosphere of nurturing. I had never been on stage with anyone who

looked at me the way he did, with total acceptance and tremendous love. I felt I was being made love to. It was a communication of mood and feeling; almost a Jungian bond. I don't know any of Bernstein's detractors, people who criticize his personal life, who did not add, 'But the performances! Life changing.' "

Bernstein's dedication to new music by contemporary composers continued to receive favorable comment. Speaking of the way he introduced a new work by Lukas Foss, called *Time Cycle,* the critic Allen Hughes observed that most conductors would have done their duty by it and returned with relief to their old work horses. Bernstein, however, gave his audiences explanations about the new work, written in "a compositional style related to that of Webern, fiendishly complex and . . . extraordinarily beautiful to perceptive listeners," Hughes wrote. This willingness to explain made the difference between an indifferent audience and a receptive one.

Bernstein's pedagogic instincts would sometimes get the better of him. Ned Rorem recalled, "Lenny is Germanic in style. He interprets music; he likes to bend it, like jazz. But my temperament is basically French, crystalline and precise. I don't go in for rubato and I don't like to have my music over-interpreted.

"In 1957 I wrote my third symphony in France, although it had not been commissioned, and showed it to Lenny. He loved it and said, 'I am looking for exactly this piece and I will do it next season on condition you rework the third movement for strings.' I said I would but I didn't, and he forgot he had asked.

"The last piece of mine that he performed was a violin concerto that had been given its premiere by Jaime Laredo. Bernstein, against my better judgment, engaged a more famous violinist, Gidon Kremer, and began to rehearse it. The sixth and final movement, called 'Dawn,' ends quietly and wistfully. Bernstein decided that the piece needed a fast ending, so we sat down and talked about it. Fink that I am, I agreed to take the last twenty measures of the fifth (toccata) movement and repeat them. But after some perceptive listeners asked me, 'How could you let that happen?' I took out the Bernstein ending. On the recording it ends the way I wrote it. There were times when he could not leave well enough alone."

As the first season in Philharmonic Hall progressed during 1962–63, Bernstein's only serious problem would appear to have been the acoustics, which had been questioned since the opening and were judged in need of radical revision. But his hydra-headed success, as Donal Henahan wrote, did not please everyone. After an almost unanimous chorus of praise during his first three or four years, Bernstein was beginning to encounter some negative reviews, criticism he may have invited by saying some years before that most music critics knew very little about music. He had reduced his own season appreciably and was doing more traveling, recording and guest conducting, which annoyed some critics. He was "spreading himself too thin," they wrote. His programs demonstrated what appeared to be a falling off in concentration, lacking the ingenuity one had come to expect. Paul Henry Lang of the *Herald Tribune,* Winthrop Sargeant of the *New Yorker* and Harold Schonberg of the *New York Times* all expressed dissatisfaction with Bernstein's work. Words such as "vulgar" (Schonberg), "disappointing" (Sargeant), "hardly merits serious criticism" (Boretz) and "quite wrong" (Alan Rich) began to appear. Lang thought the problem with Bernstein was his exhibitionism. In rehearsal, Lang wrote, his conducting was "precise and his gestures economical," but once the audience came through the doors he turned into a monster. Critics expressed irritation when he played only excerpts of Beethoven and Mahler choral works during the inaugural concert in the hall. They were exasperated when, performing Brahms's Piano Concerto No. 1 with Glenn Gould, Bernstein deferred to Gould's eccentric tempi and dynamics but disclaimed all responsibility for them in a speech beforehand. The general opinion was that Bernstein was a skilled interpreter of romantic music but lacked the temperament to conduct Haydn, Mozart and Beethoven.

As Lang had primly noted, Bernstein was too easily influenced by what other people thought of him. But when his critics were challenged, they responded with the defense that theirs was merely an opinion. Alan Rich wrote, "Mr. Bernstein . . . just cannot be satisfied with his sold-out houses and his cheering audiences. He must gear himself to total acceptance; anything less becomes total rejection." Bernstein, however, appeared to have learned an important lesson from the bruising he was receiving at that period. From about the mid-1960s he began to look for writers who would lend a sympathetic ear, who would, in effect, give him a podium when he needed one. One of them was John Gruen, who wrote a lively defense of Bernstein's position, essentially his response to his critics. Gruen's approach may be inferred from this sample description of the maestro being greeted by post-concert visitors to the greenroom: "All want to taste the presence, be close to the magnet.

In all there is the need to be near the source of excitement, the electricity and glamour that is Leonard Bernstein." His hostesses learned to be acutely aware of this potentially dangerous topic of conversation. A guest recalled that he had been invited to a dinner for Bernstein given by the writer Marcia Davenport just as Paul Henry Lang had published a negative review of a performance of *Messiah* by Bernstein and the New York Philharmonic. Everyone but Bernstein had arrived and the hostess was plainly on edge. "Please," she said, "do not talk about Handel, or conducting, or music reviewing, or anything else." Finally Bernstein appeared. He stood in the arched doorway of her Park Avenue apartment, looked slowly around the room and said, "Anyone here named Paul Henry Lang?" They all laughed and the party was a success.

Part of the critical coolness seemed to center around Bernstein's inability to embrace the new movements with the fervor that some critics thought his position dictated. When his assistant Jack Gottlieb wrote a program note for Bernstein's *Serenade* in which he stated that one of the reasons for the decline of new symphonic music was the "dissolution of tonality," Alan Rich responded: "Is it really possible that Mr. Gottlieb, or Mr. Bernstein for that matter, can let himself believe that the 12-tone system . . . cannot sustain a large musical form as logical as that of a Mozart symphony? If so, where were they the last time the Schoenberg Third Quartet was performed? Or his *Moses und Aron?* Or the Berg Violin Concerto?" Unfortunately Bernstein was too fond of saying, "There are still some reactionaries hanging around, like myself, clinging arduously to the old beloved F majors and modulatory harmonies." This was as shocking in its way as Kenneth Clark's remark, about a sentimental nineteenth-century painting, that he had "rather liked it."

Any conductor worth his salt ought to take it as a personal mission to program the new works in all their diversity, from the "group of doctrinaire post-Webern serialists, who have extended the Master's organizational precepts into every aspect of compositional technique"; to the "jazz group," emulating Gershwin; the "chance composers, the electronic buffs, the non-Webern serialists (working outward from the more conservative twelve-tone principles of Schoenberg), the post-Webern non-serialists," and so on, as Rich explained. The barrage continued even after Bernstein had programmed a two-month series of concerts as a showcase for the avant-garde in early 1964.

As might have been predicted, his earnest desire to be fair to the post-Webern serialists, the chance composers, the nonserialists and so on did not appease. Schonberg found Bernstein's attempts to jolly his audiences along with explanatory chats annoying; why couldn't he just get on with it? Rich thought Bernstein's remarks so condescending that "Leonard Bernstein tried everything short of a Flit gun in his attempt to kill off the avant-garde movement in music . . . last night." Critics with less of a polemical stake seemed to find Bernstein's talks informative, enlightening and amusing and sympathized with the audience's reactions, which varied from derisive laughter to booing and audible exits. It must have been some comfort for Bernstein to read that for five weeks he had "walked a musical high wire above the audiences . . . and never slipped once."

For in fact his critics were right. Of all those who might have provided a hospitable platform for atonal experimentation, Bernstein was perhaps least fitted by temperament and conviction. He believed that the idea of abstracting musical tones was an impossibility, because music was an abstract art to begin with. Music acquired its reality through form, and "all forms we have ever known—plainchant, motet, fugue or sonata—have always been conceived in *tonality,* that is, in the sense of a tonal magnetic center, with subsidiary tonal relationships . . . And the moment a composer tries to 'abstract' musical tones by denying them their tonal implications, he has left the world of communication." In the mid-1960s, as Schonberg later wrote in *Facing the Music,* there was a great deal of discussion about whether the symphonic form was dead. Bernstein, who also wrote about the subject, obviously believed it was, because the symphonic form depended upon "a bifocal tonal axis" which itself depended on the existence of tonality, and that was now a thing of the past.

As was becoming his pattern, when he wanted to shift direction he would let slip comments to see what kind of reaction he received and then advance cautiously. He had been putting around the word that there was "a sharp ache in my heart" because he had had to give up composing. It would be truer to say that he had not yet found the right vehicle to follow *West Side Story.* Laurents recalled that a year or so after its success he attended a meeting on the subject in Bernstein's Park Avenue apartment. Laurents brought up the idea of writing a musical about blacks but no one else was interested. Then they discussed the theme of the dybbuk, in Jewish folklore a malevolent spirit somewhere between a vampire and incubus that seeks a living body to inhabit. The theme is an old one and had been used successfully at the turn of the century by the Yiddish playwright S. Ansky, who had produced a classic. Laurents said, "Lenny, being very Jewish, knew a lot about the subject. I said I had a problem with the idea. At the time I was too much the rationalist; I've changed since. I said I could only do it with a box of salt. Lenny was willing to make the compromise but Jerry was not." (The idea later became a ballet.)

There was a further problem, Laurents said. Bernstein had acquired the notion that whatever he did next had to be "important," meaningful, impressive—and that, Laurents thought, was his Achilles heel. *West Side Story*'s success had had the paradoxical but not uncommon effect of making its creator afraid he would never do as well again, while the perfectionist in him demanded that he top himself; the result was that he was creatively blocked. Not surprisingly, a host of ideas was entertained and discarded. Brief notices appeared to the effect that Bernstein was considering an opera about the era of false Messiahs and the Hasidic movement in eighteenth-century Russia and Poland. He had also promised the BSO a piano concerto for its seventy-fifth anniversary that was now several years overdue, and wanted to get back to it. As he told an interviewer in Tel Aviv, "Yes, it's a great thing, the New York Philharmonic, but it's slavery too. Slavery! Concerts and recording sessions and television. Hard work." He wanted to return to the point he had left with *West Side Story,* or so he claimed. "If I hadn't spent the time conducting, perhaps by now I would have evolved some kind of musical theater form that I can be proud of." Soon he announced plans to take a sabbatical in 1964–65 and work with Comden and Green on a musical version of Thornton Wilder's *The Skin of Our Teeth.*

He managed to write and finish his Third Symphony, the *Kaddish,* a reference to the prayer glorifying God which is recited at the close of the synagogue service. It is also the prayer recited by children at the graves of their dead parents and can even refer to a son, sometimes called "Kaddishel," or "my Kaddish," who will be the chief mourner after his parents' death. It was going to be the prayer he offered up for everyone, Bernstein told David Diamond. As with his other works, *Kaddish* went through numerous revisions and false starts. Bernstein had intended to take as a starting point some poems written for him by Robert Lowell, but these seemed to lack the necessary dramatic impact. Then he turned to a young Jewish poet, Frederick Seidel, but, he said later, Seidel appeared to be the kind of person who wrote one word a week and erased it the next, so he was forced to write his own text.

He was working on the symphony all through 1963, an exhausting and unrewarding year, he told Diamond, that left him depressed and drained. Part of his depression had to do with the death of yet another of his idols, John F. Kennedy, a man he had extravagantly admired and loved, a "Zeus, Achilles, Apollo . . ." Roger Englander recalled that on the day of the assassination they were preparing to rehearse yet another Young People's Concert. He said, "I went up to Bernstein's office at Philharmonic Hall to go over our notes. We were next to the library and the radio was on. All of a sudden, the head librarian came in to say Kennedy had been shot. We didn't know what to do. Bernstein and I walked over to his apartment not saying much. I left him there and somehow we found out it was fatal. CBS wanted a memorial concert for November 24, so we got together an orchestra, chorus and Jennie Tourel to do a memorial telecast on a Sunday afternoon of Mahler's Second, *Resurrection*, Symphony. I remember seeing and hearing Bernstein. When he gave the downbeat, he was singing out loud. He was so angry. And Jennie Tourel made her entrance a third higher than it should have been. It was a real error and she never did that. In the control room, we didn't know what was happening, but as it turned out, just as Tourel began to sing the network had cut away because Jack Ruby had just shot Lee Oswald, and this gaffe of hers was never seen."

Bernstein's sense of loss and outrage never left him. He immediately dedicated *Kaddish* to President Kennedy's memory. "Ah, what a tragic waste, what a stupid murder, irritating as well as painful," he said a few weeks later in Israel, where he had gone for the symphony's premiere, and burst into tears. From then on, the question of whether humanity would survive obsessed him: "The only theme that interests me at this point is the great question of our time—are we headed for destruction, or is there hope . . . ?"

It was curious, he wrote later, that Wagner, the last of the great tonalists, died in 1883, the very year that Nietzsche supposedly announced the death of God. Just as one felt an "agony of longing for tonality," so, he implied, one felt the same longing for an idea of God and "a blind need to recapture it." This and other matters of a faithless age were becoming familiar themes in Bernstein's work. However, unlike *The Age of Anxiety* and *Jeremiah*, *Kaddish*, perhaps his least tonal work to date, received a very mixed response. He intended to write a work that was less a lament for the dead than "an affirmation of life in the face of death," but that is not the way his work, considered more of an oratorio or dramatic monologue than a symphony, struck his listeners. "As it turns out, indeed, the speaker is a scold, a shrew who thrusts at our Lord without piety or refinement. God is put into the position of a 'heavy' who has failed us completely, has lost faith in us, has consigned us to a void of apathy," Jay Harrison wrote in *Musical America*. He was referring to the spoken role of the protagonist, read by Felicia Montealegre. Others thought the language itself a pretentious mixture; at one stage, for instance, Montealegre is obliged to tell God, "We are in this thing together. You and I." One critic wrote, "The despair he portrays is only the despair of the prideful: drama is merely melodrama." Alan Rich thought it was Bernstein engaged in the task of cutting God down to size, "telling Him off in no uncertain terms. 'Kaddish' is a reasonable enough name for the piece but 'Chutzpah' would do just as well." The composer had his revenge a year later by means of an essay written by one of his employees, which a magazine saw fit to publish. The author lost no time in swinging to his defense. "The preponderance and type of vituperation that has been heaped upon the symphony leads one to suspect that it was the personality, rather than the music, that was being judged," he wrote. A "vendetta" by the critics was in full swing.

The American premiere of *Kaddish* in Boston early in 1964 was treated as the occasion for a great homecoming, with photographs of the local boy flanked by his parents, an arm around each of their shoulders. A former professor at Harvard, Walter Piston, now a vigorous, white-haired seventy-year-old, Olga Koussevitzky, Elliott Forbes, conductor of the Harvard and Radcliffe choruses, and scores of Cabots, Coolidges, Putnams and Saltonstalls appeared in force to congratulate the Bernsteins, ask for autographs and drink champagne. It was not the first such triumph. Two years before, in January 1962, Bernstein had been the principal speaker at a dinner and reception given by the Boston Lubavitz Yeshiva in honor of Samuel Bernstein's seventieth birthday, which eight hundred attended. Sam, wearing black tie and a yarmulkah, Jennie in something dark and slimming, Felicia, in the final months of pregnancy with their third child, Nina (who was born on February 28, 1962), Shirley, Burtie and his wife were all there. In honor of the occasion Bernstein revised one of his earliest works, which he called "Meditation on a Prayerful Theme My Father Sang in the Shower Thirty Years Ago." When he first played it at Mishkan Tefila nearly thirty years before, this Russian-Jewish folk theme had been arranged in the style of the great masters. Now it was in his own style, he said.

Father and son exchanged polite compliments, each grateful for what the other had given him.

Jennie Bernstein, her son Leonard, Sam Bernstein, and Irving and Vera Fine
at dinner in Boston, June 1961

Bernstein was also grateful that, in the twilight of their lives, his parents had finally reconciled. For years they had lived separate lives, pursued separate interests and even had separate friends. But, their daughter said, "We finally made my father go to a psychiatrist when he was over sixty. The psychiatrist told him he had an ulcer and that he was a very unhappy man. He went for about three months. Then he claimed the doctor had dismissed him, and made fun of the whole thing. It was a great waste of money, he said. But my parents became friends after that. The doctor actually got him to make friends with her, to make us weep with pleasure. One night they even went out dancing and began to see the same friends. Their marriage ended on a very different note than for most of its length, which was awful."

It was a poignant moment, and there would be at least one more before Sam Bernstein died in 1969. Bernstein again returned to Boston in 1966, this time for a concert in his honor. Again, he was surrounded by his family. Again, the emphasis was on the homespun virtues. His mother said: "Take any genius, I don't care who. If you don't give him the right background, he'll fall by the wayside." His father had an equally typical reaction: "With 'ruach Elohim' [a godly spirit] a man does not become dizzy when he reaches high places. I've tried to give it to Leonard through learning, understanding and religion." It would seem from a photograph of Sam Bernstein, bald and shrunken, all smiles and in the act of embracing his son, that the two had reconciled at last. But there is something about Bernstein's answering smile that is closer to a grimace.

Both of them knew that Sam Bernstein's seventieth birthday had marked the end of his lifespan as described in the Bible, and "in his mind, every moment thenceforward would be borrowed from God," his younger son wrote. Just as the father vacillated between delight and dread, so did his older son, who could all too easily imagine himself in the same predicament. In fact, after that birthday Sam Bernstein went into a steady decline, and had a crippling heart attack two years later, at age seventy-two, by a curious coincidence the exact age at which his son Leonard would have a heart attack.

That period of Bernstein's life seemed marked by foreboding and a sense of impending loss. Perhaps even the desire for music was leaving him. He was no longer sure whether it was even important, he wrote. He was aging along with everyone else, yet he still felt young. He felt ten years old, just as if he were still a frightened little boy singing the megillah, who was longing for the chance to make music his life.

To Have Is to Be

Drunk still with life in flood . . .

— GOETHE, "AN SCHWAGER KRONOS"

Bernstein's fears about aging tended to focus on his hair and he would examine his hairline anxiously for signs that it was receding. He engaged a hair specialist to give his scalp a regular tugging or "popping"—presumably a method that worked, but one that was in any case very fashionable among the prominent and successful, such as Kenneth Tynan and Gian Carlo Menotti—and his wife kept his hair, if anything, shorter than ever. He soon began to appear in clothes custom-tailored to his short-legged, broad-shouldered frame; a topcoat of vicuna lined with silk with a sash belt, or a suit of muted gray-and-white shepherd's check with "a shorter jacket, natural shoulders and a slightly suppressed waist," as *Gentlemen's Quarterly* described it. But then everyone knew he wore expensive clothes and loved fittings; it was said he would even invite friends to attend what were known as "Lenny's dress rehearsals."

In New York his manner of living (intimate little dinners for Mike Nichols and Franco Zeffirelli) was played out in a setting of new sophistication and splendor. In 1961 he and Felicia moved out of the Osborne, taking a sixteen-room duplex apartment on two top floors at Park Avenue and Seventy-ninth Street. One arrived at the top level, entered a small, well-appointed foyer and then a large hall, decorated in black and white, with a curved staircase leading to the family living quarters on the floor below. The living room, large enough for several separate seating areas and twin grand pianos covered with the regulation battery of photographs, was decorated in splashy floral prints, pale blue velvet and beige. The style was an eclectic mix of antiques and contemporary pieces, all found by Felicia Bernstein; she had become a passionate bargain hunter and frequently sought the advice of professional decorators. She had also started buying art and taking lessons in painting and sculpture. She maintained a small studio downtown and had cleared a corner of the library for her own use. Everything about the setting denoted the hostess's discriminating, one might say calculated, taste. The result was pretty but not too fidgety. The decor was meant to convey that, on the one hand, there was a family in residence and, on the other, that a world-famous conductor entertained here in a manner befitting his status. She herself tended to dress in pastels that complemented the decor; a "champagne blonde who moved through the rooms in visions of beige," as a visitor described her. By the mid-1960s they had a housekeeper named Julia, who had been a family servant in Chile, and the children, with the exception of baby Nina, were attending private schools. Shortly after moving, Bernstein took Shirley Rhoads Perle on a tour, "and when he got to the elevator he said, 'My God, look what I have got! Suppose I lose my job!' "

Felicia Bernstein was never photographed with a cigarette, and one could not imagine an unemptied ashtray on those handsome coffee tables stacked with the latest fashion magazines and decorated with fresh bouquets of hothouse flowers; still, smoking remained her single addiction. As Bernstein's schedule became more and more demanding, she began to let her acting career slide and, apart from the occasional speaking part, took more and more time with the children, her painting, music, needlework and Lenny's career. The role of the conductor's wife suited her temperament, to a point. Edward Alexander, a former Foreign Service officer who met them in West Berlin, said, "She was being overlooked, not even introduced." He happened to have seen her on television, and when he complimented her on her performances, her face lit up. Halina Rodzinski observed that such a life, on the surface, looks glamorous enough, with its openings, gala receptions, overseas tours, teas, dinners and continual fast changes into one beautiful outfit after another. "But in short order this . . . life develops a tedium of its own," she wrote. "There is so much of *it,* and so little time for one's own self. And paramount is the constant demand that one be a happy and loving wife when the husband one loves is himself capable of the most monstrous behavior because the pressures of this way of living are also depleting him . . .

"A woman learns to be either skillfully adept at this life or a compliant nonentity—sometimes she is both. In any case, the mortality rate of marriages to performing artists is . . . high . . ." As in the case of so many others, Bernstein's admirers measured his success in terms of how fast he traveled, how much money he made, who his friends were and how well he conformed to their image.

Said the writer John Gruen who, with his artist wife Jane Wilson became a friend of the Bernsteins', it was "an incredibly glamorous world of many celebrations, birthdays, parties, charades, singing around the piano with Lenny and I playing four-hand and wonderful Christmasses in the country. And Felicia was a glowing hostess. There was always food, generosity and merriment, word games and puzzles . . . To have been in their aura and taken up was, to say the very least, one of the most thrilling experiences of our lives, like a gift. We were bestowed with an aura that came about entirely through our being seen with them. It gave our lives a panache in those years. We met all their friends and we had the privilege of entertaining them in this very room," he looked around him, "and at this very piano. I could supply some friends, too, like Nureyev. It was a coming and going of glamour."

Felicia Bernstein had developed a great admiration for Jane Wilson's work and persuaded her to give lessons. Wilson said, "She had a playful quality in her work. She worked hard at keeping things lighthearted and worked on still lifes, mostly. One of those people with multiple talents."

Felicia Bernstein also bought a great many of Wilson's paintings. After about a dozen successful one-man shows, Wilson said, her gallery told her it was time to raise her prices. At the opening Felicia Bernstein arrived with a group of her famous friends and saw the new price list. "She looked at me in a way she had never looked before, as if I had betrayed her publicly. She was white with anger." She decided that Felicia Bernstein must have thought the prices had been raised for the benefit of her friends.

Daniel Schwartz was another artist who once taught Felicia Bernstein, along with a group of women all married to wealthy men or musicians. They met once a week for three hours to study figure and portrait painting in the classical tradition. "Felicia was very self-deprecating and modest about her work, but very smart. She took instructions well and began to show a talent, a sensitivity, a softness. She started to do some very nice things." Pretty soon Schwartz was being invited to dinner parties for eight at the Bernsteins with Jason Robards and Anthony Perkins, and weekends in the country.

"I remember once asking her why so many accomplished and beautiful women remained married to homosexuals, and she said what did it matter? Why make such an issue out of sexuality? And that Leonard was so handsome and talented she had been swept up by his enthusiasm and charm. She also admitted to having boyfriends, although she never came right out and said she had had affairs. It was all part of life. A terribly advanced marriage; beyond me. Personally I think she was very conflicted and putting on an act. Her own career was in the background. She had made a conscious choice to marry him because of the world that opened for her."

When Schwartz first met the Bernsteins, he had had four or five one-man shows. His pupil thought he should be better known and said she wanted to help him. "Knowing a bit about the celebrity world, if you don't become the success they expect, you are dropped. The first couple of years was wonderful. Then three or four years went by and they didn't see my name in the paper, and there was a cooling off." At length he was having another show on Madison Avenue and invited Felicia Bernstein to come to the opening and bring her friends. She arrived early on the night of the opening to see his work, left a bottle of champagne and a personal note. When he arrived she was gone, and none of her friends came to the show. That was, effectively, the end of the friendship.

Jane White had a similar experience. She said she was "taken up" again by Felicia briefly when she had a big success in a play and then dropped. The late Peter Mark Schifter, who would direct Bernstein's opera *A Quiet Place,* said, "People in the arts are notoriously fair-weather friends," and "If you are famous you never know what people really want, and that's where the doubt comes in."

The composer William Bolcom agreed that success had unforeseen drawbacks. "After a while the whole novelty and excitement of people writing about you wears off. The up side is that you can get things done. The down side is that your life is not your own. You get to feeling self-

Analyzing Beethoven's Fifth Symphony for "Omnibus" with the
Symphony of the Air in November 1954

A blackboard demonstration for "Omnibus"

conscious. You are not alone in your bed any more. You realize that people are not interested in you but in being able to tell their friends they were with you. They want the fame to rub off on them. It's a daunting feeling, a horrible feeling, like being raped." For Bernstein the danger appeared to be, as he wrote in a fragmentary opera, "to have is to be"; what a man owned, rather than who he was, defined his worth. In commencement speeches he began to warn students about assuming that success was more important than virtue, and a brilliant life more to be praised than a noble one. In the meantime he and Felicia continued to enjoy what Logan Pearsall Smith had aptly termed a "swimgloat," and if they thought that success exerted a further price, they gave no sign. That, as Noel Annan described it, was the "American syndrome" in broad outline. "To succeed, painters and writers had to become celebrities and celebrity destroyed them as artists."

Once while spending a weekend in the country with the Bernsteins, Daniel Schwartz was playing a game of tennis with his host. Schwartz said, "I was beating him and he knew it. Suddenly he said, 'I've had enough,' and starts walking off. I said, 'You really should finish the set,' and he said, 'How would you like to see the headlines, "Leonard Bernstein Dies Playing Tennis with Unknown Painter?" ' " To Schwartz it seemed that Bernstein was being a poor loser, but in fact the danger, though remote, was real. Although the symptoms lessened considerably as he aged, Bernstein never outgrew his childhood asthma and remained at risk of an attack from all kinds of irritants: dust mites, animal dander, molds and pollens, even such unavoidable hazards as a sudden rush of cold air. Of course he should not have lived in New York, breathing its contaminated air, and of course he should not have smoked—invariably three packs of cigarettes a day, and more when he was composing. There was something demonic about his disregard for the consequences and something heroic about it as well since, for the asthmatic, even moderate exercise can bring on terrifying symptoms of wheezing, coughing and a feeling of being suffocated, along with a rapid heartbeat, sweating and dizziness. That conductor the public saw taking endless bows, jumping down off the podium, smiling and waving would, in later years, be the man who pulled at his collar backstage, gasping for breath. For most of his life he was pushing himself to the very limit, physically as well as artistically.

Jack Kirkman, who began backstage at Avery Fisher Hall as an artist's assistant and became a personal assistant to Bernstein, said that while Bernstein was conductor of the New York Philharmonic he never saw him have an asthmatic attack but that he always needed a complete change of clothes at intermission, right down to his underwear, because he was "wringing wet." It was his job to attend backstage to all the maestro's needs (he never called him Lenny) from the moment he arrived until the moment he left in his chauffeur-driven limousine. He would have an elevator waiting so that Bernstein would not have a moment's delay, and ensure that the dressing room was stocked with everything he required. That would include coffee, water and cigarettes, at intermission and between pieces. After the performance Kirkman would have a Ballantine Scotch with ice waiting for him, along with a cigarette already lit; he favored L&M's in those days. "Occasionally he might have half a Valium or an upper after a concert, but I never saw him doing hard drugs."

Bernstein always had a chauffeur and valet in attendance, but on trips he needed even more help, and Kirkman often accompanied him. "He took me everywhere. I took care of his clothes, his scores, baton and his Scotch. I used to buy the presents—usually small things—that he brought home. I also had to tip everyone. I would get a certain amount from Helen Coates and I had to keep records. She'd check them when I returned and always tell me I was spending too much, but it took lots of tips. And Bernstein was always urging me to give people more. I remember one time bargaining for bracelets on the Ponte Vecchio and Bernstein said, 'Don't bargain. Give them what they want, because they are poor.' "

Going on tour seemed to bring out the hidden adolescent in Bernstein's nature. Ken Pasmanick joined the New York Philharmonic on one of its tours as a replacement for the second bassoon player. He recalled that Bernstein played and conducted a Mozart piano concerto that called for only one bassoon, so he would wait in the wings during that particular piece. He said, "After his performance Lenny would come off stage and grab me. 'Oh, did you hear that? I was atrocious!' and I would reassure him. This went on night after night as he played that concerto, and I finally got tired of this because I felt used. There was no end to the reassurance he needed.

"So finally one night, when he said, 'Didn't you hear that in the slow movement?' I said, 'Yeah, I guess I did,' and he didn't talk to me for three or four days."

Pasmanick told another story about the time that Bernstein, on a trip to Australia, New Zealand and Japan, played a game of touch football with the orchestra players in a vineyard outside Sydney. "I remember the first horn player saying, 'Lenny, don't run anymore, I touched you,' " Pasmanick recalled. "Lenny replied, 'You didn't, you didn't!' just like a child and stamped his feet." After all, as Bernstein wrote, any conductor was an automatic narcissist, or why else would he be performing?

It was the most marvelous experience to travel with him, Kirkman said, because he included one in everything he did. "I remember being at dinner in Lucerne and watching him reading scripts with Charlie Chaplin. I've seen him in Denmark with the king and in Monte Carlo with Princess Grace and Prince Rainier. One night we were staying at the King David Hotel in the old section of Jerusalem and I saw him with Edward Heath, prime minister of Britain, Teddy Kollek, mayor of Jerusalem, and Moshe Dayan [foreign affairs minister and hero of the Six-Day War] drinking tea and talking until the sun came up. In those days he had so much energy. We have roamed the back streets of Vienna, Berlin and London for hours . . ."

Considering that many young men would become disciples of Bernstein's, their careers crucially helped by the interest he took in their conducting, teaching and composing careers, his role as mentor began almost casually. Apart from his summers at Tanglewood—and he missed several of those in the early part of his Philharmonic career—when he was often working with students too unskilled to qualify as aides-de-camp, his participation in the advancement of young American careers was slow to develop. It was true that he had started a program of appointing three assistant conductors, with the expressed intention of training future music directors for American orchestras. However, it was obvious that he had no plan to help them during the year when they were, supposedly, there to gain experience.

Yuri Krasnopolsky was one of the Americans to be appointed. He was there for the 1962–63 season with a Frenchman, Serge Fournier, and a Hungarian, Zoltán Rozsnyai. He was the most experienced of the three, having served as associate musical director of the St. Louis Municipal Opera and musical director of the Los Angeles Civic Opera; he had also toured with American Ballet Theatre and conducted extensively in Europe. He was delighted at the opportunity, but soon frustrated. "We had to study every program, and it was nervewracking, because we assumed the conductor was not going to break a leg, and he didn't. We were supposed to have contact with Bernstein and we had none." So Krasnopolsky, the only one who spoke English, was delegated to present their position and Bernstein agreed to meet them once a week for lunch, or after a rehearsal. "The fact is that we were cogs in a very large wheel, and no one cared about us. Carlos Moseley [managing director] and Nick Webster [assistant manager] tended to refer to us as 'you characters.' When I appealed to Bernstein, he would make one of those deep sighs that come out of five thousand years of Jewish history and ask, 'What am I supposed to do for you?'

"Finally after about six months he agreed to present the three of us in a spring concert and give us seven minutes each. We went back to see him. He said, 'What's the trouble now?' We told him that giving us seven minutes each made us feel like students, and couldn't we each have half a concert? He was thunderstruck. He couldn't believe we would want more. He thought he was doing us all a favor."

No doubt Bernstein felt that if he gave them all a kind word occasionally he was doing all that was expected of him—treating them more or less as he had been treated as an assistant almost twenty years before. Matters came to a head when Krasnopolsky, in his role as gadfly, discovered that the orchestra was planning a tour to England. "One evening we cornered Webster, who was dressed in a tux and going to a reception for Sir John Barbirolli—we, of course, were not invited—and asked who was taking the tour. We found out that the chairman, David Keiser, and his wife were going. So I said that the Keisers could afford to charter their own plane and that the three of us ought to have the experience. Webster said the plan was to take only one of us. He wagged his finger at us and said that if it weren't for the David Keisers of this world, we wouldn't be here. As it turned out," Krasnopolsky said, "I added to my sullied reputation but we did get to go. Bernstein was delighted. He hadn't known anything about it."

Krasnopolsky's fear that the assistant conductorships were not going to be used as a training ground for young Americans developed into a conviction when he learned that, from 1963 on, the Philharmonic would take its yearly quota from the conductors who had won the Dimitri Mitropoulos International Music Competitions. In 1963 that competition, which was dear to Bernstein's heart and in which he had been involved since its inception, was attracting highly qualified applicants from around the world. Europeans were the candidates with the most experience, and they were sweeping the board. As Krasnopolsky rightly saw, "This meant that the job emphasis changed. It became an international forum. Bernstein kept saying what he most wanted was to establish a Socratic academy for American composers and conductors. We all saw him as our leader, but this was contradicting everything he had said for years."

In those days, Krasnopolsky said, Bernstein was friendly with the late Roger Baldwin, founder of the American Civil Liberties Union. Baldwin owned an estate on Martha's Vineyard, and the two of them went sailing. "Baldwin once said to me, 'Your boss is a very tortured man. He is so unhappy with himself that he hasn't written an opera to compare with *Porgy and Bess.*' " Having achieved the impossible feat of becoming conductor of the New York Philharmonic did not assuage Bernstein's ambition but merely removed it to a higher plane. He now wanted to become a composer as famous as Copland or Gershwin, someone who was going to make that major contribution to the cause of a uniquely American style which he had vowed to do all those years ago. Everything he had accomplished so far would be worthless if he failed in this most important of objectives. But, as his former collaborator Stephen Sondheim discovered, such a goal tends to have a miragelike aspect, and the closer one approaches it, the more it recedes. "The more you become known the more people expect of you and the more they will shoot you down," he said ruefully. It is evident that, for Bernstein, those external pressures were allied to inner pressures that were even more relentless. Once he had convinced himself that he had to do each thing better than he had ever done any of them before, as he said in 1958, the inner demand almost guaranteed failure, since nothing he did would ever be good enough. A note of self-consciousness began to enter his music, as well as a striving for significance in work that had been notable for its artless high spirits and directness of appeal. His tendency to procrastinate, put off difficult decisions and arduous tasks, along with a secret fear that he lacked the talent, almost guaranteed that what he most wanted would be the one goal that would always elude him. Yet he continued to believe, and would tell anyone who would listen, "I am not happy unless I can compose."

He found all kinds of excuses for avoiding work. Harold Prince said, "One year when he was supposed to be composing he and the family were staying in Porto Ercole and I went to visit him. The only thing I can remember vividly is a giant music stand with not a note on it. Through the years, Bernstein and I talked about producing another opera. I think it's a shame," he continued almost apologetically. "I just never had any sense he would finish it." Sometimes he was determined to be distracted. Paul Sperry, who sang many of Bernstein's songs in later years, said that he agreed to perform in a group of concerts celebrating the work of Reynaldo Hahn, the French composer of light opera and songs, during one of Bernstein's composing periods. He and Michael Wager, an actor who was also in the show, had invited Bernstein to attend a later performance but soon decided that what was evolving was inadvertent high camp. Bernstein was saying to Wager, "Maybe I should hear this," Sperry recalled. Wager replied, "Please don't!" Bernstein was not to be deterred. It was his duty to support his friends. So he appeared at a performance, listened briefly, then exclaimed, "My God, it's Florence Foster Jenkins!" He turned to Sperry and Wager and said, "You bastards made me come down for this!"

During his sabbatical season of 1964–65, a supposed time of reduced activity, he conducted a benefit performance of *L'Histoire du soldat* in January, went skiing in Aspen in February, conducted more Stravinsky in March and a new version by Jerome Robbins of Stravinsky's *Les Noces,* recorded a Mozart piano and string quartet with the Juilliard in April, flew to Denmark in May and Puerto Rico in June, where he performed before Pablo Casals. He also attended a performance of his theater songs at the Theater de Lys with Jacqueline Kennedy and agreed to become a member of the National Council on the Arts. Such activities were, in his mind, peripheral; but what did excite him in 1964 was conducting Verdi's *Falstaff,* his debut at the Metropolitan Opera, in a new production staged by Franco Zeffirelli. To conduct a performance that would then be recorded was becoming routine for Bernstein in those years, and his indefatigable determination to record everything accounts for the size of his discography, which is vast. Almost unanimously, critics welcomed Bernstein back into the theater: "There is no conceivable doubt that musical theater is his predestined *milieu,*" Irving Kolodin wrote.

During his year of idleness Bernstein also found a couple of months to toss off what would become one of his most performed works, the *Chichester Psalms* for boy soloist, chorus and orchestra, commissioned by the Cathedral of Chichester in Sussex. The settings of three psalms in Hebrew, beginning with "Make a joyful noise unto the Lord" and including "The Lord is my shepherd" and "Why do the nations rage," were a momentary distraction from the main business of the year. Perhaps because Bernstein had very little time to agonize over them, the settings were considered a great success. "They make a sequence not only of thought but also of emotion, which Bernstein has fashioned into an artistic entity by the binding strength of the musical ideas he has evolved and the warmth of the life he has breathed into them," Kolodin wrote. "A lovely enchanting work," the *New York Times* reported, and the verdict was general.

Bernstein had devoted most of the summer and late autumn of 1964 to hammering out the musical of *The Skin of Our Teeth* with Comden and Green. The production ought to have been foolproof: three old friends working together on the kind of play that seemed to cry out for translation into dance and song and with a theme that exactly expressed Bernstein's political mood. Furthermore, the Columbia Broadcasting System had provided a capitalization of $400,000, with the promise of more money if necessary. A tentative opening date had been set for September 1965. By January the whole idea had fizzled out, and Bernstein refused to explain why. A second venture, *A Pray by Blecht,* a musical adapted from Bertolt Brecht's *The Exception and the Rule,* with Zero Mostel in the leading role, also reached the production stage before being abandoned. "Don't talk to me about writing stage works," Bernstein said at about this time, "it makes me very sad."

A further disappointment of his sabbatical year centered around the legacy of Marc Blitzstein. The composer, then fifty-eight, went on vacation in Martinique in January 1964. One evening, as was his habit, he went to the waterfront bars and picked up three sailors, one from Martinique and two from Portugal. The men discovered he was carrying a sizable bundle of cash, robbed him, beat him severely, took off all his clothes except for a shirt and socks and left him for dead. He was taken to a hospital but died of his injuries a day later. Blitzstein had left behind a distinguished body of work and also three unfinished operas in various stages of completion. Two, *Idiot's First* and *The Magic Barrel,* were based on stories by Bernard Malamud, and the third, which had been commissioned by the Ford Foundation in association with the Metropolitan Opera, was to be based on the trial of Sacco and Vanzetti. At a memorial concert for Blitzstein in the spring of 1964 Bernstein announced that he would finish *Idiot's First.* He could, theoretically, have had a free hand with all three works, since he and Copland were executors of Blitzstein's musical estate. Had Bernstein been capable of finishing any of them, there is little doubt that he would have, given his enormous admiration for one of his mentors and the outrage he must have felt at the circumstances of his death. The fact that he did not, as it turned out, is another indication of how completely he felt blocked whenever the challenge of writing—or completing—an American opera loomed before him.

It was Bernstein's bad luck to be working as a composer at a moment when the world of music was in an uproar and the cult of the new was at its height. The great movements in art of the early twentieth century, cubism, futurism, dadaism and surrealism, bringing with them the belief that art must portray man's alienation from a disintegrating society, eventually had a profound effect on all the arts. Instead of the ultimate goals of truth and beauty, since truth was unknowable, modernists valued the relative ones of originality, experimentation and style. Besides style, everything depended upon how unique and daring the work was; and if it aroused outrage, so much the better. That canny arbiter of fashion, Diaghilev, had understood the new imperatives at once with his demand of Cocteau, "Étonne-moi, Jean!" The new measurement of worth had, however, problems of its own. "The artist must forever develop or die," Noel Annan wrote. "In each phase of his work he must change almost beyond recognition." If he succeeded, the artist had probably lost his audience, but he had won instant critical acclaim, almost an impregnable reputation. If he failed, he was going to be ridiculed into conforming and the kindly dismissal "at best, eclectic" was perhaps the most damning of all.

Unfortunately for him, Bernstein's temperament had put him in sympathy with the great romantic movements of the nineteenth century, and his gift was lyrical at an age when such a gift was dismissed or relegated to such minor musical tributaries as writing for the theater. Jon Deak said, "Bernstein was called a very good Broadway composer by the In crowd of the 1960s. That was the put-down. The corollary was that he was not serious. Both Bernstein and Copland were susceptible to this reasoning, i.e., that real music was an intellectual exercise, a kind of exclusive discipline shared by a few initiates, like nuclear physics, something they could not hope to understand." This attitude, as propounded in some college music departments and musicological journals, had succeeded in giving lesser men than Bernstein a conviction of intellectual inferiority, and he was struggling against this bias, on top of everything else, during his unsuccessful sabbatical year. He finally let it be known that what had been at the root of his failure was an effort to come to terms with the avant-garde. "I was writing twelve-tone music and even more experimental stuff. I was happy that all these new sounds were coming out, but after about six months of work I threw it all away. It just wasn't my music; it wasn't honest." The most common criticism of Bernstein's work was that he needed a theme, a book, a poem to get him going; he was an illustrator, a writer of "program" music and not a "pure" composer. He could write in every style from boogie-woogie to plainchant, but always in tracks that had been worn bare by others. "It has been said that, like the proverbial blonde, his music is extremely well put together and has all the obvious points of attraction, but no heart." After years of this and similar criticisms it is not surprising that he, too, believed them. "He was always making excuses for his music," John Corigliano recalled. "When he wrote *Songfest* [1977], which is lyrical and romantic, he said apologetically that it was old-fashioned music, not to be compared with the important work I was doing."

The trouble was, Bernstein liked to say, he felt helplessly suspended between the performer in himself and the creator. He identified with those of his predecessors who, in the exigencies of earning a living, had performed or conducted and snatched at rare moments to write their symphonies, operas and concerti. Of all those with whom he felt a common bond, Gustav Mahler was his beau idéal. Mahler, too, had been born Jewish, had begun as a pianist and had turned to composing and conducting. Like Bernstein's, Mahler's gifts as a conductor had raised him to prominence at an early age. Mahler, too, excelled in musical theater, and his decade as artistic director of the once-declining Viennese Imperial Opera was a series of triumphs. At the age of forty-seven he was at the peak of his conducting career and almost ignored as a composer, when not actually derided. He converted to Catholicism; Bernstein married a Catholic and would write a Mass. Mahler exhausted himself with the effort of producing performances at the Metropolitan Opera and singlehandedly attempting to revive the floundering New York Philharmonic. He conducted the latter for just two years, dying of overwork in 1911, at the early age of fifty. By then Mahler had managed to finish ten symphonies, but these works were so far outside the conventional form that they were considered insane. Mahler's two most devoted admirers, Bruno Walter and Willem Mengelberg, were almost alone in their determination not to allow the work of their master to be forgotten. Dimitri Mitropoulos was another and, from an early age, so was Bernstein. Early in 1948, when just twenty-nine years old, Bernstein gave a performance of Mahler's *Resurrection* Symphony with the New York City Symphony and repeated the program in Boston, where the work was heard for the first time in thirty years.

It was clear immediately that Bernstein had an instinctive affinity for Mahler's work. "One could only wonder why this magnificent work has been allowed to languish on the shelves for thirty years," Jules Wolfers wrote. "Within its pages there is encompassed such a wealth and variety of expression that one feels, at the end, that a lifetime of experience has been exposed . . . in a little over an hour . . . If the effect was overwhelming it was because the composer was overwhelming. This alone is enough to stamp Bernstein as a master . . ." The symphony was "a masterpiece of splendor and noble vision," Cyrus Durgin wrote, and other critics were similarly lavish in praise of the work and its interpreter. From then on, the Mahler symphonies stood at the summit of all that Bernstein hoped to achieve as a conductor. To give these massive, masterly, anguished, demanding works the most fully realized readings of which he was capable became an obsession. He programmed the symphonies repeatedly, began to record them one by one from 1960 on, and was so committed to the subject that he began to wear Mahler T-shirts and offend his friends. In 1955, when Bernstein was conducting the Symphony of the Air, Copland refused to attend the first performance of his new work for chorus and orchestra, the *Canticle of Freedom,* because, Virgil Thomson told Nicolas Nabokov, "he was mad at Lenny for sacrificing too much of his rehearsal time to a Mahler symphony." In 1960, the centennial of Mahler's birth, Bernstein scheduled performances of six of his symphonies plus numerous concerts of his songs; and in 1965, when he returned from his sabbatical, he programmed three symphonies, the Seventh, the Eighth and the Ninth. "How the wheel has turned!" a critic wrote after those performances. "The sold-out houses were knowledgeable, attentive, and, at the last, roof-raising with their cheers. Bernstein's years of devotion to Mahler have produced a totality in the art of communication of which the entire country should be proud." Another critic wrote, "Let it be said . . . that the performance of the Eighth was one of the towering moments of my life in the concert hall. Rarely have I witnessed a more blazing affirmation of faith on the part of an interpreter. Mr. Bernstein has a consuming love and understanding of Mahler, and on this occasion he placed his entire being at the service of the man and the music . . ."

Bernstein wrote that Mahler stood at a pivotal moment poised between the end of the romantic era and the beginning of the modern movement. Perhaps Mahler, as Bernstein said, had brought the symphonic era to its close. Mahler had been granted, Bernstein wrote, "the honor of having the last word, uttering the final sigh, letting fall the last living tear, making the final goodbye."

That Bernstein identified with Mahler was axiomatic. Yuri Krasnopolsky said, "After George Washington, Bernstein would have liked to be Mahler." From there it was a short step to actually believing himself Mahler reincarnated, and a belief in reincarnation is an accepted tenet of Hasidism. He certainly saw himself as buffeted by conflict as Mahler had been: "Mahler the creator versus Mahler the performer; the Jew versus the Christian; the Believer versus the Doubter; the Naïf versus the Sophisticate; the provincial Bohemian versus the Viennese *homme du monde;* the Faustian philosopher versus the Oriental mystic . . ." Mahler's Ninth Symphony was completed in 1910, a year before he died, establishing him in Bernstein's eyes as the musical prophet of the coming horrors: two world wars and weapons so destructive that humanity itself faced extinction. Bernstein believed that Mahler, in common with Thomas Mann and Carl Jung, somehow knew what the future held and that his symphony summed up his anguished responses, first to his own death (Bernstein theorized that the opening bars imitated the irregular beat of Mahler's weakening heart), then to the death of tonality, "which for him meant the death of music itself," and finally, the death of society. In that year before he died Mahler was writing "farewells to music, as well as to life." By then Bernstein had become so identified with performances of the Ninth that "one feels [he] has become Mahler," Schuyler Chapin wrote gushingly in *Musical Chairs.* After a performance of that work Chapin was always glad to see the maestro step down off the podium "in one piece."

Mahler's death in 1911 was the inspiration for *Death in Venice,* the novella Mann wrote that same year. It tells the story of Gustave von Aschenbach, a man of fifty—Mann has changed his occupation from musician to writer—who has reached his life's goal of becoming famous but no longer wants to write. "To him it seemed his work had ceased to be marked by that fiery play of fancy which is the product of joy," Mann wrote. Dreading summer alone in the country, Aschenbach decides to go to Venice. There he falls in love with Tadzio, an androgynous fourteen-year-old boy of exquisite beauty and the natural air of an aristocrat. As the days pass, Aschenbach rediscovers his youthful creativity, as personified by the beautiful boy, and begins to write again. He also tries to approach him but is overcome with embarrassment. He begins to notice that the hotel is emptying, but Tadzio's family remains. Then he discovers that there is a cholera epidemic in Venice that the authorities are trying to keep hidden for fear of destroying the tourist trade.

He begins to follow Tadzio in the streets, sit behind him in church and pursue him in a gondola, half pretending that it is all happening by chance but aware that Tadzio knows and welcomes the attention. He is tempted by orgiastic dreams and the fantasy that everyone will abandon them, leaving him alone with his beloved. Then one morning he learns that Tadzio and his family are finally leaving. He walks down to the beach and finds Tadzio playing on the sand. As he watches intently Tadzio begins wading into the water and then turns in his direction. It seems to Aschenbach that the adored figure he has so long sought is finally responding. He smiles and gestures, clearly inviting him to follow. At that moment Aschenbach dies.

Speaking of the final bars of Mahler's Ninth, Bernstein remarked that it was "the closest we have ever come, in any work of art, to experiencing the very act of dying, of giving it all up." The concluding passage was "terrifying, paralyzing, as the strands of sound disintegrate. We hold on to them, hovering between hope and submission. And one by one, these spidery strands connecting us to life melt away, vanish from our fingers even as we hold them . . ."

The Right to Fail

Dazed with billowy fire . . .

—GOETHE, "AN SCHWAGER KRONOS"

Bernstein's tenure at the New York Philharmonic is generally agreed to have been extraordinary, perhaps as significant as Toscanini's. He had not only rescued the Philharmonic from its lackluster image and established it anew as one of the most important orchestras in the country but built its audiences, its income, its repertoire, given it national and international attention and, perhaps most important, provided its musicians with their first fifty-two-week season and a handsome annual salary. (This was further augmented by recordings and television work.) He had held the post longer than any other conductor including Toscanini, and led more concerts than anyone else in the 125-year history of the Philharmonic: 736 to date. He had made the orchestra his own: "I shall always regard the Philharmonic as 'my' orchestra," he said. He had met every demand placed upon him except that of pleasing every critic, an impossible feat. He had proved that an American, given the chance, was the equal of Europe's finest musicians. He ought to have been happy.

In November 1966 he announced that he would leave when his contract expired in 1969. He was coming to a moment in his life, he said, when he wanted to concentrate on composing. The orchestra responded by inventing a new title for him, that of conductor laureate. There were the usual flowery compliments all around and there the matter rested.

Harold C. Schonberg of the *New York Times* thought that was a mistake. Since returning from sabbatical Bernstein, he wrote, had shown a new maturity. There was less of the flashy, vulgar and mannered about his performance and there was more substance. "He has not been breaking rhythms and violently changing tempi the way he used to, and while there is still a great deal of personality to his interpretations, there is in addition a sustained line that had been missing. In short, he is threatening to turn into the kind of conductor that his talent originally had indicated." He had almost graduated from being called "Lenny" by his musicians to the honorific of "maestro," Schonberg also wrote. What a pity that he should abandon a goal just as it was within reach.

Schonberg could have been right. However, Bernstein's statement about his reasons for leaving, while worded with typical circumspection, reveals a glimmer of truth. The problem went back to that sabbatical year, when a great deal of money had been gambled on his continuing ability to create a Broadway hit at a moment's notice. For the first time in his life he had taken a monumental pratfall. He was looking for exoneration and fastened on his post as music director. That left him, at best, two months off every summer. No one could compose against that kind of deadline; it was "intolerable," he said. If one idea did not materialize, he wanted to be able to start something else. He wanted, he said, "the luxury of being able to fail." To the extent that he was now willing to allow himself to make a mistake, the news was positive, but it was at best a partial victory, since too much of the pressure he felt stemmed from inner needs that were impossible of fulfillment. What he wanted was to feel young again, to be filled with the "fiery play of fancy" that was better than sex, better than one's first drink of orange juice in the early morning. He was directing his efforts to solidify his ultimate place in the musical firmament because he would soon be fifty. He said, "Permanency . . . That's my obsession. I want things to last . . . Ah, how to cope with the problem of mortality, the sense of one's own death as a reality." He had been given several commissions, including that of writing a theater work for the opening of the John F. Kennedy

Center for the Performing Arts in Washington, D.C., in 1971. He could write anything he liked, he said. For the moment he had no ideas.

As Bernstein prepared to leave the New York Philharmonic he may have been giving the impression that he planned to retreat to the life of the mind but, typically, he knew exactly what he would do next, and conducting was a prominent part of the plan. In March of 1966 he had repeated the triumph of his Metropolitan Opera *Falstaff* in a new production staged by Luchino Visconti at the Staatsoper in Vienna, with the Vienna Philharmonic in the pit. Bernstein arrived to begin rehearsals and moved into a hotel across the road from the opera house. There was a week of orchestra rehearsals, at the end of which the players broke into two minutes of spontaneous applause for the maestro. Next day he went to bed with bronchitis. The following week, rehearsals began with the singers, and it was the usual chaos. The orchestra was raucous and the singers were late with their entrances. Bernstein told them, using English, German and Italian, to watch his baton: "You can't rely on your ears alone for more than two or three bars." He exhorted the players to soften their tone. "Not so heavy—*nicht so Deutsch,* this is Italian."

On opening night, Bernstein conducted without a score and received an ecstatic reception. For every performance an anonymous admirer sent a fresh bouquet of red roses which sat on the music stand where his score ought to have been. The Vienna Philharmonic had lacked a permanent conductor since Karajan resigned in 1964, and discussions began almost immediately in the hope that Bernstein would accept the position once he left the New York Philharmonic, but he refused to commit himself. Meantime, talks were being held with Egon Hilbert, director of the Staatsoper, to engage Bernstein for several return visits. Bernstein rather added fuel to the speculations by appearing in London with his wife later that year and saying that, once he was a free man, he might buy a house in London.

It was his first guest appearance abroad for years. He soon returned, this time to conduct Mahler's *Resurrection* Symphony, pulling the "wires of concentration almost unbearably taut in establishing a scale of dynamic and tonal values equal in scope to the proportions of the work," a critic wrote. "The Philharmonic and . . . the State Opera Chorus, were driven along as though ridden by a demon . . ." Another triumph and, this time, Bernstein, with his own supply of red roses, showered them on his audience. Although he said that he could walk unnoticed in the streets of Vienna, in contrast to New York, where he could not step outside his apartment unrecognized, that was beginning to change. His

At rehearsal in 1981

face was appearing on billboards, and his recordings were being featured in the windows of music stores.

But perhaps his biggest triumph there was conducting Strauss's *Der Rosenkavalier* in the spring of 1966. Given the opera's identification with Vienna, that was an act as daring, it was said, as any since the day Daniel had put his head inside the lions' den. However, over the years the opera had been performed so often that the singers were almost walking in their sleep and "a brown soup of string tone" had blurred the fine details. Bernstein approached the work as if he were a restorer, and critics responded with encomiums far exceeding the polite phrases usually reserved for visiting celebrities. Peter Heyworth of the *Observer* wrote, "Detail emerged with unusual sharpness and the Vienna Philharmonic Orchestra played with a precision and splendour of tone that it reserves for those conductors on whom it has cast the mantle of its (not easily won) approval." He was the talk of the town, it was said, and the admiration was reciprocated. He said, "In Vienna I was worried about the reporters there, about how they would treat me. But they were wonderful. That's my city. I loved it." As for the Viennese, "We in Vienna," said Marcel Prawy, that city's famous commentator on opera, "where Beethoven, Brahms and Richard Strauss worked, consider Leonard Bernstein the greatest musician alive."

If Vienna was his city, London was not far behind. British response to the conductor's flamboyant style had been chilly, to say the least, when he appeared with the New York Philharmonic on his European tour of 1959. Four years later the atmosphere had thawed considerably, and his Festival Hall audiences were stamping and shouting in a most un-British fashion. He had become "a transatlantic hero," a newspaper commented. Bernstein was sure of a warm welcome, the middlebrow *Evening Standard* reported, because of his extraordinary musical talent and engaging personality. "His only detractors seem to be those who resent his lack of the intellectual snobbery they regard as fitting." London had even grown tolerant of Mr. Bernstein's more eccentric aspects. Sydney Edwards wrote, "I cherish the memory of the last time I met him at the airport and saw him plant a smacker on a distinguished director."

The prospect of a freer, more fluid schedule in the offing put Bernstein in a mellow frame of mind. He spent the morning of his fiftieth birthday in a London hotel room having breakfast, surrounded by vases of red roses, with piles of congratulatory telegrams at his plate, his bare feet tucked under the table, wearing blue denims and an open-necked shirt, looking like a man who has just escaped from his performing-flea routine. He liked to say, "I've long ago learned to take off Leonard Bernstein, hang him up in a closet and be myself." That he should make such a statement was revealing in light of the care he had always taken to present an image of a fully rounded human being, one without guile or calculation, while at the same time keeping his inner world very private indeed. To now claim that he had abandoned this carefully constructed facade was tantamount to elegant self-deception of a high order. Only someone who had compartmentalized his life and feelings into leak-proof containers could be so profoundly mistaken about what was actually happening to him, if indeed he believed what he said. Here, for instance, was a man who told an interviewer that, fortunately, he had just slept for three days and a moment later, in the interviewer's presence, could claim to someone else that he had not slept for weeks—and not be aware of a contradiction. Being subjected to his father's admonitions had served to perfect his ability to evade painful admissions. Denial was his defense, and he was very good at it. Now, at the moment when he was energetically proclaiming that he no longer needed a facade he was in fact constructing a new one.

Look magazine had published a flattering picture essay about him, and out of that came an idea for a picture book to mark his fiftieth birthday with a large, handsome format, a kind of coffee-table advertisement for the new Leonard Bernstein. Bernstein knew that his writer, John Gruen, would protect him from the wrong kinds of revelations, and he was about to subject his photographer, Ken Heyman, to a test with the same objective in mind. Heyman said, "Bernstein had to have approval of the photographer, so we spent a weekend together, and at the end he told me to go ahead. It was arranged that I would arrive the following Monday morning. He met me at the door in a bathrobe. We sat and had breakfast. Then he said he was going to shave, so I went along to take pictures. He had photographs of those who adored him around the walls and a British crossword puzzle beside the toilet. I was taking pictures when he suddenly turned towards me and dropped his pants. I thought to myself, 'This is a test,' and did not take that picture, although I had been snapping twenty seconds before. If I had taken the picture, it meant I wasn't his friend. It was a bit sad and pathetic, although I must say I was more shocked than sad."

Gruen had met Bernstein when he was working for the New York *Herald Tribune* as associate critic of music and art and went to interview him. "I was bowled over because here was this personage . . . Then I reviewed his concerts. I might not be kind at times, but always concluded with the obvious realization that we were listening to a great musician. Back in the sixties there were many complaints about his gyrations. He was so boisterous and a bit of a show-off. If you were in the same room you had to fight for your very existence, because he was so all-encompassing. I don't mean to say he overwhelmed you. You could talk to Bernstein, but he did most of the talking if he was interested." Then the invitation came to write the book. Gruen with his wife, Jane, their eight-year-old daughter, Julia and their long-haired dachshund, Sophie, took a villa near the Bernsteins' in Ansedonia, a small town near Rome, and began to do interviews.

Gruen said, "Our relationship was a double-edged sword." On the one hand, they were in close social contact but, on the other, Felicia Bernstein was uneasy that Gruen was a member of the press and kept saying, "You can't have it both ways, John!" He was writing for the *Times* when Schonberg's critical reviews were appearing. After each attack Bernstein would be angry and would vent his wrath on Gruen. When Tom Wolfe wrote his famous Bernstein profile for *New York*, Gruen was writing for that magazine, too. "Bernstein called me up and said, 'If you are my friend you will instantly resign,' and I replied, 'If you will go on paying my salary, I will.' "

Although *The Private World of Leonard Bernstein* incorporates a great deal of biographical material, for the most part it presents a picture of an idyllic family life: Bernstein loafing on a terrace in tailored white pants and an open-neck shirt, Felicia Bernstein in thonged sandals and a long skirt, two daughters with the same pert, finely featured profiles as their mother and Alexander as his father's indispensable companion. They swim, sunbathe and chatter. Bernstein, bare-chested, has his hair cut. Charlie Chaplin and family come for the evening. Bernstein does push-ups, Bernstein looks out over his Park Avenue terrace, Bernstein rehearses, Bernstein conducts, Bernstein relaxes, Bernstein gives a party, Bernstein watches his wife paint, Bernstein and his wife share a tender moment, Bernstein plays with his children and Bernstein becomes a country squire at Springate, the house they now own near Fairfield, Connecticut. The final photograph shows the family man all in white, with three romping children and wife, hands linked, under the trees, cavorting in the leaves: the perfect fadeout.

They all indulged in what was variously described as "serious kidding" and "the puncturing of egos," dangerous games in which each was at liberty to make cutting remarks to the others. The results showed themselves, in Bernstein's case, in an automatic defensiveness to every attack, real or imagined. Bernstein remarked to his children:

> Mummy is fond of a kind of intimate, loving, teasing
> criticism . . . It has always been a sort of duty, sworn on oath, by
> all the members of all my family, to act as bringer-downers, so
> that Daddy doesn't go off on Cloud 9 with a wildly swelled

head . . . I am constantly being brought down . . . Daddy's fat belly when he was doing a Greek dance, Daddy's this and Daddy's that. This is part of every conversation, every day. Right? Daddy's driving. Daddy's reaction to something. Daddy's wrong jacket that he put on . . . You must also admit that Mummy goes somewhat overboard in that department. Mummy is perhaps the most critical single person I've ever met in my whole life.

Shirley Bernstein said, "Of course she criticized him all the time. She'd laugh but he got the point—and he *was* excessive. You know, he used to love riding in convertibles in the fall with the top down and the heat on below—it's something we all share. This one time he was walking down Park Avenue when he saw a beautiful white Cadillac convertible in a showroom window, so he bought it then and there. Felicia had a fit. 'You're not conspicuous enough?' she said. She made him take it back." She must have felt there was a certain weary inevitability to her role. Ellen Adler, who often invited them to dinner, said, "We used to joke that he wasn't housebroken. Lenny would think nothing of putting his feet up on a table and knocking over a lamp. Felicia was constantly calling the next morning and saying, 'Let me send you a check for the lamp.' "

She was, of course, very correct. Their life was lived with a certain formality; on that she was "persnickety," Shirley Rhoads Perle thought. Richard Wilbur saw something quite old-fashioned and ladylike about her. "Once on his birthday Lenny got a lot of sycophants around and showed them blue movies, and I can imagine how Felicia felt about that," he said. "Lenny was forever verbally and in other ways, violating her ladylikeness. These things would come up at meals especially. I remember at lunch his talking about the kind of food being served at Hamburger Heaven and using the appropriate vocabulary, words like 'glop,' " for the fun of seeing how uncomfortable he could make his wife. Daniel Schwartz recalled going into the Russian Tea Room with Felicia Bernstein and coming upon her husband with several friends. He was introduced and Bernstein insisted they join them. "When the talk got around to Felicia's art, someone asked me how she was doing. I said her work was wonderful. At that point, Lenny pipes up, 'Oh, it's so sentimental and old-fashioned. Why don't you get with it and do modern painting?' It was very stupid and cruel and I had to bite my tongue. She didn't say a word, but he really put her down, and I hated him for it."

Some years earlier the Bernsteins had made their first professional appearance together in *Joan of Arc at the Stake,* the dramatic oratorio by Arthur Honegger. He conducted and she played the title role, a spoken part. Rosemarie Tauris Zadikov, who was a reporter for *Time* magazine in those days, said, "She was nervous and tense, very attentive with him. I recall that her mouth was drying up and she kept asking for water. She watched his every cue and his whispered suggestions were eagerly accepted. At one point she has to say, 'What is that dog howling in the night?' and Bernstein, to be funny, said, 'That's no dog, that's my wife.' Felicia shrugged angrily and turned away."

Rose Styron and her husband, William, saw a great deal of the Bernsteins during the 1960s, often at Martha's Vineyard, where they all spent the summers. She said, "He was the star, but Felicia, who was a kind, wonderful, gentle, shy, tasteful woman—she was the friend. He was larger than life. She was sane, calm and disciplined, the one everyone loved. I've seen him in many guises, as the warm family man, for instance. I have also seen him be rotten, in ways he didn't know were rotten, to Felicia and Alexander. Then when he'd discovered he had gone too far, he would be very contrite and go to excessive lengths to make amends."

In 1968 Felicia Montealegre was back in the theater, acting in a revival of Hellman's *Little Foxes,* directed by Mike Nichols. She was interviewed in Baltimore on her birthday and blamed herself for being too critical with her family and herself. She had just received a birthday telegram from her husband, "I love you" repeated sixteen times, with "I love you dearly" at the end. For in fact they loved each other still, despite the clash of temperaments. He was beginning to suffer from chronic sleeplessness and went to bed as late as possible. She liked to retire early and rise with the dawn. He loved the limelight; she tried to avoid public exposure. When he was agonized, she was coolly confident; when he was impatient, she was a model of self-control; when he became petulant, she assumed the role of, if not parent, at least the older, wiser, levelheaded sister. She hated the constant traveling and, although she went with him, as photographs show, up to about 1968, after he left the New York Philharmonic she slipped into the background. He began taking his children on trips and to public appearances. A rumor circulated that she had wanted to leave him while he was still with the orchestra and was implored to stay because she was the only one who could "control" him. A columnist announced in 1960 that the two were close to a divorce, then retracted it. Whatever the private battles might have been, in every way that counted she remained her husband's fiercely loyal supporter. A friend recalled a dinner with her at which everyone had to sit and listen to her describing what it was like to live with a genius. She once said, "He gives me so much love, more than any other person, that I can accept him as he is."

Part of Bernstein's private but far from secret world had to do with his resumption of his homosexual liaisons. Gossip among students in Tanglewood as far back as 1955 had it that he was attracted to both sexes and that handsome young homosexuals had a definite advantage as candidates for his conducting classes. Thomas J. Schwab, a New England attorney, was living in a bachelor house in Washington when Bernstein came to conduct at Catholic University in 1954 or 1955. "A close friend of one of my friends, very handsome, was being propositioned by Bernstein and I remember being shocked." Another observer, who would become an opera director, said, "The first intimation I had that he was gay was when I was at Yale Drama School in 1959. One of our music students stayed at Tanglewood and Bernstein had put the make on him." Disbelief and disapproval were the rule. Someone might overhear a graphic conversation in the locker room of the Yale Athletic Club and feel that his idol was crumbling before his eyes. Someone else might observe him as a visiting celebrity at a conservatory, laughing and joking with terrifying and unmistakable frankness.

A photographer recalled that he had been hired to take Bernstein's picture just before a concert. "He was wearing a cape with a red lining and looked very impressive, but the minute I pointed the camera at him he turned to stone," he said. "I didn't know how to come up with anything decent in thirty minutes. Then I thought of a strategy to warm him up. I decided to tell him how awed I was, and how afraid of him. It worked like a charm; too well. He said, 'Come over here and let's have a kiss.' That was not what I had in mind, but I made the mistake of moving toward him. He had his hands all over me and I had to extract myself again and again."

Bernstein continued to try psychoanalysis: "I've had terrible depressions and various other problems as well," he told an interviewer. In the 1950s he had consulted the late Dr. Sandor Rado, a Hungarian-born psychiatrist who was president of the New York School of Psychiatry until 1967 and had many famous patients. Exactly what problem Bernstein asked Dr. Rado about could not be determined, but it is known that the latter thought of homosexuality as a perversion and would have treated Bernstein accordingly. In any event, Bernstein never completed a course of analysis, pleading one excuse or another: the psychiatrist was not clever enough and therefore easily misled, or too clever, or overly impressed by having him as a client, or trying too hard not to be impressed. So he did his own reading and appeared to conclude that he was hopelessly torn. Maggie Smith, who photographed him for the *Saturday Evening Post,* recalled she took one picture of him in 1963 that showed him behind a pole that had more or less bisected him. She apologized for the gaffe, but he replied, "That's a perfect portrait of me. Half man, half woman."

One of the strong bonds uniting the Bernsteins had to do with their common political beliefs. He campaigned for Robert Kennedy and conducted the Adagietto from Mahler's Symphony No. 5 at his funeral on June 8, 1968. As the war in Vietnam intensified, both of them became involved in the protest movement. "I deplore it! Deplore it!" Felicia Bernstein said. "Oh, if only we could do something to stop this—this terrible destruction of human life." During Eugene McCarthy's presidential campaign she campaigned across the country with Rose Styron and Phyllis Newman, handing out leaflets at shopping centers.

At about that time, Yuri Krasnopolsky recalled seeing Jennie Tourel in Omaha, where he was conducting and she had come to do a performance of *Jeremiah.* He asked how Bernstein was. "Oh, I feel so badly about him," she said. "He's deeply troubled about Vietnam, angry and frustrated. He comes into my apartment with this enormous leonine head, in command of the world, and after a few moments he is in tears, about the war, the stupid government and his powerlessness. He falls apart." Steve Rosenfeld recalled that he went to a State Department dinner given for Bernstein. A long table, seating twenty or twenty-four, was presided over by former ambassador Robert Schaetzel. When the conversation turned to Vietnam, Bernstein gave his views and tempers began to rise. "Schaetzel began to say, 'As our secretary of state [Dean Rusk] said . . .' and Bernstein became inflamed. He said, 'Don't tell me about your secretary of state! He looks like a man who rolls condoms for a living.' "

Felicia Bernstein was also active in the American Civil Liberties Union and became concerned when she learned that twenty-one members of an extremist black organization, the Black Panthers, had been in jail for ten months awaiting trial. She was appalled that any group could be held for so long and immediately began to consider ways to help them financially—bail had been set, but none of the accused could afford it. There was no question about the sincerity of the Bernsteins'

Bernstein said of this photograph, "That's me. Half
man, half woman."

motives. However, raising money for the Black Panthers was not a particularly popular cause: those being held faced charges of plotting to kill
policemen and conspiring to blow up midtown department stores,
precinct houses, railways and the New York Botanical Garden. It would
have been more politic to send around a fund-raising letter. Instead, the
Bernsteins decided to hold what they called a meeting but that included
cocktails and canapés served by butlers and maids. The satirical possibilities were too good to miss and, as chance would have it, the ideal
writer was at hand.

"The only time I had ever laid eyes on Bernstein was in Springfield,
Massachusetts," Tom Wolfe recalled in his gentle, unemphatic and
courtly voice. "He came for a lecture series and was absolutely brilliant.

It was an illustrated lecture. He'd jump to the piano and play and illustrate, often humorously. He had just written *West Side Story,* so we had a quick interview and I mentioned that some of his critics had accused him of commercialism. He replied, 'Are the slums of New York and people dying, with blood on the sidewalk, what you call commercial?' " Wolfe said with private amusement, "Now I would say yes." He was wearing a black check suit and looking elegant and dandyish, his breast pocket handkerchief at just the right angle.

"Fast forward to 1969. That summer I was invited to a party given by Andrew Stein for Cesar Chavez and the grape workers at his seaside estate in Westhampton. All sorts of socialites with their big bouffant hairdos and their Pucci clings. Everyone was asked to close their eyes and try to imagine getting up at sunrise and having a hot dog and a Pepsi for breakfast. There they stood with their eyes closed, holding their hair to protect it from the ocean breeze, and a phrase popped into my head: 'radical chic.' " When he heard about the Bernstein meeting, he wangled an invitation. "There were a great many things going on that fell under the same heading. I was contemplating a nonfiction version of *Vanity Fair* and thought the Bernstein event might make a chapter in such a book." His report on the event became an article for *New York* magazine and, eventually, part of his book *Radical Chic and Mau-Mauing the Flak Catchers.*

Wolfe continued, "To me the cause had no particular interest. What interested me was the social phenomenon," that is to say, the juxtaposition of all those Black Panthers, with their Afro hairstyles and goatees and black turtlenecks, and the rich, chic crowd with whom they were mingling, in the Upper Bohemian living room with its Chinese yellow walls and white moldings and flotillas of family photographs on twin pianos, its butlers and maids and its host with his Black Watch plaid trousers, his navy blazer and black turtleneck with a pendant displayed on it. It was William Makepeace Thackeray resurrected on the southeast corner of Park Avenue and Seventy-ninth Street. The late Charlotte Curtis, then society editor of the *New York Times,* was also amused by the artless ironies being presented but was as interested in the fact that the meeting was being used to advance a cause of anarchy and that, far from disagreeing, the host seemed to be in supine accord. She wrote that when Donald Cox, Panther field marshal, said that if businesses refused to employ blacks they would be obliged to take the law into their own hands, Bernstein replied, "I dig absolutely." Did he really, or was it just

Bernstein being compulsively charming as usual? No one bothered to find out. The Curtis article was published a day after the meeting, and an editorial followed. The *Times* commented, "The group therapy plus fund-raising soirée at the home of Leonard Bernstein, as reported in this newspaper yesterday, represents the sort of elegant slumming that degrades patrons and patronized alike . . . Responsible black leadership is not likely to cheer as the Beautiful People create a new myth that Black Panther is Beautiful."

Although the party was treated by the press as Bernstein's idea, it had actually been his wife's. She had overcome her natural reticence and dislike of the spotlight in order to do something constructive, she thought, something that would give adequate outlet to her sense of outrage. As for her husband, he might have expected to be applauded for his liberalism and was unnerved to find himself being booed as he mounted the podium. His sister said, "I was very proud of him because during the whole period, when he was being subjected to so much criticism, it would have been so easy for him to say it had been his wife's idea, but he never once betrayed her. And the event marked his life; the term 'radical chic' followed him forever."

As might be expected, Bernstein put up his usual energetic defense. It was not true that he supported the Black Panthers. The whole affair had been grossly distorted. Their only aim had been to raise money for those accused. "As an American and as a Jew I know that freedom of religion and the freedom of the citizen go hand in hand. Strike the one and you have damaged the second. If the American society refuses to grant the Panthers their legal rights, simply because they disagree with their method—we are striking at the very soul of democracy." His wife went into political seclusion and, from then on, would only work behind the scenes, as she did for Amnesty International in Chile, according to Rose Styron. She would never place herself in such a vulnerable position again. A decade after that, Bernstein accused the Federal Bureau of Investigation of carrying on a calculated campaign of harassment against him and his wife following the Black Panther meeting, which included hate mail and spiteful attacks in the press as well as attempts to undermine his relationship with Israel. He said after her death, "None of these machinations has adversely affected my life or work, but they did cause a good deal of bitter unpleasantness, especially to my wife who was particularly vulnerable to smear tactics. For the sake of her memory if for no other reason, I should be happy to see this whole shameful F.B.I. episode exposed . . ." (The author was unable to verify the validity of Bernstein's charges, since repeated requests over a three-year period for information under the Freedom of Information Act were not honored.) He also believed he was under continuing governmental surveillance. In 1980 he said, "I'm perfectly aware that my phone is tapped by the FBI and the CIA. I talk to them, and if it's a private conversation I say the dirtiest words I can think of, and then I say an even more astonishing thing, and I hear a little click."

By then Bernstein was accustomed to being labeled as a political radical and investigated for his beliefs. A resurgence of interest in politics on his part happened to coincide with his father's death in 1969. Once he had convinced himself that, now that he had celebrated his seventieth birthday, his time was up, Sam Bernstein's body obligingly confirmed his worst fears. All manner of ailments began to plague him, and he made plans to sell his business, telling his son Burton, "I'm as good as finished." Then, at seventy-two, he was rushed to hospital for heart surgery to repair an almost-ruptured aneurysm of his aorta. He survived that but became increasingly frail. He had a heart attack in 1966 and died in the spring of 1969. Rabbi Israel Kazis of Temple Mishkan Tefila officiated at his funeral and the Bostoner *rebbe,* Levi Horowitz, officiated at the gravesite to make sure that the casket was properly covered with earth according to Hasidic custom.

Before he died Sam Bernstein reflected on the ironic fact that each generation of Bernsteins had rebelled against the wishes of the one before. His grandfather Bezalel had become a blacksmith instead of a rabbi. His father wanted to be a rabbi, not a blacksmith. He himself had escaped to America in order to become a businessman, not a rabbi. Now that what Sam Bernstein wanted was entirely beside the point, Bernstein could talk of nothing else but the fact that his father should have been a rabbi and that he himself had been born to teach. His life had been one long attempt, through the classroom, the television screen, even through conducting (since that was a form of teaching), to impart his knowledge. "Anything that is sharing of a feeling that one has or of knowledge which one may have—I don't go so far as to say *wisdom* . . . comes in the category of teaching . . ." "Rabbi," of course, was just another word for teacher, someone with the knowledge and authority to command respect. He liked to attribute the idea that he himself might be a *rebbe* to his children, publicly at least. In private he was more direct: "It was a time of his life when he wanted to be a teacher, a *rebbe,* above everything," said his friend Phillip Ramey. In due course Bernstein assumed his father's position as a prominent member of Mishkan Tefila, which by that time had moved from its Roxbury premises to a new sanctuary in Newton. Rabbi Kazis said that Bernstein came to the synagogue whenever he was in Boston and sat beside him on the pulpit. Bernstein would always be awarded an honor of some kind, such as opening the Ark during the Yom Kippur service, a privilege usually reserved for the president of the temple. Bernstein consulted Rabbi Kazis about preparing Alexander for his bar mitzvah in 1968 and went to some pains to ensure that the boy received exemplary instruction. Of Bernstein's determination to have Alexander follow him at Mishkan Tefila, his boyhood friend Mitchell Cooper said, "There weren't many of us who would have felt that tie to the degree he did."

Bernstein was preparing to give a series of lectures at Harvard while serving as Norton Professor of Poetry for the 1972–73 academic year. That was another high honor—Stravinsky, Copland, Chávez and Sessions had held the chair before him—and was thinking about his subject matter. He would, of course, deal with music as it related "to poetry, to words and especially the metaphorical aspects of words, because I consider music a language of metaphor."

While continuing to talk about how much he wanted to compose, Bernstein went on filling his time with a manic series of performances. Almost all of 1970 was completely taken up with the New York Philharmonic (including a tour of Japan), the Metropolitan Opera, the Vienna Philharmonic, the Israel Philharmonic, the Vienna State Opera (*Fidelio* at the Theater an der Wien to celebrate Beethoven's two hundredth anniversary) and the London Symphony Orchestra, summer at Tanglewood, and a dozen other such dates. Instead of conducting in one city, he was maintaining the same pace but in cities around the world, giving himself, if possible, even less free time. He nevertheless insisted that he had been composing. The Jerome Robbins and Zero Mostel project had not worked. The next challenge had been to write a score for an experimental film with Zeffirelli dealing with the conversion of St. Francis of Assisi, *Brother Sun, Sister Moon*. By the spring of 1970 that, too, had been abandoned. Then Bernstein got excited about a plan to work with the Israeli actor Topol on a project involving Brecht's *Caucasian Chalk Circle*. Unfortunately he had been obliged to stop work because of a commitment to conduct *Cavalleria rusticana* at the Met. That did not mean he was not composing. Anything might be revived at any time, including *The Skin of Our Teeth.*

Meantime he was glad of the "blessed overwork," which gave him "the lift I most need, and I need it now . . ." Spring of 1970 found him rehearsing Mahler's Third Symphony with the newly formed Orchestre de Paris. He was making regular trips to Paris and, if he was not traveling with his wife, would ring up his old friend Kiki Speyer, who by then was married to Jacques Fouré, a Parisian dentist. She said, "The first time he had the trots he said that the only person who knew how to take care of him was me." Kiki Fouré was summoned and arrived with a big bottle of paregoric. The friendship began again and was soon back on its old easy footing. She said, "We were in his dressing room one time and I was surprised to see the hair on his chest. I said, 'You never had that,' and he replied, 'Yes I did.' " Another time he arrived with a tooth missing. It seemed that, on the transatlantic flight, he had sat next to a particularly pretty girl who asked for a parting present, something that was his alone, so he gave her a false tooth. She jokingly said, "You never gave me such an expensive present!" Every year he arrived, he would introduce her anew with the words, "This is the girl I should have married."

He was beginning to feel an increasing nostalgia for his youth, filled as it had been with so many tempting options. Mildred Spiegel, now Zucker, remembered that when they met after a period of years, Bernstein immediately insisted on sitting down at the piano and launching into their favorite duet, Gould's *Rumbalero.* Annette Elkanova, who was also married by then, recalled a similar experience when she met him backstage after a concert. It was some time in the 1960s and she was upset to see that he was using an oxygen inhaler. "He said, 'Do you remember the Stravinsky concerto we used to play?' and immediately sat down and began to play it."

There was also the time that the composer William Bolcom lunched at Bernstein's apartment. "I said goodbye and just before the elevator came he gave me the strangest look, *un regard,* as the French say. It was a yearning look, as if he were asking something from me. Not a sexual message. A certain sense of, 'You have something I don't.' He would have loved to have been me. A sense of the direction he could have taken, and didn't."

Questions Without Answers

Lost in utter bewilderment . . .

— GOETHE, "AN SCHWAGER KRONOS"

If in his earlier works Bernstein had been attempting to make contact with his God, the creation of the work that opened the Kennedy Center in the autumn of 1971 has to be considered a further milestone in that lifelong quest. The commission had been suggested to him by Jacqueline Kennedy, and to take the Roman Catholic Mass as framework for a theatrical piece about the loss of faith seemed intriguing. The work has as its slight plot the story of a very contemporary young man carrying the compulsory guitar who begins as a celebrant but, as the Mass progresses, becomes increasingly embittered and disillusioned and erupts in a rage, desecrating the sacraments and tearing off his vestments. The work ends with an affirmation of faith, or a demonstration of the need for faith, by the congregation.

Bernstein worked on the new project intermittently for three years and had not yet finished as the Kennedy Center neared its opening and the production began to take shape. Julius Rudel, who was then music director of the center, said, "The thing I found rather amusing in retrospect is that we were planning to open a building that hadn't been finished with two works that hadn't been written yet." He was referring to a new opera by Alberto Ginastera, *Beatrix Cenci,* as well as *Mass,* although in the latter case that was a slight overstatement. Bernstein had conceived the work in broad outline and was collaborating with Stephen Schwartz, a young librettist who had just triumphed with *Godspell,* had chosen his conductor, Maurice Peress, and assembled an enormous cast of dancers, singers and instrumentalists. He had even found his central character, who, Schuyler Chapin wrote, had to be "young, intense, attractive, compelling and sympathetic . . ." The agent Matthew Epstein brought Alan Titus, a baritone who could also play the guitar, to audition, and he was an immediate success. Epstein said, "Bernstein liked very passionate, vibrant performers, although occasionally he'd find a technically adept singer, perhaps not so extroverted, but with a beautiful tone. His response to singing was always emotional and artistic." It is true, however, that a great deal of work needed to be done with the orchestration, and Jonathan Tunick, a brilliant young New York composer, was called in to help Bernstein's old collaborator, Hershy Kay, because the time was growing short. Wayne Dirksen, organist and choirmaster at the Washington Cathedral and himself a composer of note, was engaged to play one of the two organs for *Mass.* He recalled that Bernstein was living at the nearby Watergate Hotel, rehearsing all day and composing all night. The ending of the piece was not written until a few days before opening night. Across the road, in the Howard Johnson's, a two-room suite had been engaged for "at least" five copyists, and every day someone would go to the Bernstein suite to pick up the latest pages and transcribe the composer's scrawl into a legible manuscript. Dirksen said, "It was common knowledge that Mrs. Kennedy was paying all the bills."

Chapin, who was acting as Bernstein's manager at the time, saw other problems. After the first run-through he was sure the show was going to be "a very exciting theatrical event," but it was much too long. He voiced his concerns to the director, Gordon Davidson, who agreed but wished him good luck at getting Bernstein to part with a single note. Chapin was at his most convincing, but Bernstein would not compromise. "After the dress rehearsal all of us again landed on Bernstein, who by this time was exhausted, and finally, at some ungodly hour in the morning he agreed to Gordon's cuts," but only for the preview. Chapin knew that Felicia Bernstein would be there for the preview and pinned his hopes on her persuasive powers, but even she was unsuccessful. "Now you've all had your fun," Bernstein said afterward. "Everything goes back in tomorrow."

Chapin's thesis, that any problems inherent in *Mass* could be resolved by some judicious trimming, was not shared by the critics. No mention was made of its length in any of the reviews, although critics discovered other flaws in what would become perhaps Bernstein's most controversial work. At the opening reporters swarmed around the members of the Kennedy family—Jacqueline Kennedy was conspicuously absent—in the hope, presumably, of getting an unguarded comment or two expressing Catholic displeasure with the scene in which the altar is desecrated. Indeed, one member of the audience did call out "Sacrilege!" The Kennedys, and particularly Rose Kennedy, were not to be ambushed and murmured their support. Bernstein, naturally, dissolved into tears and hugged and kissed everyone with such abandon that Mrs. Kennedy finally had to gently beg him to desist. (Tears, he liked to explain, were proof, absolute proof, that the work had been a success.) His team of singers, instrumentalists and dancers adored performing *Mass,* thought he was without flaw and gave him reassurance whenever he seemed to need it. One of them was Amy Antonelli, a singer who struck up a warm friendship with Bernstein and acted as a de facto hostess during his Washington visit. She said, puzzled, "He should have known how good he was!" Shortly after the opening a photographer, meeting him at the National Press Club, was moved to say, "You captured everybody's hearts." Bernstein smiled and then touched him. As the reporter said, "The handful of men who'd lingered at the VIP reception stiffened . . ."

Catholic priests were naturally offended, and the archbishop of Cincinnati called it "a blatant sacrilege against all we hold sacred." Critics were sharply divided between those who, like Paul Hume of the Washington *Post,* called it "the greatest music Bernstein has ever written" and those who, like John Simon, thought it was "derivative and attitudinizing drivel." Stephen Sondheim said, "He had asked me to do the lyrics for *Mass,* but I had reached the stage of not wanting to collaborate with anyone anymore. He made me sit through it twice. He was in tears and I didn't know where to look." Bernstein insisted on some kind of reaction, so Sondheim said, "Have you thought of translating it into Latin?" Sondheim added sotto voce, "So you won't have to listen to the words," and indeed the libretto was subjected to a great deal of criticism. Simon called the lyrics "simplistic, pretentious, pedestrian and not a little distasteful," and Eric Bentley dismissed them as "subliterate rubbish." That was a serious, perhaps irreparable flaw, although great composers had been known to triumph over the crudest of conceptions. Donal Henahan thought that Bernstein had been trying to write a morality drama and a personal passion play to boot, and there was in consequence "a great deal of . . . mythic allusion and ritual transformation in *Mass,* some of it effective and some of it putting one in mind of an adult-education lecture on the Metamorphosis of the Gods." It was true that Bernstein's style was, if possible, more eclectic than ever. That was not necessarily a defect in this particular work, since a pastiche was defensible as reflective of the age. One might even write a dissertation on the ways in which Bernstein had managed to meld the Roman Catholic and Hebrew traditions, "or how skillfully [he] drops in and out of the styles of Stravinsky and Orff," or how, less successfully, he tried to adapt the latest Broadway craze, the rock-musical idiom of *Godspell* and *Hair,* to his own use. Henahan continued, "What cripples *Mass* at last, however, is less its failure to find a workable way to reconcile the popular and classical musical traditions than its inability to persuade the sympathetic listener that the banalities have been given a meaning . . . We are unmoved . . ."

Henahan had rightly called *Mass* a personal passion play. In it, Bernstein has taken his inner monologue beyond descriptions of the spiritual vacuum that accompanies a loss of faith and into open defiance: the sacrilege at the altar. But he is torn between his insistent need for self-assertion and his need for love and acceptance, and therefore his rebellion is doubly symbolic, rather than real. Not only is he play-acting at this masked rejection of his own faith (it is, after all, a piece of theater, therefore not really happening), but he has already invented the safety net of the happy ending in floods of tears, as if eternally suspended between rebellion and reconciliation. It is this insistence upon a facile solution that, from the point of view of the audience, is the basic flaw of *Mass.* Eric Bentley wrote that the culminating moment "consists of a stoppage of conflict which is arbitrary, not organic, and an equally tacking-on-at-the-end of Love Love Love Love Love as a solution that may not be questioned." The whole drama hinges on a pivot that is missing, one in which the central character will experience the necessary insight into his own spiritual malaise that will make the final affirmation of faith seem genuine and inevitable, rather than forced. This crucial omission is, however, true of every attempt at musical theater by Bernstein for which he has provided the libretto. Why Bernstein can-

With Elie Wiesel at the Tavern on the Green in 1988

not seem to write such a scene is another question. In his introduction to Ibsen's verse drama *Brand,* W. H. Auden refers to one of the characters in the play, an acquisitive mother who cannot bear the thought of dying because she does not want to part with her material possessions. He writes, "The sinner does not know what it means to be spiritually happy; he only knows that to give up his sin will be a great suffering."

Whatever one thought of *Mass,* Henahan wrote, one had to admire Bernstein's courage in attempting such an effort, "his unrepentant insistence on disclosing himself to us as an artist," which made most other contemporary composers look "intolerably timid." Henahan concluded, "*Mass* is Bernstein's attempt to embrace, in one tear-stained bear-hug, us, our children, God, and our common dilemma. Mahler, wherever he is, will appreciate the effort."

Christmas of 1971 found Bernstein back in the studio of his Park Avenue apartment, correcting galleys for the booklet to accompany the Columbia recording of *Mass.* He sat, legs crossed, "like a Jewish guru, on an overstuffed brown leather chair, wearing a pink shirt with a diamond pattern and jeans studded with metal stars . . ." wrote Robert Kotlowitz in an article describing the rehearsals of *Mass* and its aftermath. "The jeans and the shirt are at odds with the body, which is middle-aged . . . and the face has too much experience on it for the whole outfit. 'With it' is what it proclaims, and the very act of proclamation puts it in doubt." Despite mixed reviews, interest had been expressed in a less lavish traveling production, the record had been made and the same team was preparing for a New York debut in the summer of 1972 as well as a performance in Cincinnati. The agent Margaret Carson said, "Bernstein was being attacked for being sacrilegious, and he felt something needed to be done about being misinterpreted and misunderstood." They had known each other since the early 1940s, when she had tried to persuade the singer Gladys Swarthout (unsuccessfully, as it transpired) to perform his song cycle *I Hate Music,* but she had never represented him. She agreed to tackle the assignment. "The archbishop of Cincinnati had sent out a pastoral letter telling people not to go, and the production was being picketed by some solid citizens." Since she knew the archbishop had not seen a performance, she hoped to persuade him either to attend one or to withdraw his letter. Although he was perfectly charming, he would agree to do neither. Just the same, she was asked to become Bernstein's permanent press representative. Her gesture of help at an early stage "paid off" after all, she said. The Kennedy Center debut of *Mass* also introduced another new staff member. Harry Kraut, a former Boston Symphony Orchestra official whom Bernstein met at Tanglewood, replaced Chapin as Bernstein's indispensable aide-de-camp following that production. Another young man, Tommy Cothran, worked as his personal assistant, keeping track of the changes, a difficult assignment, and also helping to prepare the vocal score.

The furor over *Mass*—an organization representing almost two thousand Catholic priests in Britain expressed "disgust and distress" after *Mass* was shown on BBC-2—was effectively extinguished after an invitation came from Pope Paul VI to give a concert at the Vatican in connection with the opening there of a new gallery containing works by contemporary American painters and sculptors. Bernstein, delighted to be vindicated, arrived in the summer of 1973 to conduct the Harvard Glee Club and Newark Boys' Choir in a program ranging from Bach's Magnificat to his own *Chichester Psalms,* sung, of course, in Hebrew. Jerry Hadley said, "All the princes of the church lined up, and at the end of his concert the secretary of state for the Vatican, a cardinal, said something superlative about the concert. So Bernstein hugged him and, according to Harry Kraut, twelve rows of nuns dropped to their knees and made the sign of the cross." Bernstein was back for a return visit a decade later, in October 1983, to perform Beethoven's *Leonore* Overture and his own *Jeremiah* Symphony, with Christa Ludwig as soloist. Another friend said, "They were still operating Vatican City as an eighteenth-century royal court, with royal chamberlains in white ties, and here was this plan to play this outrageous new music by an American Jew. It was Bernstein tweaking the nose of the Catholics. The first day of rehearsals he tried to see how far he could go. He turned up in sneakers and jeans and a patchwork buckskin coat with an outrageous fringe. It was a warm October, and the first chance he could get to claim he was overheated, he stripped to the waist and walked around in those elegant rooms bare-chested."

Bernstein was tweaking numerous noses with relish from the 1970s on. He was already on the "enemies list" of President Nixon—described as a Social Register of the liberal establishment—so it really did not matter how outrageous he became. Bernstein decided to hold his own musical protest during the second inauguration of President Nixon in January 1973 to draw attention to the continuing war in Vietnam. He performed Haydn's *Mass in Time of War* at the Washington Cathedral and attracted a crowd of between nine thousand and twelve thousand, many of whom stood outside in the wind and rain, at the identical hour that the President's inaugural concert was being played at the Kennedy Center a few miles away. "Of course this is a protest," said the Reverend Peter Winterble, curate of St. John's Episcopal Church in Georgetown. "You don't think all of those people are out there to hear the music, do you?" The performance was subsequently recorded. That was also the year that Bernstein, at the Edinburgh Festival to perform with the London Symphony, once again announced that he intended to retire from the podium in order to compose.

Bernstein went out for a Chinese meal with friends just before rehearsals of *Mass* were due to begin and the group was asked who had preceded him as conductor of the New York Philharmonic. Nobody could remember. Bernstein buried his face in his hands. " 'My God,' he cries, 'the same thing will happen to me. No one will remember I was here.' " At the same time he wanted to talk about his past successes. He had just revisited *On the Town:* "It seems half-real, half-remembered to me, a very vivid dream I once had. What I love about it is its spontaneity and daring. It seems to me now such a courageous thing for all of us to have done then. And it dealt with serious things. The race with time. What is more serious? What is more important? It's the ultimate subject. But the surface of the show is all farce . . . We had an excuse for a plot, but we made a real attempt to relate it to music and ballet. It was not manufactured. If we had any commercial sense, we would never have done it . . ." As if feeling the need to surround himself with as many reminders as possible of former triumphs and, like Aschenbach with

Tadzio, recapture his magical youth, Bernstein began to drift toward an ever-younger crowd of musicians, conductors, writers and actors. One of the first for whom he would play the crucial role of mentor was Michael Tilson Thomas, whom he met in 1968 just before he made the kind of sensational conducting debut that Bernstein himself had done a quarter-century before. They resembled each other enough physically for their photographs to be published side by side (Thomas, it must be said, had wider-spaced eyes, a sharper nose and more angular features than his handsome mentor); both had followed similar musical paths, and there were some striking temperamental affinities. Bernstein began by saying that Thomas reminded him of himself at that age and then declared, "You're *me* at that age." But who was Bernstein now, exactly? Pressed to describe himself as either a composer, conductor or pianist, Bernstein had always evaded the definition and its implied criticism by insisting upon the all-inclusive term of "musician." But now even that inner conviction had deserted him. While working on *Mass,* he spent time at the MacDowell Colony in a studio in which each occupant is asked to record his stay with his signature on a board. Bernstein had scratched his name but, under the subheading of "Occupation," he simply scrawled an enormous question mark.

Tom Cothran was thin and tall, very sixties-looking, with little round glasses, usually badly dressed and very, very clever. A friend who knew him well thought Bernstein's relationship with him began during the period when he was writing his six Norton Lectures, subsequently delivered at Harvard in the autumn of 1973. He was young and Irish, from Indiana, and although Roger Englander called him "a silly, twitty boy," others thought he was delightful, a gifted conversationalist and something of a writer. In the book that followed the lectures Bernstein states, "In the beginning was Tom Cothran, whose musical sensibilities and poetic insights fertilized my every idea." Ned Rorem, who met him twice, recalled that he and Cothran had a lively exchange about war, the Quakers and pacifism; Cothran was "cute, earnest, and devoted—though I am not sure to what." It seemed clear that Cothran was utterly devoted to Bernstein at least, and the sentiment was reciprocated.

The series of lectures, called "The Unanswered Question," took its title from the short orchestral work by Charles Ives of the same name and referred to the question "Whither music?" It was quickly evident that Bernstein's philosophy of aesthetics had been formed at Harvard, thanks to his courses with Professor David Prall, who had instilled in him the wisdom of Keats's famous dictum " 'Beauty is truth, truth beauty'—that is all / Ye know on earth, and all ye need to know." To have that aesthetic overturned, even derided, had clearly brought about a major personal crisis. He recalled that some years before, when he was writing a preface to his book *The Infinite Variety of Music,* he had become convinced that music had taken a fatal wrong turn. The cause of his despair was the discovery that Stravinsky, that best and brightest hope for those composers still believing in tonality, had converted to the serial faith and the twelve-tone row. "It was like the defection of a general to the enemy camp, taking all his faithful regiments with him." That music was now to be considered an intellectual exercise and approached by means of a calculator—he called the phenomenon "almost a mathematical takeover"—was the antithesis of his lifelong conviction that music must be understood intuitively and perceived through the senses. He subsequently became convinced that to look for meaning through the beautiful was more important than ever, "as each day mediocrity and art-mongering increasingly uglify our lives." In "The Unanswered Question" he was making a tremendous intellectual effort, by far his most ambitious, combining all his gifts as musician, analyst, philosopher and critic, to rise to the defense of his art and assert its ultimate values.

Bernstein evidently decided that the best way to defeat the new music pioneered by Arnold Schoenberg, which he described as an artificial language, a theoretical construct with no actual content, would be to argue that music was not only basically tonal but universally so. Melody was, as it were, part of the human condition, as intrinsic as the first sound a baby makes when it begins to speak. If this could be demonstrated, then he would have made a major contribution to the debate; the aesthetic of music could no longer be considered as a historical construct that one could fashionably accept or reject, but an eternal and immutable fact of existence, like love and death. To launch such an argument he needed an analogy, and thought he had found one in the work of Noam Chomsky, the linguist, who believed all language could be traced to a single common origin. If one looked long and hard enough, one would be able to discover universal rules of syntax and phonology that underlay the world's four thousand or so languages. This innate grammatical competence, Bernstein said, "is a human endowment; it proclaims the unique power of the human spirit. Well, so does music." He leapt on the idea that by returning to the elementals, the basic building blocks of language, one could draw direct analogies between language and music. Music, after all, had long been described as heightened speech; by this method one could "seek analogies between linguistic universals and the natural musical universals that arise out of the harmonic series."

To take music apart just as Chomsky had dissected language, beginning with sound alone and building up through layers of meaning and, ultimately, poetic metaphor—it sounded brilliantly promising, and he devoted hours of effort to the project. However, to state a premise was one thing; to make the case for tonality as an intrinsic language was something else entirely. Chasing linguistical meanings immediately took Bernstein too far from music; describing the harmonic series and the ambiguities inherent in a Mozart symphony, too far from the parallel with language. He made a promising start when he argued that children all over the world teased each other with the same musical sing-song, but never expanded on this theme in the lectures that followed.

In that respect "The Unanswered Question" marked a distinct departure in tone from the lectures that had made him famous. In earlier lectures he spoke in easy generalities illustrated by apt and unusual examples that invariably gave a familiar subject a fresh and unexpected aspect. The new series took a properly more academic and cross-disciplinary tone but lacked the clarity of his earlier investigations. The more earnestly Bernstein pounded home his multiple points, the more enmeshed the listener became in a thicket of learned speculation, leading one to conclude that the original hypothesis had been too tenuous to bear the weight of detailed argument. At the end one had to take on faith conclusions, almost a litany of beliefs, that he enumerated but had far too seldom explored during the course of his lectures: that, as Keats wrote, there was a "poetry of earth" from which emerged a groundswell of music that was innately tonal; that from this derived a phonology of music, a universal musical syntax, musical languages with common and discernible roots; and the final belief that "our deepest affective responses to these particular languages are innate . . ."

As might have been expected, the critics praised or attacked, depending on their theoretical biases. Even those who supported his position had to agree, however, that his attempt to demonstrate that tonality was innate to the human condition had not succeeded; it had been a noble failure. By a curious coincidence Bernstein was attempting to do for music precisely what Kenneth Clark had tried to do for art during the height of the abstractionist movement. Lord Clark argued that certain pictorial motifs appeared so universally and carried such profound emotional, as well as aesthetic freight, that they could be considered basic to the human condition. They were what Walter Pater meant when he wrote of "that complex faculty for which every thought and feeling is twin-born with its sensible analogue or symbol." One might, in other words, strike the conclusive blow against formlessness in art if one could demonstrate the universality of the language of form. However, to pierce the mystery of "form and matter in their union and identity," as Pater phrased it, proved frustratingly difficult. Lord Clark worked on the problem for years and gave it up in 1970 with the comment that the subject was too enormous. "It's bigger than any of us," he said, curiously, just as Bernstein was about to begin the attempt.

Returning to Harvard was a euphoric moment for Bernstein. "I mean, I was even living in the same house—the Eliot House—in which I had resided as an undergraduate. Only then, I had a cramped little fifth floor walk-up I shared. This time, I had a five-room apartment with fireplaces in every room . . . with valets, maids and what-not. I couldn't get over it, and I just spent a lot of time being at Harvard, reliving my memories of it."

His series of lectures had been announced for the spring of 1973 but was postponed until the autumn. This did not deter his audiences, who mobbed the lectures, lining up for blocks, sometimes overnight. He had agreed to make himself accessible to the student body and took it so literally that, as soon as word spread, "they just came trooping in without stop and I found it very hard to say no," he said. "Mostly it was identity problems—what should I be doing, who am I really, how do I find out who I am. I've had lots of problems in my own life, but that particular one never . . . I finally had to call a halt at a certain point—it was getting ridiculous; my room was getting to be like a shrink's office."

"Playing shrink" was one of the things he really liked to do. Maurice Peress said, "One of his hobbies was to try to get close to people and find out their essences." What he liked best were all-night talk sessions in which he'd try to "understand and absorb all the ills of the world," another friend said, falling asleep around dawn and leaving everyone else in a state of complete exhaustion. "He was outside the law of the rest of us; that was what was wrong with him." Andrew Pincus, music critic of the Berkshire *Eagle,* who also met him in those years, said Bernstein would arrive surrounded by his staff as well as various young men, described as aides, and want to party all night. "He had no sense of what's out there. He was becoming isolated from the real world, no longer the young kid who did it all on his own." Other friends stopped accepting his invitations because, as the evening wore on, women would be firmly told that it was time for them to go home; their men were supposed to stay. Once a friend came upon Bernstein in a hallway necking with a beautiful twenty-year-old boy. His wife was sitting by herself in the living room. When asked what she was doing, Felicia Bernstein said she was waiting. "I've been waiting for Lenny all my life."

They had moved again, to a palatial twelve-room apartment in the Dakota, a famous old soot-stained Victorian Gothic stone castle at Central Park West and Seventy-second Street, which had become the fashionable address for top people. Lauren Bacall had fourteen rooms; Polly Bergen occupied eighteen; the Lennons, John and Yoko, arrived in identical his and hers silver limousines; and various arrivistes were trying to gain admittance. Felicia Bernstein happily began to decorate. The dining room, seating twenty, was fin-de-siècle; the library was charcoal and deep red, with a red harpsichord; and her bedroom, in shades of rose and green, had a splashy print upholstery along with a tiny geometric wallpaper and an iron canopied bedstead. There were books, paintings and Gothic arches everywhere. They spent weekends at Springate, their comfortable clapboard house on eighteen acres outside Fairfield, Connecticut, complete with tennis court, barn, pool, orchard and vegetable gardens. There Felicia Bernstein was interviewed in the spring of 1975 by a local reporter who asked the inevitable question, "What is it like . . . ?" Felicia Bernstein completed the sentence: ". . . to be married to Leonard Bernstein?" She did not answer because she was so amused by the triteness of the question. Or so the reporter concluded.

When the occasion demanded, Bernstein could still dress stylishly enough to please *Gentlemen's Quarterly*. He favored white suits in summer, with striped shirts, dark ties and a matching handkerchief in the breast pocket. But after an hour or so the image inevitably became frayed. A tuft of silvery gray hair would escape onto his forehead above those surprisingly small eyes and sharply lined face, the tie would lose its plumbline contours, the jacket would crumple, the knees would bag and a gangling adolescent's slouch would appear, as if beyond conscious control. His wife, by contrast, always looked as if traveling in her own invisible bell jar. Her white dresses never became wrinkled or smudged, her shoes were never streaked with mud and her little black belts always

A family portrait of Nina, Jamie, Leonard, Alexander and Felicia on
the terrace of their Park Avenue apartment in 1969

stayed precisely centered. There was, if anything, a further elaboration of
this faultless facade in these years. At a Seranak party she wore a straw
boater with a striped ribbon that fell behind, exactly bisecting her shoulder blades, dark glasses, neat little ring earrings, gloves, a buttoned-front
coat dress and a buttoned-down purse. She looked distinctly overdressed,
as if preparing for a very cold wind.

Those close to her knew how miserable she was; they also knew she
was ill. Cancer had been diagnosed in the mid-1970s and she had had a
mastectomy. Byron Bray, who was a close friend of Helen Coates, was
privy to the latter's diary for 1976. Coates wanted it known that Felicia
Bernstein had found her husband in bed with Cothran in their apartment and told him that Cothran had to leave the city that day or, "I will
make a public scandal." For her to threaten such a step was an indication of her state of mind. She was absolutely at her wit's end, telling her
friends that, up to that moment, she had refused to believe her husband
was "really a homosexual." Perhaps what she meant was she believed
that his love for her and their children was at the center of his life, and
his other entanglements would never disrupt it. For years this had been
true. But here was a relationship that really did threaten their marriage,
and they both realized it. Bernstein left for Vienna to make a film of a
Mahler symphony on October 12, and two weeks later, on October 26,
Felicia Bernstein announced that they had separated. Then she bravely
returned to the stage, after an absence of eight years, playing a minor
role in *Poor Murderer.* Her husband was not in the audience.

For someone as self-contained and reticent as she was it must have been acutely painful to have the world know that her husband of twenty-five years had moved out and into an apartment on Central Park South with an unimpressive-looking youth he called the love of his life. To find them in bed together—Bethel Leslie thought that a similar incident had ended their engagement all those years before—was not implausible, since, as has been demonstrated, it was the kind of gesture Bernstein was perfectly capable of making in the right circumstances. "She knew he had lovers, and that was all right as long as he didn't bring them into the house," Leslie said. "I do believe he felt he could get away with anything, but she was not the kind of person to lie down and be run over.

"Yes, Felicia was very grown-up in a lot of ways. She also had feelings. It was not so much a love betrayed as a trust betrayed. If you have given everything of yourself to someone else and they throw it away . . . It was terribly hurtful, and although he could sympathize, he lacked the ability to empathize. He was not ever aware of the deep hurts going on around him."

Bernstein's state of mind is harder to assess. The psychiatrist Karen Horney thought that expansive personalities like his, with their buoyancy and perennial youthfulness, gave a false impression because they took such pains to please. Their hidden expectations of others, that they be given blind admiration and devotion and be allowed to declaim endlessly about their own unique and wonderful qualities, were likely to become oppressive in close relationships. When those close to such a person tired of their self-effacing roles and the constant support and reassurance required and began to expect something from him, or react critically—and he had complained about how critical his wife was—he was likely to "explode in a burst of rage." Horney wrote, "Up to a point his resilence gives him a capacity to bounce, but on the other hand repeated failures in enterprises or human relations—rejections—may also crush him altogether." Bernstein may have thought that the burden he felt had to do with the facade required to maintain his marriage and the intolerable constraints under which he had chafed. Given the relaxed social climate of the 1970s, he could at last strike a blow for honesty and be what he felt himself to be, demand the right to live as he wished and expect others to accept it. On the other hand, given his particular personality, that might not be as easy as he expected; inner dissatisfactions stemming from his perfectionism and fury over his own failures were not likely to be affected by this change in status. Horney wrote, "The self-hate and self-contempt, successfully held in abeyance otherwise, may then operate in full force . . . Thus he may see a tragic quality to life, not the one that does exist but the one he brings to it."

Jane White said that when she heard the news of the separation she called Felicia Bernstein, or perhaps wrote her a note. Some time after that, they met by chance in Bloomingdale's and fell upon each other. "I asked her how she was and saw her pull herself up. 'I'm fine, I'm fine,' she said brightly. 'You know, I am really relieved.' That is all she would say." Angus Whyte, a musician, photographer and art dealer, who used to entertain Bernstein whenever he was in Boston, recalled that shortly after the separation Harry Kraut called to ask whether he knew of a house on the California coast where Bernstein could go with Cothran and be very private. Whyte promised to investigate, but by the time he returned the call a house had been found. "Of course the relationship didn't work," Whyte said. "Bernstein was impossibly demanding and spoiled and his life style was such that hardly anyone could live with him." Shirley Bernstein thought the Cothran affair symbolized Bernstein's repeated failures to establish relationships with men. "He'd have this fling thinking he had found the love of his life, but then he would always end up discovering this wasn't 'it.' " Her explanation was that her brother was really a bisexual. Six months after their separation, Bernstein was preparing a concert in honor of the benefactor of Alice Tully Hall at Lincoln Center and engaged his wife to perform in Walton's *Facade.* The two were photographed at work on the piece, his arm lightly resting on her shoulder. About a month after that, in April 1977, a reconciliation was effected. Bernstein and Cothran parted and he went back to the Dakota to live with his wife and family.

Bernstein had been working on a new musical to mark the Bicentennial and a cycle of songs, called *Songfest,* that was also in celebration of that event but was not performed in its entirety until the autumn of 1977. He set thirteen poems by a number of American poets, including Gregory Corso, Edna St. Vincent Millay, E. E. Cummings, Langston Hughes and Frank O'Hara, who together spanned three centuries. There was Anne Bradstreet's tender "To My Dear and Loving Husband," Millay's lament "What lips my lips have kissed," and Hughes's "I, Too, Sing America." Bernstein set a poem by Julia de Burgos, a Puerto Rican, in which she described the conflict between the poet she felt herself to be and the role society expected of her. That might seem to have some relevance to his wife's inner state, poised as she was between being Mrs. Leonard Bernstein and Felicia Montealegre. For similar reasons perhaps,

The Bernsteins photographed in their New York apartment in 1967
by John Gruen, who published a biography of Bernstein that year

Bernstein also set a poem by Walt Whitman that makes that poet's
homosexuality evident. But perhaps Conrad Aiken's "Music I Heard
with You" best expressed Bernstein's mood at the time.

> Music I heard with you was more than music,
> And bread I broke with you was more than bread;
> Now that I am without you, all is desolate;
> All that was once so beautiful is dead.

Friends thought Bernstein simply had not realized the effect of his
behavior on his wife and children or bargained for the effect of the
breakup on himself. Rose Styron said, "I think he tried awfully hard.
Felicia was always very discreet and loving and not bitter, at least not
to me. She gave me the impression that he was very contrite but so dramatic about it, and I think she had heard it all once too often."

They were back on some kind of footing, but Felicia did not feel well.
She had a cough she could not get rid of, and in July of 1977 they discovered she had lung cancer. Although she underwent numerous treatments, nothing helped. "It was a slow, painful death," said the late Irma
Lazarus, another of their close friends. "She would not take the full dose
of painkillers she needed, because she wanted to remain conscious." Feli-

cia Bernstein had stopped smoking in order to try to convince her husband to do likewise. Choral director Norman Scribner, who worked with Bernstein on *Mass,* said, "After a party in the Watergate we were the last to leave, and he told me in the vestibule how hard he had tried to give up. He talked about all the different methods he used, even hypnotism. Then he said that when he knew Felicia had cancer, he went back to smoking. He reached over and grabbed me at that point." Phil Ramey recalled a similar experience. He said, "One time in Rome Lenny said he didn't know what he would do if Felicia died, and began to weep."

Although his wife was now very ill, Bernstein seemed as curiously impervious to the effect of his behavior on her as ever. Some old friends from London, not knowing how ill she was, invited themselves to dinner. One of them said, "She looked awful. I had last seen her several years before, beautifully dressed and looking her ravishing self, out of an eighteenth-century Boucher. She was sitting there unrecognizable with a wig and wearing some kind of old dress, and knitting. She did not say a word, but she was looking at Lenny with immense dislike, almost hatred." Bernstein, the guest said, was making an obvious play for her, loudly praising her in front of Felicia and telling her how gorgeous she was. The guest thought the compliments in the worst taste and left as soon as she could. Raphael Hillyer recalled a similar incident when he and his wife went out on the town with Bernstein and Princess Grace of Monaco. He said, "Lenny was principally talking to her the whole time. Personal family questions and political name dropping. He was making very amorous physical contact. He had her very tightly with his arm around her shoulder and showered slobbering kisses on her. We ended up at his apartment in the Dakota. Felicia was in the hospital and Lenny proceeded to graphically describe her illness, including how many organs she had lost."

In an effort to brighten her final months of life, Bernstein bought her a house in East Hampton, Long Island. Once it was clear she was dying, he canceled all his concert dates to be with her. She was in the hospital and asked to go back to the new house, so, Shirley Bernstein said, "we all ran around to furnish it. People contributed curtains and furniture. Her bedroom was very beautiful, overlooking the ocean." Felicia Bernstein lived there for about three weeks and, to control her pain, was given a very powerful prescription every morning. "She was sitting there making no sense, talking gibberish with her eyes wide open," Shirley Bernstein said. Felicia Bernstein had told Antonio de Almeida when he visited her in the hospital, "Don't worry, it's not going to get me," but

Harry Kraut, at left, as usual in the background, this time following
Bernstein's acceptance of an honorary degree from Johns Hopkins
University in 1980

perhaps she was just giving one last, superb performance. Both Bernstein
and his sister were at her bedside when she died on June 16, 1978. She
was fifty-six. At her funeral Leonard Burkat went into the kitchen with
his wife and was shocked to see the Bernstein children playing cards. A
friend said to him, "Don't be. You don't know what they have been
through these past few months."

Those next six months were the worst in Bernstein's life. At night he
could not sleep: "but the rain / Is full of ghosts tonight, that tap and
sigh / Upon the glass . . ." He called it

the kind of insomnia when you can't work, you can't read, you
don't know what to do with your body, your muscles tickle and
everything itches. But during the day I slept nonstop, to avoid
living. I had fantasies about Felicia, and guilt about whether I was
in any way responsible . . . And does science know, how does med-
icine *really* know that cancer can't be caused by some great agony,
some great emotional stress . . . I mean, such a deep-rooted guilt
at the death of your most beloved person in the world which, for
me, she was . . . The most beautiful, the most gracious, the funniest, the smartest; she could also be the most vulgar, she could be

With Pat Handy, one of the first women conducting
students at Tanglewood

The famous rear porch at the Koussevitzkys' old home, Seranak, looking out
over the Berkshire hills at Tanglewood

the most racée, a wonderful mother, a marvellous wife and companion. Irreplaceable . . . And to feel that you may have had something to do with her dying . . . I went to psychiatrists but nothing helped. I thought I was finished.

Angus Whyte said, "In the summer of 1978 they were trying to get him to quit smoking. Everyone's left him, his valet left, he's grumpy and awful. Harry Kraut called me and begged me to help out for a while. Cheer him up and get him to exercise." He agreed out of friendship and admiration for Bernstein. In July they went to Tanglewood and he stayed for the first time in Seranak, Koussevitzky's old home. "We thought it would be a great place for him," said Dan Gustin, "but he said there were too many memories and ghosts." Because he was sleeping so badly, he would be tired in the mornings. Whyte said, "He'd sometimes just stay in bed and take naps. It was hard to get him moving. I did try to make him go jogging. That was quite a scene.

"He was teaching, which he loved. He'd rev up and be terrific, working on the podium with students. The minute it was over he'd collapse in a slump. He was grim. All the humor was gone. Harry Kraut came in and out. He didn't want to be around; I stuck it out." That summer Jacob Druckman was in residence at Tanglewood and writing a piece of music he called *Aureole*. Bernstein would often drop by at his composer's cottage, and Druckman was concerned about his friend's state. He decided to make a phrase from Bernstein's *Kaddish* Symphony central to his new work. "For me the piece is a very serious one which involves not so much death, as the idea of survival." Looking at Bernstein that summer, whether he would survive the blow was on everyone's mind.

Whyte said, "Part of the problem was that his sixtieth birthday was coming up, and it was not a joyful occasion. He'd always been the kid; suddenly he was gray-haired and overweight." That was the summer that a big birthday tribute was to take place in Washington, and all of his dear friends would be there: Slava and Yehudi and Isaac and Lukas and Lauren and Aaron and Bill and Elizabeth and Lillian. He knew he would have to "smile and be gracious when inside I was feeling rock bottom." Whyte remembered that trip down from Pittsfield in the Berkshires to Washington in Bernstein's private Lear jet. "He was sitting there with the score of a Beethoven symphony on his lap and he fell asleep in despair. I thought to myself, here is a man who has the world eating out of his hand and he is so sad. It was a real revelation."

Haywire

Hurl me forth into Hades' dark night . . .

— GOETHE, "AN SCHWAGER KRONOS"

This was a new Lenny, one they had not seen before. Victor Alpert, who had known him since they were both adolescents in Boston, said, "I remember he came to our house for dinner shortly after Felicia died. It was the only time when he was with us that he did not go near the piano." Leonard Altman said, "Usually when you saw him he was his public self. He put on a mask and kept it on. But after Felicia died, all of a sudden he abandoned that and was real. That summer he sat under the trees and moped and sighed. I was sitting in a restaurant one time when he came in. He greeted me and put an arm around my shoulders, but he did not join me. He went off and actually sat at a table by himself." Harry Ellis Dickson, who had lost his wife a year before, said, "When he saw me he threw his arms around me and said, 'I know what you were going through,' and cried." The large gold wedding band that he had worn ever since their marriage joined the talismanic images with which he staved off bad luck: the Mitropoulos cross, the Koussevitzky cuff links, and the obligatory cape lined with red silk. Photographs of his wife were everywhere in the Dakota and at Springate. A friend who went to work for Amberson shortly after Felicia Bernstein's death said that the whole office was in mourning and, "everything was practically draped in black." As soon as she died, Bernstein called his interior decorator, Gail Jacobs, to turn his wife's bedroom into a new study for him. She said, "He wanted it done in six weeks. I can't believe I did that. I decided on taupe walls with a parsley-looking leaf pattern, full of softness and warmth, velvet drapes in a Pompeian red and lots of warm, jewellike fabrics in pillows and upholstery." Once Felicia had left him forever, he wanted to be as close to her physical memory as he humanly could.

He had always been superstitious and renewed his interest in reincarnation and similar arcana. When he was interviewed by Mike Wallace shortly after his wife's death and the subject of his next sabbatical, in 1980, came up, he said that the decision was partly taken "through, so to speak, consulting her voice. She's with me a lot," he said, smiling, knowing he would not be believed. Then he dashed away a tear. "Whenever I detect a whine in my voice I can hear her saying, 'Are you whining?' and I stop." Before long there were rumors that he was seeing her ghost. Ed Skidmore said the National Symphony Orchestra was playing Bernstein's *Kaddish* Symphony, a work Felicia Bernstein had often performed, and Bernstein was conducting "when I heard backstage that he thought he was hallucinating because he had seen her on stage." Several people were convinced that she was haunting Springate. One of the staff said she would hear noises upstairs when no one was in the house and used to joke that Felicia was making sure the beds were properly made. Bernstein's grief was so public and prolonged that some people could not believe it was genuine; it had to be self-indulgent theatrics. A friend recalled seeing him backstage at Wolf Trap Farm Park in suburban Washington during his sixtieth-birthday celebrations, when he was moaning and shaking and declaring he could not go on. She spoke to him sharply, saying that he was a professional and had to make an appearance, and his mood instantly changed.

Disbelief—that was the clue. In spite of everything, he had wanted and expected the happy ending. Now that this lingering hope had been torn from him he was incredulous, stupefied and literally ill with grief. He went to Jamaica for a holiday at Christmas and began to recover some of his old zest. Early in 1979 he visited Mexico with President Jimmy Carter and returned feeling almost like himself. But after the opening of

A few months after Felicia's death, 1978

a new Zeffirelli film in the spring of 1979 and a party afterward, "I couldn't get out of bed," he said. "I thought I must have drunk too much the night before and called it a hangover." Finally his doctor discovered a rare virus in his throat. He consulted a tropical disease specialist, who "announced that he had never seen so many bugs in his life. They were simply eating me up in there. They had been colonizing in a cyst ever since that Mexican trip . . . before breaking out." It took him months to recover, and even in July, while touring Japan with the New York Philharmonic, he was still convalescing and unable to take requests for encores.

He had always been subject to depressions. His pronounced mood swings were curiously like those that are said to afflict other strongly creative people, who can oscillate between periods of euphoria, when their confidence is boundless, their energy unflagging and they never seem to sleep, and a depression so severe that they may actually contemplate suicide. He was certainly in good company, since Byron, Shelley, Melville, Robert Schumann, Virginia Woolf, Theodore Roethke and Samuel Taylor Coleridge all demonstrated similar patterns of varying severity. It is known that periods of exaltation and depression and self-hatred can appear at long intervals, and at times in between the artist in question will seem to be perfectly normal and in command of life; this was certainly true of Bernstein. But that the death of his wife had a profound and permanent effect on his always delicate equilibrium seems incontestable. Now, feelings of intense and long-lasting sadness would dog him for the rest of his life. Recent studies have found that heavy smokers are more than twice as likely to have had a history of depression than nonsmokers, and the greater the dependence on nicotine, the more likely the concurrent depression. Nicotine has a euphoric, stimulating effect, and when heavy smokers try to stop they usually experience a resurgence of their black moods. Heavy drinking—also associated with nicotine addiction—has a further depressive effect, and Bernstein was becoming ever more dependent on alcohol; eventually, he would seldom be seen without a drink in his hand. Added to all of this was the wear and tear on his lungs from years of heavy smoking. Phillip Ramey noticed that Bernstein began to experience fits of coughing and, as soon as one had passed, he would light up another cigarette. Ramey told him, "No one can feel sorry for you if you are killing yourself," to which Bernstein replied, "Don't act like a shrink." Ramey's opinion was shared by Sondheim and others, who said he was committing slow suicide. David Diamond said, "I saw the start of this self-consuming behavior all those years ago as soon as he arrived in New York: smoking, drinking and staying up all night. But after Felicia's death, his descent into hell really began." Aaron Copland put it even more succinctly. "Lenny," he said, "wants to die."

Bernstein went to Mexico City at the invitation of President Carter, who was on a state visit. He was invited to conduct the Mexico City Philharmonic Orchestra, and at the reception afterward he sat with Carter and President José López Portillo talking about music, the hemisphere, oil and Israel until well after midnight. He had campaigned for Carter, had coached Rosalynn Carter in a performance of Copland's *Lincoln Portrait* and was frequently invited to the White House during the Carter administration. Shirley Bernstein said that one December, when Bernstein was to receive an award at the Kennedy Center, President Carter invited him to the White House for a small reception before festivities began. When Bernstein demurred, saying that he needed to change into formal evening wear, the President offered him Lincoln's bedroom. Since his family—mother, sister, two aunts and children—were with him, Bernstein managed to get them upstairs to see the famous room. After they had admired it extravagantly Bernstein suggested they have a small ceremony to observe Hanukkah, the Festival of Lights. First his children sang a blessing in Hebrew that he had taught them. Shirley

Bernstein said, "Out came a traveling menorah that he had in his bag and a leader candle (called a *shammes*) with which to light all the others and we had our ceremony." Then the time came to leave, and they realized that, although custom decreed that they could not blow out the candles, neither could they leave the lighted candelabrum in the bedroom. "Can you see the headlines?" they asked each other. " 'Jews Burn Down Lincoln's Bedroom.' " They compromised by leaving the menorah in the bathroom.

For Bernstein, the connection with Lincoln had a special significance; he had put up a poster on the door of his study that listed the similarities between the lives of Lincoln and John Fitzgerald Kennedy. So it seemed natural and logical that, when the idea of writing a musical for the Bicentennial was first launched, Bernstein would want to write about the White House. Alan Jay Lerner, creator of *My Fair Lady* and *Camelot,* a friend of Kennedy's and an old Harvard classmate of Bernstein's, conceived the idea of writing about the occupants and their generations of servants below stairs. Lerner said he wrote the book at the height of the 1973 Watergate scandals. He was thinking about "those moments when people tried to take the White House away from us."

"Scratch that, scratch that," Bernstein said during the first day of rehearsals early in 1976. "This play has nothing to do with the contemporary scene except in the minds of those who choose to see it there." Lerner said that he was such a person. "Bernstein slapped Lerner's knee playfully. Lerner slapped Bernstein's knee playfully. Somebody had the good grace at that point to change the subject." No one mentioned that the only collaboration between Bernstein and Lerner so far, the two songs written for the glee club almost two decades before, had been a disaster. (Both works were subsequently withdrawn.) It was taken for granted that two such famous men would be bound to collaborate fruitfully, and Bernstein, who had said he wanted the right to fail, seemed to have forgotten his own caution and plunged merrily ahead in the glare of the spotlight. Other friends thought that the Achilles heel first noticed by Laurents was becoming a major stumbling block. "Lenny had a bad case of important-itis," Sondheim said succinctly. Rorem thought, "Getting better to Lenny meant getting bigger: more money, more fame, more lovers, more everything. That's very American, of course." Frank Corsaro's view was that both Lerner and Bernstein had become "so high-powered their attitude was that they could do no wrong."

By the autumn of 1975 Bernstein had already written twice the amount of music normally required, about thirty songs, and had set some scenes entirely to music by the time the official announcement was made. He was completely entranced with the idea. His wife had also loved it and urged him to accept it. The only problem was "Where's the ending?" he said. "I mean, you've got to bring it to Nixon and Ford. And I said you've got to know the end first, especially when you're doing a historical and chronological piece. And for three years [Lerner] kept saying, 'The end will come, the end will come. It will be right. Just keep writing and we'll know when the proper thing comes.' And I, like a fool, believed him." Laurents said, "I was originally hired as director and had two meetings with Alan and Lenny and the first question I asked was what it was about; and they didn't know it was about blacks. I realized that the musical was doomed." Corsaro stepped in to replace him.

Corsaro said, "I first heard the score of *1600 Pennsylvania Avenue* when we had a read-through at which Bernstein was present and some singers performed the music. Then I read the book and was absolutely perplexed, as it seemed impossible. I should have known better, but everyone was pushing me into it. I agreed against my better judgment, and it was a continual battle to try to make some sense of an impossible situation." All too late he learned that the producers, Roger Stevens and Robert Whitehead, shared his reservations. "While Roger Stevens was being adulatory beyond the pale for quotation, in private he had made a secret pact with Whitehead that while they were raising money, they would not make any advance toward a musical until we had a book that made sense." Unfortunately the Coca-Cola Company, the main backers, who knew nothing about Broadway shows, were easily convinced. While those in a position to know went into rehearsals with a feeling of dread, Bernstein concealed any private doubts he may have felt behind a facade of euphoria. "I love it," he told reporters during rehearsals in Philadelphia. "I've never been so excited about a show while I was doing it. I've never been so confident, so thrilled." He was asked whether the show would do something to restore the tarnished image of the White House. He replied, "We're not out to be missionaries. We're out to write a work we can be proud of and which we think is passionate and moving and very funny and in some ways bitter."

Corsaro, however, thought that "bitter" was the operative word. Lerner's original impulse to write the book had been his outrage over Watergate. Consequently, what ought to have been a celebration of two hundred years of democracy had become a vehicle for political protest of a particularly savage kind. The Philadelphia critics soon realized this. The

Principal cast of characters in the creation of the ill-fated musical *1600 Penn-sylvania Avenue,* from left: Robert Whitehead, producer; Alan Jay Lerner; Frank Corsaro, director; Roger L. Stevens, producer; and Bernstein, 1976

Inquirer called the musical "a heavy, bloated, gloom cloud of a show" and said, "The tone throughout is simple-minded cynicism." As for the composer, author of such wonderful lighthearted successes, he seemed to have been thrown off his stride—perhaps it was the seriousness of the theme—and the result was bombast. The producers promised immediate changes. As for the backers, Corsaro said, "I saw the representatives of Coca-Cola sitting in the bar across the street, astounded. They could not believe what was going on. Some attempt was made to pull out, but it was too late." Meanwhile, Bernstein watched in the wings at the preview performances, wanting to believe. There is a story, perhaps apocryphal, that after the first preview in Washington a young assistant director caught sight of him in the shadows, his face buried in his hands. He hurried over in order to murmur some consoling words, but then Bernstein looked up and said blearily, "It was so beautiful!"

Rewrites began at once and heads began to roll. Laurents said, "Bernstein called me the night after I bowed out and said, 'I ask you as a friend, what should I do?' and I said, 'Get out.' But he had spent too much time on it and could not accept that it was a mistake. I saw the show shortly after the opening in Philadelphia and it was still a mess in every department. Musically it was all over the place. I realized they had hoped I would direct. Instead, I suggested they get a black." Gilbert Moses and George Faison, who had worked together on the successful black musical *The Wiz,* were hired to replace Corsaro and the choreographer, Donald McKayle.

Laurents continued, "I sat with Bob Whitehead until two or three in the morning begging him to close the show, but Stevens was all for taking it to the Kennedy Center, saying they had the money they needed. I kept saying, 'Yes, but when it gets to New York Bernstein will be hurt.' We are all sensitive to reviews, but Lenny was overly sensitive, as I well knew. Whitehead didn't tell me that one of the terms with Coca-Cola was that the show had to open in New York. So they had to go through with it." The new team immediately began to clash with Lerner and Bernstein, both of whom, it was charged, overruled anyone making changes to their work. Moses actually succeeded in barring them and the producers from some of the rehearsals. Nothing helped. *1600 Pennsylvania Avenue* was, said *Newsweek,* a victim of "myasthenia gravis conceptualis, otherwise known as a crummy idea." Alan Rich of *New York* called it "an epic disaster" and added that he could not understand why Stevens and Whitehead had "worked so hard to sustain so obvious a failure. When we learn the answer to that question, we might also know why moths fly into flames."

Eventually, Bernstein was able to say he had suspected trouble all along: "I never saw anything so execrable on stage or ever heard anything so stupid." He still wanted to return to the theater but thought the main problem with *1600 Pennsylvania Avenue* was that it became too commercialized, "so now I've decided to choose my collaborators with a little more care and write an opera for the opera house, not for a commercial Broadway show." He wanted to start right away, because "what I mind is this terrible sense that there isn't much time," he said. So as soon as his next sabbatical was fixed in his mind, he launched on a new project called *Alarms and Flourishes* with his old friend Laurents. Bernstein said, "He had an original idea that excited me, so we went to work with a great will—something that I thought would be the next step towards what I'd always hoped would be an *American* opera." Laurents said, "I did an outline for a musical about a human being's desire to be free, a fairy story with balladeers, that appealed to Lenny. We worked on it at his house in Aspen, where I went to ski, and in Jamaica, but nothing seemed to be accomplished." Laurents thought one of the problems was that he had decided to write the lyrics himself, which turned out to be a mistake. Another was that Bernstein immediately wanted to jump several stages ahead and start casting and bring in his director and principal actors, before they had even put the material together. Laurents said, "I'd fly up to a meeting and leave with very heavy shoes. Where it essentially fell apart was that he was trying to turn it into an opera because he thought musical theater was not classy enough and this material would not support it. You leave a watercolor out in the rain and it just dribbles away." Bernstein's version was that, "everybody involved in it was pushing it gently and subtly in a more commercial direction." He said he was so depressed by the failure of the project that he went to a psychiatrist. Then there was the problem of alcohol. Laurents said, "Every afternoon at four out would come this tumbler full of booze. It took the edge right off his mind."

During the rest of his time off Bernstein worked on a piano piece for the Van Cliburn Competition; *A Musical Toast,* a short memorial work for the conductor André Kostelanetz; and *Divertimento for Orchestra,* in celebration of the Boston Symphony Orchestra's centennial. He also finished *Halil,* a nocturne for solo flute, string orchestra and percussion, dedicated to an Israeli flutist killed in the Sinai desert in 1973. That work would receive its first performance in Jerusalem the following year. He started thinking about a "very serious, one-act opera" that would make a sequel to *Trouble in Tahiti.* It had been, despite everything, a productive year.

Whatever he might say, returning to musical theater or even composing was more and more in the nature of a temporary deviation in those years; most of his time continued to be taken up with conducting. As soon as he learned that Pierre Boulez planned to leave as conductor of the New York Philharmonic in the late 1970s, he flirted with the idea of returning. Jon Deak recalled that he arrived back as guest conductor on one occasion and, after the obligatory hugs and kisses all around, picked up his baton, conducted for ten seconds and then put it down. "How dare you play that way?" he said. "What are they doing to my orchestra?" Shortly after that he announced, "I just want you to know this is my orchestra and I am coming back." When queried, Carlos Moseley said, "Bernstein says lots of things. Let's see if he actually means them." Indeed Bernstein did increase his appearances with the Philharmonic, but he never returned as music director, perhaps by mutual agreement. It was too taxing, and he had become accustomed to the absolute freedom to do whatever he liked and travel at will. Sometimes he crammed so much into his schedule that he would book two performances in different cities on the same night. A chauffeur, a helicopter and his own private plane would be waiting to get him there.

There were his continuing association with the Israel Philharmonic and his successful excursions into the domains long considered the exclusive prerogative of Herbert von Karajan. He had recently made his debut with the Berlin Philharmonic; "Berlin would like to have crowned Bernstein king that evening," reported *Die Welt*. He did not conduct a concert in Europe without having the performance filmed and recorded. He had recently recorded all nine Beethoven symphonies with the Vienna Philharmonic. Vienna, enthused Marcel Prawy, the indefatigable dramaturg of the Staatsoper, who translated and produced several of Bernstein's stage works, had become "the world Bernstein capital." That remark was made after the Vienna State Opera produced its own version of *Mass,* with a less saccharine ending. It was well received, if not with quite the superlatives Bernstein was accustomed to hearing in Vienna.

As a conductor Bernstein still had his detractors, those who, like Alan Rich, objected to his "bobbing and weaving and leaping as if auditioning for the local basketball team." But these were growing fewer. His performance of Beethoven's Ninth Symphony, a critic wrote, was "one of the most explosive, gut-thumping ones we've ever heard." Reviewing another performance of the Ninth, Harold C. Schonberg, who had been so disapproving in the past, wrote that it had all "his expected attributes and mannerisms. It was dramatic. It was theatrical. It was highly personal and involved. Some might have called it vulgar. Some with equal justice could have called it self-indulgent. But one thing it did have: life. This performance simply pulsated with life . . . It was a rather long performance, clocking in at well over the average, but it never felt long, and this listener admired it no end."

Instrumentalists and musicians who worked with him continued to speak in superlatives. "You have to start with the word 'unique,' " Norman Scribner said, "because there is no one else I knew like him. We all start out as children making music, and our emotion is pure. We feel our bodies dance. We have this pure and unalloyed love for music, and what makes Bernstein unique is that . . . he never veered from that childhood love. When you made music with him, you felt brought back

Conducting the Vienna Philharmonic with soloists Gwyneth Jones
and Jess Thomas in rehearsal, 1979

to the place in which you should be and from which you should never
stray—that primal state of joyful embrace."

Then there was his audience. Bernstein's *Fidelio* with the Vienna
State Opera at the Kennedy Center included a performance of the
Leonore Overture No. 3, which is traditionally inserted before the closing scene. Addice Thomas, company manager of the Washington Opera
Society, happened to be in a box for that performance. "I had never been
a particular fan of Bernstein's," she said. "But I had never seen *Fidelio*
and was very curious about it. The *Leonore* overture began and I had this
almost transfiguring experience of seeing light bouncing off the walls.
I actually thought I saw it bouncing, like a strobe. I have had that experience before listening to a singer, but never a conductor, and it lasted
through the entire overture. I felt in the presence of greatness and I
remember thinking, 'So that's what it's all about.' "

Bernstein was being showered with honors and awards. He received honorary doctorates in humane letters from Johns Hopkins University, Cleve-

land State University, the University of Warwick and Boston University; he had honorary doctorates in music from Harvard and Yale and doctorates in philosophy from Tel Aviv University and Hebrew University in Israel. Foreign governments had awarded him their decorations, including Chile, West Germany, Italy and Israel, and he had been made an *officier* in the Legion of Honor by France. (He would become a *commandeur* in 1985.) His Vienna recording of Beethoven's Ninth received a Grammy in 1980, as did his performance of Shostakovich's Fifth. His recording of Gershwin's *An American in Paris* received repeated Grand Prix du Disque Classique awards, the most recent being 1981, and there were numerous Emmy and other television awards through the years, as well as arts and civic awards on an international scale. It should be noted, however, that Bernstein never won a Pulitzer Prize. William Bolcom, who was awarded a Pulitzer in 1988, said, "One thing he never got was respect from his peers, and the peer thing is absolutely important in the composing world, because nobody else gives a damn. *West Side Story* might be the greatest musical ever, but that was 'popular' music, therefore not considered serious." It was an omission that always rankled. At dinner with George Perle, another Pulitzer Prize winner, Bernstein made a slighting reference to the fact, then said, "Everyone has a fucking Pulitzer Prize but me!"

What was also disappointing was that, although there had been a festival of his music at Butler University in Indianapolis in 1976, there was a general lack of interest in the subject. However, the following year, 1977, the Israel Philharmonic celebrated its fortieth anniversary by giving Bernstein a thirty-year retrospective and, in two weeks, played almost every major Bernstein score. Two years after that, in 1979, Maurice Peress, conductor of the Kansas City Philharmonic, organized a similar festival, which began with four pieces Bernstein had written at Harvard and ended with one of his most recent, *Songfest*. Then in 1980 he, along with Agnes de Mille, James Cagney, Lynn Fontanne and Leontyne Price, was a recipient at the third annual Kennedy Center honors. At the awards ceremony and the performance that went with it, Bernstein heard his good friend Lauren Bacall expatiate on his life story and his daughter Jamie sing a song she had written for the occasion.

Everyone was honoring him except *Grove's Dictionary of Music and Musicians*. This famous work, published in London, the largest music reference book in use throughout the English-speaking world, was about to appear in a new edition in the late autumn of 1980. For the first time since its original publication in 1878, *Grove's* not only would be annotated and amended but would be completely rewritten. The effort had taken twelve years and cost some $7 million; there were twenty volumes and some 22,500 references.

Joan Peyser said, "At the time I was editor of *Musical Quarterly,* and I devoted an entire issue to *The New Grove.* In general my contributors gave it high marks, but there were two areas I thought problematic. One was German music; the Nazi connections in the lives of von Karajan and Elisabeth Schwarzkopf, for instance, had been glossed over. The second area was the dismissive treatment accorded American composers, and particularly Jewish composers, in the musical theater, and I zeroed in on Bernstein." His treatment in that august publication was, she said, "horrible." It was a verdict Bernstein shared. He expressed his disapproval in a typically oblique way when the publishers, Macmillan of London, held a party to celebrate the event in the Starlight Room of the Waldorf-Astoria Hotel in New York.

Bernstein arrived in a too-tight tuxedo, the buttons of which were already popping open to reveal a bare stomach, a silk scarf slung around his neck. Susan Koscis, a former director of publicity for CBS, was at the party and recalled, "He was incoherent and rambling. It was surreal." After dismissing the publication with the remark that any further encomium from him would be superfluous, Bernstein noted that the seventeenth anniversary of Kennedy's assassination had passed without a single reference in the *New York Times* two days before. That, he said, was because Americans had forgotten all about the great man. He dropped sinister hints about a conspiracy at the highest levels and began to elaborate on his next theme, that the country had been sliding downhill ever since, when hisses were heard in the audience. "Eric Lloyd, an assistant managing editor of the *Wall Street Journal,* stood up and walked toward Mr. Bernstein, shouting 'Rubbish! Rubbish! Americans have not forgotten John Kennedy!' " Then he told Bernstein to sit down, but by then Bernstein was unstoppable. Kennedy was his personal friend; he was the greatest president since Franklin Roosevelt. Then he began to cry. His very real anger over being slighted, as he felt, one he had not dared to express, and his feeling that he was destined to be forgotten, had transferred themselves to his grief over loss of another kind. To the audience, however, he simply seemed disheveled and obviously drunk.

There were other indications that the Lenny everyone knew was changing. Ned Rorem recalled that Bernstein performed one of his works, a suite in eight movements called *Sunday Morning,* early in 1981. This was on a program with Copland's *Old American Songs* and Schuman's Third Symphony, and all three composers were sitting in a box for the first of four scheduled performances. Rorem said, "During the second movement, which is slow, something weird happened. Bernstein had been coughing and the first cellist looked up anxiously. Lenny put down his baton and left the stage. He didn't come back. There was no announcement of a five-minute break, nothing. The audience was getting restless. Shirley Bernstein, who was sitting nearby, went backstage and eventually returned to tell us he was okay. Lenny came back, began where he left off and went on to the end." Rorem learned that Bernstein had just had a throat biopsy, which showed no malignancy, but had been coughing up some blood during the performance. So he went out "to get a cigarette, so as to cough better," Rorem said wearily. The Bernstein they once knew would never have walked off the stage without a word.

Bernstein had always traveled in the company of someone, his sister, his wife or his secretary, but now the size of the entourage was conspicuously enlarged. Dana Kruger, a singer who performed in several of Bernstein's works, said, "There were always three or four people around him and they all looked alike and handsome. There to light his cigarette, hold his coat and do anything he wanted. I remember one time overhearing him say, 'Gee, this is bothering me,' reach into his mouth and take out part of a bridge. A young man put his hand out and he put it right in the guy's hand."

Dana Kruger first met Bernstein when she was singing in the tenth-anniversary performance of *Mass* at the Kennedy Center in 1981. "A bunch of us were on stage late one afternoon in the Opera House when something happened, the air changed, because Bernstein walked in. That was the effect he had on everyone, the power of his presence. Then he came to dinner and drank all our Scotch. My husband ran next door to borrow some more and our neighbor gave him his Chivas Regal. 'Anything for Leonard Bernstein,' he said. Another time I was just outside the rehearsal room when Bernstein came up behind me and took his fist and jammed it up inside my shirt. A very odd thing to do, but he had that kind of power, and it was a big problem. We all called him the eight-hundred-pound gorilla.

"I remember while we were doing *Songfest* in Los Angeles, his son Alex's birthday party was going on in the other room and I heard Bernstein had put his fist through the birthday cake. It was awful, but it was exciting too, because you never knew what he'd do next. One of the things you think is, 'Poor Lenny.' "

The brief beard, in 1976

He had tried wearing a beard; it was silvery gray when it appeared, and he fretted that it made him look older. He wanted to look like Tchaikovsky, who was a beautiful person, not Hemingway. That was soon abandoned, but the faded denim jackets with matching bell-bottom jeans, the saddle shoes, the too-tight blazers, the red kerchiefs at the neckline, the heavy silver-and-turquoise Indian bracelets and the Mickey Mouse watches, replaced the camel-hair coats and designer ties he once wore. His stomach began to look distended, and he was shrinking, as could clearly be seen: his head seemed to be disappearing into his neck. There was something almost gnomelike about the bulletlike head above a striped cotton matelot jersey open to the navel, something unsettling about the way his tongue would flicker out from between his teeth. He appeared in films at the wheel of a big white convertible with some delighted boy seated beside him, still making the grand entrance at Tanglewood just as Koussevitzky had done. He would, Helen Epstein wrote in an article, "Listening to Lenny," interject sexual innuendo at every turn of the conversation, however innocent. "He appeared at rehearsals dressed as everything from a beachcomber . . . to a punk rocker . . . talked about self-discipline and carried on like a six-year-old. 'Everybody out of the closet, bam-bam,' he began chanting one afternoon to a gathering of students, colleagues . . . and waiters in a local restaurant . . . 'Why does he behave like that?' students kept asking each other while they vied for seats in his classes, seats at his rehearsals, a chance to meet with him for a few minutes by themselves." A young piano teacher recalled she was a student at Tanglewood after Felicia Bernstein died and was dating a boy in the conducting class, which was very small. They were walking down a country road hand in hand when they saw Bernstein's Mercedes coming toward them and her boyfriend "actually dropped my hand," she said. She was furious.

Dick White said, "He came back to the National Symphony Orchestra soon after his wife died and he had aged ten years in a few months. The spark was gone." Ken Pasmanick noticed that, at a morning rehearsal, a bottle of Scotch would be prominently displayed on the piano and the player invited to have a drink. White also thought Bernstein was experimenting with cocaine, because the drug narrows the pupils "and I have seen him when his pupils were pinpoints." Kenneth Mirkin began to notice problems with memory and wrong beat patterns in performance, and rehearsals during which he would be wheezing and using an inhaler. He said, "Next year he'd come back as good as ever. You'd see him going up and down, coming back from the edge."

A theory evolved that Bernstein's behavior largely depended upon his intake of alcohol and that in turn had to do with whoever was mixing the drinks in the little silver cup that was always at his side. If the person in charge gave him a well-diluted Scotch, all was well. But someone else in the constantly changing role of personal assistant and valet might be pouring straight Scotch all day long, and that was when the trouble started.

Phillip Ramey, who was a close friend of Copland's, recalled that during one Wall-to-Wall performance of Copland's music in Symphony Space, New York, in 1980, which was a live radio broadcast, Bernstein arrived late as usual. Then he wanted to know where the "boy of the hour" was and subsequently announced to the audience, and nationwide, that Copland was out "taking a pee." People began to remark upon his striking change of manner whenever he was drunk. What Arthur Laurents considered to be Bernstein's outrageous side had always been there, but now that he was in his early sixties there was a new attitude; he seemed immune to any understanding of the embarrassment he was causing. Given his compulsive need to be loved, Bernstein was bound to conceal and swallow his angers and resentments, as the incident involving Jerry Robbins's additions to the *West Side Story* score demonstrated; but then, he had no outlet for these feelings. Alcohol gave him such an outlet. After having enough to drink (and given his fondness for mixing pills and alcohol indiscriminately, with who-knows-what synergistic effects), he no longer cared whom he offended and could unleash the dark side of his personality with all its pent-up angers and resentments. Gone was the careful diplomat who weighed each word, the gregarious charmer, the charismatic teacher and performer, and in his place was a crude, critical, sarcastic and demanding figure who bored his friends when he did not offend them, straining everyone's patience to the breaking point. After having invited him to dinner and listened to the usual monologue, Rorem wrote, "You can't set forth an idea without Lenny's poohpoohing it, then putting you straight by merely rewording the idea in his own style. The style is built around non-stop impersonations (of Boulanger, of Giscard d'Estaing, of Rosalynn Carter, of people present), accurate, and cutting . . . The content is that of He Who Sees Clearly, anecdotes from the Inside interlarded with the Suddenly Serious Stance about the Great Problems." He was exasperating, but the trouble was that Lenny was also "the world's most generous creature," as Rorem reminded himself next day. One veered between irritation, admiration and reluctant affection. He'd be impossible and then go on one of his "hugging orgies," and one would be swept into the sodden embrace despite oneself.

Something of that sort happened to the pianist and conductor William Huckaby, who was summoned at the last moment to accompany singers James McCracken, Richard Stilwell and others in a recital following a formal White House dinner. Bernstein was then conducting *Fidelio* at the Kennedy Center; Huckaby was vaguely aware of this but did not know he was in the audience. After the performance Huckaby was standing on the dais chatting with President Carter when, in mid-sentence, "I felt these hands clamped on my shoulder, I was whirled around and engaged in a deep kiss of the French variety and Bernstein was saying, 'I haven't heard such virile piano playing for fifteen years. It was magnificent.' President Carter watched all this with his mouth open and then walked away. I was charmed in a way, but in retrospect one has to concede he was crude."

Bernstein inspired the same struggling mixture of feelings in every-one. "He was surrounded by sycophants, people trying to anticipate his every need. A swirling mass of craziness," Jerry Hadley said. "Many times I've seen him before a concert looking like the wreck of the Hesperus, with a cigarette in one hand and a drink in the other. Yet as soon as he reached the stage thirty-five years would melt away and he would become this ageless sylph who loved music; his whole body would pulsate. He was the most utterly human, most exasperating, petulant, the most maddening person to be around, and the most stimulating and fulfilling musician I have ever encountered.

"I had an experience with him recording the Mozart Requiem in Germany in a tiny baroque church and was later invited to a party given by the widow of Carl Orff. The whole Bernstein retinue and soloists were staying in a pretty hotel about twenty-five kilometers away on a lake. Somehow, Bernstein and I were the last to leave the party. I got a ride back to the hotel in his chauffeur-driven car, sitting in the back seat with him. It was three in the morning. Suddenly he reached over and grabbed my hand with his bony old fingers, and I am sitting there thinking, 'Please don't let it happen.' He stared out of the window looking at the stars. Then he said, 'I really hate the middle of the night. This is when I realize how lonely I am.'

"Nothing happened. We went to the hotel and got our keys. He turned to me, smiled and said, 'You're a good kid,' and went up the stairs."

Amberson

Now let clamour of horn
Din of the clattering hoof . . .

— GOETHE, "AN SCHWAGER KRONOS"

Among the angers and resentments that were expressed after Felicia Bernstein's death was the cavalier treatment he felt he had received from the one orchestra that ought to have wanted him as resident conductor and had never engaged him as such. Bernstein continued to appear regularly as guest conductor of the Boston Symphony Orchestra and, whether by accident or design, managed to lengthen his rehearsals regularly enough to alarm its management almost as often as he had antagonized the New York Philharmonic's managers. Mary H. Smith, who worked for BSO management at the time, said, "Yes, we would let him do overtime. I don't think anyone knew how to stop it. At one point they were doing a morning rehearsal at Tanglewood and the board of trustees and overseers of the orchestra were having lunch on the grounds nearby. Everyone was so delighted at this beautiful music washing over them, and I remember looking at my watch and thinking they had no idea what they were paying for it."

The problem first began back in the summer of 1974 when Bernstein was rehearsing for a performance of Tchaikovsky's Fifth at Tanglewood. Joseph Silverstein, who was the orchestra's concertmaster for twenty-nine years, recalled that the problem was always the same. "Whenever Lenny would come to us, the first fifteen minutes were taken up with personal greetings, so there was never enough time to rehearse. The first-chair players were all members of the faculty, and we had to teach in between double rehearsal days, from one to three in the afternoon. He was puttering around that morning, and at the break I said that we had to leave on time at 12:30 p.m. He replied, 'Joe, baby, don't worry about it.' Then at 12:30 he said, 'I think we will go through that slow movement again.' I objected, 'We have to teach,' at which he replied in a very patronizing way, 'You have to teach, but I have to teach *you*.' I had to leave the stage long enough to let my pupils know I would be late, which is perhaps why the story got around that I walked out. It was a matter of license on his part, but we were crusty, and he took it as a personal affront that a rehearsal only lasted two and a half hours."

The concert was a great success and the incident was forgotten. Then, at Aaron Copland's eightieth birthday party at Seranak in November 1980, there was another incident. Bernstein had not been conducting at Tanglewood for a while and felt that "we should do something," Silverstein recalled. "He sat down at Koussevitzky's piano and began to play Gershwin's *Rhapsody in Blue.* 'My God, we should record this piece along with the Concerto in F!' Bernstein said." The respective managers were called in to discuss how a Tanglewood recording session might be accomplished during the summer of 1981. Recording in the open-air shed was obviously impossible. Taking the orchestra back to Boston for a recording session was impractical, so the managers looked for a suitable recording hall in the area and thought they had found one in the Koussevitzky Auditorium at the Berkshire Community College in Pittsfield. Silverstein continued, "At that point there were scheduling problems, and management finally said, 'We really can't do it.'

"Bernstein was very angry. He did an all-Bernstein program by way of substitution that included the Symphonic Suite from *On the Waterfront.* The parts were full of mistakes and he had a terrible temper tantrum and walked off the stage." Richard Dyer of the Boston *Globe* also recalled the incident. "Bernstein said, 'I have been treated in a cavalier fashion,' and went on and on about all the things he had done for the orchestra and said he had helped them buy Seranak in 1977 or '78. Just before the concert began Bernstein opened all the windows of the conductor's room and began to practice *Rhapsody in Blue,* in case anyone should miss the point."

A few months later Bernstein canceled his only winter appearances with the Boston Symphony Orchestra: he was to have conducted a Hindemith work as part of the orchestra's centennial celebration. The following year, the summer of 1982, he did not return to Tanglewood but spent his time conducting and teaching at a new summer school, the Los Angeles Philharmonic Institute; he called it "Tanglewood West." He also recorded *Rhapsody in Blue,* but with the Los Angeles Philharmonic, not the BSO. Silverstein said, "Nobody was at fault. Everybody was trying to do this for him and it just couldn't work out. Instead of being understanding about it, he thought he was being done in." The rift was repaired in 1983, when, to celebrate Bernstein's sixty-fifth birthday, the BSO threw a lavish party for him in Seranak. He finally deigned to arrive at two in the morning. The soufflés had long since fallen, and the chef was in a fury.

Bernstein's contretemps with the Boston Symphony Orchestra illustrates not only the way his injured feelings would lead him to look for ways to get even but also that by 1981 his company, Amberson Enterprises, had become the major influence on his career. It was his unvarying practice that, every time he mounted the podium, the effort would pay off three ways: the concert itself, a recording and also, if possible, a film of the whole event. All that had been dictated by the realities of the classical music business, and his company had grown from its modest beginnings in ways he could not have imagined.

One of the earliest factors shaping Amberson's expansion was the departure of Arthur Judson from Columbia Artists Management in October 1963. Harry Beall, who became his business associate, believed he either was fired or left in a pique. Judson's name had been given to Columbia's concert hall on West Fifty-seventh Street, and he asked that it be removed. The day he left CAMI he announced that he was establishing a new company, Judson, O'Neill, Beall and Steinway. He gave prominent mention to the fact that he would manage the career of Leonard Bernstein. Three months later, a letter from Bernstein to Judson was leaked to the press. In it Bernstein denied he had engaged Judson and asked his old manager (by then aged eighty-two) not to use his name. Beall said, "I don't think they ever exchanged words again."

It would have occurred to Bernstein that, if he needed a manager, his new company could represent his interests more faithfully than someone with Judson's notorious ability to pursue his own interests at the expense of his client's. At a single stroke he had dispensed with the payoff he owed Judson, via Bruno Zirato, every time he took an outside engagement—usually 10 percent to the presenting manager plus a further 5 percent to Judson. (He had complained that by the time he paid his traveling expenses, especially in Europe, and paid off his managers, there was nothing left.) Removing that continual drain on his income would be a great relief. Bernstein's strategy seems remarkably clear-minded and consistent: first to dispense with the middleman as publisher, then with the middleman as manager and finally to remove the middleman as impresario. This last issue also arose in 1963. Bernstein learned that Sol Hurok, who had once tried to hire his services, was presenting what he called "A Leonard Bernstein Gala!" that spring. It was all perfectly aboveboard, as performance rights to the opera, ballet and Broadway works were available from the publishers who still owned them. Bernstein would receive some royalty payments, but the size of those would be trivial compared to the potential profits to be made from taking such a show on the road. In any event, Bernstein had a stake in ensuring that the production met his artistic standards but no control over it and, in fact, the gala was not a success, receiving poor to middling reviews. Walter Gould, the actual producer of the show (Hurok only guaranteed the costs and took a percentage of the proceeds), said he had received verbal permission from Helen Coates. However, Bernstein had subsequently learned that a friend of his, Johnny Green, wanted to put on a similar evening. According to Gould, Bernstein called Hurok and asked him to drop his plans. Hurok refused and Bernstein could not legally prevent him. Helen Coates subsequently wrote that the event took place over Bernstein's strong objections. The moral needed no underlining: if he were to have artistic control over his own stage works, Bernstein had to become his own producer.

What Bernstein needed next was someone with more than Helen Coates's limited talents or even the expertise in contract negotiation provided by his faithful lawyer, Abe Friedman. He needed an experienced arts administrator. As luck would have it, Schuyler Chapin, who had worked with Bernstein while he was supervisor of the Masterworks series at Columbia Records, was leaving his job at Lincoln Center just as Bernstein was leaving the New York Philharmonic and, in 1969, he agreed to join Amberson as first director of a new production company. All that was then needed was a company to do the actual work of filming. Chapin negotiated with Unitel of Munich and plans began to make a film of Mahler's Ninth Symphony with the Vienna Philharmonic; other contracts would follow for the remaining Mahler symphonies and the four Brahms symphonies.

That was in 1971, and by then Amberson Productions had already produced a film about the making of an opera production, Bernstein's *Fidelio* at the Theater an der Wien, and also made a television program of his London performance of the Verdi Requiem, using St. Paul's Cathedral as a backdrop. Bernstein's innovations, while ingenious, were not unique. His rival Herbert von Karajan had come to the same conclusions and, as conductor of the Berlin Philharmonic, was making use of his commercial opportunities as assiduously as Bernstein; both men were filming with Unitel. Music, in their view, was something to be promoted and sold like any other commodity. A friend said, "The wisdom was that classical music was on the threshold of a video explosion, and Bernstein was obsessed with keeping up with Karajan. Look at the later portraits— the turtleneck sweater, draped around his shoulders, looking down at the score, the rumpled hair in profile . . ." Bernstein had found yet another model to imitate and beat at his own game.

After leaving the New York Philharmonic, Bernstein had shifted his business activity to Europe. The Vienna Philharmonic made this an easy choice, but there were other reasons. To maximize his company's profits he needed to record everything he performed as well as film it. His reputation as a composer, conductor and pianist had been built by his very early access to recordings. Even relatively unknown works such as his Clarinet Sonata and his piano pieces *Seven Anniversaries* had been considered sellable, in the early postwar years, as well as his better-known music from *Fancy Free* and his First Symphony, the *Jeremiah*. Bernstein's association with Columbia Records began in 1950 and developed rapidly after he became conductor of the New York Philharmonic, which was already under contract to Columbia. When his contract came up for renewal, one Columbia executive argued that the company had too much invested in Bernstein's future to let him go elsewhere; the terms extracted were munificent. It was thought to be the first time that a conductor had managed to get a clause in his contract giving him the right to record anything he liked. That turned out to be expensive for Columbia on occasion. Another former executive said, "Bernstein was always having sudden enthusiasms. One time he insisted they record Justus Frantz playing the Grieg Piano Concerto, and it wasn't released for ages, as there was no market for this unknown pianist."

Over the years Bernstein recorded over six hundred performances, many under the Columbia Masterworks label. "Not since the sunset years of Toscanini and the NBC Symphony has a conductor been so voraciously recorded," Roland Gelatt wrote. "Every Bernstein performance, no matter where in the world, is almost inevitably followed by a session before the microphones. Whether it be Nielsen in Copenhagen, Verdi in Vienna, Mahler in London or Ives in New York, the documentation proceeds at a furious pace." His best-selling records included *West Side Story,* Gershwin's *An American in Paris* and *Rhapsody in Blue, The Joy of Christmas,* Mahler's Symphony No. 9, and Handel's *Messiah.* He received, it is believed, an advance against royalties plus a 10 or 15 percent royalty on each record sold. In many cases his records sold over a million copies; assuming that a royalty on such a best-seller might be twenty cents, a conservative estimate, that would mean that a single record could earn $200,000.

With his departure from the New York Philharmonic Bernstein's lucrative relationship with Columbia slowly came to an end. He was anxious to make his mark as an operatic conductor, but after sales of his recording of his Vienna *Rosenkavalier* with Christa Ludwig as the Marschallin proved disappointing in 1971, Columbia refused to record the Vienna *Fidelio.* The company also refused to record his Metropolitan Opera *Carmen* with Marilyn Horne in the title role in 1972. A record company executive said, "Operas cost $225,000 to record, which was very expensive then, so Deutsche Grammophon made the recording instead of Columbia, and I heard that they took a bath on *Carmen;* there were hundreds of thousands of sets not sold." (Just the same, the record won a Grammy as best opera recording two years later.)

For the fact was that American classical music recordings, which had nurtured the careers of so many brilliant young Americans, were disappearing. In part this was due to the increased costs of recording American orchestras, with their higher wage scales, when there were plenty of cheap foreign orchestras available. It was also due to the record industry's discovery that there were enormous profits to be made quickly from pop music albums, versus the smaller profits to be made over a longer period for classical albums. Such elegant figures as Columbia's Goddard Lieberson, a one-time student of the Eastman School of Music and a trained composer, whose choices of repertoire reflected his informed tastes, were being replaced by managers who might know almost nothing about repertoire but who knew how to maximize profits. In Europe, by contrast, the demand for classical recordings was brisk. A former executive said, "It was a question of Columbia being penny wise and pound foolish. They had monster pop acts making hundreds of millions and they wouldn't spend the trifling amount to keep Bernstein; they were only interested in the bottom line."

Bernstein was understandably resentful, and the relationship ended acrimoniously in 1975 when he signed a contract with Deutsche Grammophon to record with the Vienna Philharmonic, the Boston Symphony, the London Symphony and the Czech Philharmonic; that contract became an exclusive one six years later. Shortly before Bernstein died he made a new contract with DG for a new batch of recordings which he must have known he would not live to see. Bernstein's departure from Columbia did not prevent him from making one more lucrative business deal with them before severing his relations entirely. Peter Munves, a former CBS executive, recalled meeting Bernstein by chance in a record shop in 1979. Bernstein turned to him and said, "Peter, we have got to save the catalogue," meaning all the records he had made for Columbia, most of them out of print. Munves came up with the idea of a "Great Performances" label, and out of a hundred reissues thirty-three were from Bernstein. They were best-sellers all over again.

Schuyler Chapin was invited to go to the Metropolitan Opera as assistant general manager in 1971, and by then the next chief executive of the enterprising Amberson firm was waiting in the wings. He was Harry Kraut, who had worked on *Mass* and known Bernstein while he was with the Boston Symphony Orchestra management and at Tanglewood. Kraut was the son of a prominent Brooklyn banker, of German Protestant origin, and would combine his twin interests in business and music during his undergraduate years at Harvard. He sang with the glee club and later became its graduate manager. He can be glimpsed in numerous films about Bernstein, balding, neatly dressed, with rimless glasses and a narrow fringe of beard, hovering in the background at parties and waiting to greet Bernstein whenever he came off stage. He bears a superficial resemblance to Samuel Bernstein. Those who knew him in his Harvard days remember him as immensely competent.

Harry Kraut was one of the organizers for the Harvard Glee Club's tour of Europe in 1956. William G. Dakin, another organizer of that trip, recalled that everything ran like clockwork except for the time when the group checked into a Paris hotel and there were not enough beds for everyone. Dakin, whose French was fluent, offered to translate, but Kraut would have none of that. He fixed the concierge with a steely eye and tried to tell her that every singer had to have a mattress (*mate-las*), but unfortunately he used the word *maîtresse* instead, which caused a stir. Dakin also recalled planning the English and Dutch appearances for the tour, which included a performance in Westminster Abbey as well as the opening of a festival in Holland. He was chagrined that no one complimented him on his expertise. Kraut replied, "Never do any-thing for gratitude." That showed, Dakin concluded, that Kraut was much more sophisticated than he was. Kraut also enjoyed what another friend called "skull and bones" tactics. Noel Tyl, who would go on to a career as an operatic bass, said, "There was something very fragile and reticent about Harry Kraut. People who are alone in this world some-times look for jobs in which they can feel important. He was austere and powerful, even at that age. One evening, on the boat coming back from Europe, we played chess together and had some drinks. Then, to be sure we would not be overheard, Harry escorted me out on deck to tell me that I had been chosen as the next glee club manager."

From Bernstein's point of view, Kraut's credentials were impecca-ble, but at the same moment that he was probably negotiating to pro-mote Kraut, Bernstein, in typical fashion, also found a way to put his new employee on the defensive. Jack Kirkman had learned that Chapin was leaving Amberson and immediately contacted Bernstein in Vienna to ask to be considered for Chapin's job. Bernstein suggested they talk when he returned. When the moment came, Bernstein did not take Kirkman to lunch himself but sent Kraut. Kirkman made his proposal and slowly realized that he was applying for a job Kraut also wanted. In any event, Kraut was chosen. Kirkman said he never had a reply to his application and never knew how to raise the subject with Bernstein afterwards.

Friends thought Kraut was the ideal temperamental foil for Bern-stein, secretive and inscrutable. Businessmen who dealt with him praised his ability to protect his employer's interests. He was "a very tough nego-tiator" and "brilliant at what he did." One record executive said that Kraut was extremely adroit at the poker-playing game required when contracts were being negotiated. "His method of operation is only to tell a certain amount. Each person gets a piece of the puzzle, and the rest his opponent has to find out somehow." Kraut would tell each person, "You are the only one who knows this, and if there is a leak, I will know where it came from." His passion for secrecy even extended to Amber-son employees, who were required to sign legal contracts agreeing not to discuss what transpired during their period of employment. "He is into total control," the same record executive said. He was also the one who, like Helen Coates, had to become famous for saying no. "He has to say, 'I'm sorry, it's forty thousand dollars or Bernstein doesn't show.' 'I'm sorry, Bernstein has to have the whole top floor' when they go to a hotel," another friend said. W. Stuart Pope, who retired in 1984 as president of Boosey and Hawkes, which would become Bernstein's publisher, and knew Kraut well, said, "He had a reputation for being tough, but he had a difficult master, too." Pope said that Bernstein liked to spend money, and "one had to keep the coffers well lined."

Kraut was a close friend, perhaps Bernstein's only real confidant, observers agree. He had a personal set of keys to Bernstein's Dakota apartment. He also became his financial advisor. When the Bernsteins separated in the autumn of 1976, Kraut was appointed one of the trustees of the property in Fairfield, Connecticut. Subsequently, as Chapin's memoir made clear, Kraut, Bernstein's new lawyer Paul Epstein and Chapin were the ones making such important decisions as how much money should be given to Bernstein's children, and Chapin described the tactics he used to get Bernstein to sign his will. All three men were named trustees of the estate in the will. Chapin claimed he did not know this when he urged Bernstein to sign it.

To their children, Kraut became a surrogate uncle; to Bernstein he was all things: manager, confidant, even social secretary. Angus Whyte, their Boston friend, said, "Harry is very conservative with a twinkle in his eye, very smart and engaging. He also likes to have his own way. He'd come back from Russia with a tin of fresh caviar and I would supply the champagne and boiled eggs. We were friendly for many years." He continued, "I had a house on Beacon Hill that was pretty small, and Harry would call and say, 'We are coming up. Why don't you have a party?' " so Whyte would entertain Bernstein and his entourage. That, however, was a bit unpredictable. The first time he had Bernstein as a guest he gave a dinner for twelve, which was the most he could seat. Bernstein arrived late with three unannounced guests, then declared that he hated sit-down dinners and went upstairs to the living room, where he sat with a plate of food on his knee. The next time, Whyte thought he had better have a buffet, and Bernstein took a plate of food and sat down at the dining table; there was no predicting how he would react. Their friends believed that Bernstein treated his chief assistant in his usual mercurial fashion, both extremely well and badly. One of them said, "There was always this gray area between the personal and professional worlds." Others agreed that Bernstein would try to make friends of all his employees until the moment when he needed them to do something, at which point they were rudely reminded they were there to carry his suitcases. One friend said that Kraut had to swallow "dumpster loads of shit" from Bernstein. But when the chips were down, "Harry knew Bernstein would be on his emotional knees and Harry would be there to pick up the pieces."

Money, as Norman Lebrecht observed in *The Maestro Myth,* is the last taboo. "The maestro's task is to commune with superior levels of spirituality, to shed light on cosmic mysteries. If he was seen to be pursuing material wealth as greedily as the stockbroker in row 16, his priestly myth would be dispelled." Bernstein's actual earnings have never been made public, but it is possible to make an educated guess, since it is known that conductors' top fees for a performance in the United States are around $20,000 and 30 to 50 percent more in Europe. In Japan, fees triple and quadruple; Lorin Maazel allegedly received $80,000 a night to appear in Tokyo, and Bernstein made frequent appearances in Japan. Riccardo Muti and André Previn, according to Lebrecht, could expect to make $2 million in an average year. Given the extra income to be derived from so many sources: films, television, recordings, publications, Broadway and performance royalties and miscellaneous rights, which Bernstein pursued relentlessly, it seems reasonable to suppose that Bernstein's yearly income was between $2 million and $3 million.

One reliable source believed that when Kraut became executive vice-president of Amberson Enterprises in 1972, the company was valued at $55 million; its value had probably doubled by the time Bernstein died. Like its founder, Amberson was street smart. It is said that when there was some doubt a check might be forthcoming, the word came from Amberson in advance of the performance that the maestro was feeling unwell and might not be able to appear; a check would arrive that afternoon by messenger. Kraut also knew how to increase the suspense by throwing up further objections or refusing to act. An executive with the National Symphony Orchestra, who had to work with Kraut directly, complained that whenever Bernstein was due to make an appearance, he would keep them dangling for months and, "we'd have the feeling he wanted us to beg for it."

Bernstein's own private fiefdom was seen as either an enchanted kingdom or a Borgia court, depending on one's perspective. Both those pro and con agreed that Bernstein's definition of loyalty included being loyal to the friends of his friends, finding work for them as his father had done with the family business, tolerating their personal shortcomings and defending them when necessary. The same kind of loyalty was expected from them. Jonathan Tunick, to whom Bernstein generously gave free composition lessons, was subsequently approached to supervise a crew of students who were being organized to orchestrate a work of Bernstein's. "There was no mention of a fee," Tunick said. "I was willing to do it but not crazy about the idea, and I never heard anything more from them." Tunick also received requests for a charitable contribution in Felicia Bernstein's name, to which he responded. However, the way in which recipients of Bernstein's favors were expected to act might not be clear until it was too late. A famous conductor who had enjoyed a close working relationship with Bernstein recalled that, after conducting numerous performances of one of Bernstein's musicals, he had to step down because of previous commitments. He had already coached his successor carefully in the score when Bernstein let it be known that he had someone else in mind. In the conductor's view the young replacement was completely unprepared, and he said so. He won the argument but, he said, from then on his days with Amberson were numbered.

The same conductor, who signed numerous contracts with Amberson, said that as a company to deal with they were "brutal." Conductors and singers who worked on their projects had to sign "buy-out" contracts. "He wanted a legacy unencumbered," the conductor said. "If you were a collaborator, you ended up being a gun for hire and gave up all future royalty or performance rights. Bernstein was a very tough hombre and their attitude was, 'This is the deal; take it or leave it.' You're dealing from power; what can I say? I've done it myself and I know what it's like." A pianist who was hired to work on an opera recording in Rome encountered the same attitude. "I think the offer was fair, but I remember asking about a per diem because I knew the singers were getting one. Harry Kraut denied this. He said he wanted the paper signed and returned the next day or someone else would get the job." The bargain might be a poor one but too many people were willing to accept because, "it was worth doing even if I had lost money. Just the idea of having been exposed to Bernstein and under his guidance for that amount of time."

One of Amberson's important functions was to be prepared to go to court to defend Bernstein's interests. The largest piece of unfinished business, and one that must have grated on Bernstein, was the fact that his music publishers, G. Schirmer in particular, still owned the copyrights to his works and had absolute control over their disposition. As the years went by Bernstein continued to take steps to wrestle those back from their owners. Under the copyright law that prevailed until 1976, copyright reverted to its original owner after twenty-eight years, and Bernstein was able to get back from Warner Bros. some of his earliest works, including *On the Town* and *Fancy Free*. He also signed a contract with Boosey and Hawkes in 1975 retaining his copyright but giving that company distribution rights. Some time later he set up a company, JALNI Publications (the acronym was derived from his children's first names), to ensure that these royalties would be paid directly to them. However, that still left a great many copyrights, the bulk of his compositions during his most active period, in the hands of Schirmer, so Amberson initiated a lawsuit against that publisher in 1985–86. The suit was finally settled and all copyrights reverted to Amberson except a few worldwide print rights to *West Side Story*. Bernstein continued to claim that money meant nothing to him and that he did not bother to read his contracts.

Another of Amberson's functions was to make sure that milestones in Bernstein's life—he was sentimental about such things—were properly acknowledged and celebrated by the world at large. When Bernstein was about to become sixty-five, the word went out that his birthplace of Lawrence, Massachusetts, wanted to celebrate that birthday of August 25, 1983. A newspaper reported that the whole affair was very "hush-hush" but that Bernstein was about to give his consent. As Bernstein said on the great day, "I think there is nothing so dumb or pompous as celebrating your own birthday. But to have it celebrated FOR you is pretty nice." His remarks would imply he did not know that his own company had organized this supposedly spontaneous demonstration of affection, but such was the case. One of those working on the project said, "The idea was to mastermind what would appear to be a grass-roots celebration of Lenny's hometown, but it had to look as if Mickey and Judy were doing everything. We had a local committee, but they were straw figures. Everything came from Amberson's offices." Bernstein subsequently spent a full day there and also wore a blue armband, another Amberson initiative, to signify he was making an appeal for nuclear disarmament that day. Musicians around the world were invited to join in the protest, and many did.

The Lawrence birthday party was only one of many seemingly independent "tributes" to Bernstein the origins of which could be traced to his company. Amberson not only had become generator of public-relations affairs but remained in charge, since experience had taught Bernstein the danger of leaving anything to chance. He was his own best promoter and packager of the "product"—himself. Harry Kraut said later, "Lenny and I talked quite a bit . . . about the idea of putting out an image. Otherwise, the person whose image it is doesn't control it. That's what I was in charge of." But if Amberson was necessary to the performer who wanted to manipulate the public perception of his accomplishments, his "image," its usefulness to him as a creative artist is less clear. Hal Prince, who also employs an office staff, said, "This operation is not about 'Let's make more money,' because, as you grow, there are so many strings and so many people tugging at them" that the company takes on a life of its own and starts to direct the course of the artist it was founded to serve. There are pressures to repeat in formulaic form what had been hard-won victories of the imagination and to make artistic compromises instead of venturing into unknown waters. But the very fact of employees to feed and mortgages to pay had to have its incalculable effect upon an original mind that sought, not success or financial reward or even fame, but the realization of its own possibilities. That Bernstein's imaginative powers had suffered could not be denied, as the failure of *1600 Pennsylvania Avenue* had demonstrated; that the demands of business were directly responsible was only a conjecture, but a plausible one. It seemed likely the composer himself was aware that he was losing touch with some essential part of his gift. As early as 1969, when he left the New York Philharmonic, he declared that he was tired of "cutting his life up into chunks and selling them," but this was what he continued to do. Amberson could give him every kind of material reward, but it could not give him satisfaction, so from that point of view his bargain was Faustian.

That his conscience troubled him is possible. Jacques Barzún believed, "As in every contact of art with trade . . . contamination, not of morals but of art, has ensued; for in our unyielding social order the only way to fight exploitation and monopoly is to exploit and monopolize in return." It is true that, as time passed, Bernstein became increasingly cynical; "his view was that everyone was on the make," a friend said. He began to suspect the people working for him, questioning their loyalty. Gustav Meier, Tanglewood's resident opera conductor, recalled that he once rang up Bernstein to wish him a happy New Year. Bernstein was quite touched, but then he asked, "Is that all?" He could not believe Meier did not want something from him. His mood was consistently somber. A friend recalls that he and Bernstein attended a performance of Alban Berg's opera *Lulu,* about moral degeneracy. Bernstein had talked all the way through the performance, and at the moment when one of the characters, a depraved marquis, has to speak a line, "Der Schmutz!" ("The filth!"), Bernstein spoke it with him.

A similar incident occurred at Tanglewood in 1980, the year that Copland's eightieth birthday was being celebrated. A friend recalled, "Bernstein had had a lot to drink and started telling stories about the early days with Copland. Although he was drunk he insisted on driving. We were going down a road that borders the lake. It was very twisting and I was frightened for my life. What happens is that the road comes to a dead end. There is a hill or berm there and you have got to turn right. He suddenly slammed on the brakes with such force that I hit my head on the windshield. His hand was on his head and he was saying, 'My life is all wrong. I have become a tool of the networks!' It was two or three in the morning and the silence was deafening. We finally went back to his hotel. He stormed in, demanding a drink, and started to cry."

Tadzio

So the landlord of Hades may hear us . . .

—GOETHE, "AN SCHWAGER KRONOS"

The suspicion that he had lost his way, commercialized and degraded the art that was most sacred to him and which alone made life worth living, was perhaps Bernstein's most poignant fear. Typically, he looked for something or someone to blame. Some vast impersonal corporate machine still held him hostage—this was the thought that appalled and comforted him. By looking outside himself he could avoid staring too closely at that other fear, that the person he had been, with his boundless hopes and dreams, had gone forever.

It was to this that he referred (obliquely, as ever) when he said, speaking of Mahler's music, "He wrote of what was so beautiful about life when it was young and which can never be recaptured." He was Mahler reincarnated, or perhaps Mahler as represented by Aschenbach, transfixed by the allure of youth, mourning its loss, repelled by the "adventures of the spirit and mind" that life had etched on his face, as Mann said of Aschenbach. His pursuit was, perhaps like Aschenbach's, of "an ultimate mysterious fulfillment," a dream of glory without end. It was "a dark illimitable ocean," as Milton wrote, untroubled by any thought of personal shortcomings and all-too-human limitations. He would do it all, not just well but to absolute perfection. He would become a composer to rank with Mahler, a conductor such as the world had never seen, the self-appointed teacher of mankind, the loving friend, moral guide, seer, visionary, tzaddik . . . And success was so easy, so effortless at the beginning that his ambition fed upon it and grew ever more voracious. It became "a demoniacal obsession, almost like a monster swallowing up the individual who has created it," as Karen Horney wrote, which was what made rejection and failure so mortifying. The ravenousness of this inner demand made the fact of his own mortality seem all the more poignant as time grew short. He was growing old feeling that he had never achieved what he set out to do. Since his need for praise and reassurance was bottomless, he felt that no one had given him the recognition he deserved. No wonder he was in such torment. No wonder he feared death so much, or, at moments, half wished for it. Once when the subject of the dangers of plane travel was raised, he replied he rather liked the idea of falling out of the sky. It would solve so many of his problems.

The irony was that this heroic, almost demonic striving after the unattainable took Bernstein to a higher level of accomplishment than any American musician had achieved before. Although he constantly compared himself to Mahler, in his effect on his age it would be just as apposite to compare him with Hector Berlioz. Like that astounding composer and conductor, he too "ranged over his whole domain . . . and . . . bore the brunt of fighting for the modern art of his epoch," as Barzun wrote. If Berlioz taught all of Europe whenever he picked up his baton or his pen, so too did Bernstein instruct, inform and enlighten his own ignorant age. Like Berlioz, he left the stamp of his uncommon personality on everyone he met. He, too, was on easy terms with princes, or their modern equivalents. He, too, towered over his contemporaries. He, too, was the subject of intense controversy. As happened to Berlioz after death, there is a similar belated awareness that a figure of enormous stature has left the stage, by general agreement the most gifted musician in America of the twentieth century.

As a youth Bernstein entertained the notion that he had lived some seventy-five years before, which would have made him a romantic composer. This is an appealing parallel. Like Berlioz, who was not a child prodigy either, Bernstein acquired a conscious inner life at an early age. He showed, like other artists besides Berlioz, the power to feel intensely, and retained those first visions of childhood in their original freshness and vigor throughout his life. As with Berlioz, the most striking aspect of Bernstein's personality was his swiftness in associating ideas. With that was combined a great capacity for passionate expression and an unusual ability to enter rarified realms, to seek for and find a supreme revelation through art. His life, like those of the other romantic heroes, spanned every extreme from the vulgar to the sublime. For him, art had been elevated to the status of religion. He shared with the romantics the "insight that a continuity existed between life and art comparable to transubstantiation in a sacrament," Barzun wrote.

Kenneth Clark wrote that romanticism's dark side was its restlessness and death wish. He was speaking of Byron and Géricault, but he could just as well have been speaking of Bernstein. If music was the ennobling focus of his life, it was a particularly capricious Muse for someone who was so much in need of reassurance, since, as Barzun wrote, "even performance cannot compare with the fullness of effect of a book which may be reread and studied at will; nor with the canvas which, though not always on view, is at least stationary and reproducible." His art might bear as profound a relationship to life, but it existed only in the ear of the hearer and by virtue of that most fallible of human faculties, the memory. Music needed to be constantly imagined, constantly reinvented, constantly pursued. In the nineteenth century the ideal heroine for romantic composers usually took the name of Estelle or Stella. Being a child of his time, Bernstein's muse was Felicity (Felicia), a symbol of that inner tranquility he would forever and vainly seek. And so he fretted about how much was still to be done and how little time was left, and was prey to accidents. During a rehearsal of the Orchestre National de France in Paris he stabbed his hand with his baton and spattered blood all over his score. At about that same time, following concerts in Milan, Venice and Washington, he was forced to go to bed for a week suffering from exhaustion. Then, during a performance of the Israel Philharmonic in Houston he did what audiences had been predicting for years and fell off the podium during a performance of Tchaikovsky's *Francesca da Rimini.* He landed on his knees, assured his audience he was not hurt and scrambled back to his feet. To die on the podium; that, he told his friends, was all he wanted.

Bernstein still took time off for periods of composing, traveling up to Springate in a beautiful old Mercedes-Benz with a mahogany dashboard and leather seats, or a convertible with MAESTRO license plates. Like his father before him, Bernstein was a terrible driver who seems to have escaped ever having a serious accident, although he thoroughly alarmed his passengers. Peter Mark Schifter recalled that he once took a car trip with Bernstein in which he finally had to ask him to pull over. The same thing happened to Stephen Somary (son of the New York choral conductor Johannes Somary), who came to know him well during his later years. He said, "We were driving up to Fairfield one time when I saw him take both hands off the wheel going seventy-five miles an hour. Finally I screamed, 'Stop the car!' and he pulled over so fast he almost killed us. I yelled 'Get out!' and he did. I got into the driver's seat and took us the rest of the way. He didn't say a word, and at the end of the trip he said I was a good driver and went off by himself for an hour. After that he was fine."

Bernstein's studio was a converted barn with an extra bedroom; it was relatively sparsely furnished with early nineteenth-century antiques and some Chilean influences. "He could not be alone, so I would usually go up once a week," Somary said. " 'Baby-sitting,' he called it." He liked to work at the kind of high-Jeffersonian style of desk that would allow him to write standing, and would return either very depressed "or jubilant, because he had managed to write eight bars," his sister said. He was always planning to conduct less and compose more once life quietened down, which it never seemed to do. He was going to write an autobiography. "I have to say we were quite nervous about that," she said. They were all sure it would be indiscreet. Bernstein got as far as a working title, *Blue Ink,* the meaning of which no one could decipher, but never actually wrote a word.

In his studio he liked to be surrounded by familiar objects, all kinds of knickknacks and mementos, and his assistant's main job, when he traveled, was to turn his hotel suite into a temporary home filled with familiar books, ashtrays, cigarette filters and pictures of his wife and children. The demands placed on such an assistant were erratic and could be anything from writing letters to picking up wet underwear off the bathroom floor. Nevertheless the position had its attractions. As was his custom, Bernstein treated a young aide as part lackey, part personal friend, and, when on tour, expected him to take a lavish life style for granted. One assistant said, "They told me they paid for everything except presents and sex." The biggest problem when traveling was getting him somewhere on time. The same assistant said, "I consider myself the world's greatest procrastinator and I am an amateur compared to him. I would have to physically drag him to where he had to go."

All his life Bernstein was a self-medicator and took all kinds of pills: pills to go to sleep, pills to wake up, vitamins and whatever else took his fancy. It is known that he tried lithium for depression and also Halcion for his chronic insomnia, a drug thought to have such possible side effects as paranoia, depression and hallucinations. However, his sister said he did so only briefly and did not suffer any ill effects. Whenever Bernstein met a new doctor, he would question him closely about the latest discoveries. He had a friend in Munich who was a homeopath and regularly prescribed exotic remedies. His lifelong pattern, of taking an almost obsessive interest in his health while continuing to abuse it regularly, continued. What was even stranger, he sternly forbade his friends from taking the kinds of risks to which he habitually exposed himself. Arthur Laurents once recalled seeing him swallow an amphetamine along with a tumbler of Scotch at four one afternoon. When he wanted to try the same thing, Bernstein was horrified. While at home he lived, the assistant claimed, a quieter life than most people would have believed. He got up as late as possible. He wanted to sleep all day and be up all night writing and reading. Because he got hungry, two refrigerators were kept well stocked with cold cuts, fruit and milk. For breakfast he would have a soft-boiled egg, toast, orange juice and strong coffee, made by Julia in an old coffee pot that turned it to mud.

Julia liked to maintain the idea of the back and front of the apartment; in her own precinct, his housekeeper was the secret ruler, directing the staff and watching over the family. She was a good South American cook, but for entertaining or just evenings at home Bernstein employed a professional. One of his former cooks said that Bernstein liked "homey" cooking, perhaps even a meat loaf. He loved lobster and fresh corn with a passion and, for dessert, anything made of chocolate. Dinner could be set for eight o'clock, but that was fairly meaningless; it might be as much as three hours later, so the cook had to plan menus that could be prepared at the last minute. She never knew whether there would be four for dinner or fourteen. When at home he usually entertained a small circle of friends: Comden and Green, Lauren ("Betty") Bacall and Michael ("Mendy") Wager. His former assistant said, "He and Mendy used to do a lot of intellectual sparring, and it wasn't good-natured. He once said of himself that he never had to win, which was wrong. He always had to win. He also thought of himself as never mean, which wasn't true either. I remember one time having an argument with him in Vienna. He was eating pea soup and flung it at me from a spoon. I looked longingly at a bowl of whipped cream, and left."

As always, Bernstein took a close interest in his children's welfare and the benevolent point of view, one friend said, that they were all geniuses. Jamie and Nina went to Brearley, a top girls' school; and they all went to Harvard, spending their summers working at Tanglewood. In a memoir Jamie subsequently wrote for the *Radcliffe Quarterly* she described a happy childhood, for which she thought her sister must envy her, as by the time Nina arrived their parents were much less happy together. Alexander was physically delicate as a child, subject to severe colds, perhaps an asthmatic condition, and was taken by his mother to Arizona and Chile in an attempt at a cure. When he returned from Chile he had forgotten much of his English and had a crucifix, which predictably horrified his father.

All three experimented with careers in the theater. For a while, Nina was going to be an actress; she and Alexander performed in their father's *West Side Story* recording. Jamie was a songwriter-singer. In the best show-business tradition, she was given a brief moment during her father's television interview with Mike Wallace, and Bernstein confidently declared in another film of the same period (1980) that she was on the brink of a meteoric career—a prophecy that was not to be fulfilled. With Alexander, Bernstein tended to be more critical. A friend recalled attending a dinner after a Bernstein concert in Los Angeles during which Bernstein insisted that his son stand and deliver a lengthy lecture about the Passover to the assembled guests. Alexander was clearly ill at ease, and the friend thought the episode inappropriate and insensitive. While loving their father, his children would have readily conceded that he was not the easiest person to live with. Two years before he died, Jamie Bernstein, by then married to David Thomas and mother of a baby girl, said, "Our family is like a solar system with Pop as the sun. Sometimes it's very difficult to figure out your own identity as a planet while you're circling him."

Jamie, whose ambitions dovetailed most directly with her father's, clashed with him so often as an adolescent that Alexander gave them both boxing gloves in an attempt to defuse the situation. Alexander himself went through a period of about two years in his mid-teens when he too was in revolt and refused to speak to his father. This appeared to be connected with the discovery that his father was bisexual and that it was causing his mother much suffering; but then, they all reproached their father for that. Like others in his life, they were alternately exasperated (to Alexander, it was inconceivable that his father should still be talking about what he was going to do when he "grew up") and disarmed by his ability to sweep differences aside. Alexander recalled that while he was away at school he was listening to jazz and rock but also his father's Beethoven recordings. "And I came home and the *Pastoral* Symphony was on and I was singing along. He ran over and gave me a great hug . . ."

By the early 1980s the Bernstein children were, for the most part, independent; still, sister Shirley had stepped into the breach and wanted them to call her "Mommy." Her pet name for her brother was "Big Ben," a reference to his sexual attributes, perhaps ironic—no one dared to ask. Life in the Dakota was secure and uneventful, with one exception. After John Lennon was killed in December 1980, Alexander was watching television one night in their second-floor apartment when someone climbed up a tree and shot at him through a window. He was unharmed, but the next day all the windows on the Central Park side were replaced with bullet-proof glass and a private security guard was hired. Bernstein, like Yoko Ono, took to coming and leaving through the back door. Despite his protected passage from apartments and hotels to concert halls and airports in stretch limousines, Bernstein suffered the normal hazards of modern life. He was robbed at gunpoint while having dinner with Michael Tilson Thomas in 1983. One night in Munich, walking back to his hotel, he was knocked down and bloodied by two American blacks who took his money and watch. He continued to be as fearless as ever. Somary came across him at eleven-thirty one night on Seventy-second Street with Copland. He had stopped to talk to a bum. Somary said he had "decided to play shrink, which he loved to do. He kept him there for half an hour trying to find out why he was homeless and wouldn't go to a shelter, and eventually quite a crowd of people had gathered around. The bum asked for money. Bernstein put his hand in his pocket and pulled out a string of credit cards but no cash. Copland had to lend him five dollars."

Those who saw him after an absence of years were startled at the physical change. Julius Grossman, a conductor who had helped to found New York's High School for the Performing Arts, met Bernstein as a young man and said, "He had dark hair, an aquiline nose and extremely beautiful eyes. I told my wife I had never seen a face like that." But when they met again years later, "If you didn't know it was him you wouldn't recognize him; the contrast was so marked." Another New Yorker, Marion Weil, saw Bernstein in the 1950s when he was staying with Marc Blitzstein and his wife in the same hotel in Cuba as she and her husband and friends. They were all "impressed by how compactly he was built, how coordinated and how attractive." Then years later she saw him on a New York street corner, wearing "a sweeping black cape, standing like some brooding bird . . ."

Young men in Bernstein's life took to dropping in at the Dakota, part of a "whole new world of parties and receptions," one of them said, but were sometimes uncomfortable about it. They might be merely friends but felt that others assumed differently. Daron Aric Hagen, a young opera composer and teacher, was one of them. He had seen Bernstein spending drunken evenings at Tanglewood, always surrounded by younger men and asking at the top of his voice whether someone was "straight or gay," and embarrassing everyone, Hagen said. "After that, I kind of kept my distance from Bernstein. I felt sad that I couldn't spend a lot of time with him. Even if you didn't have sex with him, you had to sleep with him in the same bed, and I never wanted that. This is what everyone doesn't want to talk about. Right away everyone assumes you are gay. It's guilt by association, and Bernstein was too important in this business for me to get into a situation where I had to say no."

However, Bernstein went to Milwaukee in 1986 to attend a performance honoring his work and Hagen spent an evening with him. "We talked from nine at night until six the next morning," he said. "It was the most amazing night of my life. We kept drinking—I think he must have drunk three-quarters of a bottle of Ballantine's—I sat in my chair and he was deep in an armchair with a glass of Scotch poised on his tummy, and it was the bull session I'd always hoped to have. He made me feel special by taking me so seriously. I saw his loneliness and need for emotional intimacy; it radiated from him. He was forty years older than I and he inspired feelings of wanting to protect him from his failures and encourage his talent. All of Bernstein's friends, young and old, saw his qualities and wanted to protect him to a fault.

"I believe he was intensely lonely. I could see him thinking at any second, 'This could be the love of my life.' And it was so seductive. You could totally lose yourself in the guy. At the same time, you would feel that who you were was being completely trivialized. He'd forge these rock-solid, supposedly deep relationships just like that, and then expect you not to feel emotionally raped.

"I always knew how to be safe with him, and that was to get him to become a composer. He got real. He was very humble about that. Composing was the one thing no one would give him respect for. I loved his work and I loved his lapses in taste. Whenever he started moving in for the kill and his tongue would go like *that* at me, I'd get him onto composing. I'd tell him that music is what I am, and he'd give up. It goes back to extracting payment, because I'd feel, despite my deep gratitude, that because Bernstein was putting it on the sexual level he was extracting payment. And if I was cannon fodder, that meant I wasn't a serious composer."

The amount of alcohol Bernstein could consume without apparent effect was one indication that he was becoming completely dependent upon it. In addition, the times when he was loudly and flamboyantly drunk were becoming more frequent. A press agent who accompanied him on that trip to Milwaukee remembered meeting him at the VIP lounge in the airport at three or four in the afternoon and thinking he was already in his cups. They got him into a first-class seat and he tried to order drinks before the take-off. He drank nonstop during the flight. They checked into his hotel, called the Pfister, at which point he walked up to a bellboy and remarked, "Welcome to the fist fuck hotel." He was, she said, "humiliating and wretched and drunk all the time." On the final day of their stay they went to an afternoon performance of the Milwaukee Ballet and he sat in the darkened auditorium with his Scotch and put out his cigarette on the carpet. "I turned to his assistant and said, 'Get him an ashtray.' I was struggling with myself. Should I get up and tell him not to smoke, or not say anything? And I said to myself, 'You are as bad as everyone else. Everyone tiptoes around the master.' "

Such public incidents were becoming common. Susan Koscis remembered attending a performance of *Aida* in Newark with Plácido Domingo as Radames. Bernstein was seated directly in front of her, next to Franco Zeffirelli, and she overheard him talking about doing a performance of *Aida* in front of the Pyramids. "During Act Two he began whispering, which got to be a low murmuring. He was essentially singing, conducting and giving a running commentary as the opera progressed, and I was mesmerized by the show in front of me. At intermission, someone in front of him turned around to him and said, 'Sir, with all due respect, if someone was doing to you what you are doing, you would stop the performance. I beg you to have the respect for the performers you would want them to have for you.' During Act Three he was quieter, and later slumped over with his head on Zeffirelli's shoulder."

Bernstein arrived in a similar state, late as usual, for a dinner party honoring Alistair Cooke given at the Carlyle. At some point during the evening he was to perform with James Galway, the famous flutist. When the moment came Bernstein walked up on stage, went up to Galway and started kissing his neck and nibbling on his ear. "He turned back to the audience and said, 'This won't be bitonal but it is bisexual,' and you could hear the clatter of dropped cutlery all over the room," said John McLennan, another guest at the dinner. What was very sad was that Bernstein's clothes were actually dirty. "He had an old scarf he wore everywhere and a smoking jacket with silvery black piping, with spots all over it and his tie tied all wrong."

Bernstein was now being as ostentatious about his attraction to men as he had been studiedly heterosexual in the early days of his marriage. But one never quite knew, Shirley Rhoads Perle said, how much was genuine and how much play-acting, even at this late stage. "He reminds me of the character of Jupien in Proust. There is a scene in a courtyard describing the body movements of Jupien, who is trying to seduce Charlus, and Bernstein would get that way in front of these young men." Yet at other times, finding himself in such a crowd, he was capable of turning to her and saying, "What am I doing here with these people? Why did I want to fool around with any of them?" On the other hand, "At a party a year or so before he died my son was there. Bernstein was interested in a young man called Matt. My son told me later that he stayed quite late. At a certain point Bernstein looked at him and said, 'This man means a great deal to me. Do you understand and can you accept that?' In a certain mood, you felt he wanted to rub it in everybody's face."

What was also disturbing was that Bernstein, who had always had endless patience with new orchestras and a seemingly effortless ability to win them over, seemed no longer willing to make the effort. In the spring of 1982 he was making his debut with the BBC Symphony Orchestra in London's Royal Festival Hall, performing Elgar's *Enigma Variations* and the London premiere of his *Songfest*. The concert was being broadcast live simultaneously on radio and television. Dr. Cormac Rigby, now a Catholic priest, was then the announcer for the program and took detailed notes of what transpired. Dr. Rigby said that Bernstein habitually arrived half an hour late for the start of rehearsals and then insisted on going overtime. He was boorish and rude and looking for a fight. "On the morning of the concert the rehearsal was held in a sulphurous atmosphere and there was a major wrangle with the trumpet player," who was made to repeat a phrase ad nauseam. The player "won the orchestra's hearts by declining to be browbeaten by megastar status and gutter language."

Bernstein's interpretation of the famous English work did not help matters. The BBC Symphony had played the *Enigma Variations* under Sir Adrian Boult, who had made a more or less definitive recording of the work with the London Philharmonic, and had themselves made a famous recording of it under Toscanini. Bernstein, of course, took the view that he alone knew how it should be played, adopting tempi so slow that they were "nothing short of a caricature," the influential magazine *Gramophone* reported.

At the end of the concert's first half Bernstein decided he wanted to watch the interval feature. "The backstage monitor had no sound, so he invaded the radio cubicle, shirtless and smoking, and wouldn't be budged till it was over." The intermission dragged on and Dr. Rigby was forced to improvise while Bernstein got himself dressed in his usual leisurely way. Bernstein told the orchestra he never wanted to work with them again, and the feeling was reciprocated. But then, as he also said at about this time, conducting had lost its charms. Henry Fogel, manager of the Chicago Symphony, recalled one performance in Japan of a Mahler symphony when "the sparks just flew. When I complimented him on it he said, 'So what? Five years from now, who will know we have done this?' " And he also made the astonishing assertion that "I never had a career. Conducting is really just a thing."

There was a further problem: one could no longer trust him to be exquisitely well prepared. Michael Barrett, a young conductor who became one of his last protégés, recalled that he was one of the producers for an evening celebrating the work of Marc Blitzstein and that Bernstein had agreed to sing one of his songs, "doing his Marlene Dietrich act." Barrett had seen him perform the song but knew he always got the words wrong. On the day of the dress rehearsal he went straight to Bernstein's apartment, explaining he was there to make sure he knew his song. "Oh, come on, let's have a drink," Bernstein said. Barrett replied, "No, we have a concert to do and you can't have a drink until after the concert. That's the rule." So Bernstein practiced his song, and although it took several tries "he finally got it right and stole the show." Increasingly Bernstein would bring in Barrett or others to substitute and take rehearsals, particularly early-morning ones and usually at a moment's notice.

His old friends were beginning to lose their patience. Verna Fine said, "We all went to a party for Aaron's eightieth birthday which was held in a hotel. On my way to the ladies' room I noticed Lenny with two or three boys. He had begun to drink heavily. He called me over and put his arm around me. 'Oh, Voina,' he said in a sarcastic 'Toidy-toid Street' voice, and then turned to the boys and said, 'A day doesn't go by when I don't think of Irving,' speaking of my late husband. I was offended by the fake sentiment in his voice. So I turned to him and said, 'I don't

Copland and Bernstein at Tanglewood in the summer of 1984

believe you. I want you to know that many days go by when *I* don't
think of Irving,' and went to the ladies' room."

Gary and Naomi Graffman, who were by then living in Bernstein's
old apartment building on West Fifty-seventh Street, recalled inviting
him to a party "very reluctantly," she said, since Bernstein had a reputation for bringing uninvited guests and it was a sit-down dinner. He
was loud and argumentative during the meal, and at the end of a long
evening in no hurry to leave. "Finally he's standing in our foyer. My husband offers him a cognac and he keeps standing there for twenty minutes. Then he says, 'It was in this very house that I wrote *West Side Story!*'
and I am thinking, 'Go away, please, little man, go away.' "

Richard Wilbur said, "He would come down to Key West with a
whole entourage of cowed people, always hopping with drugs and alcohol. He was losing emotional control. He put me off; he insisted on kissing me on the mouth in front of a lot of people." David Diamond did
not like the way Bernstein would linger at parties with those "dreadful
girl-boys." He was incoherent on the phone and had stopped listening
to what a person had to say; "he spoke through you," he said, "giving a

With Kitty Carlisle Hart at the Tavern on the Green in 1988

nonstop sermon." Richard Dyer thought Bernstein required a degree of adulation that was almost sickening. At a Tanglewood party, Dyer recalled, Bernstein was sitting in the middle of two descending staircases. "The only way to approach him was on your knees, and I saw Andrew Porter [former music critic of *The New Yorker*] actually do that, and I am never going to let him forget it." Kiki Speyer Fouré said, "Over the years I found him more and more vulgar, brazen and yelling and screaming and jumping around. I was embarrassed by him and for him." Ned Rorem said, "Gide's comment that Victor Hugo was a madman who thought he was Victor Hugo applies here."

The composer Joan Tower, who had never met Bernstein, recalled being taken to a party with Phillip Ramey early in the 1980s. "It was some kind of farewell party for a French orchestra, and Bernstein was surrounded by lots of young guys. And Ramey said, 'We'll get to him,' and kept insisting, but I wasn't that interested and certainly didn't want to push myself on him, but I did have a couple of questions I would like to ask, as one composer to another. Finally the party was coming to an end. We had gone to get our coats and Ramey saw him coming down the stairs. 'This is it!' he said and rushed up to introduce me. There I was in this little circle, so I asked what his new opera, *A Quiet Place*, was about. He started going off as if he was giving Hamlet's soliloquy, 'It's about men and women,' and he begins to intone, 'and women and men, and men and men, and women and women . . .' and I realized he was performing in this mega way as if he were on stage. There was something very sad about this, something very tragic in his face. He was holding on for the last performance."

Bernstein's final opera, *A Quiet Place*, was written as a triple commission from the Kennedy Center, the Houston Grand Opera and the Teatro alla Scala in Milan. It was to be a sequel to *Trouble in Tahiti*; Bernstein said "he was interested in looking at the characters of that opera as if they had lived on into the present and brought up their children . . ." The work was supposed to have a workshop production early in 1982 at Indiana University, where Bernstein spent a few weeks as fellow of its new Institute for Advanced Study, but reports stated that only parts of the opera were performed.

The libretto was being written by Stephen Wadsworth, a tall, good-looking writer who was managing editor of *Opera News* and a contributing editor of *Saturday Review*. Wadsworth had met Bernstein's daughter Jamie at Harvard and sent a letter proposing to interview Bernstein for *Saturday Review*. He happened to mention that he also wrote libretti and had an idea for a sequel to *Trouble in Tahiti*. Bernstein's first reaction was, " 'You, callow youth?' Here was this kid less than half my age." He agreed to look at a synopsis, however, and Wadsworth provided a draft which showed that "his ideas jibed with mine." They had both shared a recent loss; for Bernstein it was his wife and for Wadsworth, his sister Nina. So they both saw an opening scene of a funeral, that of Dinah, who had died in an apparently suicidal car crash. Other characters were Dinah's husband, Sam; their forty-year-old son, Junior; Junior's sister,

Dede; her husband, François, who was once Junior's lover; and Dinah's brother, Bill.

As portrayed in the sequel, nothing much has happened to improve the family or allay its members' individual neuroses. Sam is facing the bitter results of having rejected Junior, who has become mentally ill and walks around waving a gun. The daughter, also rejected, has married a man who cannot make love to her. The characters trade insults and recriminations and mourn their various dilemmas. But, as with Bernstein's *Mass,* the librettist waves his magic wand and at the end they all reconcile. "Son and daughter are able to tell daddy they love him, and daddy accepts not only them but François, too. Somehow, in a way not made clear, François also is redeemed by the family crisis: he suddenly finds he is able to lust after his wife for the first time. Really," Donal Henahan wrote. As before, Bernstein was concluding his latest work, as Elia Kazan observed of Clifford Odets, "with a trumpet solo of romantic hope, however falsely based."

Peter Mark Schifter said he was recommended for the position of director by people Wadsworth and Bernstein knew; although he had met Bernstein through Jamie, Bernstein did not remember him. Schifter thought of him as "a bona fide genius and incredibly powerful and romantic figure. Sort of Byronic, standing on the heath with the wind blowing. Physically, by the time I met him he was very unprepossessing, very short, with jackets too small and buttons popping, going to seed." As for the libretto, although both men denied it had autobiographical overtones, Schifter thought Bernstein was closest to the character of François, the person around whom the opera revolved, a kind of "bisexual saint" who reconciled the family members. "Bernstein was a very tormented guy and his sexuality was a big thing. In a way he wanted to sleep with the world. It wasn't just sex but a deep hunger for connectedness."

By the time Schifter arrived on the scene, Bernstein and Wadsworth had been working for a couple of years. "They were very much into word games and puzzles that were completely over my head. They were intensely connected, like twin souls, but they were also fighting. Bernstein used to make Stephen as crazy as everyone else. Extraordinarily demanding at three in the morning. As long as you were working with him, you were his." Schifter thought that Wadsworth was playing a unique and curious role in Bernstein's life, analogous to that played by Hilda Wangel, the young woman who appears late in the life of the central character of Ibsen's *Master Builder.* She repairs the great man's wounded ego, convinces him that his powers have not waned and urges him to make one final effort to produce a work of genius. Each was dependent on the other, and Schifter felt his role was to mediate, find a way to produce the work as clearly and faithfully as possible. But he discovered that Bernstein needed a more forceful personality as a director. "I didn't want to say 'What is this shit?'" he said. "In retrospect, it would have helped, and I misjudged him. I should have told him it was not going to work."

Schifter really became aware of the opera's shortcomings about two weeks after rehearsals began. "The maestro arrived and demanded a run-through of the first two acts, which were not really ready. In addition, the last act had not been written. Somehow we put it together on forty-eight hours' notice. This very talented, committed cast started in the morning and the first two scenes ran for an hour and a half. It went well, but the reaction I thought was overly emotional. There was all this keening and crying going on. I had to stop the rehearsal, and I remember looking at the stage manager, and he looked at me. We were the only ones who weren't dissolved in tears, and I realized that the opera had careened out of control. The line had been crossed into psychodrama." Because they were so personally involved, Wadsworth and Bernstein had not seen that the work's emotional content had not been conveyed to the audience. It was "written in code," Schifter said. "It's for him and Stephen but not for anyone else."

That fact became painfully clear after the first reviews. Donal Henahan called the work "a pretentious failure," with a libretto seemingly left over "from discarded episodes of 'All My Children' . . . The music that Mr. Bernstein drapes over this heavy-breathing but barely alive body of an opera is thoroughly eclectic and craftily put together. Yet it continually shudders on the edge of sounding more than cosmetic, but more frequently its portentous and epic tone is wildly inappropriate . . . The opera, in fact, is one long series of cliches, musically and dramatically . . ."

Jerry Hadley recalled that he attended a party with Bernstein at the American embassy in Rome in the summer of 1986. Bernstein was "well in his cups" and at some point turned to the ambassador's wife and said, "You know what's made me really distraught? I am only going to be remembered as the man who wrote *West Side Story*." Someone was heard to remark, "Well, that's better than being remembered as the man who wrote *A Quiet Place*." Bernstein passed it off with a smile and continued to defend the work: "I feel that in time, people will come to praise my own music as much as they have praised my conducting," he said. But the failure of *A Quiet Place* must have been devastating, coming as it did after *Mass* and *1600 Pennsylvania Avenue,* and the repeated disappointments had taken their toll. A young Washington soprano, Nancy Scimone, recalled seeing the final version at the Kennedy Center. After the performance she was walking down the stairs when she came across Bernstein, wearing a pair of blue polyester pants, Reeboks and a baggy sweatshirt, holding a cigarette with a long ash on the end of it. He was surrounded by a crowd of people telling him how wonderful the opera was. He was saying, "This opera affected everyone who saw it all over the world" (an exaggeration, as by then the opera had been performed only in Italy and the United States) "even though they couldn't speak English, because these are the things people feel and experience." Scimone replied, "Yes, Mr. Bernstein, but when you are this high," indicating a child, "you don't know that." It seemed a fairly obvious remark, but, in his fragile state, Bernstein chose to find it full of profundity and smothered her in a tearful embrace. It was clear that the reaction of critics had taken its toll. During his interview with Bernstein, Mike Wallace read a comment from a San Francisco critic who wrote that Bernstein needed and wanted to be recognized as a major composer, but this had not happened. He had failed to fulfill his promise, the critic said. The camera caught Bernstein's pain and bewilderment, the look of a man who sees his world crumbling, lost and stunned.

As part of his effort to leave a legacy Bernstein decided to record *West Side Story.* If the original cast recording had been made with dancers who could sing, the time had come to make a new recording with opera singers. His decision seems to have been part of a trend, as Jonathan Yardley wrote, to reconsider the great Broadway musicals of the past not just as high popular culture but as high art, "attaching pretensions to Broadway that, on the merits, it simply cannot sustain." These musicals might be classics, but by no stretch of the imagination could they be called work that reflected the highest aspirations of their culture, "elevated and glorious and maybe even eternal" i.e., classical. However, "in a culture devoid of genuine seriousness, we solve the problem by ascribing seriousness to the frivolous and evanescent and amiable." No one wanted to discover a profundity of meaning in his work more than Bernstein did, and he was therefore vulnerable to the urging of his advisors that *West Side Story* should have a new and grander presentation as befitted a work of art. Kiri Te Kanawa was engaged to sing Maria, José Carreras for Tony and Tatiana Troyanos for Anita, with Marilyn Horne brought in to sing "Somewhere"; Bernstein would conduct. The album was recorded by Deutsche Grammophon (it became a best-seller), and the rehearsals were filmed by Unitel in association with Amberson; the film was subsequently seen on public television in the United States and in Europe. The singers were interviewed and, as might be expected, were effusive. Working with Bernstein was "very exciting," Troyanos said; "a dream for me," said Carreras; and as for Te Kanawa, it was "sort of like having Mozart with you—you're getting it from the master." But although the documentary had been prudently trimmed, "there were reports during the sessions that some of the more emotional screaming matches could be heard several blocks away without benefit of microphones," according to the *New York Times*. Te Kanawa, a New Zealander, had to affect a Puerto Rican accent, but the main problem stemmed from the fact that "Pepe" Carreras, a Spaniard, could not provide a convincing American accent as Tony. Matthew Epstein said, "I did not cast for Bernstein on that project. What happened was that the recording company wanted a superstar name in every role." However, Epstein knew that Plácido Domingo had been approached to sing Tony and had declined. So had Neil Shicoff, the second choice; he had scheduling conflicts. Jerry Hadley was proposed but, at the time, was thought not to be well enough known, so Carreras was hired instead. Epstein allowed cautiously that commercial considerations outweighed artistic ones in coming to this decision. It was a bad one.

Finding he had made a mistake, Bernstein took it out on Carreras. The documentary showed moments when Carreras was dropping final consonants as he sang and Bernstein was grimacing at the results, his hands over his face, saying, "No, you are ahead of me. Look at me, and if you sing the wrong words, we'll go back." The voice of a producer could be heard prompting Carreras, and Bernstein said, "Please don't do this! Don't give elocution lessons over the mike!" Carreras began again and hit a wrong note. There was a shot of Bernstein listening to the tapes and saying out of the side of his mouth, "I am afraid we need a retake." Back again to Carreras, who had one hand to an ear as the other waved in time to the music. Bernstein was mouthing advice, trying to nod his head, but his approval seemed forced and his irritation and disappointment were palpable. And then, finally, "How many times do I have to tell you? Carreras," he sang, caricaturing the final bars of "Maria," "I'll never stop singing Carreras!"

Bernstein called himself "a tired, aging maestro." At other times he would say brightly, "I am feeling very up and young, the way I wrote it.

It sounds to me as if I just wrote it yesterday!" Then he said, "It's not as fresh as Mozart is time after time. But who's in his class? None of us!" Some moments of spoken dialogue were to be included, and Bernstein cast Alexander as Tony and Nina as Maria. Nina sat through rehearsals and was particularly affected by Te Kanawa's performance of "One Hand, One Heart," the moment when the young lovers pledge that their love is stronger than death. Afterwards Bernstein wanted everyone to know that his daughter had been moved, little Nina who was so "hard-boiled." He was very proud of the fact that she had burst into tears. If she were thinking of her parents' failed hopes, he made no mention of it.

"Little by little the bad news dribbles in . . ." Bernstein said at one point during the recording of *West Side Story*. In 1988 the bad news was that he reached the biblical limit of seventy. "Seventy—I loathe the sound of it! Don't utter it in my presence!" The whole year was devoted to celebrations, not just the great day itself. There were so many that one music reviewer groaned that Bernstein's seventieth birthday went on interminably and the joke was that he did not bother to attend half of them. The biggest of them all was at Tanglewood that summer, culminating in a concert with Lauren Bacall, Van Cliburn, Lukas Foss, Frederica Von Stade and Yo-Yo Ma, with new works composed for the occasion by Rorem, André Previn, Sondheim and Michael Tilson Thomas. Guests like Mstislav Rostropovich flew in from Europe, and others, like Malcolm Forbes and Elizabeth Taylor, arrived by hot-air balloon. At another of those celebrations in the early spring of 1988, William Bolcom and his wife, Joan Morris, filled in at the last moment to perform "What a Movie," one of the songs from *Trouble in Tahiti*. Bolcom said, "What struck me immediately was that he was much shorter and quite stocky and a little sweaty and very pale." He was not looking well. Everyone said it and he indirectly acknowledged it: "God knows I should be dead by now. I've been smoking forever; I drink; I stay up all night; I'm overcommitted everywhere." People were astounded at his physical stamina. John Corigliano recalled that, a year before Bernstein died, he was still vigorous enough to attempt sit-ups on a boat deck leaning at a forty-five-degree angle over Lake Michigan and nearly fell in. Then he insisted that they all go swimming in near-freezing temperatures. Schifter said, "His appetite for drugs, sex and alcohol remained immense. He was amazingly vital and wild and out of control." Those who had once worked for him, meeting again after an absence of months, would shake their heads in disbelief and say, "He's still alive!"

Tanglewood, 1990

And there at his door be found
Hospitable welcome!

— GOETHE, "AN SCHWAGER KRONOS"

In the spring of 1990 Bernstein learned that he was going to die. Shortly after making this discovery he wrote a poem in blank verse in which he tried to bargain with God for enough time to write the One Important Piece he had been attempting obsessively since leaving the New York Philharmonic two decades before. He was negotiating for a deal, as he called it—he dedicated the poem to Harry Kraut—but on the surface only. In some part of himself he had expected this to happen, just as his father had before him, and seemed almost grateful.

He had lost his Felicia and was losing Tommy Cothran, who had become ill some time after they parted and was dying slowly from a form of leukemia he had contracted in India. The two had kept in touch after Cothran returned to Indiana. For a time it seemed that expensive treatments might save him, so Bernstein brought him to New York and paid for an apartment. By then, Cothran had become a close friend and confidant (they never tried to repeat their domestic experiment) but to see him slowly fading must have been painful, if not agonizing. Perhaps because of Cothran, Bernstein generously supported AIDS causes. There is no confirmation of the rumor that he was HIV-positive. True to form, Bernstein continued to disregard his health and grumble about it: "Lenny's morning prayer," it was said, was his daily complaint that he had not slept. Just the same, it was clear that his hold on life was weakening. The danger signs had been visible for months: the terrible shortness of breath after the least exertion, the paroxysms of coughing, the constant use of inhalants for emphysema, the cylinders of oxygen and the fatigue that showed clearly enough that his stores of energy were being exhausted at last. Matthew Epstein said, "In the spring of 1990 I went to a premiere of the Paul Taylor dance company with Bernstein and Rorem. At the end of the evening Lenny actually said he was tired and had got to go home. I was very worried." He added, "It was his last real night out, and he seemed in very good form, sweet and affectionate; serene in a way."

He continued to imagine himself writing another opera. For a while he was intrigued by the subject of Nabokov's *Lolita,* but he abandoned the idea after reflecting that having a leading character with nothing original to say would be an almost insurmountable obstacle. Then he wanted to tackle the Holocaust, in a five-language version, and was crushed when Stephen Wadsworth said he did not have time to work on it. There was a concerted effort by some old friends to convince him to take up the musical adaptation of Brecht's *Exception and the Rule* that he had previously abandoned. Jerome Robbins was the main force behind the effort, a workshop production of the musical, now named *The Race to Urga,* with a new script by the playwright John Guare and lyrics by Sondheim. It was performed in the spring of 1987 before an invited audience that included Bernstein and his sister. Ken LaFave, who played in the production, said, "Robbins's only goal was to convince Bernstein that it was good enough to get him to come back and work on it. Bernstein was not impressed." Then he was going to write a ballet for Martha Graham, but that came to nothing. The year he died he was working on another opera, called *Babel,* in Key West. He seemed amazingly cheerful. John Wells, the English playwright who had worked on the final version of *Candide,* said he spent five weeks in Key West, most of them listening to Bernstein telling stories. "In almost all of them he appeared as the hero—jumping on a riderless horse after a battle with the Arabs in Israel, playing the piano alone at a concert in Berlin when it was too wet for the orchestra to go on stage—but he had such a wonderful gravelly voice, he was such a brilliant mimic, and the richness of his intelligence and learning was so great that I could have listened to him for ten times as long . . ."

As well as last-ditch attempts to write the One Important Piece, Bernstein seemed obsessed by the idea that the right kind of assessment of his life needed to be made, hence his sporadic attempts to write *Blue Ink*. It was widely rumored that Joan Peyser's biography, published in 1987, had not been a success in Amberson circles. Although Bernstein claimed to have promised his children that he would never read it, Shirley Rhoads Perle recalled that, some time after the biography was published, the subject arose in a conversation with him. "He came at me with his fist clenched, waving it in my face and saying, 'If I ever see Joan Peyser . . .' I felt for a moment as if, in his mind, I had become Peyser. It was a very unpleasant feeling."

There were bleak moments to which Bernstein would refer with the comment "I'm all wrapped up in elf's thread," an anagram for "self-hatred." But most of the time, Wells wrote, "he had the purest child-like enjoyment of life, thumping on the breakfast table and shouting, 'I want my honeybear!'—a plastic honey pot in the shape of a bear that squirted honey out through a hole in the top of its head—or walking along the beach with a sponge in the shape of an inverted bird's nest on his head, declaiming Lear." He was mostly not working, while fretting about not working, and turned gratefully to conducting and travel.

After the Jonathan Miller production of *Candide* was performed in the West End of London and received the Olivier Award for best musical, Bernstein decided to record the work and conduct it himself for the first time. The plan was to give *Candide* in concert form with the London Symphony Orchestra at the Barbican and videotape that performance. Then there would be four days of recording in studios on Abbey Road before the cast went home for Christmas in December 1989. Perhaps in response to previous criticisms, the *Candide* casting was made with great care. Jerry Hadley was engaged for the title role and June Anderson, as Cunégonde. The part of Dr. Pangloss was taken by Adolph Green, and Christa Ludwig surprised everyone with an unsuspected talent for broad comedy in the role of the Old Lady, whose adventures with the Moors and Turks literally cost her a buttock. Kurt Ollmann, a baritone who was also in the cast, said, "Bernstein did not know the voice, and his casting was sometimes erratic, but this was ideal. It looked like being a dream performance. Then one after another of us got sick with a virulent flu—'the royal flu,' Bernstein called it, with fever, vomiting and nausea." It was one of the worst epidemics in Britain since the end of World War I. During the Barbican rehearsals the orchestra members were the first to get sick. Then Green and Ollmann dropped out; Anderson was next; and Hadley, leaving the stage one night, discovered he had a fever of 103 degrees. It was several months before he was well enough to dub in his part; the same was true for Ludwig. Bernstein was also beginning to feel unwell but managed to appear at Tower Records in Piccadilly Circus to sign autographs, hear an audition of a young Russian baritone and go to a performance of *Miss Saigon.* Then he, too, succumbed. He was feverish and at a low ebb; he looked like "a ghost with shoes," Hadley said. Still he insisted on continuing, pushing himself relentlessly, "and was not particularly forgiving of those who couldn't do the same," said Alison Ames. However, he was obliged to agree to record the orchestral parts and have his absent singers dub in their parts later.

Although he had hardly recovered, Bernstein went straight to Berlin from London to conduct three days of performances of Beethoven's Ninth in celebration of the demolition of the Berlin Wall. His sister said, "He never thought of refusing, but it took an enormous effort." The concerts took place in East and West Berlin, the latter timed to end at midnight on Saturday, December 23, 1989, when West Germans were allowed to cross the border without visas for the first time. The symphony was chosen because of the symbolism of the final movement, in which Schiller's "Ode to Joy," with its plea for universal brotherhood, is sung by soloists and chorus. For the word "joy" (*Freude*) Bernstein substituted "freedom" (*Freiheit*). Sherry Sylvar, an oboist who played in the concert, said, "When the chorus sang the word '*Freiheit*' . . . I shall always remember how his face lit up." It was one of the crowning moments of his life, but it exacted a high price. His sister said, "He came home crawling with exhaustion."

Bernstein slowly began to feel better but was having lower back pains. Since he had always been prone to them, neither he nor his doctor was very concerned. He rested and took painkillers, but the pains increased. Bernstein took the matter up with his doctor, who again dismissed their importance and the patient had to talk his doctor into getting a scan, Shirley Bernstein said. It was then that they discovered he had a malignant tumor on the pleural lining of his left lung, a condition called mesothelioma. This particularly virulent and rapid cancer is believed to be caused by exposure to asbestos, sometimes decades before, although what exposure Bernstein could have had that brought this about was never determined.

Shirley Bernstein said, "I remember it was the end of April, because I went to Fairfield for the weekend and stayed over the following Monday, the thirtieth, because I knew he was getting the results of the tests. When the doctor called to break the news he didn't feel sick anymore and couldn't believe it."

Peter Pan, Donal Henahan of the *New York Times* noted, had finally become a Grand Old Man. He had graduated to those peaks of distinction and eminence invariably accorded to conductors at the end of their lives and was no longer capable of a musical sin. "People who formerly jeered or smiled indulgently at Mr. Bernstein's exuberance and choreographic antics on the podium . . . now greet his super-heated performances as the ripened interpretations of a revered master . . . It is now generally agreed that his exhorting glances and dramatic gestures are not only effective showmanship, but the necessary eruptions of an overpoweringly musical nature . . ." While there were still grumblings about tempi that seemed erratically fast or slow to the point of perversity, and arbitrary interpretations, the disapproval was drowned out in the general chorus of admiration. As a conductor he had reached that indefinable moment when he had joined the ranks of the masters. John Rockwell observed that most of the great conductors had once been composers, a tradition that had fallen into disuse since avant-garde composers had either "given up the orchestra altogether" or were composing in "idioms too abstruse for audiences to understand and too complex for orchestras to play." Bernstein was unusual as a conductor in that he had come from a tonal American symphonic tradition and "conducts the classics with a present-day rhythmic alacrity and sense of color and drama that most other conductors, aping one past conducting style or another, grievously lack."

Whatever compromises he might have made, whatever white lies he learned to tell, whatever "smart esthetic definitions" he might have learned to spout, Bernstein remained true to Koussevitzky's concept that in music, the composer was the most exalted of all. The composer partook of the divine because he reached for the Note; and it was "this reach, this leap, aspiration, thrust . . . [that] Koussevitzky held most sacred . . ." When he exhorted students at Tanglewood to remember Koussevitzky's "central line," meaning "the line to be followed by the artist at any cost, the line leading to perpetual discovery, the mystical line to truth," he was speaking of his own ideal and one to which he had dedicated his life.

As for Bernstein the composer, that remained a sensitive subject. Bernstein had continued to undervalue his own easy victories as a young man and the magical scores he had written for *Fancy Free, Peter Pan, On the Waterfront, On the Town,* and *West Side Story.* If he was returning to *Candide* belatedly, that might have been fueled by the realization that, with enough polishing, *Candide* had the best chance of enduring as a successful blending of the vernacular and classical traditions that was his unswerving operatic ambition. More than one music critic thought it a pity that Bernstein had not followed up the triumph of *West Side Story.* Rockwell wrote, "He would surely have enjoyed a more straightforward success if he had stuck to Broadway . . . Then all the plaudits that have accrued to Stephen Sondheim, his one-time librettist and avowed disciple, might have fallen to him." Harold C. Schonberg thought his gift was for sophisticated entertainment and that he could have become the American Offenbach. Henahan thought the problem was that since *Candide,* Bernstein had seldom found collaborators who inspired him to write his best work. "Looking back over the last quarter century . . . it does seem that he has been our Sullivan in search of his Gilbert, our Offenbach in search of his *Tales of Hoffmann.*" And perhaps the major issue was the ambitious nature of Bernstein's goals at that time: "the American theater-going public of a quarter-century ago apparently was not ready to demand great things of Mr. Bernstein or anyone else. It had neither the musical sophistication nor the taste necessary to draw the best from its favorite composers. As a result, it can be argued, our chance for a golden age was missed, or at least seriously delayed . . ."

If his works for the popular stage were too serious-minded, it could be argued that his works for the concert stage were too full of "rhythmic dash and syncopated swagger," too theatrical, in short, to be taken seriously. This was perhaps what Copland believed in 1949 when he called it "conductor's music—eclectic in style and facile in inspiration." That was the main reason given for dismissing Bernstein as a serious composer; there was a further reservation having to do with his determination to switch between genres. He said, "People say I don't belong in the concert hall. What's wrong with theater in the concert hall and concert hall in the theater?" It seemed like a reasonable objection, yet, as Leon Botstein wrote in "The Tragedy of Leonard Bernstein," Bernstein's actions "challenged a rigid historical pattern. It is hard to recall a composer of great or even memorable 'art' music who also tossed off catchy scores for Broadway and Hollywood . . . Twentieth century composers such as Ernst Krenek, Hans Werner Henze, even Sergei Prokofiev and Paul Hindemith, have failed to end the self-conscious distinctions between popular culture and high culture. And often they have failed despite ideological convictions that regard that gulf as a matter of snobbery and prejudice . . ." Gershwin came as close as anyone; Aaron Copland succeeded with *Appalachian Spring* and *Billy the Kid;* and Kurt Weill, after writing "art" music, made a successful transition to theater but never returned to writing symphonies. As for Bernstein, Botstein thought the harder he tried to write serious, important works, the more fatuous and bombastic he became.

Yet another objection, that his conservative adherence to tonality demonstrated how threadbare his ideas were, the fashionable verdict of the 1950s and 1960s, had been robbed of its power to wound in recent years. Rockwell wrote, "Now, in a climate of 'new Romanticism,' Bernstein begins to look like a prophet." The composer David Schiff wrote that a parlor game for the decade might be to transform Bernstein's

> modernist vices into postmodern virtues. Bombast and theatricality can now be called "performative." The lack of originality now looks like a gift for "appropriation." The absence of stylistic unity and the penchant for eclecticism become "intertextuality." The dependence on gesture—call it "semiotic." And the ultimate modernist putdown, that the music is easy to listen to, can now be termed "legibility" . . . The advantage of a postmodern paradigm shift is that it allows us to view Bernstein in sympathetic terms . . . Today, when the wildly eclectic and theatrical music of David Del Tredici, Corigliano, Adams and Alfred Schnittke wins critical approval, Bernstein can look like a harbinger of the postmodern.

Radiation treatments were prescribed even though mesothelioma is not curable and some medical opinion, Shirley Bernstein claimed, holds that radiation can even hasten its course. Bernstein kept to a reduced schedule. He canceled his appearance at the opening of the Spoleto U.S.A. Festival in Charleston, South Carolina. He also canceled a planned concert at the Curtis Institute, giving as his reason a bout with pleurisy. This news was received with some relief at the music school by those who found the requirements of his staff particularly exacting and had nicknamed the event "the Gorilla Concert." Bernstein continued to perform in Vienna, where he enjoyed an exalted status, perhaps unique for a Jew

With Friedelind Wagner in Bayreuth in the
spring of 1990

in a city in which anti-Semitism had once flourished. To the surprise of
some fellow musicians he continued to appear there despite urgings that
he refrain from doing so in order to protest the alleged Nazi past of Austria's president, Kurt Waldheim. (He would conduct the Vienna Philharmonic for the last time at Carnegie Hall early in March.) Similar
criticisms had been voiced when Bernstein refused to boycott the music
of Richard Wagner, a notorious anti-Semite. Bernstein defended that
decision in an article that was published posthumously in the *New York
Times.* He also visited Wagner's granddaughter Friedelind (who left Germany after Hitler took power) at Bayreuth on April 6, and was photographed with his arm around his silver-haired hostess.

After a month of cancer treatments, his sister said, he was visibly
weaker. He had a bout of pneumonia and then broke out in shingles. In
an attempt to gain relief he tried acupuncture, which was such a success
that he took the therapist with him to Czechoslovakia, where he conducted Beethoven's Ninth. His press agent, Margaret Carson, went with
him and recalled that he looked ashen and was having trouble breathing. Just walking through the airport was too stressful, and he would
have to sit down at intervals to catch his breath. He persevered. The big
events that year were a trip to Sapporo, Japan, to inaugurate the Pacific

Music Festival with Michael Tilson Thomas, and teaching and performing at the fiftieth anniversary of the Tanglewood Music Festival,
one of the great moments of his life. That was to be followed by an
orchestra tour of Europe later that summer. In Japan he was having
severe back pains, developed a new lung infection and was in such an
exhausted state that his New York physician, Dr. Kevin Cahill, flew
there to examine him. He was ordered to cancel his remaining four performances with the London Symphony and return home to rest. For a
while no one knew whether he would be well enough to go to Tanglewood. It was finally decided that he would go for a shorter visit and then
accompany the student orchestra on an abbreviated, two-week tour of
six European cities at the end of August.

"Tanglewood's brought back a breath of my youth," he once wrote.
"Stravinsky and Mozart, Beauty and Truth . . ." James E. Whitaker,
chief coordinator at Tanglewood, said, "I saw him when he first got
here. He drove up, I guess that was on a Thursday night, and he was
already exhausted. He almost wanted to go home but convinced himself to stay. Students always seemed to pep him up. He did Copland's
Third the following Tuesday, and it was a fun performance, but he
never recovered. From then on he looked gray and drawn; he just
couldn't get his breath." Lukas Foss recalled, "I remember saying to
him, 'Lenny, how do you feel?' because he looked terrible. And he said,
'Well, at least I'm upright.' And I said, 'Well, unlike a piano, you're
both upright and grand.' " He claimed to have stopped smoking and
was chewing nicotine gum, but at Tanglewood he was "gasping for
breath and puffing on a cigarette," Whitaker said. Ralph Gomberg
said, "At a Tanglewood gathering I was shocked to see [Tanglewood
administrator] Richard Ortner holding a cigarette, and my first
thought was, 'What is he doing smoking in front of a man with
emphysema?' Then I realized he was holding Bernstein's cigarette—it
was a pathetic attempt to fool us."

Dan Gustin said that Bernstein was renting a white clapboard
country house in Great Barrington, with "not a right angle in the
place, and that's what he liked." There were shelves of the most interesting books, and he was reading *Treasure Island.* He still came to the
conducting seminars, Gustav Meier said. He might not have studied
the music, but "it was right there. And it was growing; I could not
believe that. He never lost that." But he was obviously so ill that
Meier was shocked. "I have four children, and if I was in that
state . . . I shall never understand why his children didn't stop him.

My God, the man could hardly get to the podium, and they are talking about a tour, going to Europe! I said, 'This is never going to happen.' " He was still seen on the grounds and, one day that summer, visited Highwood Manor, a nineteenth-century farmhouse that was being used for offices and practice rooms on the Tanglewood grounds. As luck would have it, this was the summer that the office staff claimed to have had encounters with an invisible spirit which turned lights on and off, opened and closed doors, walked around at night, especially on the second floor, and had actually lifted the very long hair of Highwood's manager from the front of her shoulders to the back. Two girls witnessed the event and ran screaming. The manager, Marcia Duncan, was so scared that she did not talk for several days. Curiously, Bernstein encountered the same invisible presence. He was sitting in a second-floor window seat when, Duncan said, he suddenly leapt up, threw up his arms and asked, "What is it that's here? Who is that here?" He felt something or someone sitting right next to him. He left shortly afterward.

A former assistant said, "He was still telling stories and singing songs about Koussevitzky. I came in and changed his shirt and we joked about the good old days. But he was there with a nurse and medical apparatus, and it was clear that he was just a shadow of what he had been. Bernstein had always had this unbelievable clarity in his eyes, and—it wasn't there anymore. It made me very sad." Shirley Rhoads Perle, who saw him for the last time that summer, said, "I knew he was sick, although it was not generally known. Nevertheless it was a shock to see him. His body was so changed it was horrible." He had begun rehearsals for the performance of Copland's Third Symphony with the student orchestra, and it was soon clear, said Mark Stringer, one of the conducting fellows, that the orchestra did not know the work. Shirley Rhoads Perle said, "I saw him after the rehearsal and he was upset because he didn't have the energy to teach it to them.

"I looked at him and he said to me, 'Don't cry.' I said, 'I'm not crying,' and he said, 'Yes you are,' and it was true. I knew it would be the last time I would ever see him."

Stephen Somary said, "Tanglewood was usually his happiest time of year. He would get so stimulated and want to stay up till all hours talking to students. But this time he looked terrible. He was coughing up blood and his whole demeanor had changed. But he was still saying he would fight on."

Leon Fleisher, Tanglewood's artistic director, said that rehearsals were under way for the European tour. He was to appear in performances of Ravel's Piano Concerto for the Left Hand, and several of the programs were to be conducted by two of the other conducting fellows. Fleisher was in the piano room warming up one day when, hearing Berlioz's *Roman Carnival Overture* in progress, he went out to listen. As the overture came to an end, Bernstein appeared wearing his Koussevitzky cape. "He grabbed my hand and said, 'Come with me.' You know the stage is raked enormously behind the trombones and tubas. There is a certain spot where you can sit and watch the conductor between the instrumentalists' chair legs. To all intents and purposes you are completely hidden. Bernstein said, 'When I was a kid I used to come here and watch Koussevitzky conducting.' So we sat there and he held my hand as we watched and listened. It was an extraordinary moment of communion."

Bernstein's last concert at Tanglewood took place on the afternoon of Sunday, August 19, 1990. It was the annual Serge and Olga Koussevitzky Memorial Concert. He was conducting the Boston Symphony in the Four Sea Interludes from Britten's *Peter Grimes,* Beethoven's Symphony No. 7 and a new collection of songs for mezzo-soprano and baritone that he had written in 1988 for four-hand piano accompaniment. These had been given an orchestral setting by the young composer Bright Sheng. Bernstein had originally planned to conduct the work himself, but again it was clear that some basic work was needed, and the orchestra was prepared and eventually conducted by the young conductor Carl St. Clair.

If *Songfest,* with its setting of a poem to homosexual love and its poignant memories of past relationships, was an accurate mirror of his state of mind in 1977, *Arias and Barcarolles,* with its songs exploring various aspects of conjugal life, can be said to be an accurate indication of his state of mind in those final years. The climax of the work is the memory of a wedding, a setting of a poem in Yiddish by Yankev Yitskhok Segal. It recounts the appearance at a wedding of an itinerant violinist, a klezmer, who performs with such virtuoso skill that the listeners are moved to tears. Michael Barrett, who played the four-hand piano version with Bernstein, recalled the composer telling him "that a musical catalyst and inspiration to him as a boy came from his father's Hasidic friends, who would dance and sing and play with great rhythmic vitality and emotional abandon. He thought perhaps that this was how he had first learned 'how music goes.' " The work reflected Bernstein's late compositional style, John Rockwell wrote, "erratic, self-indulgent but capable of telling, moving beauty."

Andrew Pincus, music critic for the Berkshire *Eagle,* said, "I saw him at the first student orchestra concert and thought he was weak, shaky and bloated, but he gave a fine performance. I came out believing the European tour really would take place. But five days later, when he conducted the BSO, he was noticeably weaker. In the Four Sea Interludes I had the feeling of icy foreboding. I could feel death in the music. Then came the *Arias and Barcarolles,* with a fairly long interval, and he came on to conduct the Beethoven.

"Others have praised the performance, but I thought there were a lot of hesitations. The tempi were much too slow. Usually he could make a work glow and burn even while developing it at this extremely slow pace, but this time it did not happen. Then came the famous moment in the third movement when he could not conduct at all. He leaned back against the podium rail, pulled a bandanna from his back pocket and had a coughing fit. He kept the orchestra going by nodding his head. I truly thought he would die right then and there. I wrote the review as a eulogy. It was a tremendously moving concert, but not for musical reasons." As Pincus remembered it, Bernstein did not make his usual repeated returns to the podium for bows but came out only as far as the violas and waved. The last photographs show his retreating back, his white head and stooped shoulders. Dan Gustin said, "When he came off he was standing, but gasping for breath like a drowning man." Roger Englander, who arrived too late for the concert but went to the party afterwards in Seranak, found Bernstein sitting in a chair. "I hadn't seen him for six months and I was shocked," he said. "I looked at him, kissed him and left. I couldn't say a word."

The orchestra tour was canceled and Bernstein went first to Springate and then the Dakota. In mid-September his doctors gave him the astonishing news that he was free of cancer. Shirley Bernstein said, "Everybody believed it and we were overjoyed and thrilled, including Lenny." The doctors were tragically mistaken. By the end of September he had lost the use of one lung and could no longer walk upstairs. His remaining lung was under severe strain, and the cancer was spreading. On his next visit, Stephen Somary found him in bed, joking about how Dvořák had stolen from *West Side Story.* "I talked to him the week before he died. I got a message to call because I had sent a card. He sounded better and said, 'Don't worry, everything will be fine.' " True to his pattern, Bernstein refused to make any concessions to his illness such as giving up alcohol or cigarettes. Arthur Laurents recalled having dinner with him and watching him undergo a spasm of acute pain. Laurents was very concerned, but Bernstein deliberately cut off the subject with an irrelevant question. Laurents said, "You're going to beat this. You've always been lucky." Bernstein agreed; "but my luck has run out."

Bernstein was still talking about the work he was writing, but nobody believed him. Philip Setzer, violinist with the Emerson Quartet, said they met at a party following the performance of the Vienna Philharmonic in Carnegie Hall. Great numbers of people wanted to talk to him, but he concentrated on the quartet for over an hour. He had agreed to write for them and told them he had completed the opening but, after his death, nobody could find anything on paper. Bernstein had also committed himself to writing a new choral work in celebration of the twenty-fifth anniversary of Washington's Choral Arts Society, to be performed at the Kennedy Center in the summer of 1990. But as the June 3 date drew nearer and nothing had been received, Norman Scribner, the director, flew to Vienna. He attended a Bernstein concert and patiently waited in line for his chance to speak to Bernstein after the performance. Scribner said, "I ran into Harry [Kraut], who said, 'Norman, Lenny has written your piece and lost it.' When I got to him he looked like a shell of a person, so tired and old. 'Oh, Norman, I have lost the piece.' He looked at me. He was so far down that I was kneeling beside him. 'Oh, Norman, what am I to do?' "

Then, early in October, the announcement came that he was retiring from the concert stage because of ill health, canceling a string of concerts and recordings with the New York Philharmonic, the Israel Philharmonic, the Vienna Philharmonic and the London Symphony. As soon as the announcement was made, friends said, they received phone calls from Bernstein's staff. Rorem wrote, "Harry said both 'He's not dying' and 'He doesn't have AIDS,' but at different times. I'd never said he *did*." His former assistant said, "Everyone knew the retirement announcement was a death announcement. Bernstein would never retire."

Bright Sheng was visiting New York from Chicago on the weekend of October 13 and 14 and called the Dakota on Saturday to see whether he could visit. Sheng said, "I literally tried hour by hour. It was arranged for Saturday afternoon, so I went there around three or four and they said, 'No, he's really tired and sleeping.' I was very disappointed since I was leaving the next day, so they suggested I try Sunday morning. Next morning I called and the answer was still no. I was really pushing for a few hours. I tried again around one in the afternoon, and Bernstein suggested I come in at four. He was in the apartment with his son, Alexander, and Mendy Wager. They were watching David Zinman conducting in a performance with Yo-Yo Ma. He was sitting on a La-Z-Boy chair with an oxygen tube beside him and smoking. He was lively and humming along. He had scheduled to play a work of mine with the New York Philharmonic on my thirty-fifth birthday in December and was so sorry he could not conduct my piece and apologizing for it." Although Bernstein was having obvious difficulty breathing, Sheng said, only once did he refer to his illness. "He told me, 'All of a sudden the body is giving up.' " Sheng was the last visitor Bernstein would see.

At about six that evening, Bernstein's doctor arrived to give him a routine shot. He was being helped to walk, with his doctor on one side and Wager on the other, when he suddenly threw back his arms, stopped and said, "What is this?" Then he had a heart attack, collapsed and died. It was 6:15 on October 14, 1990.

Alison Ames had a curious experience. She said, "That Friday before he died I encountered someone close to the inner circle who told me he was really dying. I had a friend who was a therapist and also a nurse, and I told her I could not bear the thought of his suffocating. She reassured me that this would not happen, because his heart would give out first. That weekend I was working on my apartment, and early that evening there was a flash across my mind. I saw it as a headline: 'Leonard Bernstein Will Die of a Heart Attack.' It was just around 6:15. Then I went off to a dinner party." That same night Kiki Speyer Fouré, in Paris, had a dream about Bernstein that she could not shake off. She awoke to the news that he had died.

No one could believe it. Leonard Slatkin recalled that he and his wife were performing chamber music that evening in Cherry Hill, New Jersey, and had included a work from *Songfest,* "A Julia de Burgos." He said, "I thought the audience reaction was strange, and when we came offstage I asked whether there was something wrong. There was a stack of messages when we got back to the hotel at midnight." When she learned at midnight that Bernstein had died, Ames, who lived close to the Dakota, walked over and sat on the curb looking up at the windows of his apartment. "It was the worst news," Ellen Adler said. "It was the most painful, ghastly loss, like being stabbed. It was agonizing to everyone. I'll never forget the pain of losing Lenny." The New York Philharmonic flew its flags at half-mast. Carnegie Hall announced that its concerts for the coming week would all be dedicated to Bernstein, and radio stations played his music and recordings.

Jerome Robbins said, "The loss is too great to consider," and Yehudi Menuhin said, "No one has done more for music." Tim Page wrote in *Newsday,* "Perhaps Bernstein's most important influence was the example he set for American musicians . . . He elected to build a career in the United States—studied here, made his debut here, lived here all his life. This choice had something of the same effect on our native musicians that Ralph Waldo Emerson's lecture 'The American Scholar' did on nineteenth-century literati. It was a declaration of independence . . . and eventually, Europe came to Bernstein and, by extension, to America."

All accounts agree that, to the very end, Bernstein was alert, aware and involved. As Herold said of his own subject, Madame de Staël, "Neither pain nor weakness, nothing short of absolute death could still the urge to think, to speak, to communicate, to inspire." To have him cut down in mid-sentence was all the more shocking, unthinkable to those who had known him in all his eager vitality, as someone who had the ability not only to charm and stimulate but to inspire. Bernstein had given his contemporaries a glimpse of a wider and richer world.

It is true that he was a man of large faults, narcissistic and vain, erratic in his judgments, intolerably demanding, pettish and unpredictable; tiresomely preaching the virtues of a disciplined life while seemingly unable to direct his own, faults magnified by the public figure he presented to the world. But one could nevertheless give him credit for consistency in his goals and achievements, for taking part in the great debates of his age, for being committed and involved to the last. Even his strongest detractors had to concede that Lenny never lost his enthusiasm. It is a word derived from the Greek *"enthousiasmos,"* meaning divine possession or inspiration: God-inspired.

Here, perhaps, is the point at which Bernstein would have judged himself. If he had aspired to be a Tzaddik, inheriting the mantle of his father and forebears and taking his rightful place as spiritual mentor, the exuberant exponent of a message of hope and faith, he had failed; that failure would have been a constant reproach, if not a reflection on his human worth, in his own eyes. As a child of his age, doubtful and disbelieving, he had been tortured by a need to believe that never left him. Perhaps he had never seen the world "appareled in celestial light." He had, however, found a vision almost as beatific in music and celebrated, in his art, his own communion.

Notes

Index

Notes

ABBREVIATIONS

F *Findings,* Leonard Bernstein, 1982

FM *Family Matters,* Burton Bernstein, 1982

HOR *Understanding Toscanini,* Joseph Horowitz, 1987

INF *The Infinite Variety of Music,* Leonard Bernstein, 1962

JOM *The Joy of Music,* Leonard Bernstein, 1959

JP *Bernstein: A Biography,* Joan Peyser, 1987

M *Maestro: Encounters with Conductors of Today,* Helena Matheopoulos, 1982

MC *Musical Chairs: A Life in the Arts,* Schuyler Chapin, 1977

MT *Music Talks: Conversations with Musicians,* Helen Epstein, 1987

P1 *Copland, 1900 Through 1942,* Aaron Copland and Vivian Perlis, 1984

PW *The Private World of Leonard Bernstein,* John Gruen, 1968

ROD *Our Two Lives,* Halina Rodzinski, 1976

SH *Philharmonic: A History of New York's Orchestra,* Howard Shanet, 1975

UA *The Unanswered Question,* Leonard Bernstein, 1976

YPC *Leonard Bernstein's Young People's Concerts,* Leonard Bernstein, 1992

THE TZADDIKIM

3 "Faster, my Kronos, give your horses the whip": "An Schwager Kronos" (To the Postilion Kronos), poem by Johann Wolfgang von Goethe, translated by Richard Capell; set to music by Franz Schubert, D. 369.

3   "In the beginning was the Note . . .": F, p. 211.

4   Planted a fist on the keys: *Time,* February 4, 1957.

Practicing fingerings on the windowsill: Boston *Post,* November 21, 1943.

". . . a new kind of communion . . .": *The Joys of Yiddish,* Leo Rosten, pp. 73–74.

". . . music heightened spiritual awareness . . .": *Holy Days,* Lis Harris, pp. 78–79.

5   "The 613 *mitzvot* . . .": *World of Our Fathers,* Irving Howe, p. 13.

"sang and acted out the old story . . .": Boston *Post,* November 21, 1943.

"reached the ideal of communion . . .": *Holy Days,* p. 82.

6   ". . . hunched over his books . . .": FM, p. 20.

". . . no question was too small . . .": FM, p. 24.

He was severely beaten: FM, p. 24.

7   ". . . they cough and cough . . .": *World of Our Fathers,* p. 7.

8   ". . . cleaning two tons of fish": Boston *Post,* November 21, 1943.

". . . anything could happen in this America": FM, p. 33.

". . . I studied and scrimped . . .": Boston *Post,* November 21, 1943.

9   ". . . had fallen in love with a Gentile . . .": interview with author.

". . . a good story to tell": FM, p. 51.

". . . disdained their women,": *In Search of History: A Personal Adventure,* Theodore H. White, p. 21.

Moved back with her parents: interview with Shirley Bernstein.

11   "spread-eagled himself against the door": ditto.

". . . the old religious orthodoxy . . .": *In Search of History: A Personal Adventure,* p. 25.

12   "a prison": FM, p. 28.

". . . scenes at the dinner table . . .": interview with author.

". . . said about salt . . .": PW, p. 39.

"a man's prestige . . .": *World of Our Fathers,* p. 8.

". . . not one syllable . . .": FM, p. 83.

". . . the father is God": F, p. 174.

Awaited the transformation: *ASCAP Today,* July 1972.

Talked in grown-up sentences: New York *Post,* June 1, 1960.

"I live to give . . .": Boston *Sunday Post,* November 21, 1943.

13   Skinny and scared: *Time,* February 4, 1957.

14   "I couldn't fight back": New York *Post,* June 1, 1960.

". . . the Mighty Wurlitzer itself . . .": *Time,* February 4, 1957.

"They were rigorous . . .": *In Search of History: A Personal Adventure,* p. 21.

". . . memory cut grooves . . .": ditto, p. 22.

"not only verbatim but backward": *New Yorker,* January 11, 1958.

A "thoroughgoing kid": interview with author.

15   "It wasn't any beauty . . .": Boston *Sunday Post,* November 21, 1943.

"And I remember *touching* it . . .": *SoHo News,* September 2, 1981.

". . . wanted to feel my muscles": *Time,* February 4, 1957.

Jumped up and down in excitement: Boston Latin School *Register* LXXXVII, June 1967.

16   "interdisciplinary cognition . . .": *New York Times,* November 22, 1984.
      ". . . a very strong school spirit": Boston Latin School *Register,* June 1967.
      ". . . made an incredible impression . . .": ditto.
      Quite useful for a businessman: essay dated September 24, 1934.

17   ". . . drifters, odd types . . .": *Joys of Yiddish,* p. 183.
      ". . . 'Lenny Bernstein had a father' ": *New Yorker,* January 11, 1958.
      ". . . an enmity, a hatred . . .": MT, p. 58.
      ". . . only the fingers moving": *New Yorker,* January 11, 1958.

20   ". . . he was still playing . . .": New York *Post,* June 1, 1960.
      ". . . selling apples in Times Square": MT, p. 55.

21   ". . . they were indescribably rich": Leonard Burkat and Elaine Lubell, interviews with author.
      There had been no music: Boston Latin School *Register,* June 1967.
      ". . . infant intellectuals and artists": interview with author.
      ". . . one tiny, malformed ear": interview with author.
      ". . . this exquisite music": Boston *Sunday Herald,* May 12, 1963.

22   ". . . a man of great enthusiasms . . .": interview with author.
      ". . . I was his audience": New York *Post,* June 1, 1960.
      A brilliant career: letter from Samuel Bernstein to Helen Coates, June 26, 1933, Library of Congress.
      Hoped he would not become a musician: letter from Samuel Bernstein to Helen Coates, July 20, 1934, Library of Congress.
      A mammoth piano concerto: *New Yorker,* January 11, 1958.

23   " 'Damn you, Lenny' . . .": Boston *Sunday Post,* November 21, 1943.
      Parents left the house: *Collier's,* October 13, 1945.

24   The whole family was upset: Leonard Bernstein to Mildred Spiegel, August 1936.
      Screamed the leading roles: New York *Post,* June 1, 1960.
      ". . . I'd reject the person": PW, p. 146.
      "absolutely positively idolized . . .": Elaine Lubell, interview with author.

25   "crazed with curiosity": FM, p. 74.
      "protect the palace . . .": *Defenders of the Faith,* Samuel Heilman, p. 320.
      Female flesh was *trayf*: FM, p. 93.
      Would not roll up her sleeve: FM, p. 95.
      ". . . two-dollar whores": FM, p. 71.
      ". . . as if I was a whore . . .": interview with author.

26   ". . . Get out of my office!": FM, pp. 65–66.
      "I did love Millie Long . . .": F, pp. 168–69.
      ". . . as though I didn't exist . . .": *Time,* February 4, 1957.
      Performing the Grieg Piano Concerto: on May 14, 1934.
      ". . . used to fake the runs": interview with author.

28   ". . . gave him some records": interview with author.
      An audition with Iturbi: from correspondence of Leonard Bernstein to Beatrice Gordon and Mildred Spiegel.
      ". . . so much to say": Jerome Lipson interview with Andrew Pincus.
      ". . . I got a good mark": ditto.

29   ". . . sort of light, easy . . .": ditto.
30   Watching the impromptu ballet: *Newsweek*, April 10, 1944.
          ". . . I work hard": *New Yorker*, January 18, 1958.
          Performance of *H.M.S. Pinafore*: on August 29, 1936.
31   ". . . screaming for hours . . .": *Opera News*, September 1972.
33   "I was like a big sister . . .": interview with author.
34   "He made a dent . . .": interview with author.
          A 1930–ish nostalgia: letter from Leonard Bernstein to Elaine Newman
          from Cuernavaca, May 4, 1951.
36   "You little trollop . . .": New York *Journal American*, September 25, 1962;
          JP, pp. 301–02.
          ". . . he liked women too much": interview with author.
          Brusquely put in his place: letter from Leonard Bernstein to Mildred Spiegel,
          July 21, 1941.
          ". . . starts your musical blood . . .": New York *Herald Tribune*, February 5,
          1961.
          ". . . saved up for two or three months . . .": *Ovation*, May 1981.
37   Writing sonatinas: *New Yorker*, January 18, 1958.
          ". . . a delicious summer afternoon . . .": New York *Herald Tribune*, February
          5, 1961.

ROCKING THE CRADLE

38   "For short-lived is the day . . .": "An Schwager Kronos," translated by
          Richard Capell.
          Some quiet roommates: interview with author.
39   "That's the best school . . .": Lipson interview with Andrew Pincus.
          "he could do it all . . .": interview with author.
          The minimum in music courses: *New Yorker*, January 11, 1958.
40   ". . . pre-Beethoven and post-Wagner . . .": F, p. 304.
          ". . . a big thwack . . .": Shapero interview with Andrew Pincus.
41   ". . . waved his hand and walked out": letter by Alan S. Evans to author, Feb-
          ruary 8, 1992.
42   ". . . We fought and drank . . .": interview with author.
          The piano was a wreck: interview with author.
          Bernstein's repertoire: as recorded by Mildred Spiegel.
          "of pleasing richness": Boston *Post*, June 13, 1935.
          ". . . unlimited technique . . .": *Christian Science Monitor*, November 1, 1937.
43   An outstanding young pianist: Manchester *Leader*, November 7, 1938.
          "A new world of music . . .": *Listen*, December 1963.
          ". . . I'll teach it back to you": ditto.
          Guaranteed to "empty rooms": *High Fidelity/Musical America*, November
          1970.
44   ". . . 'ne Ravelons plus' ": P1, p. 337.
45   ". . . Take these two bars . . .": *High Fidelity/Musical America*, November
          1970.

"I learned such works . . .": ditto.

". . . 'destined for success' ": ditto.

46   "one steady push . . .": "On Gershwin," F, p. 305.

". . . harmonically truthful . . .": ditto.

47   Died of a brain tumor: on July 11, 1937.

". . . the power of music . . .": Chicago *Tribune,* June 27, 1976.

". . . no such thing as a bass voice . . .": *Opera News,* September 1972.

48   "a series of stirring dissonances . . .": *New Yorker,* January 11, 1958.

Captain of the baseball team: *Seventeen,* August 1946.

". . . on the baseball field he was hitless . . .": Seymour Wadler, letter to the *New York Times,* October 17, 1990.

". . . the smart thing to do": interview with author.

". . . never entered my mind . . .": MT, p. 58.

He intended to apply: from a letter to Beatrice Gordon, October 1, 1936.

49   Stared in disbelief: Hanna Saxon, interview with author.

50   He might as well go in: *New Yorker,* January 18, 1958.

It had been arranged: JP, p. 36.

". . . electric blue eyes . . .": from a filmed interview with Paul Hume, 1980.

"incredible hypnotic quality . . .": *New Yorker,* January 18, 1958.

". . . a great and awful love . . .": F, p. 29.

51   "Mitropoulos seduced him . . .": interview with author.

". . . That was the gate that opened": interview with author.

"Do not sleep . . .": Paul Hume interview.

"I want you . . .": F, p. 34.

Went to Minneapolis for a week: from Bernstein correspondence with Mildred Spiegel.

52   ". . . capitalism destroying itself . . .": *Our Age,* Noel Annan, p. 180.

"a composer functions . . .": F, p. 39.

53   Bernstein never appeared: Thomas A. Goldman, letter to author, July 20, 1991.

Copland came to a meeting: P1, p. 224.

Marc Blitzstein's "The Cradle Will Rock": Mark the Music, Eric A. Gordon, p. 143.

54   ". . . I thought it was pure trash . . .": From interview and memoir by Harold W. Williams.

55   "We all thought he was so far superior . . .": ditto.

"My parents knew nothing . . .": New York *Post,* June 2, 1960.

They did not seem to mind: interview with author.

56   "the theater erupted . . .": From interview and memoir by Harold W. Williams.

". . . a hell of a splash": New York *Post,* June 2, 1960.

WRONG NOTE RAG

57   "Heart and brain . . .": "An Schwager Kronos," translated by A. H. Fox Strangways and Steuart Wilson.

57   "the most talented student cast . . .": Boston *Globe,* May 28, 1939.
        ". . . had the professional touch . . .": Boston *Transcript,* May 29, 1939.
58   ". . . what 'on consignment' meant": from a filmed interview with Paul
        Hume, 1980.
        Turned his father down: *New Yorker,* January 18, 1958.
59   Had nothing to offer: P1, p. 339.
        ". . . $4 left in my pocket": ditto.
60   A clarinet in a pawn shop; ". . . It was the beginning of the end . . .": filmed
        interview with Hume.
        Born to be a conductor: MT, p. 59.
        ". . . in my loneliness and despair"; ". . . this is terrible": P1, p. 339.
63   ". . . 'Do you think you can play it?' ": MT, p. 60.
66   ". . . He never smiled": filmed interview with Hume.
        ". . . an overstuffed battleship . . .": *I Really Should Be Practicing,* Gary
        Graffman, p. 36; ". . . sang a duet . . .": ditto, p. 60; ". . . accents every so
        many notes . . .": ditto, p. 43; "shouts, screams, threats . . .": ditto, p. 42.
        ". . . the greatest gift . . .": MT, p. 60.
67   "the laziest conductor . . .": Jacques Margolies, interview with author.
        ". . . absolutely basic . . .": *Arts Guardian,* August 12, 1974.
        ". . . what the composer meant": filmed interview with Hume.
        ". . . analyzing . . . in detail . . .": M, pp. 13–14.
        An A from Reiner: letter from Bernstein to Mildred Spiegel, February 28,
        1940.
68   A grand total of seventy-five dollars: from a letter by John W. Walker to
        Bernstein, November 18, 1940, Library of Congress.
69   ". . . wouldn't know the most obvious things": interview with author.
        in "short pants"; ". . . all irrelevant": F, p. 320; the police were called: ditto,
        p. 321.
70   ". . . all-night bull sessions . . .": ditto, pp. 318–19; "Obsessing our private
        lives . . .": ditto, p. 319.
71   Temporized in close relationships: interview with author.
72   Wants him to come to Minneapolis: Leonard Bernstein, letter to Mildred
        Spiegel, February 1, 1940.
        "the sexual life . . .": as quoted in JP, p. 57. "It cannot be . . .": ditto, p. 57;
        letter written on June 4, 1940.

TANGLEWOOD, 1940

73   "Forth! Stumble your way . . .": "An Schwager Kronos," translated by A. H.
        Fox Strangways and Steuart Wilson.
        ". . . Distracts the stray look . . .": "Gare du Midi," by W. H. Auden.
74   "He wasn't a real person . . .": MT, p. 59.
        They had met before: Leonard Bernstein, postcard to Mildred Spiegel,
        undated.
        ". . . a great shock . . .": *Berkshire,* June–July 1991.

"Vatch that boy . . .": New York *Post,* June 3, 1960.

75   Gave Tanglewood its name: *Tanglewood,* James R. Holland, p. 10.

76   ". . . break down the . . . barriers . . .": Boston *Globe,* June 5, 1951.

". . . awfully not togedder": *Tanglewood,* Herbert Kupferberg, p. 41; "Nuts to you!": ditto, p. 41.

". . . you give me something nothing"; ". . . you're not the corpses": interview with Lukas Foss by Tom Godell, Koussevitzky Recordings Society.

77   ". . . No one will play such work . . .": *Tanglewood,* pp. 74–75.

". . . how on earth . . .": interview with author.

78   "[Jazz] was the one thing . . .": filmed interview with Paul Hume, 1980.

He was not identified: the photograph, by the Berkshire *Eagle,* was published in *Newsweek,* August 26, 1940.

". . . We couldn't believe it": interview with author.

79   ". . . cut his movements down"; ". . . like being beaten up . . .": interview with author.

". . . a beautiful setup . . .": FM, p. 136.

". . . Up all night . . ."; ". . . my happiest hours . . .": MT, p. 60.

80   ". . . sexuality incarnate . . .": interview with author.

81   ". . . wasn't his fault . . .": interview with author.

"One is Dionysian . . .": *Berkshire,* June–July 1991.

The draft was imminent: letter dated July 26, 1940.

Soothing wounded sensibilities: letter dated August 27, 1940.

82   Not in the surviving correspondence: at the Library of Congress.

He was being groomed: Leonard Bernstein to Serge Koussevitzky, September 30, 1940, Library of Congress.

83   ". . . don't come back here . . .": *Esquire,* February 1967.

Urged him to return: telegram dated September 10, 1940, Library of Congress.

An all-black symphony orchestra: letter from Bernstein to Helen Coates, November 11, 1940, Library of Congress.

84   ". . . original and refreshing . . .": May 26, 1941.

A good impression: Helen Coates to Bernstein, October 20, 1940, Library of Congress.

His tremendous progress: Helen Coates to Bernstein, December 1, 1940, Library of Congress.

Bored and out of sorts: Bernstein to Coates, January 10, 1941, Library of Congress.

"The first time I met . . .": interview with author.

85   Hoped his friend would feel better: Bernstein to David Diamond, November 4, 1940.

"We always knew . . .": interview with author.

90   ". . . I always looked . . .": interview with author.

". . . 'the old bubbe' . . .": interview with author.

91   ". . . I can hear him now . . .": F, p. 341.

93   ". . . might as well be dead": interview with author.

". . . Lenny raised hell . . .": Lipson interview with Andrew Pincus.

94   Two more bows; Fiedler apologized: letter from Bernstein to Mildred
      Spiegel, July 21, 1941.
      ". . . a repertoire of pieces . . .": interview with author.
      Making the same shifts: F, pp. 312–13.
      "Judson stormed out . . .": interview with author.
96   ". . . a little bit pederastical": ditto.
      ". . . It was so traumatic . . .": Evelyn Saile, interview with author.
97   Hoping to be deferred: Bernstein to Mildred Spiegel, July 21, 1941.
      Ideal for the position: Koussevitzky, letter dated October 29, 1941, Library
      of Congress.
      American Jewry rallied: *The Land That I Show You,* Stanley Feldstein, pp.
      328–29; "had brought my Jewishness . . .": ditto, p. 370.
      ". . . the end from Hitler": *Serge Koussevitzky,* Moses Smith, p. 303.
      ". . . crying as though . . .": Boston *Sunday Post,* November 21, 1943.
      ". . . Thanks be to God . . .": JP, p. 68.
98   ". . . I would have laughed . . .": *Radio and TV Mirror,* May 1962.
      Could not get the necessary waiver: *Serge Koussevitzky,* p. 294.
      ". . . 'for heaven's sake drop in' ": New York *Post,* June 3, 1960.
      ". . . two hands on eight pianos . . .": *New Yorker,* January 18, 1958.
      ". . . more or less stale . . .": F, pp. 50–51.
      "There's that wonderful boy!": interview with author.

PAID WITH INTEREST

99   "Fair, grand, boundless . . .": "An Schwager Kronos," translated by A. H.
      Fox Strangways and Steuart Wilson.
      " 'I'm a *very good* conductor' ": New York *Post,* June 5, 1960.
101   ". . . a bit of a philistine": *P.M.,* February 18, 1943.
      Bernstein appeared with Copland: on May 11, 1942.
      League of Composers twentieth anniversary celebration: on December 10,
      1942.
102   Appeared at a Town Hall performance: on May 18, 1943.
      Bernstein wrote to Helen Coates: on February 19, 1943, Library of Congress.
103   ". . . he . . . contrives to look like him . . .": August 2, 1943.
      His debut as a composer: on March 14, 1943.
      "jazzy, rocking rhythms": April 22, 1942.
      "meaty, logical harmony . . .": on March 14, 1943.
105   ". . . the happiest days of my life": interview with author.
      He received twenty-five dollar weekly royalties: JP, p. 76.
      Working around the clock: *Collier's,* October 13, 1945.
107   ". . . a chief concern of my life": *ASCAP Today,* July 1972.
      Klemperer angered Judson: HOR, p. 183.
      ". . . Poppa financed the boy's career . . .": interview with author.
      ". . . did not have enough money . . .": interview with author.
      ". . . pursued the powerhouses . . .": Milton Goldin, letter to author, August
      3, 1991.

108   Bought the job for her husband: Richard Bales to author.
        Became his wife: in 1947.
109   ". . . inverse chauvinism . . .": HOR, p. 17.
        ". . . a passionate lack . . .": *I Really Should Be Practicing,* Gary Graffman, p. 97.
        "an emerging . . . middle-class . . .": Milton Goldin, letter to author,
        August 3, 1991.
110   ". . . I was overwhelmed . . .": interview with author.
111   ". . . the most exciting . . .": *P.M.,* September 10, 1943.
        "living in love . . .": ROD, p. 208.
        "Take Bernstein": JP, p. 83.
        ". . . just to get away . . .": interview with author.
        Agreed to serve for one year: Bernstein to Koussevitzky, undated, Library of
        Congress.
113   "Here we go!": quoted JP, p. 83; the original announcement was pasted into
        one of his scrapbooks and is now in the Library of Congress.
        "absolute agony": Providence (Rhode Island) *Journal,* November 19, 1944.
        ". . . forbid Lenny to enter . . .": ROD, pp. 240–41.
114   ". . . a heavy drinker . . .": interview with author.
        Asked to compose: *New Yorker,* November 27, 1943.
115   ". . . it will be years . . .": Boston *Sunday Post,* November 21, 1943.
        ". . . the great virtuosos . . .": November 15, 1943.
        Why not ask Bernstein?: ROD, p. 240.
117   ". . . a deliberate decision . . .": interview with author.
        ". . . I was scared . . .": *Cue,* April 12, 1944.
        "Did a Bernstein . . .": Boston *Sunday Post,* November 21, 1943.
        First-chair members were called in: New York *World-Telegram,* November
        15, 1943.
118   Radio programs were important: ROD, p. 240.
        "I was so shaky . . .": New York *Post,* June 5, 1960.
        ". . . a great electric shock . . .": PW, p. 106.
        ". . . stood up and cheered . . .": interview with author.
119   ". . . another lifetime . . .": *Time,* January 15, 1945.
        His definition of God: JOM, p. 29.
        ". . . ecstatic and baffled": *Reflections,* a film by Peter Rosen, United States
        Information Agency, 1978.
120   ". . . keep those dates": St. Louis *Globe-Democrat,* February 15, 1945.
        "four scotches . . .": *Current Biography,* February 1944.
        ". . . you paid me back . . .": Boston *Sunday Post,* November 21, 1943.

ALL-AMERICAN BOY

121   "And when peak calls to peak . . .": "An Schwager Kronos," translated by
        A. H. Fox Strangways and Steuart Wilson.
        ". . . American success story . . .": November 16, 1943.
        ". . . He made it": *Newsweek,* April 10, 1944.
122   ". . . a secret rebate . . .": *Against the American Grain,* Dwight Macdonald, p. 67.

122   ". . . entire cast of characters . . ."; a convincing show of grief: *New Yorker,* January 11, 1958.

123   "He always cries . . .": interview with author.
". . . fume and rage . . .": INF, p. 284.
". . . it takes me so long . . .": MT, p. 52.
". . . it was magical . . .": *Lord Beaverbrook,* Anne Chisholm and Michael Davie, p. 503.

124   "First timesies?"; all seventeen songs: *New Yorker,* January 11, 1958.
". . . in five minutes . . .": interview with author.
". . . how to risk and return . . .": interview with author.
A letter of protest: *New Yorker,* January 11, 1958.

125   Would prove them all wrong: *Connoisseur,* September 1991.
". . . no security . . .": interview with author.
". . . he wants success . . .": David Diamond, interview with author.
". . . A fine kid": *Mark the Music,* Eric A. Gordon, p. 261.
"How can I be blind . . .": *New Yorker,* November 27, 1943.
"purely atmospheric . . .": New York *Herald Tribune,* December 4, 1943.
As guest conductor: SH, p. 302.

126   "his cues are clean . . .": Pittsburgh *Post-Gazette,* January 29, 1944.
". . . will destroy himself . . .": *Sun Telegram,* January 29, 1944.

127   ". . . Leonard Bernstein day . . .": Boston *Herald,* February 19, 1944.
" 'Hats off . . . a genius!' ": Boston *Post,* February 19, 1944.
Predicting great things: New York *Herald Tribune,* February 19, 1944.
". . . all steamed up . . .": *P.M.,* May 14, 1944.

128   Their method of working: *Dance Magazine,* January 1980.
". . . these black dots": ROD, p. 249.
". . . just like that . . .": INF, p. 286.
"There's no future . . .": *A Smattering of Ignorance,* Oscar Levant, pp. 246–47.

129   "Compare for a moment . . .": INF, p. 275.
". . . a fancy bit of choreography": *P.M.,* April 19, 1944.
"expertly scored . . .": *New Yorker,* April 29, 1944.

130   Took him by the throat: PW, pp. 130–31.
". . . dashed for a train . . .": Boston *Evening Globe,* May 5, 1944.
". . . young and fortunate . . .": Chicago *Sun,* July 5, 1944.
". . . supplicant and truculent . . .": Chicago *Daily Tribune,* July 5, 1944.

131   "eloquence and fire . . .": Chicago *Daily Tribune,* July 7, 1944.
". . . flair for the dramatic": *New York Times,* July 15, 1944.
Appeared with Levant: on August 26, 1944.
His twentieth year: on May 16, 1944.
Helped sponsor a new orchestra: on November 22, 1944.
Appeared at a benefit concert: on May 14, 1944.
A concert of *Jeremiah:* on April 27, 1944.

132   On ten political committees: *American Hebrew,* November 9, 1945.
Supported a national health program: *New York Times,* December 1, 1945.
Sending musical instruments: *New York Times,* December 23, 1945.
Improving department store wages: *Daily Worker,* October 17, 1946.

A program of Russian music: on April 13, 1945.

A Victor Red Seal contract: in March 1945.

"The aim of the performer . . .": *Mademoiselle*, October 1944.

133 ". . . sings and dances . . .": *Time*, January 8, 1945.

"The 'Future,' of course . . .": *New York Times*, October 31, 1971.

135 ". . . I'd hate to tell you . . .": *Tomorrow Magazine*, May 1945.

136 "If you are writing . . .": Associated Press, February 4, 1945.

"the worst ten days . . .": Pittsburgh *Press*, January 12, 1945.

". . . most engaging . . .": *New York Times*, December 28, 1945.

Earned $100,000: *New Yorker*, January 18, 1958.

". . . It's madness . . .": INF, p. 283.

To avoid being mobbed: *Calling All Girls*, February 1946.

137 Buttons torn off: Pittsburgh *Press*, January 12, 1945.

". . . the critics weren't there . . .": interview with author.

". . . a mental hazard . . .": St. Louis *Globe-Democrat*, February 15, 1945.

138 ". . . a thrilling ovation . . .": New York *Daily News*, May 15, 1945.

"MUSIC I HEARD WITH YOU"

139 "Music I Heard with You": title of a poem by Conrad Aiken, set to music by Bernstein in *Songfest* (1977).

"See by the roadside . . .": "An Schwager Kronos," translated by Richard Capell.

Was judged good-looking: this comment was made by Cecilia A. Vogel, who used to see him on the elevators; letter to author, July 19, 1991.

140 ". . . You don't keep hours . . .": Hollywood *Citizen-News*, September 26, 1960.

141 ". . . boring everyone stiff . . .": *P.M.*, September 26, 1945.

"There's an opening . . .": interview with author.

"You're hired": interview with author.

142 ". . . the biggest stink . . .": New York *Sun*, November 19, 1945.

"exceptional brilliancy": *New York Times*, October 9, 1945.

"innate resourcefulness . . .": *New York Times*, October 23, 1945.

Included a reference: on December 1, 1945.

"Do Re Mi . . .": New York *Mirror*, November 23, 1945.

". . . exactly and clearly . . .": *Music News*, March 1945.

143 ". . . touring Italian bandmasters . . .": New York *Herald Tribune*, October 16, 1946.

". . . lots of slapping down": *Selected Letters of Virgil Thomson*, Tim Page and Vanessa Weeks Page, p. 204.

"I think a lot of . . .": *The Memoirs of an Amnesiac*, Oscar Levant, p. 13.

Waving his arms around: Barbara Lewis, interview with author.

One of "America's Great . . .": in 1945.

144 Steinberg to Pittsburgh: 1952.

Paray to Detroit: in 1952.

"he hadn't accomplished . . .": New York *Post*, June 6, 1960.

144   "... Then you'll be ready ...": PW, p. 107.

145   "In those days ..."; "Sadly, he was right ...": interview with author.

146   "I have never conducted ...": interview with author.

"... I never was ...": letter to author from Mrs. L. P. Bachmann, July 19, 1991.

147   "I wasn't in love ...": interview with author.

"They all went to bed ...": interview with author.

"I don't know if ...": interview with author.

148   "We ... like real men": interview with author.

"... effete American queens ...": JP, p. 426.

"... I thought he required ...": interview with author.

149   Felicia Montealegre's background: New York *Post,* June 6, 1960.

"... My biggest thrill ...": St. Louis *Post-Dispatch,* October 23, 1961.

150   "I got the feeling ...": interview with author.

"... completely bowled over ...": *Radio and TV Mirror,* May 1962.

151   "... virtually alone ...": interview with author.

"a lovely woman ...": interview with author.

"Felicia was so private ...": interview with author.

"... sat up straighter ...": interview with author.

"I was crazy ...": interview with author.

"... a class act": interview with author.

"... this great-looking girl ...": interview with author.

152   "... She'd never believe ...": *Radio and TV Mirror,* May 1962.

153   "... enormously respectful ...": interview with author.

Performance was bad: Bernstein to Koussevitzky, June 22, 1946, Library of Congress.

A stern letter in reply: Koussevitzky to Bernstein, December 23, 1946, Library of Congress.

154   "... raised what I needed": interview with author.

Insisted on paying: interview with author and letter, July 11, 1991.

"... absolutely sizzling ...": interview with author.

156   "... going to make an opera ...": interview with author.

The ninth international festival: September 15–22, 1946.

"... their inner emptiness ...": New York *Herald Tribune,* October 25, 1946.

"... like a shuttlecock ...": *Time,* November 4, 1946.

157   "... a wonderful imitation ...": *Selected Letters of Virgil Thomson,* p. 197.

"... tremendously alive ...": interview with author.

"As I recall ...": interview with author.

160   "... Jewish ethics ...": interview with author.

161   "They were upset ...": interview with author.

THE ELEGANT CONSTRUCTION

162   "And a welcome is waiting ...": "An Schwager Kronos," translated by A. H. Fox Strangways and Steuart Wilson.

163   "... in his pajamas ...": *New Yorker,* January 11, 1958.

"... talented and Jewish": *New York Times,* May 2, 1947.

164 "I found myself weeping ...": ditto.

"I gave a downbeat ...": New York *Post,* May 8, 1947.

"It could become ...": *New York Times,* May 2, 1947.

"... the most brilliant ...": June 12, 1947.

"We ended up ...": interview with author.

165 He conducted naked: Tanglewood *Trumpet,* July 21, 1947.

166 "This is the lady ...": *Every Friday,* Cincinnati, July 18, 1947.

It sounded better: New York *Post,* June 28, 1947.

"... If he ever does marry ...": New York *World-Telegram,* May 6, 1947.

"We had a house ...": interview with author.

Considered quite shocking: Howard Shanet, interview with author.

"We all loved her ...": interview with author.

"... glared at me": interview with author.

167 "... very-well-behaviorized ...": F, p. 122.

She would divorce: interview with author.

"he proposed to absolutely ...": interview with author.

168 "the scaly and scummy ...": F, p. 107.

"... The elegant construction ...": F, p. 123.

169 "... they still cheer ...": *Harper's Magazine,* February 1948.

Bernadotte was assassinated: on September 17, 1948.

"... a sort of half-crouch ...": Boston *Globe,* December 10, 1948.

"... um-cha, um-cha ...": San Francisco *Chronicle,* March 15, 1950.

170 "... a ten-ton truck"; "Fiddles are not ...": New York *World-Telegram,* December 30, 1949.

"interpreter in excelsis": *New York Times,* October 28, 1947.

"His treatment of ...": *New Republic,* March 20, 1950.

"... made the transition": *New Yorker,* December 17, 1949.

"I remember having ...": interview with author.

With a fluegelhorn: New York *World-Telegram,* March 2, 1948.

171 How dared he call him brash? *Harper's Magazine,* February 1948.

Plotted its overthrow: New York *World-Telegram,* March 13, 1947.

Protested the firing: March 3, 1947.

Concert dedicated to Eisler: Providence (Rhode Island) *Bulletin,* March 30, 1948.

172 "Any attempt to curb ...": *New York Times,* October 24, 1947.

Copland's work dropped: in January 1953.

"Dupes and Fellow ...": *Life,* April 4, 1949.

Doing nothing well: Baltimore *Sun,* June 6, 1948.

"I'm the logical ...": *Harper's Magazine,* February 1948.

"I wrote the jazz ...": New York *World-Telegram,* February 25, 1950.

173 "I suppose I told ...": interview with author.

Comparing mountains to Beethoven: JOM, p. 22.

174 "... she was wonderful ...": interview with author.

175 "He was obviously propositioning ...": interview with author and letter dated June 28, 1991.

175   "a sort of tinsel . . .": *New York Times,* February 24, 1950.
"I meant every note": A Talk with Leonard Bernstein, Phillip Ramey, taped December 4, 1973.

176   "a virtual dance . . .": letter to author, August 8, 1991.
". . . vigorous and ebullient . . .": August 13, 1949.
"It is a triumph . . .": *Newsweek,* April 18, 1949.
". . . the sincere expression . . .": *New York Times,* February 24, 1950.
"It really has . . .": *Newsweek,* March 6, 1950.
One of ten: *Life,* May 5, 1952.

177   Was still attached: interview with author; "an enormous reunion": ditto.
"She's by herself . . .": interview with author.
The reconciliation that led to their marriage: Shirley Bernstein.
Would like to "settle down": Pittsburgh *Post-Gazette,* January 6, 1950.
The wedding was called off: Walter Winchell, January 12, 1950.
"I'm worn out . . .": Washington *Star,* January 31, 1951.

178   Tchaikovsky's *Queen of Spades: Tanglewood,* Herbert Kupferberg, p. 132.
"He knew something . . .": F, p. 151; letter dated November 14, 1959.
Died in his arms: filmed interview with Paul Hume, 1980.

179   ". . . I was going to divorce . . .": interview with author.
". . . her wedding dress": interview with author.
He formally proposed: Washington *Post,* August 14, 1961.
"it must be a signal . . .": San Francisco *Chronicle,* August 22, 1951.
Concentrating on composing: Boston *Sunday Advertiser,* September 9, 1951.
"He had had a lot of therapy . . .": interview with author.
". . . I'd be dead": interview with author.

180   " '. . . not one of us' . . ."; "she balanced Lenny . . .": interview with author.
"In stillness, every . . .": F, p. 328; ". . . the two are not separate . . .": ditto, p. 174.

THE WHITE SUIT

181   "Quaff your fill . . .": "An Schwager Kronos," translated by A. H. Fox Strangways and Steuart Wilson.

182   Disconnected and adrift: F, p. 122. Written in 1948.
"myself, reincarnated": Boston *Herald,* May 12, 1944.
"This reach, this leap . . .": F, p. 211.
"I wanted to fling . . .": PW, p. 55.
"They were exasperated . . .": interview with author.

183   "a terrible mistake . . .": ditto.
". . . denouncing or flattering . . .": JOM, p. 41; ". . . we can arrive . . .": ditto, p. 45.
". . . a happy man": F, p. 129.
"conductor's music . . .": *Copland on Music,* Aaron Copland, pp. 172–73.

185   ". . . a muffled thud": *Saturday Review,* November 29, 1952.

". . . to make them laugh . . .": interview with author.

186 ". . . thinnest of thin ice": *Saturday Review,* November 29, 1952.

". . . a silver moon . . .": *New Yorker,* November 29, 1952.

He would be photographed: by the *Knickerbocker News,* July 15, 1953.

". . . my bride will be . . .": Boston *Sunday Advertiser,* September 9, 1951.

"burst into tears": *Time,* February 4, 1957.

". . . the spirit of youth . . .": New York *Post,* June 7, 1960.

187 "most maturely eloquent . . .": March 8, 1952.

". . . What is happening . . .": *Christian Science Monitor,* June 13, 1952.

188 ". . . would run screaming . . .": *Berkshire County Eagle,* May 21, 1952.

"Mr. Tanglewood": *Holiday,* June 1953.

189 "Who does he think . . .": as told to author by Leonard Marcus; ". . . more than music . . .": interview with author.

Training for the real world: *Holiday,* June 1953. "One of the things . . .": ditto.

190 Zita Carno's amazing ear: from a letter to author by Marcia Kraus, July 1, 1991; ". . . a well-known test . . .": ditto.

a "Kraft Television Theatre" production: October 28, 1952.

191 He simply did not know: letter to Irving Fine, October 20, 1952.

"I called Felicia . . .": interview with author.

"I always remember . . .": interview with author.

She "gentled" him: interview with author.

193 " 'curbed' is more like it": interview with author.

194 "When I am sitting . . .": interview with author.

". . . I was coming . . .": interview with author.

196 ". . . I don't think we left . . .": *Holiday,* October 1959.

197 "memorably versatile . . .": *New York Times,* February 26, 1953.

"to disseminate ideas . . .": New York *Daily News,* April 1, 1953.

"step out of . . .": New York *Daily News,* March 9, 1953.

198 ". . . must now pass political . . .": New York *Herald Tribune,* March 27, 1953.

"lengthy Communist-front record": March 6, 1954.

". . . very happy investors": March 16, 1953.

unlikely to be ". . . favorites . . .": March 17, 1953.

His next mock dialogue: JOM, p. 52. (In 1955.)

"a devil at his back . . .": INF, p. 272.

". . . you itch to conduct": *Time,* December 21, 1953.

"WOW, I'M FAMOUS!"

199 "Downhill now and away . . .": "An Schwager Kronos," translated by Richard Capell.

". . . were getting clobbered . . .": *New York Times,* July 11, 1954.

200 ". . . the best . . . background music . . ."; "I found myself . . .": *New York Times,* May 30, 1954.

"a curiously piercing . . .": *Time,* February 4, 1957.

201   "all rigid thinking . . .": New York *Herald Tribune,* November 25, 1956.
       ". . . phony moralism . . .": *New York Times,* November 18, 1956.
       ". . . equated with a callous . . .": New York *World-Telegram,* December 3, 1956.

202   ". . . the most characteristic . . .": *Landmarks in French Literature,* Lytton Strachey, pp. 163, 165.

203   ". . . there's nothing official . . .": New York *Herald Tribune,* February 12, 1954.
       "It's an amusing . . .": Los Angeles *Times,* May 9, 1954.
       Some frothy melodies: letter to David Diamond, May 20, 1954.
       Melodic and romantic: ditto, August 17, 1954.
       In two months: ditto, November 25, 1954.

204   Quite a challenge: ditto, May 25, 1956.
       "He never had . . .": interview with author.
       ". . . attractively self-forgetful . . .": *Berkshire,* June–July 1991.
       ". . . austere woman . . .": January 14, 1955.

205   ". . . the very hardest work . . .": *Vineyard Gazette,* July 16, 1954.
       More FBI agents: John Duffy to author.

206   "'Twas love, great love . . .": *Lillian Hellman,* Carl Rollyson, p. 365.
       ". . . a failure of nerve": ditto, p. 364.
       "Opera fans did not go . . .": interview with author.

209   "I know that when . . .": *Newsday,* April 21, 1974.
       ". . . skittering of ideas . . .": *Time,* March 25, 1974.
       ". . . grandest, wittiest . . .": *New York,* October 25, 1982.

210   A standing ovation: *New York Times,* October 14, 1982.
       ". . . quite harmonised with the set": letter to author, June 26, 1992.

211   "There's more of me . . .": interview with author.
       Hoped he would not try: *Sondheim & Co.,* Craig Zadan, p. 54.

212   Its Washington premiere: on August 19, 1957.
       ". . . a classic myth . . .": *Holiday,* October 1959.

213   ". . . If you're looking . . .": INF, p. 286; the conscious, controlling part: ditto, p. 269; ". . . and then you're doing . . .": ditto, p. 283.
       ". . . it wasn't for them": Laurents, interview with author.
       "The music was so rich . . .": interview with author.

215   His claim to fame: letter to author, July 9, 1991.
       ". . . We had a famous audition . . .": interview with author.

216   Never had a failure: *Life,* September 16, 1957.
       "Lenny didn't want . . .": interview with author.
       Found the needed money: Philadelphia *Inquirer,* August 25, 1957; *Sondheim & Co.,* pp. 17–18; interview with Harold Prince.

217   "Lenny was a marvelous . . .": interview with author.
       A great education: *Sondheim & Co.,* p. 25.
       "The last scene . . .": New York *Herald Tribune,* September 22, 1957.
       ". . . he destroys you": *Sondheim & Co.,* pp. 18–19.

218   ". . . He was terrified . . .": interview with author.
       Something of a procrastinator: letter to author, September 10, 1993.
       ". . . five shots of whisky . . .": *SBI,* February 1962.

"... and kept clapping,": interview with author and letter to author, December 7, 1993.

Robbins called it an accident: Jerome Robbins, letter to author, November 29, 1993.

219   "I remember him saying . . .": interview with author.

Did not know which part: *New York Times,* September 22, 1957.

"She's exactly seventeen": Rochester *Democrat-Chronicle,* December 1, 1957.

220   "He didn't trust . . .": interview with author.

"Music is a cause . . .": *New Republic,* September 9, 1957.

". . . really quite lovely . . .": *New Yorker,* October 5, 1957.

". . . nervous, flaring scores . . .": *New York Times,* September 27, 1957.

He had capitulated: *New York Times,* October 13, 1957.

"The big money . . .": *Sondheim & Co.,* p. 29.

221   "Wow, I'm famous!": interview with author.

". . . started taking bows . . .": interview with author.

THE OMNIPOTENT ONE

222   "Ere old age . . .": "An Schwager Kronos," translated by Richard Capell.

"a born conductor": Parkersburg *News,* November 14, 1944.

"the first American-born . . .": Boston *Herald,* November 25, 1944.

223   Being groomed to succeed: *New York Times,* April 29, 1956.

"Does anyone imagine . . .": New York *Herald Tribune,* January 5, 1958.

". . . the inferiority complex . . .": *New York Times,* November 25, 1957.

224   The orchestra was slipping: *New York Times,* April 29, 1956.

225   Loaned to the artists: *The Music Makers,* Milton Goldin, p. 169.

"harness their orchestras . . .": *The Maestro Myth,* Norman Lebrecht, p. 309.

226   Ormandy took a train: Richard Bales, interview with author.

"Stokie was Judson's . . .": ROD, p. 281.

There was a photograph: Richard Bales, interview with author.

". . . something very cold . . .": ROD, p. 145.

"You asked, 'How high?' ": interview with author.

". . . a barroom Irishman . . .": interview with author.

227   Box-office poison: *Leopold Stokowski: A Profile,* Abram Chasins, p. 126.

He could not get work: ROD, p. 279.

". . . argued at cross purposes . . .": ROD, p. 280.

228   Paying Judson under the table: Richard Rodzinski.

"the worst musical racket . . .": *New York Times,* September 12, 1956.

"a courageous gesture": *Newsweek,* February 17, 1947.

229   ". . . would not tolerate . . .": *New York Times,* April 29, 1956.

". . . a bad influence"; "Somebody had a brilliant . . .": interview with author.

230   "The real function of form . . ."; "Form is not a mold . . .": JOM, p. 75; "a delicate lady . . .": ditto, p. 78.

"living truths": JOM, p. 24; "those syncopations and twists . . .": ditto, p. 85.

231   "We live in a world . . .": ditto, p. 91; ". . . shouting for freedom . . .": ditto, p. 114.

232   "a perfect summary . . .": ditto, p. 134; ". . . just another airport": ditto, p. 135.
". . . a tremendous adventure . . .": *New York Times,* November 21, 1954.
There was a cue sheet: *Leonard Bernstein: The Television Work,* Museum of
Broadcasting, p. 39.

234   Had sunk to tenth: New York *Herald Tribune,* May 2, 1947.
". . . It seemed a slap . . .": interview with author.
". . . The Philharmonic is *it*": *New York Times Magazine,* December 22, 1957.
". . . Use your teeth . . .": Memphis *Commercial Appeal,* January 15, 1957.

235   Imaginative and rejuvenating: *Saturday Review,* January 12, 1957.
". . . a sense of structure": Boston *Daily Globe,* April 16, 1955.
". . . your mussy hair": Boston *Daily Globe,* November 24, 1957.
"He plays too hard . . .": *Time,* February 4, 1957.
". . . this is a frightening . . .": *Milwaukee Journal,* December 4, 1957.

237   ". . . Why doesn't *ANYONE* . . .": New York *Post,* November 13, 1955.
". . . I have been waiting": Boston *Daily Globe,* November 24, 1957.
". . . like a child . . .": Jersey City *Journal,* November 29, 1957.
". . . some real corny jazz . . .": *Mayfair,* March 1958.
". . . her own identity . . .": *Milwaukee Journal,* December 4, 1957.
Working on needlepoint: *Jewish Times,* July 26, 1956.

238   ". . . yellow marvelous?": New York *Post,* June 7, 1960.
He was on a diet: Jersey City *Journal,* November 29, 1957.
He was getting old: *Newsweek* and *Time,* November 25, 1957.
". . . a great deal of boldness . . .": *New York Times,* December 22, 1957.
". . . each thing better . . .": *Pageant,* December 1958.
He was soon bored: *Milwaukee Journal,* December 4, 1957.
"Lonely Men of Harvard": interview with Thomas Beveridge.

239   ". . . and patted the floor . . .": interview with author.
Urged him to settle: *New Yorker,* January 18, 1958.
A symbolic change: *Saturday Review,* January 1958.

240   ". . . an educational mission . . .": *New York Times Magazine,* December 22,
1957.
Welcomed by Taubman: SH, p. 329.

241   Original and stimulating; ". . . the Philharmonic is awake . . .": *New York
Times,* December 22, 1957.
"far from the bite . . .": *Time,* January 13, 1958.
". . . a sense of poise . . .": *New York Times,* January 4, 1958.
"I am a happy man": *New Yorker,* January 18, 1958.

MAESTRO

242   "Ere limbs begin to totter . . .": "An Schwager Kronos," translated by
Richard Capell.
". . . honor the intellect . . .": Remarks made at "Bernstein / 60," benefit
concert at Wolf Trap Farm Park for the Performing Arts, Vienna, Virginia,
August 25, 1978.

243   On nationwide television: December 1, 1957.
245   Had never been seen on television: SH, p. 321.

"... I love the silence ...": *Newsweek,* March 2, 1959.

"... He wanted to be pleased ...": interview with author.

In twenty-nine countries: SH, p. 341.
247   Enrolled at birth; "I don't talk ...": *New York Times,* January 22, 1967.

An integral part: F, p. 223.

"... a *dream* of a cathedral ...": YPC, p. 182; "the way it makes you feel ...": ditto, p. 28; "... notes instead of words": ditto, p. 28.
248   "... an Erector Set": ditto, p. 113; the right result: ditto, p. 114; a time of elegance: ditto, p. 119; "Shave and a haircut": ditto, p. 122; "ghastly wrong notes": ditto, p. 143; "... a very puzzled look": ditto, p. 145; "rude noises": ditto, p. 146.
249   "... you feel his head ...": New York *Herald Tribune,* February 5, 1961.

"When you know that you're reaching ...": *Newsweek,* March 2, 1959.

"I want him to be ...": interview with author.

"You fought a good ...": *Time,* October 13, 1958.

"it's a positive ...": *Harper's Magazine,* May 1959.
250   "... a most unusual phenomenon ...": New York *Herald Tribune,* March 1, 1959.

"the most socially ...": New York *Journal American,* October 4, 1958.
251   More subscribers: *Harper's Magazine,* May 1959.

"The orchestra played ...": *New Yorker,* October 11, 1958.

"the nervous tension ...": Portland (Maine) *Express,* February 19, 1959.

His rising income: *New Yorker,* January 11 and 18, 1958.
252   "... they are so tragic ...": interview with author.

"... bookkeeper's eye ...": Milton Goldin, interview with author.
254   "I was in the midst ...": Arthur Shimkin, letter to author, July 1, 1991.
255   *Carousel* was an opera: Washington *Post* and Washington *Star,* September 19, 1957.
256   Founding of Amberson: February 20, 1959.

"... a very small world ...": interview with author.

"... you have to be horizontal ...": interview with author.

Deliberately changed: interview with author.

Sexually propositioned: interview with author.
257   "There is a certain ...": interview with author.

"... sexual fantasy ...": *The Maestro Myth,* Norman Lebrecht, p. 263.

"... maintain a facade ...": ditto, p. 263.

Preferring the Baldwin: *New Yorker,* May 10, 1958.

An exclusive contract: MC, p. 209.
258   "a handsome monetary donation ...": ditto, p. 239.

"... their musical pedigree ...": *Boston Review,* February 1985.
259   a "luxury tax": ditto.

"We always hope ...": interview with author.

"... it's a game": interview with author.

259   The price went up: Robert Kreis, interview with author.

"You might have found . . .": interview with author.

261   Mitropoulos was in tears: State Department dispatch written by Jacob Canter, September 19, 1958.

Toppled from the podium: *New York Post,* November 2, 1960; *New York Times,* November 3, 1960.

262   The Mitropoulos cross: After Bernstein's death, Diamond asked for the return of the cross and was informed that during a hospital visit Bernstein's ring, wristwatch and cross all had been stolen.

Had died in his arms: filmed interview with Paul Hume, 1980.

An ambitious tour: *New York Times,* February 27, 1959.

The Reiner cancellation: *Time,* March 9, 1959.

263   "great cheering": *New York Times,* February 27, 1959.

"A new god . . .": *Time,* September 7, 1959.

264   ". . . tried to shut him up . . .": interview with author.

266   Felt no identification: Paris *Herald Tribune,* September 19, 1959; *National Jewish Post and Opinion,* October 23, 1959.

268   An explanatory lecture: *New York Times,* September 26, 1959.

". . . a musical revolution . . .": *Time,* September 7, 1959.

". . . a hill of beans . . .": *Newsweek,* September 7, 1959.

269   ". . . this fantastic music": Washington *Post,* March 4, 1988.

THE KISSING BANDIT

270   "Blind in the sunset": "An Schwager Kronos," translated by A. H. Fox Strangways and Steuart Wilson.

". . . virtuosos and waiters": New York *Herald Tribune,* September 24, 1962.

271   A properly religious fervor: ditto.

In plain English: *Newsweek,* September 24, 1962.

272   ". . . the slamming of a gate": interview with author.

"You're the only man . . .": *Showcase,* May 1992.

". . . the symbol of music . . .": *Esquire,* February 1967.

273   "Lenny never does . . .": *Saturday Evening Post,* June 16, 1956.

Income estimates: *Science* (London), February 18, 1963; *Bravo,* January–February 1962.

274   ". . . a cultural symbol . . .": *Science,* February 18, 1963.

An extended contract: New York *Herald Tribune,* February 10, 1961.

275   The rehearsal was a success: *New Yorker,* January 11, 1958.

". . . a special ray of sunshine . . .": *Esquire,* February 1967.

". . . intensely private . . .": interview with author.

"a fraternal gulp . . .": *Musiques,* September 1979.

". . . the most remarkable mind . . .": New York *Post,* May 31, 1960.

276   "He said I could!": interview with author.

". . . enormously intelligent . . .": interview with author.

". . . wiping tears from their eyes . . .": interview with author.

". . . a great gift . . .": interview with author.

"open to you . . .": *New York Times,* August 23, 1981.

277 An international figure: *New York Times,* September 29, 1974.
". . . commanding presence . . .": *New York Times,* November 27, 1960.
". . . a kind of sculptor . . .": *New York Times,* September 29, 1974.
". . . a cast-iron stomach . . .": New York *Herald Tribune,* May 21, 1961.

278 A radiant personality: *Esquire,* February 1967.
"a fearsome reputation . . .": *The Maestro Myth,* Norman Lebrecht, p. 178.
"laughing so hard . . .": interview with author.

279 "It is easy enough . . .": *Esquire,* February 1967.

280 ". . . pleased and delighted . . .": interview with author.
". . . wearing pink tights . . .": *Newsweek,* September 24, 1962.
". . . how I had played it": interview with author.
A hand on each head: Ken Pasmanick, interview with author.
". . . I'd get almost resentful . . .": interview with author.
Explain and philosophize: interview with author.
"Toscanini would never . . .": interview with author.

282 ". . . Forget what we did . . .": interview with author.
". . . some joke horoscope . . .": interview with author.

283 ". . . think of their union . . .": M, p. 10.
". . . atmosphere of nurturing . . .": interview with author.

284 ". . . extraordinarily beautiful . . .": *Musical America,* January 1961.
". . . crystalline and precise . . .": interview with author.

285 Knew very little: *Argonaut* (San Francisco), February 21, 1958.
". . . spreading himself . . .": *New York Times,* April 16, 1961.
Lacking ingenuity: *New York Times,* March 4, 1962.
Turned into a monster: New York *Herald Tribune,* November 18, 1962.
Disclaimed responsibility: New York *Herald Tribune,* April 7, 1962.
No gift for the classics: New York *World Journal Tribune,* February 19, 1967.
Too easily influenced: New York *Sunday Herald Tribune,* May 11, 1961.
". . . cannot be satisfied . . .": New York *World Journal Tribune,* February 26, 1967.

286 ". . . electricity and glamour . . .": New York *World Journal Tribune,* February 19, 1967.
"do not talk . . .": Alan Miller, interview with author.
". . . a large musical form . . .": New York *Herald Tribune,* March 6, 1966.
". . . clinging arduously . . .": *Saturday Review,* January 18, 1964.
"group of doctrinaire . . .": New York *Herald Tribune,* September 22, 1963.

287 Annoying chats: *New York Times,* January 3, 1964.
". . . a Flit gun . . .": New York *Herald Tribune,* January 3, 1964.
Enlightening and amusing: Harriett Johnson, New York *Post,* January 3, 1964.
". . . a musical high wire . . .": Indianapolis *Star,* February 16, 1964.
". . . he has left the world . . .": INF, pp. 12–13.
"a sharp ache . . .": Detroit *News,* August 12, 1960.

288 ". . . a box of salt . . ."; had to be "important": interview with author.
". . . it's slavery, too . . .": *Ma'ariv,* December 13, 1963.

288   ". . . some kind of musical theater . . .": Baltimore *Morning Sun*, January 5, 1967.

The chief mourner: *The Joys of Yiddish*, Leo Rosten, p. 162.

A prayer for everyone: letter to David Diamond, January 10, 1963.

Depressed and drained: letter to David Diamond, October 13, 1964.

289   A man he had loved: *Ma'ariv*, December 13, 1963.

". . . a third higher . . .": interview with author.

". . . what a tragic waste . . .": *Ma'ariv*, December 13, 1963.

". . . is there hope? . . .": Baltimore *Morning Sun*, January 5, 1967.

The death of God: INF, p. 13.

"an affirmation of life . . .": *Time*, February 7, 1964.

290   ". . . without piety or refinement . . .": May 1964.

"The despair he portrays . . .": *Time*, February 7, 1964.

". . . 'Chutzpah' would do . . .": New York *Herald Tribune*, April 10, 1964.

A critical "vendetta": Jack Gottlieb, *Colloquy and Review*, Fall–Winter 1965.

A great homecoming: on February 1, 1964.

His own style: Boston *Herald*, January 8, 1962.

291   ". . . my parents became friends . . .": interview with author.

". . . the right background . . .": Boston *Morning Globe*, February 21, 1966.

". . . does not become dizzy . . .": *Jewish News*, January 1966.

292   ". . . borrowed from God": FM, p. 193.

A sense of loss: F, p. 153.

Longing for the chance: speech delivered February 2, 1959.

TO HAVE IS TO BE

293   "Drunk still with life . . .": "An Schwager Kronos," translated by Richard Capell.

Would examine his hairline: there are numerous references in the Bernstein correspondence with David Diamond.

A scalp "popping": as described to author by Joan Vanoni, who once performed that service for him.

". . . slightly suppressed waist": spring 1958.

"Lenny's dress rehearsals": Atlanta *Journal-Constitution*, March 22, 1959.

294   ". . . visions of beige": Joan Vanoni to author.

In private schools: *New York Times*, November 22, 1965.

". . . what I have got! . . .": interview with author.

". . . being overlooked . . .": interview with author.

295   ". . . the mortality rate . . .": ROD, p. vii.

". . . incredibly glamorous . . .": interview with author.

". . . a playful quality . . .": interview with author.

296   ". . . very self-deprecating . . .": interview with author.

"People in the arts . . .": interview with author.

298   ". . . not alone in your bed . . .": interview with author.

"To have is to be": F, p. 134; success was more important: ditto, p. 249.

". . . had to become celebrities . . .": *Our Age*, Noel Annan, pp. 292–93.

"I was beating him . . .": interview with author.

Three packs a day: (Virginia) *Express,* March 4, 1966.

Terrifying symptoms: *New York Times,* March 28, 1993.

299 ". . . because they are poor' ": interview with author.

". . . he didn't talk . . ."; ". . . just like a child . . .": interview with author.

300 An automatic narcissist: F, p. 212 (in 1963).

302 ". . . this was contradicting . . .": interview with author.

"The more you become . . .": interview with author.

"I am not happy . . .": Manchester *Guardian,* December 4, 1966.

". . . a giant music stand . . .": interview with author.

303 ". . . it's Florence Foster Jenkins": interview with author.

". . . his predestined *milieu . . .*": *Saturday Review,* March 21, 1964.

". . . an artistic entity . . .": *Saturday Review,* July 31, 1965.

304 "A lovely . . . work": Howard Klein, January 30, 1966.

Reached the production stage: *New York Times,* October 10, 1968.

"Don't talk to me . . .": Manchester *Guardian,* December 4, 1966.

Died of his injuries: on January 22, 1964.

305 "The artist must forever . . .": *Our Age,* p. 54.

". . . he was not serious . . .": interview with author.

". . . it wasn't honest": St. Paul *Pioneer Press,* November 5, 1978.

306 ". . . the proverbial blonde . . .": *Time,* February 4, 1957.

". . . it was old-fashioned . . .": interview with author.

The first time in thirty years: February 6 and 7, 1948.

307 "One could only wonder . . .": *Jewish Advocate,* February 12, 1948.

"a masterpiece . . .": Boston *Globe,* February 12, 1948.

". . . mad at Lenny . . .": *Selected Letters of Virgil Thomson,* Tim Page and Vanessa Weeks Page, p. 291 (on December 8, 1955).

". . . years of devotion . . .": *Cue,* January 1, 1966.

". . . one of the towering moments . . .": London *Times,* December 17, 1965.

308 "the honor of having . . .": *New York Times,* January 7, 1968.

". . . would have liked to be . . .": interview with author.

". . . the Faustian philosopher . . .": *High Fidelity,* September 1967.

"farewells to music . . .": UA, p. 317.

"in one piece": MC, p. 259.

"fiery play of fancy . . .": *Death in Venice,* Thomas Mann, p. 7.

309 ". . . the very act of dying . . .": UA, p. 321.

THE RIGHT TO FAIL

310 "Dazed with billowy fire": "An Schwager Kronos," translated by A. H. Fox Strangways and Steuart Wilson.

More concerts than anyone to date: March 11, 1966. He would perform his one thousandth concert in December 1971.

"I shall always . . .": *New York Times,* November 13, 1966.

311 ". . . a sustained line . . .": *New York Times,* November 13, 1966.

Attained the honorific: *New York Times,* May 22, 1966.

311   "... being able to fail": *New York Times,* November 27, 1966.
        "... the problem of mortality ...": Jamaica *Daily Gleaner,* January 8, 1972.

312   No ideas: *New York Times,* November 27, 1966.
        "... *nicht so Deutsch* ...": Anatole Shub, *New York Times,* March 10, 1966.
        A house in London: *New York Times,* November 25, 1966.
        "... ridden by a demon ...": New York *Herald Tribune,* June 13, 1967.
        His own red roses: *New York Times,* June 12, 1967.

314   "Detail emerged ...": April 28, 1966.
        "... That's my city ...": Providence (Rhode Island) *Bulletin,* June 6, 1966.
        "... the greatest musician ...": *New York Times,* November 29, 1971.
        "... plant a smacker ...": April 9, 1966.
        Performing-flea routine: London *Evening Standard,* August 31, 1968.
        "I've long ago ...": Providence (Rhode Island) *Bulletin,* June 6, 1966.

315   Contradictory statements: *New York Times,* December 19, 1971.
        "... more shocked than sad": interview with author.
        "I was bowled over ...": interview with author.
        "... bringer-downers ...": PW, pp. 93–94.

317   "Of course she criticized ...": interview with author.
        "... wasn't housebroken ...": interview with author.
        "... blue movies ...": interview with author.
        "... stupid and cruel ...": interview with author.

318   "... nervous and tense ...": interview; also article, *Time,* May 5, 1958.
        "... she was the friend ...": interview with author.
        Blamed herself: Baltimore *News-American,* February 23, 1968.
        Close to a divorce: Newark *Star-Ledger,* April 29, 1960.

319   "... I can accept ...": Antonio de Almeida, interview with author.
        A definite advantage: Marcia Kraus, letter to author, July 1, 1991.
        "A close friend ...": interview with author.
        "The first intimation ...": interview with author.
        A photographer recalled: interview with author.
        "I've had terrible depressions ...": M, p. 9.
        Treated for a perversion: Dr. Bluma Swerdloff, interview with author.
        Shortcomings of psychiatrists: M, p. 9.

320   "Half man, half woman": interview with author.
        "... this terrible destruction ...": Baltimore *News-American,* February 23, 1968.
        "... I feel so badly ...": Yuri Krasnopolsky, interview with author.
        "... who rolls condoms ...": Steve Rosenfeld, interview with author.

321   "The only time ...": interview with author.

322   "I dig absolutely": *New York Times,* January 15, 1970.

323   "... elegant slumming ...": *New York Times,* January 16, 1970.
        "... marked his life ...": interview with author.
        "... soul of democracy": *Ma'ariv,* March 27, 1970.
        "... shameful FBI episode ...": *New York Times,* October 22, 1980.

324   Requests not honored: as of March 1994.
        "I'm perfectly aware ...": filmed interview with Paul Hume, 1980.

"... as good as finished": FM, p. 196.

Death of Samuel Bernstein: April 30, 1969; FM, p. 197.

Properly covered: Mrs. Israel Kazis, interview with author.

The generational ironies: FM, p. 199.

Should have been a rabbi: on a 1981 television program about Beethoven.

"... sharing of a feeling ...": *New York Times,* June 11, 1972.

"... he wanted to be ...": Phillip Ramey, interview with author.

At some pains: Rabbi Israel Kazis, interview with author.

325   "... felt that tie ...": interview with author.

326   "blessed overwork": *New York Times,* January 25, 1970.

       "... should have married": interview with author.

       "... began to play it": interview with author.

       "... could have taken ...": interview with author.

QUESTIONS WITHOUT ANSWERS

327   "Lost in utter ...": "An Schwager Kronos," translated by A. H. Fox Strang-ways and Steuart Wilson.

328   "... rather amusing ...": interview with author.

       "... compelling and sympathetic ...": MC, pp. 266–67.

       "... emotional and artistic": interview with author.

       A last-minute ending: Norman Scribner, interview with author.

       "It was common knowledge ...": Wayne Dirksen, interview with author.

       Much too long: MC, p. 268.

329   "Everything goes back ...": ditto, p. 269.

       Hugged and kissed: *Newsweek,* September 20, 1971.

       "the handful of men ...": Washington *Post,* May 31, 1972.

       "a blatant sacrilege ...": *New Yorker,* June 10, 1972.

       "the greatest music ...": Washington *Post,* September 9, 1971.

       "... attitudinizing drivel": *New York,* July 17, 1972.

       "... He made me sit ...": interview with author.

       "simplistic, pretentious ...": *New York,* July 17, 1972.

330   "subliterate rubbish": *New York Times,* July 9, 1972.

       "... We are unmoved ...": ditto.

       "... Love Love Love ...": ditto.

331   "The sinner does not ...": *Brand,* Henrik Ibsen, pp. 36–37.

       "... a Jewish guru ...": *New York Times,* December 19, 1971.

       Her gesture "paid off": interview with author.

332   His personal assistant: Maurice Peress, interview with author.

       "disgust and distress ...": Dublin *Evening Press,* July 10, 1973.

       "... dropped to their knees ...": interview with author.

       "... stripped to the waist ...": interview with author.

       A social register: London *Sunday Times,* July 1, 1973.

       The identical hour: Washington *Post,* January 20, 1973.

333   Intended to retire: Glasgow *Herald,* August 28, 1973.

       "... No one will remember ...": *New York Times,* December 19, 1971.

333   "... half-real, half-remembered ...": ditto.

"You're *me* ...": *New York Times,* October 24, 1971.

334   A question mark: Washington *Star,* August 20, 1973.

"... silly, twitty ...": interview with author.

"cute, earnest, and devoted ...": letter to author, January 9, 1992.

" 'Beauty is truth ...' ": "Ode on a Grecian Urn," stanza 4.

Stravinsky had converted: INF, p. 419; "... a mathematical takeover": ditto, p. 420.

335   "... each day mediocrity ...": ditto, p. 53.

An artificial language: UA, p. 283; basically tonal: ditto, p. 291; "... a human endowment ...": ditto, p. 8; "seek analogies ...": ditto, p. 53.

336   "our deepest affective responses ...": ditto, p. 424.

"It's bigger than any of us": Kenneth Clark, interview with author.

337   "... a shrink's office": Washington *Post,* October 3, 1976.

"He had no sense ...": interview with author.

"I've been waiting ...": Paul Sperry, interview with author.

338   "What is it like ... ?": Bridgeport *Post,* June 1, 1975.

339   Refused to believe: the late Mrs. Irma Lazarus to author.

A minor role: the play opened on October 17, 1976.

340   "... the deep hurts ...": interview with author.

"may ... crush him ...": *Neurosis and Human Growth,* Karen Horney, pp. 194–95; "... a tragic quality ...": ditto, p. 196.

"... That is all ...": interview with author.

341   "... impossibly demanding ...": interview with author.

"He'd have this fling ...": interview with author.

His arm resting: New York *Daily News,* March 16, 1977.

"I think he tried ...": interview with author.

342   In July of that year: *Leonard Bernstein, Notes from a Friend,* Schuyler Chapin, p. 164.

"After a party ...": interview with author.

"One time in Rome ...": interview with author.

"... sitting there unrecognizable ...": interview with author.

"... amorous physical contact ...": interview with author.

343   "... making no sense ...": interview with author.

"... You don't know ...": interview with author.

"... I was finished": M, pp. 6–7.

344   "... too many memories ...": interview with author.

"... idea of survival": *Trackings,* Richard Dufallo, p. 248.

346   "... feeling rock bottom": M, p. 6.

"... asleep in despair ...": interview with author.

HAYWIRE

347   "Hurl me forth ...": "An Schwager Kronos," translated by A. H. Fox Strangways and Steuart Wilson.

"... did not go near ...": interview with author.

"... his public self ...": interview with author.

"... threw his arms around ...": interview with author.

348   "... I can't believe ...": interview with author.

"... thought he was hallucinating ...": interview with author.

Making sure the beds: interview with author.

Mood instantly changed: interview with author.

349   "... eating me up in there ...": M, p. 8.

Mood swings of the creative: *New York Times,* October 12, 1993.

350   Problems of heavy smokers: *Good Health* magazine, *New York Times,* October 4, 1992.

"No one can feel ...": interview with author.

"... descent into hell ..."; "... wants to die": interview with author.

Well after midnight: James Reston, *New York Times,* February 18, 1979.

351   " 'Jews Burn Down ...' ": interview with author.

"... tried to take ...": *New York Times,* September 17, 1975.

"Bernstein slapped ...": Washington *Post,* January 21, 1976.

"... important-itis": interview with author.

"... more money, more everything ...": interview with author.

"so high-powered ...": interview with author.

352   "... believed him": Washington *Star,* October 16, 1977.

"... until we had a book ...": interview with author.

"... in some ways bitter": Philadelphia *Inquirer,* February 22, 1976.

353   "... simple-minded cynicism": Washington *Post,* February 28, 1976.

Result was bombast: Philadelphia *Sunday Bulletin,* March 7, 1976.

"... They could not believe ...": interview with author.

Looked up and said blearily: Peter Mark Schifter, interview with author.

354   "... too much time ...": interview with author.

"... a crummy idea": *Newsweek,* May 17, 1976.

"an epic disaster": May 17, 1976.

"I never saw ...": Boston *Globe,* July 12, 1981.

"... now I've decided ...": Washington *Star,* October 16, 1977.

"... this terrible sense ...": Washington *Post,* January 7, 1976.

"... an original idea ...": Boston *Globe,* July 12, 1981.

355   "... out in the rain ...": interview with author.

"... gently and subtly ...": Boston *Globe,* July 12, 1981.

Its first performance: on May 27, 1981.

"very serious, one-act ...": Boston *Globe,* July 12, 1981.

"I am coming back ...": interview with author.

356   His own private plane: *New York Times,* December 24, 1979.

"the ... Bernstein capital": *International Herald Tribune,* March 6, 1981.

"bobbing and weaving ...": *New York,* November 19, 1979.

"gut-thumping ...": San Diego *Tribune,* October 30, 1979.

all "his expected ...": *New York Times,* October 31, 1979.

357   "... that primal state ...": interview with author.

"... this ... transfiguring experience ...": interview with author.

358   "... not considered serious": interview with author.

358   ". . . a fucking Pulitzer . . .": Naomi Graffman, interview with author.

359   ". . . I zeroed in . . .": interview with author.

       ". . . incoherent and rambling . . .": interview with author.

       ". . . Rubbish! Rubbish! . . .": Baltimore *Sun,* November 29, 1980.

360   ". . . put down his baton . . .": interview with author.

       ". . . you think . . . 'Poor Lenny' ": interview with author.

361   Made him look older: Washington *Post,* October 3, 1976.

362   ". . . 'Why does he behave . . .' ": MT, pp. 49–50.

       "actually dropped my hand": interview with author.

       ". . . The spark was gone": interview with author.

       A bottle of Scotch: interview with author.

       ". . . coming back from the edge": interview with author.

       "taking a pee": interview with author.

363   "You can't set forth . . .": *Nantucket Diary,* Ned Rorem, pp. 177–78.

       "hugging orgies": Washington *Post,* January 21, 1976.

       ". . . he was crude": interview with author.

364   ". . . 'You're a good kid' . . .": interview with author.

AMBERSON

365   "Now let clamour of horn . . .": "An Schwager Kronos," translated by A. H.
       Fox Strangways and Steuart Wilson.

366   ". . . they had no idea . . .": interview with author.

       Rehearsing for a performance: July 21, 1974.

       ". . . a personal affront . . .": interview with author.

       ". . . a terrible temper tantrum . . .": interview with author.

367   ". . . began to practice . . .": interview with author.

       Winter appearances canceled: for December 3, 4 and 5, 1981.

       "Nobody was at fault . . .": interview with author.

       The chef was furious: Edward Birdwell to author.

       Fired or left: interview with author.

       A new company: *New York Times,* November 15, 1963.

       Not to use his name: *New York Times,* February 16, 1964.

       "I don't think they . . .": interview with author.

368   There was nothing left: Leonard Bernstein to Bruno Zirato, September 1,
       1950, New York Philharmonic Archives.

       Could not legally: Walter Gould, interview with author.

       His strong objections: noted in one of the Leonard Bernstein scrapbooks at
       the Library of Congress.

       Other contracts would follow: This relationship is described in Schuyler
       Chapin's memoir *Musical Chairs: A Life in the Arts,* published in 1977, and
       in his largely repetitive memoir *Leonard Bernstein: Notes from a Friend,* pub-
       lished in 1992.

369   Using St. Paul's: in 1970.

       Music a commodity: MC, p. 36.

       ". . . obsessed with keeping . . .": interview with author.

       Too much invested: interview with author.

"... sudden enthusiasms ...": interview with author.

370 "... voraciously recorded ...": *Reporter,* February 22, 1967.

"Operas cost ...": interview with author.

Demand was brisk: Peter G. Davis, *New York Times,* January 13, 1980.

371 "Penny wise and pound foolish ...": interview with author.

"... we have got to save ...": interview with author.

372 The word "*maîtresse*": interview with author.

"... very fragile and reticent ...": interview with author.

He was applying: interview with author.

Extremely adroit: interview with author.

373 "He has to say ...": interview with author.

"... coffers well lined": interview with author.

A personal set of keys: interview with author.

One of the trustees: on December 23, 1976.

Signing the will: *Leonard Bernstein: Notes from a Friend,* pp. 13, 165.

"Harry is very ...": interview with author.

374 "dumpster loads of shit": interview with author.

"The maestro's task ...": *The Maestro Myth,* Norman Lebrecht, p. 318.

Around $20,000: interview with Henry Fogel, manager of the Chicago Symphony Orchestra.

$80,000 a night: *The Maestro Myth,* p. 320.

Could expect to make $2 million: ditto, p. 319.

Became executive vice-president: on January 24, 1972.

Had probably doubled: Jack Kirkman to author.

A check arrived: Tim Page, interview with author.

"... he wanted us to beg ...": interview with author.

375 "... no mention of a fee": interview with author.

His days were numbered; "... I know what it's like": interview with author.

"... the offer was fair ...": interview with author.

376 Signed a contract: on August 9, 1975.

All copyrights reverted: based on interviews with Leonard Burkat, James Mosher, W. Stuart Pope and others.

Very "hush-hush": Boston *Herald,* May 30, 1983.

"... nothing so dumb ...": Lawrence *Eagle-Tribune,* August 26, 1983.

"... straw figures ...": interview with author.

377 "... putting out an image ...": *New York,* August 30, 1993.

"This operation is ...": interview with author.

"cutting his life ...": *Life,* February 21, 1969.

"... exploit and monopolize ...": *Berlioz and the Romantic Century,* Jacques Barzun, vol. 1, p. 538.

Could not believe: interview with author.

378 "... started to cry": interview with author.

TADZIO

379 "So the landlord ...": "An Schwager Kronos," translated by Richard Capell.

"... what was so beautiful ...": *Life,* February 21, 1969.

379   "... spirit and mind": *Death in Venice,* Thomas Mann, p. 15.
380   "... ultimate mysterious fulfillment": *Neurosis and Human Growth,* Karen
Horney, p. 24; "a demoniacal obsession ...": ditto, p. 31.
No one had given him: interview with author.
Falling out of the sky: *Life,* February 21, 1969.
"ranged over his whole domain ...": *Berlioz and the Romantic Century,* Jacques
Barzun, vol. 1, p. 5.
381   "... a continuity existed ...": ditto, p. 396.
Romanticism's dark side: *The Romantic Rebellion,* p. 177.
"... performance cannot compare ...": *Berlioz and the Romantic Century,* vol.
1, p. 8.
Stabbed his hand: Washington *Post,* November 30, 1981.
Suffering from exhaustion: Washington *Post,* June 28, 1982.
Landed unhurt: on May 11, 1982.
382   "We were driving ...": interview with author.
"... managed to write eight bars": interview with author.
"... paid for everything ...": interview with author.
383   Tried lithium for depression: Alison Ames to author.
Halcion's side effects: *New York Times,* January 26, 1992.
Bernstein was horrified: interview with author.
Four or fourteen: interview with author.
"... wasn't good-natured ...": interview with author.
384   Horrified his father: MC, p. 22.
A meteoric career: filmed interview with Vivian Perlis, 1980, Kennedy Center collection.
Inappropriate and insensitive: Judy Gordon Gassner to author.
"Our family is like ...": *Life,* September 1988.
385   "... a great hug ...": London *Daily Telegraph,* September 25, 1993.
A sexual reference: interview with author.
John Lennon was murdered: on December 8, 1980.
Knocked down and bloodied: interview with author.
"... lend him five dollars": interview with author.
"... contrast was so marked": interview with author.
386   "... some brooding bird ...": letter to author, October 5, 1991.
"... guilt by association ...": interview with author.
387   "... fist fuck hotel": interview with author.
"... have the respect ...": interview with author.
388   "... clatter of dropped cutlery ...": interview with author.
"... the character of Jupien ...": interview with author.
"... a sulphurous atmosphere ...": Dr. Cormac Rigby, letter to author,
June 19, 1992, and diary, April 14, 1982.
389   "... a caricature": in December 1982.
Feeling was reciprocated: Dr. Cormac Rigby, op. cit.
"... 'So what? ...' ": interview with author.
"I never had a career ...": Washington *Post,* July 15, 1984.
"... let's have a drink": interview with author.

"... the fake sentiment ...": interview with author.

390 "... in this very house ...": interview with author.
"... hopping with drugs ...": interview with author.
"he spoke through you": interview with author.

391 "... on your knees ...": interview with author.
"... brazen and yelling ...": interview with author.
"... Victor Hugo was a madman ...": interview with author.

392 "... some kind of farewell ...": interview with author.

393 "... François also is redeemed ...": *New York Times,* June 18, 1983.
"... a trumpet solo ...": *Elia Kazan: A Life,* Elia Kazan, p. 352.
"a bona fide genius ...": interview with author.
"bisexual saint": *New York Times,* June 18, 1983.

394 "written in code": interview with author.
"a pretentious failure": *New York Times,* June 20, 1983.
"... made me really distraught ...": interview with author.
"... will come to praise my ... music ...": *New York Times,* July 15, 1984.

395 "This opera affected ...": interview with author.
"... frivolous and evanescent ...": Washington *Post,* January 6, 1992.

396 "... like having Mozart ..."; "... emotional screaming matches ...": *New York Times,* May 17, 1985.
Commercial considerations: interview with author.

397 "... Don't utter it ...": *Life,* September 1988.
Went on interminably: *New York Times,* February 18, 1989.
Filled in at the last minute: on February 29, 1988.
"... a little sweaty ...": interview with author.
"... I should be dead ...": *Life,* September 1988.
Attempting sit-ups: interview with author.
"... amazingly vital ...": interview with author.

TANGLEWOOD, 1990

398 "And there at his door ...": "An Schwager Kronos," translated by Richard Capell.

399 "... his last real night out ...": interview with author.
He was crushed: *New York Times,* August 31, 1986.
"... was not impressed": interview with author.

400 "... I could have listened ...": letter to author, June 26, 1992.
"I'm all wrapped up ...": *USA Today,* August 23, 1988.
"... a sponge ... on his head ...": John Wells, letter to author, June 26, 1992.
"... his casting was ... erratic ...": interview with author.

401 "a ghost with shoes": interview with author.
"... not particularly forgiving ...": interview with author.
Dubbed their parts later: *Connoisseur,* September 1991.
"... never thought of refusing ...": interview with author.
"... how his face lit up": *New York Times,* October 16, 1990.

401   Discovery of mesothelioma: interview with author.

402   "People who formerly jeered . . .": *New York Times,* August 21, 1988.

        ". . . a . . . rhythmic alacrity . . .": *New York Times,* August 31, 1986.

        "smart esthetic definitions": *New York Times,* August 21, 1988.

        "this reach, this leap . . .": F, p. 211; ". . . the mystical line . . .": ditto, p. 274.

403   ". . . might have fallen . . .": *New York Times,* August 31, 1986.

        The American Offenbach: *The Virtuosi,* Harold C. Schonberg, p. 463.

        ". . . Looking back over . . .": *New York Times,* October 24, 1982.

        ". . . syncopated swagger": *New York Times,* August 31, 1986.

        ". . . I don't belong . . .": Boston *Sunday Globe,* February 2, 1964.

404   Fatuous and bombastic: *Harper's,* May 1983.

        ". . . like a prophet": *New York Times,* August 31, 1986.

        ". . . harbinger of the postmodern": *Atlantic,* June 1993, p. 65.

        Radiation treatments: interview with author.

        "the Gorilla Concert": Naomi Graffman to author.

405   Defended that decision: *New York Times,* December 26, 1991.

        Having trouble breathing: interview with author.

406   An abbreviated tour: from news releases.

        ". . . a breath of my youth": F, p. 238.

        ". . . already exhausted . . .": interview with author.

        ". . . 'upright and grand' ": *Berkshire,* June–July 1991.

        Claimed to have stopped smoking: *Connoisseur,* September 1991.

        ". . . a pathetic attempt . . .": interview with author.

407   ". . . 'This is never . . .' ": interview with author.

        Ghost at Highwood: Marcia Duncan, interview with author.

        ". . . unbelievable clarity . . .": interview with author.

        ". . . the last time . . .": interview with author.

        ". . . would fight on": interview with author.

408   ". . . an extraordinary moment . . .": interview with author.

        ". . . 'how music goes' ": *Forward,* New York, August 31, 1990.

        ". . . self-indulgent . . .": *New York Times,* August 20, 1990.

409   ". . . not for musical reasons": interview with author.

        ". . . gasping for breath . . .": interview with author.

        ". . . kissed him and left . . .": interview with author.

        ". . . we were overjoyed . . .": interview with author.

        Had lost a lung: *Connoisseur,* September 1991.

410   ". . . luck has run out": interview with author.

        Nothing on paper: interview with author.

        ". . . what am I to do?": interview with Norman Scribner.

        He was retiring: *New York Times,* October 10, 1990.

        ". . . 'He doesn't have AIDS' . . .": letter to author, September 12, 1991.

        ". . . a death announcement . . .": interview with author.

        "I literally tried . . .": interview with author.

411   ". . . 'All of a sudden . . .' ": *People,* October 29, 1990.

        Presentiment of his death: Alison Ames, interview with author.

        A dream about Bernstein: interview with author.

". . . a stack of messages . . .": interview with author.

". . . like being stabbed . . .": interview with author.

412   "No one has done more . . .": London *Times,* October 16, 1990.

". . . the example he set . . .": *Newsday,* October 15, 1990.

". . . still the urge to speak . . .": *Mistress to an Age,* J. Christopher Herold, p. 470.

"appareled in celestial light": *A History of God,* Karen Armstrong, p. 336.

Index

Numerals in *italics* indicate illustrations.

Abbott, George, 133, 135, *194,* 196
Academy Awards, 200, 220
Adler, Ellen, 167, 249, 317, 411
Adrian, Max, 205, 207
Agee, James, 204
agents, music, 107–12, 224–7, 255–9, 367–78
AIDS, 399, 410
Aiken, Conrad, 342
Albéniz, Isaac, *Seguidilla,* 42
Alexander, Cris, *134*
Alexander II, Tsar of Russia, 7
Alexander III, Tsar of Russia, 7
Almeida, Antonio de, 96, 147, 226, 343
Alpert, Dorothy, 29–30, *32*
Alpert, Victor, 28, 29, 33, 347
Altman, Leonard, 21–2, 30, 52, 125, 347
Amberson Enterprises, 256, 348, 367–8, 396, 400
American Ballet Theatre, 300

American music, 52, 76, 77, 109, 128, 211, 240–1, 256, 413; business, 107–12, 224–7, 255–9, 367–71; folk songs, 52, 83, 248; inferiority complex with Europe, 109, 223, 359; musical theater, 128, 183, 211–21; 1930s social agendum for, 52–3; opera, 183; *see also specific composers, periods, and works*
Ames, Alison, 275, 401, 411
Anderson, June, 400–1
Anderson, Maxwell, *Winterset,* 143
Annan, Noel, 52, 298, 305
Anouilh, Jean, *The Lark,* 201, 205
Ansermet, Ernest, 223
anti-Semitism, 96, 144, 405
Aristophanes: *The Birds,* 55, 59, 84; *Peace,* 84
Arrau, Betty, 150, 161
Arrau, Claudio, 148–59, 161
Arthur, Jean, 183
Athens, 263

Athens Symphony, 49
Atkinson, Brooks, 197, 220
atonal music, 286–7, 335–7
Auden, W. H., 73, 173, *174,* 331; and
    Bernstein, 173–6
Auer, Leopold, 68
Auric, Georges, 128
Austin, A. Everett, Jr., 102
Australia, 299–300
Austria, 7, 163
Avery Fisher Hall, New York, 270
"Avol Presents" (radio program), 30
Ax, Emanuel, 259

Baalbek Festival, Lebanon, 263
Bacall, Lauren, 338, 358, 383, 397
Bach, Johann Sebastian, 39, 41, 75,
    110, 111, 146, 248, 332; *Brandenburg*
    Concerti, 240; Double Concerto, 78;
    Prelude and Fugue in F Minor, 42
Bachmann, Bettina, 145, 146
Baez, Joan, 276
Baldwin, Roger, 302
Baldwin pianos, 257
Bales, Richard, 74, 77, *86,* 107
Ballet Theatre, 114, 127–9, 300; *Fac-*
    simile production, 156–7; *Fancy Free*
    premiere, 128–9
Barak, Ann, 280
Barber, Samuel, 68, 76, 131
Barber, Stephanie and Philip, 276
Barbirolli, John, 223, 227, 301
Barlow, Howard, 125
Barrett, Michael, 389, 408
Barrie, J. M., *Peter Pan,* 183
Barrymore, Ethel, 157
Bartók, Béla, 94, 241; Music for
    Strings, Percussion and Celesta, 169
Barzin, Leon, 225–6
Battles, John, *134*
BBC Symphony Orchestra, Bernstein's
    performances with, 388–9
Beaverbrook, Lord, 123
Beecham, Thomas, 146, 223, 277, 278
Beethoven, Ludwig van, 16, 17, 24, 40,
    60, 67, 75, 76, 123, 130, 150, 169,

170, 173, 231, 232, 285, 346,
    356–7; *Egmont* Overture, 130; *Fidelio,*
    258, 325, 357, 363, 369, 370; Fifth
    Symphony, 230, 234, 281, 297;
    Leonore Overture, 332, 357; Missa
    Solemnis, 85, 86, 271; Ninth Sym-
    phony, 356, 358, 401, 405; Op. 131
    in C-sharp Minor, 49, 93; *Pastoral*
    Symphony, 247, 385; Piano Concerto
    No. 1, 34, 84; Piano Concerto No. 2,
    169; Piano Concerto No. 4, 187;
    Seventh Symphony, 282, 408, 409;
    Sonata in D Minor, 42; *Waldstein*
    Sonata, 26, 42
Belafonte, Harry, 237
Belgium, 163, 223, 225, 245
Bentley, Eric, 330
Berg, Alban, 170, 241, 286; *Lulu,* 378
Berghof, Herbert, 150
Berkshire *Eagle,* 176, 264, 337, 409
Berkshire Music Center, 75–83; *see also*
    Tanglewood
Berlin, 75, 401
Berlin Philharmonic, 264, 356, 369, 401
Berlioz, Hector, 232, 380–1; *Roman*
    Carnival Overture, 408; *Symphonie*
    fantastique, 278
Berns, Walter, 174–5
Bernstein, Alexander Serge, 235, *236,*
    316, 318, 325, *339,* 344, 360, 373,
    384–5, 397, 410–11
Bernstein, Bezalel, 6
Bernstein, Burton, 6, 9, 11, 12, *18,* 25,
    90, 114, 173, 186, 237, 290
Bernstein, Felicia, *see* Montealegre, Felicia
Bernstein, Jamie, 188, 190, 194, 203,
    235, *236,* 247, 316, *339,* 343–4,
    358, 373, 384–5, 392
Bernstein, Jennie Resnick, 8–9, *10,* 11,
    13, 52, 84, 87, *88,* 114, 182, 266,
    291, *291;* marriage to Sam Bernstein,
    8–11, 185, 291; relationship with
    son Leonard, 22–3, 50, 87, 185
Bernstein, Leonard, *10, 13, 23, 27, 31,*
    62, 64, 70, 71, 86, 89, 91, 92, 100,
    106, 110, 116, 134, 149, 155, 158,

159, 165, 192, 194, 195, 200, 214, 233, 236, 240, 246, 251, 253, 254, 265, 266, 267, 273, 274, 275, 283, 291, 297, 313, 321, 331, 339, 342, 344, 345, 349, 360, 390, 391, 405, 412; aging of, 292, 293, 346, 359–64, 380–92, 397–411; and Amberson Enterprises, 256, 367–78, 396, 400; asthma and allergies of, 13, 21, 48, 63, 97, 125, 165, 298–9; on atonal music, 286–7, 334–6; and W. H. Auden, 173–6; on avant-garde art, 286–7, 305–6; awards and honorary degrees of, 273, *274*, 358–60, 370; beginnings in conducting, 48–9, 59–69, 77–97, 115–20; birth of, 9; and Marc Blitzstein, 53–6, 101, 125, 304–5, 389; cancer of, 401–2, 404–11; childhood of, 3–5, 9–36; and Comden and Green, 132–6, *194–5, 196–7*, 288, 304, 383; commercialism of, 128–9, 142–3, 153, 198, 211, 354, 369–79; conducting mistakes, 146, 381; conducting style and views, 79, 94, 119, 141–3, 146, 190, 233, 241, 250, 264, 277–87, 311, 355, 357, 381, 402–3, 409; and Aaron Copland, 43–6, 59, 60, *62*, 63, 80, 87, *92, 96, 100*, 101–2, 128–31, 170, 180, 183, 273, 307, 350, 360, 362, 366, 378, 385, *390*, 403, 406; courtship of Felicia Montealegre, 150–2, 157–61; critics of, 142–3, 153, 156, 170, 172, 183, 197–8, 220, 281, 285–90, 306, 311, 316, 329–32, 336, 354, 394–5, 402–3; as cultural hero, 109, 242–3, 274–8, 413; at Curtis Institute, 60–72, 83–5; death of, 411–13; death of his wife, 342–50, 352, 365, 398; depressions of, in later life, 347–50, 359–64, 380–92; and David Diamond, 154, 192, 203, 221, 261–2, 288–9, 350, 390; dissatisfaction with his own compositions, 198, 288, 302, 304–6, 403; drinking, smoking, and pill-taking of, 114, 124, 170, 299, 343, 350, 355, 359–64, 378, 383, 387–90, 397, 406; early pianistic technique, 17, 21–2; early professional appearances, 28–37, 42–3, 72, 83–4, 93; education, 14–25, 38–56, 60–72, 74–98; engagement to Felicia Montealegre, 161, *165*, 166, 177–9; in Europe, 153, 156, 163–5, 259–69, 299–300, 312–14, 332, 356, 388–9, 400–1; fame of, 73, 121–5, 136–8, 143, 221, 251–2, 262, 272–6, 296–8, 312–13, 377, 413; as a father, 188, 193–4, 203, 235, *236, 247*, 316–18, 384–5, 397; first piano of, 15; and George Gershwin, 46–7, 162, 366–7; at Harvard, 24, 28–9, 34, 38–57, 69, 238, 334–7, 351, 358; and Lillian Hellman, 201–11, 275; Hollywood connections, 156–60, 162, 199–221, 325; homosexuality of, 36, 51–5, 72, 95–6, 111, 145–52, 160–1, 167–8, 179–80, 193–4, 256–7, 296, 315, 319–20, 337, 339–41, 362, 363, 384–92, 398–9; hypochondria of, 124–5; and instrumentalists, 278–84, 328, 356–7, 388; Jewish heritage of, 4–12, 96, 105–7, 123, 131–2, 144, 160, 163–9, 182, 288–92, 308, 324–5, 332, 350–1, 404–5, 408; and Arthur Judson, 94, 107–12, 117, 120, 125, 130, 144–5, 229, 239, 367–8; and Herbert von Karajan, 369; and the Kennedys, 271–2, 289, 303, 320, 327–9, 351; and Serge Koussevitsky, 74–98, 103, 105, 110–11, 120, 126–8, 131–2, 139, 143–4, 153–4, 160–2, 171, 178–82, 188, 234, 235, 250, 262, 276, 402, 407, 408; and Harry Kraut, 371–7, 398; in Latin America (1958), 259–62; and Alan Jay Lerner, 238, 351–4; and Gustav Mahler, 306–9, 379–80; marital troubles of, 318–20, 339–42; mar-

Bernstein, Leonard (*cont.*)

riage to Felicia Montealegre, 179–83, 186–93, 203, 235–8, 243–4, 250, 264, 293–8, 316–20, 338–50; method of writing music, 136, 170, 172–3, 204, 212–13, 220, 235, 302–5, 330–1, 382; and Dmitri Mitropoulos, 49–52, 59–60, 67, 72, 83, 94, 125, 137, 147, 222–3, *233*, 234, 259–62; musical education, 3, 14–24, 38–56, 60–72, 74–98; musical influences on, 36–7, 43–7, 73, 176, 208, 306–9, 330; and the music business, 251–9, 367–78; New York apartments of, 190–1, 294, 338, 373, 385, 390; New York City Symphony conductorship, 141–5; New York Philharmonic guest conductorship, 115–26, 131, 137, 175, 355–6; New York Philharmonic principal conductorship and musical directorship, 222–4, 234–40, *240, 242,* 244–51, *251, 253,* 259–87, 299, 310–12, 325, 349, 369, 410; in New York as a young man, 59, 97–121; as Norton Professor of Poetry, 325, 334–7; personality of, 41–2, 80–1, 85–7, 104, 122–5, 143, 167, 170, 180, 238, 264, 273–8, 311, 315–20, 340, 380–1, 413; philanthropic activities, 131–2, 154, 252; physical appearance, 45, 73, 80, 85–6, 113, 188, 191, 232, 238, 243, 272–4, 293, 299, 314, 319, 320, 338, 346, 359, 360, 369, 385–8; politics of, 52–3, 70, 97, 128–32, 171–2, 198, 201–2, 320–4; press on, 42, 46, 57, 78, 84, 103, 106, 121–31, 136–7, 142–3, 153, 156, 163–4, 170, 175–6, 183–7, 193, 197–8, 200, 205, 209–10, 220, 232–5, 239–41, 250–1, 274, 285–90, 311, 314–16, 322–3, 329–31, 354–7, 389, 394, 402–3, 408–9, 413; procrastination of, 282–3, 302–3, 366; in psychoanalysis, 319–20; public facade of, 122–5,

143, 314–15, 347; relationship with his father, 12, 16–17, 20–6, 30, 41, 45, 57–9, 83, 87, 97, 106–7, 115–20, 163, 167, 168, 180, 185–6, 290–2, 324–5; relationship with his mother, 22–3, 50, 87, 185; relationship with his sister Shirley, 24, 90, 105, 126, 131, 140, 163, 177, 179, 182–3, 360, 385; retirement from New York Philharmonic, 311–12, 318, 333, 355–6, 369, 370, 377; and Jerome Robbins, 127–9, 143, 156, 172, 175, 204, 211–21, 234, 325, 363, 399, 413; and Artur Rodzinski, 109–19, 125–30; role as mentor, 300–2, 334, 413; in Russia (1959), 264, *265, 266–7, 267,* 268–9; sabbaticals, 303–11, 348, 354–5; seventieth birthday celebrations, 397; sight-reading ability of, 69, 80, 84; and Steven Sondheim, 213–21, 329, 350; and Stephen Spender, 173–5; and Kiki Speyer, 85–97, 111, 114–15, 160, 166–7, 170, 178–9, 326, 411; at Tanglewood, 74–83, 85, 89, *93,* 94–7, 110, *110,* 143, 153–4, *155,* 156, 166, 175–90, 276, 300, 319, 325, *345,* 346, 365–7, 390, 397, 402, 406–9; wealth of, 136, 173, 251–6, 273, 373, 374; in the White House, 271–2, 350–1, 363; and women, 25–6, 33–6, 52, 80, 85–90, 95–7, 104, 111, 145, 148–62, 165–8, 179–80, 326, 360; and World War II, 96–7; *see also* Bernstein, Leonard, works of

Bernstein, Leonard, works of: *Age of Anxiety* Symphony, 172–6, 234–5, 268, 289; *Alarms and Flourishes,* 354–5; *Arias and Barcarolles,* 408–9; Aristophanes' *The Birds,* 55, 59, 84; Aristophanes' *Peace,* 84; ballet compositions, 127–9, 156, 172–6, 234; BBC Symphony performances, 388–9; Beethoven's *Fidelio,* 258, 325, 357, 363, 369, 370; Beethoven's symphonies, 230, 234, 247, 281,

297, 356–8, 401–9; Berlin Philharmonic performances, 356, 401; Blitzstein's *The Cradle Will Rock,* 53–7, 84; *La Bonne Cuisine,* 172; Boston Pops performances, 93–4, 130; Boston Symphony performances, 102–3, 110, 126–7, 130, 143–4, 153, 162, 166, 169, 175, 187, 235, 306, 355, 365–7, 371, 408–9; Brandeis University performances, 187–8; Britten's *Peter Grimes,* 153–6, 408; *Candide* score, 12, 201–6, 207, 208–11, 215, 219, 255, 263, 280, 400–1, 403; Carnegie Hall performances, 107–25, 132, 162, 175, 237–8, 240, 241, 244, 270; Cherubini's *Medea,* 191–3; Chicago Symphony performances, 130–1; *Chichester Psalms,* 303–4, 332; Columbia recordings, 234–5, 331, 369–71; Concerts Symphoniques performances, 131; copyright ownership, 255–7, 376; Czech Symphony performances, 153, 163, 371; Deutsche Grammophon recordings, 371, 396; European tours, 153, 156, 163–5, 259–69, 299–300, 312–14, 332–3, 356, 388–9, 400–1; *Facsimile,* 156–7, 160, 185; *Fancy Free,* 127–9, 133, 141, 153, 156, 183, 234, 255, 369, 376, 403; in films, 156–60, 162, 199–221, 325, 369, 396; first compositions, 29, 34; foreign sheet-music sales, 255–6; *Halil,* 355; "Highlights from *West Side Story,*" 255; Hollywood Bowl performances, 131–2; *I Hate Music,* 34, 111, 114, 332; Institute of Modern Art performances, 101; Israel Philharmonic performances, 168, 169, 178, 243–4, 325, 356, 381, 410; *Jeremiah* Symphony, 59, 85, 105–7, 114, 126–7, 131, 138, 141, 163, 289, 320, 332, 369; *The Joy of Music* (book), 274; *Kaddish* Symphony, 288–90, 346, 348; Kennedy Center commissions and performances, 327–33, 350,

357–8, 360, 363, 392–5, 410; *Lamentation,* 105; League of Composers performances, 101, 103; Lenox Library concerts, 110; Lincoln Center performances, 270–1, 284, 341; London Philharmonic performances, 153; London Symphony performances, 325, 333, 369, 371, 400, 410; "Lonely Men of Harvard," 238–9; Los Angeles Philharmonic performances, 367; Mahler symphonies, 175, 261, 289, 306–9, 326, 339, 369, 370, 389; "Maria," 221, 396; *Mass,* 110, 327–33, 356, 360, 393, 395; Metropolitan Opera performances, 303, 312, 325, 326, 370; musical theater scores, 128, 132–6, 183–7, 194–8, 201–21, 288, 304, 351–5, 403; *A Musical Toast,* 355; Music for the Dance, 43; Music for the Dance II, 34; Music for Two Pianos No. 1, 43, 103; as narrator and commentator, 102, 156, 188, 229–32, 244–9, 297, 334–8; NBC Symphony performances, 153; New York City Symphony performances, 141–3, 145, 148, 153, 156, 162, 166, 241, 306; New York Philharmonic performances, 115–26, 131, 137, 175, 222–4, 234–53, 259–87, 299, 310–12, 325, 349, 355–6, 369, 410; Norton Lectures, 325, 334–8; "Omnibus" series, 229–33, 234, 243, 251, 274; *On the Town,* 103, 132–3, 134–5, 136, 154, 156, 251, 255, 333, 376, 403; *On the Waterfront* score, 199–201, 203, 366, 403; in operatic form, 183–6, 204, 296, 302, 354, 392–5, 403; Palestine Symphony performances, 163–4; *Peter Pan* score, 183, 403; Piano Trio, 103; Pittsburgh Symphony performances, 126, 144, 173; poetry and short stories, 26, 33–6, 50–1, 168, 182; popular music, 46, 98, 128, 132–6, 156, 183–6, 194–200, 211–21, 288, 358, 395, 403–4; *A Pray by Blecht,*

Bernstein, Leonard, works of (*cont.*)
304; *Prelude, Fugue and Riffs,* 197; *A Quiet Place,* 296, 392–5; Ravel Concerto performances, 94, 130, 131, 163, 164, 171; record contracts, 132, 138, 234–5, 255, 331, 356, 368, 367, 369–71, 395–7; Residentie Orchestra performances (Holland), 164–5; *Rhapsody in Blue* recording, 367, 370; Rochester Philharmonic performances, 145–8, 153, 162, 166; Rorem's *Sunday Morning,* 359–60; La Scala performances, 191–3; Schuman's *American Festival Overture,* 93–4; "Selections from *West Side Story,*" 255; Serenade for Solo Violin, String Orchestra, Harp and Percussion, 203, 235, 286; *Seven Anniversaries,* 131, 369; "Sinfonia *Geremia,*" 156; *1600 Pennsylvania Avenue,* 351–4, 377, 395; *The Skin of Our Teeth* score, 288, 304, 326; Sonata for Clarinet and Piano, 103, 105, 114, 255, 360, 369; *Songfest,* 306, 341–2, 358, 388, 408, 411; "Songs from *West Side Story,*" 255; Stravinsky's *Petrouchka,* 190; Tchaikovsky's Fifth Symphony, 94; television peformances, 229–34, 239, 243, 244–51, 255, 258, 358, 369, 388, 396; *Trouble in Tahiti,* 183, *184, 185*–7, 211, 255, 355, 392, 397; Verdi Requiem, 369; Victor Red Seal recordings, 132, 138; Vienna Philharmonic performances, 163, 258, 264, 276, 312–14, 325, 356–7, *357,* 358, 404–5, 410; *West Side Story,* 156, 204, 211–13, *214,* 215–21, 234, 239, 243, 255, 269, 287, 288, 322, 358, 363, 370, 376, 384, 390, 394–7, 403; *West Side Story* recording, 395–7; *Wonderful Town,* 194–5, 196–8, 234, 255; Young People's Concerts, 244–5, *246,* 247–9
Bernstein, Nina, 290, 294, 316, *339,* 344, 373, 384–5, 397
Bernstein, Samuel Joseph, 4–9, *10,* 11, *13, 31,* 55, 60, 84, 87, 90, 97, 114, 182, 266, *291;* business of, 9, 20, 25, 45, 57–9; death of, 291–2, 324; emigration to U.S., 7–8; marriage to Jennie Resnick, 8–11, 185, 291; relationship with son Leonard, 12, 16–17, 20–6, 30, 41, 45, 57–9, 83, 87, 97, 106–7, 115–20, 163, 167–8, 180, 185–6, 290–2, 324–5
Bernstein, Shirley Anne, 9–12, *13,* 23, 26, 31, 33, 55, 70, 80, *81,* 87, 90, 94, 114, 146, *155,* 237, 290–1, 317, 341, 343, 350, 383, 401–2, 409; in *On the Town, 134,* 136; relationship with brother Leonard, 24, 90, 105, 126, 131, 140, 163, 177, 179, 182–3, 360, 385
"Bernstein and the New York Philharmonic," 273
Bernstein (Samuel) Hair Company, 9, 20, 46, 57–9
Bezalel, Dinah Malamud, 6, 26
Bezalel, Yudel ben, 6
Bible, Frances, *273*
Bing, Sir Rudolf, 258
Bizet, Georges, *Carmen,* 31, 370
Black Panthers, 320–3
Blitzstein, Marc, 53–6, 102, 132, 157, 187, 206, 276, 304, 385; *Airborne Symphony,* 146–7, 153; and Bernstein, 53–6, 101, 125, 304–5, 389; *The Cradle Will Rock,* 53–7, 84; death of, 304; *Idiot's First,* 304
Bloch, Ernest, *Three Jewish Poems,* 125
Blumenthal, Ann, 245
Bock, Helen, 33–4
Bok, Mary Curtis, 67, 96
Bolcom, William, 296, 326, 358, 397
Bolet, Jorge, 68
Bolivia, 259–60
boogie-woogie, 111, 144, 170
Boosey and Hawkes, 373, 376
Boston, 8–9, 47, 60, 74, 98, 103, 109, 204, 290, 291, 325

Boston *Evening Transcript,* 78
Boston *Globe,* 57, 103, 176, 256, 366
Boston *Herald,* 187
Boston Lubavitz Yeshiva, 290
Boston Pops Orchestra, 36–7, 93; Bernstein's performances with, 93–4, 130
Boston *Post,* 42, 127
Boston Public Latin School, 15–16, *18,* 21, 22, 33, 34, 42
Boston Public School Symphony Orchestra, 26, 34, 42
Boston Symphony Orchestra, 29, 37, 50, 72–9, 82, 131, 141–4, 151, 160, 224, 229, 257, 262, 355, 365; *Age of Anxiety* premiere (1949), 175, 176; Bernstein as guest conductor, 102–3, 110, 126–7, 130, 143–4, 153, 162, 166, 169, 175, 187, 235, 306, 355, 365–7, 371, 408–9
Bottesini, Giovanni, 72
Boulez, Pierre, 355
Boult, Sir Adrian, 223, 388–9
Bowles, Janes, 84, 102
Bowles, Paul, 44, 84, 102, 103, 125, 128, 131
Brahms, Johannes, 102, 109, 110, 131, 232, 369; *Academic Festival* Overture, 63; Piano Concerto No. 1, 148, 285; Rhapsody in G Minor, 42; Second Piano Concerto, 78; Second Symphony, 141, 270, 369; Variations on a Theme of Haydn, 78; Violin Concerto, 28
Brailowksy, Alexander, 163
Brandeis University arts festival, 187–8
Brando, Marlon, *158,* 199
Braslavsky, Solomon, 11, 14
Bray, Byron, 146–7, 339
Brecht, Bertolt, 211; *Caucasian Chalk Circle,* 325; *The Exception and the Rule,* 304, 399
Britten, Benjamin, 173; *Peter Grimes,* 153–4, 173, 408; Violin Concerto, 142; *Young Person's Guide to the Orchestra,* 189, 246
Brooklyn Academy, 162–3

Brother Sun, Sister Moon (film), 325
Browne, Gaylord, 77
Burckhardt, Rudy, 44
Burgin, Richard, 77, 103
Burkat, Leonard, 21, 30, 51, 60, 93, 94, 166, 344
Butler University, Indianapolis, 358

Caesar, Irving, 98
Calin, Mickey, 219
Callas, Maria, 193, *193*
Cantelli, Guido, 223, 229
Carnegie Hall, New York, 107, 113, 128, 139, 244, 411; Bernstein's performances at, 107–25, 132, 162, 175, 237, 238, 240, *241,* 244, 270; Young People's Concerts, 244–5, *246,* 247–9
Carno, Zita, 189–90
Carreras, José, 395–6
Carson, Margaret, 331, 405
Carter, Jimmy, 348, 350, 363
Casals, Pablo, 303
Cassidy, Claudia, 130
Chadwick, George Whitefield, 240
Chapin, Schuyler, 257–8, 308, 328–9, 332, 368–74
Chávez, Carlos, 98, 241, 325; *Sinfonía India,* 261
Chelsea Theater Center, Brooklyn, 208–9
Cherubini, Maria Luigi, *Medea,* 191–3
Chicago *Daily Tribune,* 130
Chicago Symphony Orchestra, 126, 162, 262–3, 389; Bernstein as guest conductor, 130–1
Chile, 148–9
Chopin, Frédéric, 17, 22, 34, 42, 43, 50, 102, 110, 130, 263; C-Minor Etude, 67; Nocturne in F-sharp Major, 28; Scherzo in B-flat Minor, 28
Christian Science Monitor, 42
Cincinnati Symphony Orchestra, 66, 126
City Center, New York, 141–3, 216, 234, 255
City College of New York, 136

Cliburn, Van, 267, 355, 397

Coates, Albert, 146

Coates, Helen, 22, 29, 30, 30, 42, 59, 67, 79, 84, 102, 113, 160, 339; as Bernstein's secretary, 140, 147, 152, 166, 191, 235, 252, 273, 299, 368

Cobb, Lee J., 199

Cohen, I. B., 43

Cohn, Clemencia, 148, 152, 182

Cohn, Roy, 148, 149

Colonial Theatre, Boston, *On the Town* performances at, 136

Columbia Artists Management, Inc. (CAMI), 107, 147, 225–8, 258–9, 367–8

Columbia Broadcasting System (CBS), 59, 114, 224–5, 245, 289, 304; New York Philharmonic television appearances, 244–51

Columbia Concerts, 224–5

Columbia Records, 224, 234–5, 257, 331, 368, 369–71; Masterworks series, 368, 370

Comden, Betty, 58, 98, 104, 111, 171, 213, 237; and Bernstein, 132–6, 194–5, 196–7, 288, 304, 383

Communism, 52–3, 171; anti-Communist purges (1950s), 171–2, 197–8, 201, 205

Composers Collective, 53

Concerts Symphoniques, Montreal, 131

Cook, Barbara, 205, 207

Cooper, Mitchell, 14, 15, 17

Copland, Aaron, 14, 27, 44, 52–3, 76, 85, 94, 100, 102, 104, 110, 131–2, 142, 155, 187, 256, 276, 302–5, 325, 360, 404; and Bernstein, 43–6, 59–60, 62, 63, 80, 87, 92, 96, 100, 101–2, 128–31, 170, 180, 183, 273, 307, 350, 360, 362, 366, 378, 385, 390, 403, 406; *Billy the Kid,* 45, 46, 268, 404; *Canticle of Freedom,* 307; *Danzón Cubano,* 101; *Fanfare for the Common Man,* 128; film work, 157; House Committee on Un-American Activities investigation of, 171–2; *Lincoln Portrait,* 172, 350; Music for

the Theatre, 248–9; *Of Mice and Men,* 45; *Our Town,* 45; *An Outdoor Overture,* 45, 78, 141; Piano Concerto, 156; Piano Sonata, 45, 101, 102; Piano Variations, 43, 44, 70; *Quiet City,* 45; *El Salón México,* 43, 101–2, 231; *Second Hurricane,* 100, 101; at Tanglewood, 77, 104; Third Symphony, 45, 406, 407; *Vitebsk,* 83

copyright ownership, 255–7, 376

Corigliano, John, 245, 306, 397

Corsaro, Frank, 351–3, 353, 354

Cothran, Tom, 332, 334, 339–41, 398–9

Cowan, Lester, 157, 162

Crawford, Cheryl, 215–16

Cultural and Scientific Conference for World Peace (1949, New York), 172

Cunningham, Merce, 188

Curtis, Charlotte, 322–3

Curtis, Edgar, 103

Curtis Institute of Music, Philadelphia, 39, 48, 49, 60, 62, 63, 64, 65, 77, 104, 137, 404; Bernstein at, 60–72, 83–5

Curtis Publishing Company, 67

Czech Philharmonic, Bernstein as guest conductor of, 153, 163, 371

Dabrowski, Waldemar, 64

Daily News, 121, 197

Dakin, William G., 371–2

Dalí, Salvador, 128

Daniel, Clifton, 163

Davis, Bette, 154

Davis, Peter G., 209

Deak, Jon, 280–2, 305, 355

Debussy, Claude, 43, 114, 169; *L'Après-midi d'un faune,* 37, 281; "La Cathédrale engloutie," 42; "Poisons d'or," 42

Denby, Edwin, 44, 100

Depression, 20, 52, 128, 133, 196, 240

Detroit Symphony Orchestra, 126, 143–4

Deutsche Grammophon, 275, 370–1, 396

Diaghilev, Sergei Pavlovich, 305
Diamond, David, 33, 51, 72, 84–5, 95, 115, 125, 147, 171, 192; and Bernstein, 154, 192, 203, 221, 261–2, 288–9, 350, 390
Diamond, Irene, 157, 158
Dickson, Harry Ellis, 93, 347
Dirksen, Wayne, 328
Domingo, Plácido, 396
Dorsey, Tommy, 128
Downes, Olin, 117, 142, 175–6
Drucker, Stanley, 280, 282
Druckman, Jacob, 346
Duke, Vernon, 132
Dunham, Marian Chase, 157
Durgin, Cyrus, 176, 235, 307
Dyer, Richard, 256, 366, 391

Eastern European Jews, 4–8, 17, 106–7
Eastman School of Music, 146, 370
Edinburgh Festival, 333
Edwards, Sydney, 314
Ehrlich, Jesse, 79
Einstein, Albert, 69, 172
Eisenhower, Dwight D., 172, 263
Eisler, Hanns, 171
Eisner, Alfred, 131
Elgar, Edward, Enigma Variations, 388–9
Elie, Rudolph, 187
Elkanova, Annette, 64, 68–9, 83, 85, 160, 326
Ellis Island, New York, 8
Emmy Awards, 232, 273, 358
Engel, Lehman, 194
Englander, Roger, 144, 154, 156, 245, 289, 334, 409
Epstein, Helen, 361
Epstein, Matthew, 211, 258, 396, 399
Evans, Alan, 40–1
Evett, Robert, 220

Faison, George, 354
Falkove, Albert, 64
Farrand, Noel, 146, 179
Federal Bureau of Investigation, 323–4
Federal Theatre, 53, 128

Feigay, Paul, 133
Feinstein, Martin, 110
Fiedler, Arthur, 35, 37, 93–4
Fiedler, Johanna, 259
Fields (Joseph) and Chodorov (Jerome), My Sister Eileen, 196
film, 128; Bernstein's work in, 156–60, 162, 199–221, 325, 369, 396
Fine, Irving, 187, 190, 204, 291, 389–90
Fine, Verna, 178, 191, 291, 389–90
Finkler, Elizabeth, 151
Fleisher, Leon, 124, 407–8
Florence, 192
Fogel, Henry, 389
Foldes, Andor, 175–6
folk songs, 52, 83, 247–8
Fontaine, Joan, 157
Forbes, Elliott, 290
Ford Foundation, 229, 304
Foss, Lukas, 68, 77, 82, 86, 93, 103, 155, 175, 397, 406; Time Cycle, 284
France, 60, 107, 165, 201, 247–8, 358
Franck, César, 16
French, Charlie, 39
Friedman, Abraham, 256, 368
Friends of the Philharmonic, 250
Frost, Robert, 271
Fugitive Kind, The (film), 158

Galway, James, 387–8
Garbo, Greta, 237
García Lorca, Federico, 102, 157
Garrison, Lloyd, 239
Gauk, Alexander, 268
Gebhard, Heinrich, 21–2, 29, 42–3
Geller, Edwin, 38–40
Germany, 7, 60, 245, 255, 356, 358, 364, 401; Nazi persecution of Jews, 96; in World War II, 97, 109
Gershwin, George, 46–7, 52, 98, 131, 157, 286, 302, 404; An American in Paris, 46, 358, 370; and Bernstein, 46–7, 162, 366–7; death of, 47; Porgy and Bess, 46–7, 85, 302; Rhapsody in Blue, 42, 46, 131, 168–9, 366–7, 370

Gershwin (George) Memorial Contest, 132

Ghostley, Alice, *184*

Gibbs, Wolcott, 220

Gilbert and Sullivan, 31–3, 40, 47, 208; *H.M.S. Pinafore,* 31; *The Mikado,* 31; *The Pirates of Penzance,* 47

Ginastera, Alberto, 229, 328

Glazer, David, 27, 79

Goberman, Max, 85

Goethe, Johann Wolfgang von, 231; "An Schwager Kronos," 3, 38, 57, 73, 99, 121, 139, 162, 181, 199, 222, 242, 270, 293, 310, 327, 347, 365, 379, 398

Goldin, Milton, 107, 225

Goldman, Thomas A., 52–3

Goldovsky, Boris, 77, 102, 189

Gomberg, Ralph, 141, 406

Goossens, Eugene, 143, 146

Gordon, Aaron, 16

Gordon, Beatrice, *32, 33,* 48, 160

Gottlieb, Jack, 245, 286

Gould, Glenn, 285

Gould, Morton, *Rumbalero,* 34

Gould, Walter, 368

Graf, Herbert, 77

Graffman, Gary, 66, 68, 109, 390

Graham, Martha, 399

Grammy Awards, 358, 370

Grand Prix du Disque Classique awards, 358

Great Britain, 60, 109, 111, 128, 153, 163–4, 206, 208, 256, 263, 312, 314, 332–3, 388–9, 400–1

"Great Performances" recordings, 371

Greece, 263

Green, Adolph, 48, *58,* 59, 98, 101, 104, 111, *134, 194–5,* 213, 232, 237, 249, 400; and Bernstein, *132–6, 194–5,* 196–7, 241, 288, 304, 383

Grieg, Edvard, Piano Concerto, 28, 42, 153, 369

Griffith, Robert, *214,* 216, 218

Grossman, Julius, 385

Group Theatre, 128

Grove's Dictionary of Music and Musicians, 358–9

Gruen, John, 185, 285–6, 295, 315–16, 378

Gruenberg, Louis, 101

Guggenheim, Peggy, 102

Gustin, Dan, 151, 276, 406, 409

Guthrie, Tyrone, 204, 205

Hadley, Jerry, 283–4, 364, 394, 396, 400–1

Hagen, Daron Aric, 386–7

Hahn, Reynaldo, 303

Hammerstein, Oscar, II, 129, 211, 213, 216

Hammond, Earl, 151–2

Handel, George Frederick, 111, 272; *Messiah,* 234–5, 286, 370; *Passion According to Saint John,* 272

Handy, Pat, *345*

Hanson, Howard, 131

Harms, Inc., 98, 255

Harper's Bazaar, 125, 137

Harris, Roy, 52, 59, 76, 78, 80, 94, 128, 131, 142, 171

Harrison, Jay, *Musical America,* 290

Hart, Alfred, 145

Hart, Kitty Carlisle, *391*

Hart, Philip, *Orpheus in the New World,* 107

Hart, Richard, 177

Harvard Classical Club, 55

Harvard Glee Club, 238–9, 332, 351, 371–2

Harvard Orchestra, 48–9

Harvard University, 15, 16, 84, 128, 238–9, 242, 249, 290, 358, 371, 384; Bernstein at, 23, 28, 33, 38–57, 69, 238, 334–8, 351, 358; Bernstein's Norton Lectures at, 325, 334–8; *The Cradle Will Rock* performance (1939), 53–7

Hasidism, 4–5, 11, 25, 308, 408

Hawthorne, Nathaniel, 75

Hayden, Melissa, 42

Haydn, Franz Joseph, 142, 183, 248, 282, 285; *Mass in Time of War,* 333; Sinfonia Concertante, 78

Hecht, Ben, 97, 157, 160

Heifetz, Jascha, 132

Heinsheimer, Hans, 101

Hellman, Lillian, 172, 201, 202, 263; and Bernstein, 201–11, 275; *Candide,* 201–11; *The Lark,* 201, 205; *The Little Foxes,* 206, 318

Henahan, Donal, 330–1, 393, 394, 402

Hendl, Walter, 85

Herman, Woody, 197

Heuberger, Richard, 21

Heyman, Ken, 276, 315

Heyworth, Peter, 314

Hilbert, Egon, 312

Hill, Edward Burlingame, 39, 45

Hillyer, Raphael, 42, 43, 45, 49, 79–81, 94, 221, 234, 343

Hindemith, Paul, 40, 69, 76, 85, 94, 142, 241, 367, 404; at Tanglewood, 77, 79

Hitler, Adolf, 53, 70, 97

Holiday, Billie, 24, 48, 103

Holland, 163–5

Holliday, Judy, 104, 132, 171–2

Hollywood, 156–60, 162; Bernstein's work in, 159–60, 199–221, 325

Hollywood Bowl, 141; Bernstein's performances at, 131–2

Holmes, Oliver Wendell, 75

homosexuality, role in music business, 256–7

Honegger, Arthur, 128, 229, 318

Hope, Constance, 186

Horne, Lena, 237

Horne, Marilyn, 370, 395

Horowitz, Joseph, 109, 122

Horowitz, Vladimir, 122

Houseman, John, 53

House Committee on Un-American Activities, 171–2, 198, 205

Houston Grand Opera, 392

Howe, Irving, 5

Huckaby, William, 363

Hughes, Allen, 284

Hume, Paul, 329

Hurok, Sol, 49, 110, 368

Inge, William, 154

Institute of Modern Art, Boston, 101

Internal Revenue Service, 255

International Music Festival, Prague, 163

Israel, 164, 167–9, 243–4, 259, 289, 300, 355, 358

Israel Philharmonic: Bernstein as guest conductor, *168, 169,* 178, 243–4, 325, 356, 381, 410; Bernstein retrospective (1977), 358

Istomin, Eugene, 59, 68, *116, 137,* 271–2

Italy, 156, *192, 193,* 245, 248, 256, 332–3, 358

Iturbi, José, 28, 145–6, 160

Ives, Charles, 52, 94, 229, 247, 334; Symphony No. 2, 249; *The Unanswered Question,* 268, 334

Jacobi, Frederick, 101

JALNI Publications, 376

James, Henry, 75

Japan, 245, 255, 325, 349, 374, 389, 405–6

jazz, 40, 43, 98, 197, 230–2, 234, 237, 268, 269, 276, 286

Jerusalem, 163–4, 169, 244, 300, 355

Jews, 4–9, 11, 96, 105–7, 131, 287, 308; customs, 11–12, 25; emigration to U.S., 6–8; Nazi persecution of, 97, 109

Jiampietro, Lilia, 31–3

Johns, Clayton, 21

Johnson, Thor, 77

Joint Anti-Fascist Refugee Committee, 131

Jones, Gwyneth, *357*

Joyce, Eileen, 153

Judson, Arthur, 94, *112,* 146, 224–9, 256–9; and Bernstein, 94, 107–12, 117, 120, 125, 130, 144–5, 229, 239, 367–8; as manager of New York Philharmonic, 224–9, 240–1; and Artur Rodzinski, 109–10, 227–8

Judson, O'Neill, Beall and Steinway, 367
Juilliard, 59, 258, 303
Jung, Carl, 308

Kabelevsky, Dmitri, 268
Kahn, Erich Itor, 115
Kalfin, Robert, 208–9
Kansas City Philharmonic, 358
Kapell, William, 151
Karajan, Herbert von, 223, 259, 264,
    277, 281, 312, 356, 359, 369
Karp, Frieda, 15, 17
Kassman, Nickolai, 80
Kay, Hershy, 64, 328
Kaye, Nora, 156
Kazan, Elia, 133
Keiser, David, 229
Kellogg, Cal Stewart, 256, 259
Kelly, Gene, 129, 135
Kennedy, Jacqueline, 271–2, 303, 327–9
Kennedy, John Fitzgerald, 15, 271–2,
    289, 351, 359
Kennedy, Robert, 320
Kennedy, Rose, 329
Kennedy (John F.) Center for the Per-
    forming Arts, Washington, D.C.,
    311–12, 327; Bernstein's commis-
    sions and performances at, 327–33,
    350, 357–60, 363, 392–5, 410
Kent, Rockwell, 83
Kern, Jerome, 98
Kert, Larry, 217, 219
Kirkman, Jack, 298–300, 372
Kleiber, Erich, 49
Klemperer, Otto, 223, 277
Kolodin, Irving, 141, 185, 303, 304
Kondrashin, Kiril, 268
Koscis, Susan, 359, 387
Kostelanetz, André, 355
Kotlowitz, Robert, 331
Koussevitzky, Nathalie, 75, 76, 108, 131
Koussevitzky, Olga, 108, 178–9, 290,
    408
Koussevitzky, Serge, 16, 36–7, 49, 67,
    71, 72, 74–83, 86, 91, 101, 107–8,
    252, 256, 277–8, 346, 408; and

Bernstein, 74–98, 103, 105, 110–11,
    120, 126–8, 131–2, 139, 143–4,
    153–4, 160–2, 171, 178–82, 188,
    234, 235, 250, 262, 276, 402, 407,
    408; as a conductor, 76, 90–1, 178;
    death of, 178, 182, 188; at Tangle-
    wood, 74–97, 110, 153, 178, 188,
    345, 360, 366, 408
Koussevitzky Foundation, 154, 203
Koussevitzky Orchestra, 75
Kraft, Victor, 44, 87
"Kraft Television Theatre," 190, 237
Krasnopolsky, Yuri, 218, 219, 300–2,
    308, 320
Kraus, Marcia, 189–90
Kraut, Harry, 332, 344, 371–7, 398, 410
Kremer, Gidon, 284
Krenek, Ernst, 404
Kriza, John, 129
Kruger, Dana, 360
Kruskall, Sarah, 28, 32

La Guardia, Fiorello, 96, 140
Lancaster, Osbert, 263
Landowska, Wanda, 64, 68
Lang, Dorothy, 98
Lang, Harold, 129
Lang, Paul Henry, 223, 229, 250, 270,
    285, 286
Langner, Lawrence, 133
Latin America, New York Philharmonic
    tour in (1958), 259–62
La Touche, John, 203
Laurents, Arthur, 204, 211, 214, 276,
    287–8, 351–5, 362–3, 383, 409–10,
    413; and West Side Story, 212–21
Lawrence, Carol, 219
Lawrence, Frieda, 173, 174
Lawrence, Mass., 8–9, 52, 376
League of Composers, New York, 101,
    103
Lebanon, 263
Lebrecht, Norman, The Maestro Myth,
    225, 257, 278, 374
Lees, Benjamin, 256
Lehár, Franz, 208

Leigh, Vivien, 237
Leinsdorf, Erich, 143, 145–6, 257
Lennon, John, 338, 385
Lenox Library concerts, 110
"A Leonard Bernstein Gala!" 368
Lerner, Alan Jay, 238, 351–3, *353*, 354
LeRoy, Kenneth, 219
Leschetizky, Theodor, 121
Leslie, Bethel, 152–3, 179, 340
Leuona, Ernesto, *Malagueña*, 28–30, 33
Levant, Oscar, 131, 143
Levy, Harry, 7–8
Lewis, Robert, 206, 208
Library of Congress, 76
Lieberson, Goddard, 370
Life magazine, 125, 172, 176, 250
Lincer, William, 117
Lincoln, Abraham, 350–1
Lincoln Center for the Performing Arts, New York, 263, 368; Bernstein's performances at, 270–1, 284, 341; inaugural concert (1962), 270–1
Lipkin, Seymour, *155*
Lipson, Jerome, 29, 39, 93
Liszt, Franz, 23, 42, 43, 110, 131, 157; *Consolation* No. 6, 42; *Faust Symphony*, 93; Piano Concerto No. 2, 26
"Live from Lincoln Center" telecasts, 271
London, 75, 128, 153, 312, 314, 358, 388–9; *Candide* productions, 206, 208, 210–11, 263, 400–1
London Philharmonic, 389; Bernstein's performances with, 153
London Symphony Orchestra, Bernstein's performances with, 325, 333, 369, 371, 400, 410
Longfellow, Henry Wadsworth, 75
Look magazine, 125, 315
Los Angeles Civic Opera, 300
Los Angeles Philharmonic, 189, 227; Bernstein's performances with, 367
Los Angeles Philharmonic Institute, 367
Lowell, Robert, 288
Lubell, Robert, 30, 36, 40, 43, 48, 50, 60
Ludwig, Christa, 370, 400
Luskin, Leo, *64*

Ma, Yo-Yo, 259, 397, 411
Maazel, Lorin, 189, 374
MacArthur, Charles, 157
McCarthy, Joseph, 171–2, 205
McCarthy, Mary, 206
Macdonald, Dwight, 122
MacDowell, Edward, 240
MacDowell Colony, 334
McLennan, John, 149–50, 154, 161, 256, 388
Madison Trio, 29, *32*
Madrid, 75
Mahler, Gustav, 183, 261, 285, 306–9, 379–80, 389; Eighth Symphony, 307; Fifth Symphony, 320; Ninth Symphony, 307–9, 369, 370; *Resurrection* Symphony, 175, 261, 289, 306–7, 312; Third Symphony, 261, 326
Mailer, Norman, *158*
Malden, Karl, 199
Malipiero, Gian Francesco, 40
Malraux, André, 271–2
Mann, Thomas, 69, 172, 308, 379; *Death in Venice*, 308–9
Mantle, Richard, 210
Marcus, Leonard, 189, 252
Margolies, Jacques, 118, 280
Markevitch, Dimitri, 94
Markevitch, Igor, 94, 223, 277
Marson, Philip, 16
Martha's Vineyard, Mass., 203, 302, 318
Martinu, Bohuslav, 101
Marxism, 52, 53
Massachusetts State Symphony, 42
Maugham, Somerset, 157
Maxwell, Elsa, 250
Mayer, Martin, 279
Meier, Gustav, 377, 406
Melville, Herman, 75
Mengelberg, Willem, 306
Menotti, Gian Carlo, 68
Menuhin, Yehudi, 131, 413
Mercury Theatre, 53
Merrill, Edys, 104

Merritt, A. Tillman, 39, 40–1

Metropolitan Opera, 131, 132, 145, 258, 279, 303–4, 306, 371; Bernstein's performances at, 303, 312, 325–6, 370

Mexico, 183, 186–7, 260–1, 348–50

Mexico City Philharmonic Orchestra, 350

MGM, 135

Milan, 191–3, 261, 262

Milhaud, Darius, 101, 111, 128, 241; Concerto for Two Pianos, 142

Miller, Jonathan, 210

Milstein, Nathan, 164

Minkler, Bud, 39

Minneapolis Symphony, 51–2, 60, 72, 225–6

Mintz, Ouida, 27, 28, 30, 33

Miquelle, Renée Longy, 68

Mirkin, Kenneth, 282–3, 362

Mishkan Tefila, Newton, Mass., 11, 14, 27, 28, 36, 43, 290, 325

Mitchell, Henry, 234

Mitropoulos, Dimitri, 49–52, 60, 61, 84, 99, 107, 112, 144, 154, 252, 306; and Bernstein, 49–52, 59–60, 67, 72, 83, 94, 125, 137, 147, 222–3, 233, 234, 259–62; death of, 261; as New York Philharmonic conductor, 222–4, 228, 229, 234, 259–62

Mitropoulos (Dimitri) International Music Competitions, 301

Monroe, Vaughn, 132

Montealegre, Felicia, 148–52, 157–61, 165, 192, 205, 232, 236, 263, 267, 268, 271, 273–5, 290, 294, 328–9, 339, 342; acting career of, 176–7, 190, 237, 294, 296, 318, 339; Bernstein's courtship of, 150–2, 157–61; cancer of, 339, 342–4; death of, 342–50, 362, 365, 398; engagement to Bernstein, 161, 165, 166, 177–9; marital troubles of, 318–20, 339–42; marriage to Bernstein, 179–83, 186–93, 203, 235–8, 243–4, 250, 264, 293–8, 316–20, 338–50; as a

mother, 188, 193, 203, 235, 236, 294, 316–17, 384

Monteux, Pierre, 76, 108, 223, 277

Montreal, 126, 131

Moral Re-Armament movement, 111

Moscow, Bernstein's performances in, 265, 266–7, 267, 268–9

Moscow Philharmonic Society, 75

Moseley, Carlos, 272, 275, 301, 355

Moses, Gilbert, 354

Mostel, Zero, 304, 325

Mozart, Wolfgang Amadeus, 72, 114, 183, 248, 285, 299, 303, 336; "Linz" Symphony, 163; A Musical Joke, 248; Piano Concerto in G Major, 263, 267; Requiem, 123–4, 364; Symphony No. 40 in G Minor, 49

Munch, Charles, 144, 187, 191, 223, 277

Murrow, Edward R., 245

Museum of Modern Art, New York, 102–3

Music at Work, 101

Music News, 142

Mussorgsky, Modest Petrovich, Pictures at an Exhibition, 247

Muti, Riccardo, 374

National Council on the Arts, 303

National Gallery Orchestra, Washington, D.C., 77

National Society of Arts and Letters, 273

National Symphony Orchestra, 278–80, 348, 362, 374

NBC, 83, 225

NBC Symphony Orchestra, 147, 370; Bernstein as guest conductor of, 153

Netherlands Radio, 164

New England Conservatory of Music, 17, 28, 105

Newman, Elaine, 35, 36, 160

New Opera Company, 99

Newsweek, 78, 125, 354

Newton, Mass., 20, 20, 21

New York Chamber Symphony, 259

New York City Ballet, 175

New York City Opera, 209

New York City Symphony, 96, 141, 166; Bernstein as conductor, 141–5, 148, 153, 156, 162, 166, 241, 306

New Yorker, The, 122, 125, 198, 285, 391

New York *Herald Tribune,* 103, 125, 285, 315

New York *Journal-American,* 198

New York magazine, 316, 322, 354

New York Music Critics Circle Award, 126

New York Philharmonic, 107–9, 112–21, 137, 144, 227–8, 245, 306, 411; assistant conductors, 300–2; Bernstein's conducting debut, 115–22, 125; Bernstein as guest conductor, 115–26, 131, 137, 175, 355–6; Bernstein as principal conductor and musical director, 222–4, 234–40, 240, 241, 244–51, 251, 253, 259–87, 299, 310–12, 325, 349, 369; European tour (1959), 259–69; Festival of Stravinsky, 254; Arthur Judson as manager of, 224–9, 240–1; Latin American tour (1958), 259–62; Taubman's reviews of, 224–5, 228–9, 240–1; television shows, 244–51; Young People's Concerts, 244–5, 246, 247–9

New York *Post,* 125

New York Times, 41, 111, 117, 121, 125, 142, 163, 170, 197, 223, 234, 250, 285, 304, 311, 316, 322–3, 359, 396, 402

New York University, 103, 258

New York *World-Telegram,* 166, 171

Nicholas I, Tsar of Russia, 7

Nichols, Mike, 318

Nietzsche, Friedrich Wilhelm, 280, 289

Ninth Festival of International Contemporary Music, Venice, 156

Nixon, Richard, 333, 352

Norton, Eliot, 57

Ollmann, Kurt, 400–1

"Omnibus" (TV program), 229–33, 234, 243, 251, 274

Ono, Yoko, 338, 385

opera, 23–5, 99, 189, 211, 248, 255; American, 183; Bernstein's work in, 183–6, 204, 296, 302, 354, 392–5, 403

Opéra-Comique, Paris, 111

Oppenheim, David Jerome, 103, 114, 147, 167

Orchestre de Paris, 326, 381

Ormandy, Eugene, 51, 226, 279

Osato, Sono, *135*

Pacific Music Festival, 405–6

Paderewski, Ignacé, 257; *Cracovienne fantastique,* 42; Fantasy, 15

Page, Ruth, 156

Palestine, 60, 131–2, 163–4, 167

Palestine Symphony Orchestra, Bernstein as guest conductor of, 163–4

Paley, William S., 245

Paray, Paul, 144

Paris, 75, 111, 128, 164, 165, 167, 262, 326, 381

Parker, Dorothy, 171, 204

Pasmanick, Ken, 280, 281, 299–300, 362

Pasternak, Boris, 267, 268–9

Paul VI, Pope, 332

Pelletier, Wilfrid, 244

Pennario, Leonard, *116*

Peress, Maurice, 122, 328, 337, 358

Perle, George, 71, 358

Perle, Shirley Rhoads (née Gabis), 70, 70, 71, 104, 148, 294, 317, 388, 400, 407

Perry, Thomas D., Jr., 71–2

Perry, Tod, 191, 257

Peyser, Joan, 359, 400

Philadelphia Orchestra, 119, 224, 226, 229, 262

Philharmonic-Symphony Society, 113

Piatigorsky, Gregor, 77

Pic, 125

Picard, Roger, 179

Pickford, Mary, 157, 162

Pincus, Andrew, 337, 409

Pisa, *192*

Piston, Walter, 39, 45, 76, 77, 84, 94, 101, 131, 171, 290
Pittsburgh Symphony Orchestra, 66, 114, 144; Bernstein as guest conductor, 126, 144, 173
Pix, 125
Plato, *Symposium,* 203, 235
PM, 125
Poland, 5, 70, 263–4
Pope, W. Stuart, 373
popular music, 46, 98, 128–9, 132–6, 211
Porter, Andrew, 391
Porter, Cole, 34
Portnoi, Henry, 79
Poulenc, Francis, 128
Prall, David, 43, 335
Prawy, Marcel, 356
press, 270; on Bernstein, 42, 46, 57, 78, 84, 103, 106, 121–31, 136, 137, 142–3, 153, 156, 163–4, 170, 175–6, 183–7, 193, 197–8, 200, 205, 209–10, 220, 232–5, 239–41, 250–1, 274, 285–90, 311, 314–16, 322–3, 329–31, 354, 356–7, 389, 394, 402–3, 408–9, 413; *see also specific publications*
Previn, André, 374, 397
Prince, Harold, 208–9, 302–3, 377; and *West Side Story, 214,* 216, 220
Prokofiev, Sergei, 40, 94, 171, 268, 404; *Classical* Symphony, 36, 248; Piano Concerto No. 3, 83
Provincetown Playhouse, 157
publishers, music, 98, 101, 255–6, 373, 376
Puccini, Giacomo, *La Boheme,* 123
Pulitzer Prize, 358
Purcell, Henry, 231

Rachmaninoff, Sergei, 111
radio, 109, 118, 132, 137, 141, 146–7, 164, 362, 388
Rado, Sandor, 319–20
Rameau, Jean, 114
Ramey, Phillip, 343, 350, 362, 392

Ravel, Maurice, 42, 43, 44, 102, 128, 131; *Boléro,* 36, 250; Piano Concerto in G Major, 42, 94, 130, 131, 163–4, 170; Piano Concerto for the Left Hand, 408; *Rapsodie espagnole,* 94
RCA, 257–8
Read, Gardiner, 78
Reiner, Fritz, 60, 62, 63, 66–9, 82–3, 90, 94, 99, 107, 114, 126, 144, 223, 262–3, 277–9
Residentie Orchestra, Bernstein as guest conductor of, 164–5
Respighi, Ottorino, 76; Toccata for Piano and Orchestra, 49
Revueltas, Silvestre, 102
Rice, Elmer, 198
Rich, Alan, 285–7, 290, 354, 356
Rigby, Dr. Cormac, 388–9
Rimsky-Korsakov, Nikolai, 75, 114, 171; *Scheherazade,* 60, 78
Robbins, Jerome, 127, 133, *214,* 303; and Bernstein, 127–9, 143, 156, 172, 175, 204, 211–21, 234, 325, 363, 399, 413; and *West Side Story,* 212–21
Robeson, Paul, 131, 172
Rochester Philharmonic Orchestra, 29, 126, 145–7, 257; Bernstein as guest conductor, 145–8, 153, 162, 166
Rockefeller, John D., III, 271
Rockefeller, Nelson, 132
Rockwell, John, 402–4, 408
Rodgers, Mary, 191, 193, 245
Rodgers, Richard, 216
Rodgers and Hammerstein, 129, 211; *Carousel,* 211, 255; *Oklahoma!,* 133, 211
Rodzinski, Artur, *108,* 109–15, *116,* 119, 125, 126, 144; and Bernstein, 109–19, 125–30; and Arthur Judson, 109–10, 227–8; as New York Philharmonic conductor, 227–8
Rodzinski, Halina, 109, 113, 118, 128, 226, 227, 294
romanticism, 231–2, 305–6, 380–1, 404
Rome, 75, 332–3
Ronell, Ann, 157, 160, 166

Roosevelt, Franklin D., 52, 132

Rorem, Ned, 46, 103–4, 284, 334, 351, 359–60, 363, 391, 397, 399, 410

Rosenfeld, Jay C., 176, 264

Rosenfeld, Steve, 264–9, 320

Ross, Hugh, 77

Ross, Irene, 99

Rossini, Gioacchino Antonio, *The Barber of Seville,* 37

Rosten, Leo, 4, 17

Rostropovich, Mstislav, 397

Rounseville, Robert, 205

Roxbury, Mass., 11, 14

Roxbury Memorial High, 28, 34

Rózsa, Miklós, 117

Rubenovitz, Herman H., 11

Rubin, David M., 258–9

Rubinstein, Arthur, 187

Rudel, Julius, 328

Ruggles, Carl, 240

Rukeyser, Muriel, 43–4

Russell, Rosalind, *194, 195,* 196–7

Russia, 7, 66, 75, 76, 132, 171, 241, 262; Bernstein in (1959), 264, *265,* 266–7, *267,* 268–9; Hitler's invasion of, 97

Russian Tea Room, New York, 170

Russian War Relief, 101, 171

Saarinen, Eliel, 79

Saint, Eva Marie, 199–200

St. Clair, Carl, 408

St. Louis Municipal Opera, 300

St. Louis Symphony Orchestra, 138, 154, 223

Salzburg Festival, 261, 264

Sanders Theatre, Harvard University, 49, 55

San Francisco Opera, 145

San Francisco Symphony, 126, 157, 169, 178

Sargeant, Winthrop, 285

Saturday Evening Post, 320

Scala, La, Milan, 261, 392; Bernstein as guest conductor at, 191–3

Scarlatti, Alessandro, 102

Schaeffer, Pierre, 188

Schiff, David, 404

Schifter, Peter Mark, 296, 382, 393–4, 397

Schippers, Thomas, 223, 264

Schirmer, G., 101, 255–6, 376

Schoenberg, Arnold, 70, 176, 286, 335

Schonberg, Harold, 234, 241, 277, 285, 287, 311, 316, 356, 403; *Facing the Music,* 287

Schorr, Daniel, 164

Schubert, Franz Peter, 42, 232; Op. 19, No. 1, 3

Schulberg, Budd, 199

Schuman, William, 59, 76, 94, 131, 229, 242, 360; *American Festival Overture,* 93

Schumann, Robert, 169, 232, 282, 349; *Manfred* Overture, 117, 118, 241; *Novelette* in E Major, 42; Symphony No. 2, 94

Schuster, Joseph, 117

Schwartz, Daniel, 296, 298, 317

Schwartz, Stephen, 328

Scott, Cyril, *Danse Nègre,* 42

Scottish Opera, *Candide* production by, 210–11

Scribner, Norman, 343, 356, 410

Serkin, Rudolf, 66, 68

Sessions, Roger, 52, 171, 229, 325; Violin Concerto, 250

Setzer, Philip, 410

Shapero, Harold, 37, 40, 79, 101; Four-Hand Piano Sonata, 101

Shapiro, Karl, 188

Sharon, Mass., 20, 29–34

Shaw, Robert, 147

Shelkan, Gregor, 11

Sheng, Bright, 408, 410–11

Shimkin, Arthur, 252–4

Shostakovich, Dimitri, 48, 76, 142, 171–2, 241, 267–8; First Symphony, 141; Piano Concerto No. 2, 241; Symphony No. 5, 267, 358

Show Business, 198

Sibelius, Jean, 76, 131; First Symphony, 130

Silverstein, Joseph, 366–7
Simon, Henry, 101, 129
Simon, John, 329–30
Sinatra, Frank, 135, 137
Singher, Martial, 273
Skidmore, Edward, 278–9, 348
Smit, Leo, 142
Smith, Bessie, 24
Smith, Moses, 57
Smith, Oliver, 127–9, 133, 156, 205
Smith, Warren Storey, 127
Sokolow, Anna, 43
Solov, Zachary, 41–2
Solti, Georg, 277
Somary, Stephen, 382, 385, 407–9
Sondheim, Stephen, 140, 151, 204,
    209, 214, 256, 302, 351, 397, 399,
    403; and Bernstein, 213–21, 329,
    350; and West Side Story, 213–21
Soria, Dorle, 117
"So You Think You Know Music?"
    (radio program), 132
Spain, 70, 102, 107, 131, 248, 255
Spender, Stephen, 173–5
Sperry, Paul, 123, 303
Speyer, André, 78, 85, 124, 141
Speyer, Kiki, 51, 85–7, 88–9, 90, 94,
    95–7, 111, 114–15, 160, 166, 167,
    170, 178–9, 326, 391, 411
Speyer, Louis, 78, 85, 86, 130
Spiegel, Mildred, 29, 32, 33–4, 37, 43,
    45, 52, 160, 326
Spoleto U.S.A. Festival, 404
Springate (Bernstein's Connecticut
    home), 338, 348, 373, 381–2
Starr, Herman, 98
Steell, Susan, 135
Steiger, Rod, 199
Stein, Gertrude, 102
Steinberg, William, 144, 277
Steinfirst, Donald, 106
Steinway pianos, 67–8
Stern, Isaac, 107, 146, 258
Stevens, Roger, 215–16, 352, 353, 354
Stokowski, Leopold, 68, 119, 140–1,
    144, 223, 226, 234, 250

Strachey, Lytton, 202
Strauss, Richard: Also Sprach Zarathus-
    tra, 280–1; Don Juan, 232; Don
    Quixote, 117–19, 241; Elektra, 227;
    Der Rosenkavalier, 313–14, 370
Stravinsky, Igor, 40, 76, 94, 169, 176,
    241, 254, 303, 325–6, 330, 335;
    Concerto for Piano and Wind Instru-
    ments, 268; Concerto for Two Solo
    Pianos, 83; Firebird Suite, 126; L'His-
    toire du soldat, 78, 303; Les Noces, 188,
    303; Oedipus Rex, 142; Petrouchka, 190;
    La Sacre du printemps, 36, 84, 231, 268
Stutch, Nathan, 281–3
Styron, Rose, 318, 320, 323, 342
Sullivan, Ed, 197
Symphony of the Air, 297, 307
Symphony Space, New York, 362
Szell, George, 143, 222
Szigeti, Joseph, 130, 148

Tams-Witmark, 255
Tanglewood, Mass., 27, 28, 46, 71,
    75–83, 85, 104, 155, 178, 257–8,
    345, 384; Age of Anxiety premiere
    (1949), 175, 176; Bernstein at,
    74–85, 89, 93, 94–7, 110, 143,
    153–4, 155, 156, 166, 175–90, 276,
    300, 319, 325, 345, 346, 365–7,
    390, 397, 402, 406–9; Koussevitzky
    at, 74–97, 110, 153, 178, 188, 345,
    360, 366; Peter Grimes premiere
    (1946), 153
Taos, N. M., 173–5
Tappan, William A., 75
Taubman, Howard, 220, 223, 232;
    New York Philharmonic reviews,
    224–5, 228–9, 240–1
Taylor, A. J. P., 123
Taylor, Davidson, 59
Tchaikovsky, Peter, 16, 23, 40, 75, 130,
    131, 360; Concert Fantasy for Piano
    and Orchestra, 142; Fifth Symphony,
    95, 146, 366; Francesca da Rimini,
    281, 381; Pathétique, 124, 282; Queen
    of Spades, 178; Romeo and Juliet, 131

Tchaikovsky Conservatory, Moscow, 265, 266–7, 267, 268
Tchaikovsky International Piano Competition, 267
Te Kanawa, Kiri, 395–7
Tel Aviv, 163–4, 243–4, 358
television, 190, 237; Bernstein's work on, 229–33, 234, 239, 243, 244–51, 255, 258, 358, 369, 388, 396
Terry, Walter, 156
theater, musical, 127–9, 132–6, 194–8, 211; Bernstein's work in, 128, 132–6, 183–7, 194–8, 201–21, 288, 304, 351–5, 403
Theater Guild, 133, 195
Thiede, Alexander, 42, 84
Thomas, Jess, 357
Thomas, Michael Tilson, 334, 385, 397, 406
Thompson, Randall, 64, 68, 69, 72, 83, 171; Second Symphony, 78
Thomson, Virgil, 44, 54, 102, 104, 115, 127–8, 153, 157, 228, 229, 307; on Bernstein, 142–3
Tilson, Vera, 80
Time magazine, 125, 156, 170, 200, 227, 318
Tiomkin, Dimitri, 200
Titus, Alan, 328
Toch, Ernst, The Juggler, 42
Topol, 325
Toscanini, Arturo, 91, 107, 113, 122, 147, 163, 223, 227, 249, 274, 277–80, 310, 389
Tourel, Jennie, 111, 114–17, 126, 148, 149, 172, 271, 289, 320
Tower, Joan, 392
Town Hall, New York, 101–2, 150, 244
Trenerry, Walter, 215
Troyanos, Tatiana, 395, 396
Tudor, Antony, 156, 216
Tunick, Jonathan, 328, 375
Turkey, 263
Twentieth Century Music Group, 83
Tyers, John, 184

United Hebrew Charities, 7
United Nations, 164, 169
Unitel, 369, 396

van Remoortel, Edouard, 223
Varèse, Edgar, 84
Vatican, 332
Vauclain, Constant, 64
Vengerova, Isabelle, 63, 66–8, 83–4
Venice, 156, 203, 221, 308
Venice Festival (1954), 203
Verbrugghen, Henri, 225
Verdi, Giuseppe, 40, 208; Aïda, 33, 387; Falstaff, 279, 303, 312; Requiem, 369
Victor Records, 28
Victor Red Seal Recordings, 132, 138
Vienna Philharmonic Orchestra, Bernstein as guest conductor of, 163, 258, 264, 276, 312–14, 325, 356–7, 357, 369–71, 404–5, 410
Vienna State Opera, 264, 356; Bernstein's performances with, 325, 357
Viereck, Peter, 188
Vietnam War, 320, 333
Village Vanguard, New York, 48, 59
Visconti, Lucchino, 312
Vivaldi, Antonio, 241, 246
Vogue magazine, 125, 142, 236
Voltaire, Candide, 201–11

Wadsworth, Stephen, 392–4, 399
Wadsworth Atheneum, Hartford, Conn., 102
Wagner, Friedelind, 405, 405
Wagner, Joseph, 84; Concerto in G Minor, 42
Wagner, Richard, 40, 109, 111, 231, 232, 289, 405; Die Meistersinger, 93, 117, 118; Tristan und Isolde, 31, 68
Waldheim, Kurt, 405
Wallace, Mike, Bernstein interviewed by, 348, 384, 395
Walter, Bruno, 114–15, 116, 117–18, 125, 131, 144, 222, 277, 306
Warner Bros., 98, 157, 376

Warsaw, 263–4

Washington Opera Society, 110

Washington *Post*, 329

Webern, Anton von, 286

Weill, Kurt, 211, 404; *Threepenny Opera*, 187, 211

Weiner, Marcella, 33, 37

Welles, Orson, 53, 170, 171

Wells, John, 210, 399

Welsh National Opera, 258

West Side Story (film), 255

Wharton, Edith, 75

Wheeler, Hugh, 209

Whitaker, James E., 406

Whitcraft, William A., Jr., 39

White, Dick, 278–9, 362

White, Jane, 150–2, 177, 296, 340

White, Theodore, 9, 11, 14, 16

Whitehead, Robert, 352, *353, 354*

Whyte, Angus, 341–6, 373

Wieniawski, Henri, D-Minor Concerto, 29

Wilbur, Richard, 203–6, 317, 390

Wilder, Alec, 252–4, 255

Wilder, Thornton, *The Skin of Our Teeth,* 288, 304

Wilford, Ronald, 258

Williams, Harold W., 53–6

Williams, Tennessee, 148

Williams, William Carlos, 188

Wilson, Jane, 295

Wolfe, Tom, 316, 321–2

Wolffers, Jules, 307

Women's Symphony Orchestra, Boston, 84

Woodstock, N.Y., 60, 62

Woodworth, G. Wallace, 77, 86, 103, 143

Works Progress Administration, 53

World War II, 7, 60, 69–70, 96–7, 109, 240

Wright, Frank Lloyd, 172

Yale University, 358

Yehuda, Yosef ben, 5–8

Young People's Concerts, 244–5, *246, 247–9*

Youth Arts Forum, 83

Zeffirelli, Franco, 303, 325, 349, 387

Zighera, Bernard, 103

Zimbalist, Efrem, *65,* 68

Zinman, David, 411

Zirato, Bruno, 111, 113–14, 117, 125, 368

Photographic Credits

Meryle Secrest, 18, 20, 27, 29; Ouida Mintz, 27; David Diamond, 30, 192; Mildred Zucker, 32; Barbara Firger, 32; Johanna Fiedler, 35; Elaine Lubell, 35; The Boston Symphony Archives, 44, 71, 149, 159, 201, 345; Yale Music Library, 54; William Trotter, 61; Curtis Institute of Music Archives, 62, 63, 64, 65; Shirley Rhoads Perle, 70; Richard Bales, 86; Frances McLaughlin, 86; Jacqueline Speyer Fouré, 88, 89; Vogue, copyright © 1944 (renewed 1972) by the Condé Nast Publications Inc., 91; Evelyn Saile, 92; Maggie Smith, 106, 321; New York Philharmonic Archives, 108, 112, 116, 174, 193, 214, 233, 236, 247, 251, 253, 254, 273, 274, 275, 283, 297, 361, 413; Eugene Istomin, 116; New York Public Library, 134, 135, 184, 194, 195, 207, 246, 266, 353; William P. Gottlieb, 134; Erika Stone, 135, 165; Irene Diamond, 158; copyright the Washington Post, reprinted by permission of the D.C. Public Library, 168, 214, 349, 353, 357; Eileen Darby, 195; Life, 240, 265; Peter Schaaf, 313; Roy Stevens, 297; Pat Handy, 345; Peabody Conservatory Archives, 344; Bettina Cirone, 391; John Gruen, 339, 342; Prints and Photographs Division, Library of Congress, 19, 202; the Leonard Bernstein Archive, the Aaron Copland Collection and the Irving Fine Collection, Music Division, the Library of Congress, 10, 13, 18, 31, 58, 62, 81, 88, 85, 100, 158, 291.

A NOTE ON THE TYPE

The text of this book was set in a postscript version
of Garamond No. 3, a modern rendering of the type
first cut by Claude Garamond (c. 1480–1561).
Garamond was a pupil of Geoffroy Tory and is
believed to have based his letters on the Venetian
models, although he introduced a number of important differences, and it is to him we owe the letter
which we know as "old style." He gave to his letters
a certain elegance and a feeling of movement that
won for their creator an immediate reputation and
the patronage of Francis I of France.

Composed by North Market Street Graphics,
Lancaster, Pennsylvania

Printed and bound by Quebecor Printing Martinsburg,
Martinsburg, West Virginia

Designed by Iris Weinstein